Man
Eaters

Man Eaters
True Tales of
Animals Stalking,
Mauling, Killing, and
Eating Human Prey

EDITED BY
LAMAR UNDERWOOD

THE LYONS PRESS

Printed in the United States of America

10 9 8 7 6 5 4 3 2 1

Design by Compset, Inc.

The Library of Congress Cataloging-in-Publication Data is available on file.

Permissions Acknowledgements

Thomas B. Allen, "The Shadows Attack" from *Shadows in the Sea*. Copyright © 1996 by Thomas B. Allen. Reprinted with the permission of The Lyons Press.

Robert H. Busch, "Cougar Attacks on Humans" from *The Cougar Almanac*. Copyright © 1996 by Robert H. Busch. "Grizzly Attacks" from *The Grizzly Almanac*. Copyright © 2000 by Robert H. Busch. Both reprinted with the permission of The Lyons Press.

Peter Hathaway Capstick, "African Attacks" from *Death in the Long Grass*. Copyright © 1977 by Peter Hathaway Capstick. Reprinted with the permission of St. Martin's Press, LLC.

Jim Corbett, "Man-Eating Leopards" from *The Man-Eating Leopard of Rudraprayag*. Reprinted with the permission of Oxford University Press, New Delhi, India.

Ben East, "White Fury on the Barrens" and "How It Feels to Die" from *Danger!: Explosive True Adventures of the Great Outdoors* (New York: E. P. Dutton, 1970). Copyright © 1970 by Ben East.

Hugh Edwards, "Fatal Encounters" from *Crocodile Attack*. Copyright © 1989 by Hugh Edwards. Reprinted with the permission of HarperCollins Publishers, Inc.

Brian Herne, "The Elephant Charge You Can Watch on TV" and "Close Calls" from *White Hunters*. Copyright © 1999 by Brian Herne. Reprinted with the permission of Henry Holt and Company, LLC.

Stephen Herrero, "Sudden Encounters with Grizzlies" and "The Predaceous Black Bear" from *Bear Attacks: Their Causes and Avoidance*. Copyright © 1985 by Stephen Herrero. Reprinted with the permission of The Lyons Press.

J. A. Hunter, "Rogue Elephant" from *Hunter*. Copyright 1952 by J. A. Hunter, renewed © 1980 by Hilda Hunter. Reprinted with the permission of HarperCollins Publishers, Inc.

C. J. P. Ionides, "Man-Eaters," and "Mambas" from *Mambas and Man-Eaters*. Copyright © 1965 by C. J. P. Ionides. Reprinted with the permission of Henry Holt and Company LLC.

A. E. Maxwell and Ivar Ruud, "Bears of the Year-Long Day" from *The Year-Long Day: One Man's Arctic* (New York: J. B. Lippincott, 1976). Copyright © 1976 by A. E. Maxwell and Ivar Ruud. Reprinted with the permission of John Hawkins Associates, Inc.

Thomas McNamee, "Anatomy of a Tragedy: The Yellowstone Grizzly" from *The Grizzly Bear*. Copyright © 1982 by Thomas McNamee. Reprinted with the permission of The Lyons Press.

Bill McRae, "Dying to Photograph Grizzlies" from *Sports Afield* 198, no. 3 (September 1987). Reprinted with the permission of the author.

James A. Oliver, "Aggressive Snakes" from *Snakes in Fact and Fiction*. Copyright © 1958 by James A. Oliver, renewed 1987 by Ruth N. Oliver. Reprinted with the permission of Scribner, a division of Simon & Schuster, Inc.

Pardesi, "The Scourge of a District" from *Blackwood: Tales from the Outposts*. Copyright © 1933 by William Blackwood and Sons.

Jack Denton Scott, "Deadliest Creatures on Earth" from The Best of *Sports Afield* (New York: Atlantic Monthly Press, 1996). Reprinted with the permission of Mary Denton Scott.

Lee H. Whittlesey, "Death in Yellowstone" from *Death in Yellowstone: Accidents and Foolhardiness in the First National Park*. Copyright © 1995 by Lee H. Whittlesey. Reprinted with the permission of Roberts Rinehart Publishers.

Acknowledgments

"Death in Yellowstone" reprinted by kind permission of Roberts Rinehart. "Dying to Photograph Grizzlies" reprinted by kind permission of Bill McRae. "White Fury on the Barrens" reprinted by kind permission of E.P. Dutton. "Bears of the Year-Long Day" reprinted by kind permission of J.B. Lippincott. "Man-Eaters" reprinted by kind permission of Henry Holt. "Fatal Encounters" reprinted by kind permission of HarperCollins. "African Attacks" reprinted by kind permission of St. Martin's Press. "In the Jaws of a Tiger" reprinted by kind permission of Doubleday. "The Scourge of a District" reprinted by kind permission of William Blackwood & Sons. "Man Eating Leopards" reprinted by kind permission of Oxford University Press. "Rogue Elephant" reprinted by kind permission of HarperCollins. "The Elephant Charge You Can Watch on TV" reprinted by kind permission of Henry Holt. "Close Calls" reprinted by kind permission of Henry Holt. "Aggressive Snakes" reprinted by kind permission of Macmillan. "Deadliest Creature on Earth" reprinted by kind permission of Mary Louise Scott. "Mambas" reprinted by kind permission of Henry Holt. "How It Feels to Die" reprinted by kind permission of E.P. Dutton.

Contents

Man
Eaters

Introduction

Ever been stung by a wasp? It hurt, didn't it? And—tell the truth now—you probably felt a bit of anger. As a card-carrying member of Homo sapiens, you're not only accustomed to being at the top of the food chain, but are also used to striking the first blow against pesky creatures, great or small. Then comes this dumb wasp that gets in a sneak punch, and immediately you would delight in smashing the little bugger or blowing him away with an aerosol bomb.

Actually, wasps don't fly around town looking for targets of opportunity. You likely provoked the attack, and there's a lesson here if you're prepared to face it: You could have done a lot worse. Without half trying, you might have aggravated something that could bite off a leg, arm or your head—or possibly fill your veins and arteries with poison so lethal it would make the wasp's calling card a mere itch in comparison.

Consider this scenario:

You have spent much of the day hiking into the Yellowstone Park backcountry and now, at sunset, you are enjoying the immensely pleasing sense of satisfaction that comes from the ritual of making camp. Your tent has been erected, packs tucked away, sleeping bag rolled out for a good night's rest. Supper is over, utensils cleaned and put away, and your food pack has been cached high in a tree many yards from your campsite. Now, pleasantly weary, you sit and stare across the small lake before you, watching the occasional swirl of a feeding trout. This is a good camp, you reflect, a clean camp. You are no amateur out here. In fact, you are a varsity backpacker, well aware of the possibilities of an encounter with bears and other wildlife and dedicated to avoiding an unfortunate confrontation. The sunset is magnificent in grandeur, and as you watch it you marvel at your good fortune on being here, doing your thing. There are more campsites ahead, more sunsets to come.

But you are wrong. This is your final sunset.

Tomorrow morning you will be dead. Killed and partially eaten by a marauding grizzly bear.

1

"Never happen!" you say. "No way that could happen to me."

Well, the scene just depicted really did happen. If you like wilderness trails and camps, why couldn't it happen to you? Are you exempt from bad luck? I don't think so.

So long as people go into wilderness—and, God willing, we will all go on doing just that—the possibilities, however remote, of a tragic encounter with potentially dangerous wildlife will always be a reality. Compared to the odds of having our tickets punched by an automobile accident, heart attack— or even running into some lunatic on a remote trail or campsite—the odds of being mauled by a grizzly are minuscule. And yet . . .

Well, we all know it could happen. We just keep hoping it won't happen to *us*. Like soldiers and marines, we always assume it's the *other guy* who's going to get it.

When we consider wildlife attacks on humans, the words "Man Eater" so frequently used to dramatically label the assailants are misleading and unfair in many instances. A bear—or lion, tiger, or any creature, for that matter—that charges a hunter is hardly a man eater in the same sense of a lion or tiger grown accustomed to living on human flesh, knocking off the occasional local resident for dinner. And snakes that kill many humans don't actually *eat* their victims, hence aren't man eaters in the strict sense of the words. However, we have included both types of those incidents in this book, under the general *Man Eaters* title, because the attacks described are intense dramas in which claws and fangs are turned against man. Whether they are provoked attacks or the plain-old bad luck of running into the admittedly-rare beast that's ready, willing and able to eat you, the accounts on these pages are of man eater intensity, whether or not the victim was consumed.

When it comes to reflecting on the unfortunate fates of others, most people can't help becoming rubber-neckers. The little voice saying, "There but for the grace of God, go I," has us eyeing accident sites with keen interest, instead of turning away. And if even a fender-bender on the turnpike can cause people to gawk, imagine what would happen if they had a chance to see a grizzly-ravaged campsite. People didn't flock to see the movie *Jaws* because it had great pictures of people swimming.

One example of mankind's obvious and perfectly natural (it seems to me) fascination with dramatic, even macabre, violence has emerged in recent years in documentary filmmaking and television viewing habits. Nature programs were once the province of Bambi-like depictions of nature as a peaceful realm where brethren of the wild were gentle, doe-eyed creatures all peacefully coexisting. Every scene was filled with mawkish sentimentality about harmony. Occasionally, a predator such as a hawk might make a pass at a prairie dog, or some such critter. Always, the hawk would fail. The program would end on a beautiful sunset shot, with music from the likes of the Mormon Tabernacle Choir in the background, and shots of the hawk wheeling in the sky and the prairie dog standing beside his hole. A narrator's voice would proclaim the end of a perfect day.

It was inevitable, I suspect, that this GP-rated, childishly naïve view of the natural world should pass from public favor. As anyone who has the slightest real interest in the natural world knows, it's a jungle out there. Yes, there is harmony, in the sense of nature's delicate balance being maintained. Still, it's an eat or be-eaten world.

Eventually, enterprising filmmakers began to discover that John Q. Public wanted to see the real stuff—the terror of the chase and the kill, the world of red claws and fangs. Producers started giving viewers what they were looking for—killer whales splashing onto shore to gulp down seals, crocodiles snatching unsuspecting wildebeests from the edge of a waterhole, lions and leopards outflanking and running down gazelles, the occasional python or anaconda embracing and then swallowing a monkey. [Just last night, I watched a tv nature film that showed a king cobra killing and completely swallowing a 12-foot-long rat snake. It looked as amazing as it sounds.]

Television producers of these fresh-air smorgasbords have achieved their goals: higher ratings. Other than in programs especially targeted to small children, I doubt that we'll ever see any more films depicting a silly fantasy world in which wild creatures never eat one another.

If you are interested in the realistic tv nature documentaries being aired on cable today, I have a hunch you're going to find the accounts offered here to be both gripping and illuminating. Here are the stories of accidental and provoked encounters in which men and women faced the most unforgiving moments of their lives. The terror and pain of their confrontations are staggering. The endings are not always happy ones.

The reports and eye-witness accounts presented here span many years and varied global settings ranging from desolate to breathtaking Edens where the beauty of the land belies the atmosphere of tragedy. Some of the stories are legendary—*The Man-Eaters of Tsavo*, for instance. Some, like the grizzly attacks in national parks, were once newspaper headlines. Many others are obscure events of individual heroism and ordeal, no less gripping for their obscurity.

The rewards of the outdoor life touch something deep and undeniably satisfying inside many of us. The wild country that can sustain bears and other magnificent creatures looms in our thoughts constantly, pulling us beyond pavement's end. We follow the trails taken by countless kindred spirits, including philosophers and naturalists such as John Muir, who urged, "Climb the mountains and get their good tidings. Nature's peace will flow into you as sunshine flows into trees. The winds will blow their freshness into you, and the storms their energy, and cares will drop off like autumn leaves."

Well said. We can only add that while pursuing the spiritual and physical gratification made possible by wilderness experiences, that we devoutly respect the fact that other creatures must share the same ground. A high priority for us all must be the sensibilities and woodsmanship by which we can avoid ugly and unfortunate collisions with those inhabitants which have no place else to go.

—*Lamar Underwood*
Springtime, 2000

Part One:
In Bear Country
Grizzly Bear, Black Bear, Polar Bear
Zip Up Your Tent!

1   Death in Yellowstone

BY LEE H. WHITTLESEY

Beginning in 1970, with the closure of the last Yellowstone garbage dump, the stepping up of the government's transporting program for roadside beggar-bears, and the installation of "bearproof" (odor-preventing) trash cans, the numbers of injuries to park visitors by bears began to drop dramatically. But the park's fourth human fatality involving a bear occurred in 1984. The victim was a young woman from Switzerland.

On July 29, 1984, ranger Gary Youngblood was on duty at Canyon Ranger Station when a woman hiker came into that office. She was pretty, with dark, shoulder-length hair, about 5'5" tall, and around 120 pounds. Youngblood issued the woman a backcountry permit for site 5-B-1 (north of Fern Lake) for the night of July 30. He warned her against hiking alone in Yellowstone country, and about bears particularly and foods in camp generally. Youngblood noted that the woman, Brigitta Claudia Fredenhagen, 25, of Basel, Switzerland, appeared intelligent and spoke near-perfect English. District ranger John Lounsbury, sitting in the next office, remembers that she was attractive and that she got a good bit of bear information from Youngblood.

On July 31 at 6:00 p.m., Brigitta's brother, Andreas Fredenhagen, reported to Lake area ranger Mark Marschall that his sister had failed to meet him and his wife as scheduled at Pelican trailhead. A search was begun with two persons traveling through Pelican Valley, and the following morning Ranger Marschall began a patrol of the area on horseback.

At 11:20 a.m., Marschall found Brigitta's camp. He noted that something spooked his horse there; the horse would approach no closer than twenty yards. So Marschall walked to the green dome tent that he saw pitched some sixty feet from the shore of White Lake in campsite 5-W-1. He noticed immediately that the tent fly had rip marks in it near the door and saw a sleeping pad, parka, and other gear inside undisturbed. But outside the tent, Marschall found

7

a piece of scalp with hair on it and a piece of what he thought was muscle tissue. A sleeping bag lay nearby. He radioed for assistance and then continued to search for Brigitta. He could not find her but did locate her food cache thirty yards away. It had been pulled down by a bear and the food partially eaten.

Sensing they had a bad incident on their hands, rangers Dave Spirtes and Tim Blank were helicoptered to the scene at 12:06 p.m. and began a hasty search of the area. Near the sleeping bag they found a piece of Brigitta's lip, and the rangers' faces grew grave. They searched the area between the trail and the lake. Recent thundershowers had cleansed the landscape of obvious drag trails, so the rangers swept north for about a quarter of a mile. At 12:57 they spotted a bloody article of clothing. From there a trail of more bloody clothing and human tissue led to Brigitta Fredenhagen's body, 258 feet from her tent. Quite a lot of it had been eaten by the bear.

Shaken by their discovery, the rangers continued the investigation. From blood on and a puncture in the woman's sleeping bag, it appeared to them that the bear had ripped the tent and pulled her out either by the left side of her neck or the top of her head while she slept. There was no sign of a struggle; her hiking clothing was neatly folded inside of the tent and all other items were undisturbed. Six feet outside she either slid out or was pulled from her sleeping bag. About twenty feet northwest of the tent, rangers found a rectangle of discolored grass where substantial blood and tissue had fallen, and this was deemed to be the site where Fredenhagen died. Because she was first attacked at her neck and face, the rangers decided she had probably died quickly, perhaps without really waking up.

The bear had climbed twelve feet up a tree to get to the woman's food cache, the same way she had put the cache up—both her climbing marks and the bear's claw marks could be seen. Most of the food cache had been eaten. The tree-climbing marks and other evidence seemed to indicate a subadult male grizzly, light in color.

The rangers and autopsy people attempted to piece together what had happened. Fredenhagen had hiked 8.5 miles, camped several miles short of her permitted site, boiled water for tea, and ate precooked or cold food for dinner. She hung her food, arranged her clothing and other items neatly, crawled into her sleeping bag with her feet facing the east and her head toward the lake, and was apparently asleep when the attack occurred sometime after 10:30 p.m. on July 29. The bear was never identified or captured. It apparently left the site within twelve hours, because the woman's body was not semi-buried in the fashion that feeding grizzlies often practice, and because there was no scat near the body. The rangers found scats containing human remains several miles north and again several miles east of the site, and postulated that the bear had returned once to feed on July 31. Rain had destroyed much of the evidence; in fact, it was probably raining at the time of the attack or just shortly afterward.

In attempting to piece together reasons for the attack, Rangers Mike Pflaum and Mark Marschall spent several nights in the area sleeping nervously in a bear trap made from a culvert (arguably one of the only safe places) and hoping that the bear would return. It never did.

But in the final analysis no one could be sure what the reasons were. The victim was not menstruating. The tent did contain two-thirds of a 100-gram chocolate bar wrapped up inside a pack. Other odorous tent items included lip salve, Micoren pills, and a butane cigarette lighter. If the bear was attracted by these items, perhaps it felt secure because Fredenhagen was hiking *alone,* a discouraged practice in Yellowstone country and probably her biggest mistake. Even the widespread thunder and lightning in the area for several days previously was suggested as somehow tying into the attack, but in the end no one knew. The woman's hanging of her food, possession of four bear-warning pamphlets given her by ranger Youngblood, bear bells in the tent, and her signature at a trail register where three bear-warning signs were posted, all attested to her knowledge of and concern for precautions in bear country. In fact, on August 2, while going through her belongings, Brigitta's brother and sister-in-law found a notebook in which Brigitta had made a diary-type entry, written while at the campsite. Eerily the entry noted that she had taken "all precautions."

The Fredenhagen death was partially responsible for the Pelican Valley area being restricted to day use only hiking (no overnight camping), a regulation that had been considered for some years before that.

Like Fredenhagen, William J. Tesinsky was alone when a Yellowstone grizzly killed him on or about October 4, 1986. Tesinsky, 38, a Great Falls, Montana auto mechanic, was an avid wildlife photographer who was also an expert woodsman and hunter. Chief Yellowstone ranger Dan Sholly has described him as "cocky, confident, and used to getting what he wanted." He has been characterized as able to maintain a pace in his outdoor travels that would wear out most anyone else; in fact, he usually traveled alone because he felt most people could not keep up. His attitude about hiking by himself proved to be his undoing.

Tesinsky had been somewhat successful at selling his wildlife photographs. But he had not yet photographed a grizzly bear and he was determined to do so. Sometime on or about October 4, Tesinsky became aware that a grizzly (bear 59 in park parlance) was frequenting the Otter Creek area near its junction with the Yellowstone River. Leaving his car in a pullout on the main road, Tesinsky began to stalk the bear all by himself and carrying his camera and tripod. Just how or when he confronted the sow grizzly we will never know, but his final moments must have been frightening ones and it is likely that he struggled, at least for a short time.

Bear 59 was a semi-habituated bear; that is, a bear which had had some contacts with humans and human foods. But she had never even approached a human aggressively. She had two cubs earlier in the season when the park transported her to Cub Creek, but did not have them by October. Tesinsky apparently "crossed over that fine line between being just another pesky photographer and being a potential threat or food source competitor."

After Tesinsky's blue car had been parked at the Otter Creek pullout for several days, the park began checking on him. Ranger Alice Siebecker, armed with license plate information, made calls to Tesinsky's home at Great Falls and found that he had missed work. On October 6, ranger Tom Olliff scouted the area on horseback but found nothing. Then ranger Jeff Henry talked to bear researcher Steve French and discovered that bear 59 had been in the area at least since October 4. Indeed, Jeff had seen her himself at LeHardys Rapids about October 1.

Thus, on October 7, Rangers Mona Divine and John Lounsbury, followed later by Jeff Henry, Tom Olliff, Dick Divine and Joe Fowler, began a genuine search up Otter Creek. From the top of a small hill, Mona Divine and John Lounsbury spotted bear 59 feeding on something. Henry and Fowler walked into the old Otter Creek campground to join them. Through his rifle scope, Jeff Henry saw legs lying on the ground and knew that the bear was feeding on Tesinsky. Divine and Lounsbury saw it too. Because a grizzly was in the area feeding, the rangers were very nervous. Over their radios came the voice of bear specialist Gary Brown: "Are you in a position to destroy that bear?" "Yes, we are," replied Lounsbury. Brown gave the order, and Ranger Fowler shot bear 59.

The rangers, still well armed with shotguns and rifles, moved into the area cautiously. Jeff Henry remembers that the scene was one of a classic carcass feeding, with coyotes, ravens, and magpies all waiting on the fringes for their turn. The group walked into a small meadow about one quarter mile from the main road and found Tesinsky's remains. And remains is what they were. All that lay on the ground were Tesinsky's legs and pelvic parts. His entire upper half was missing. Jeff remembers thinking that it looked as if someone had chainsawed him in two at the belt. Lying on site were Tesinsky's camera and tripod. It was evident from the large amount of blood around the collars of Tesinsky's jacket and shirt, found later, that the bear had gone for his neck from the outset. In fact, Tesinsky's entire neck was missing, probably the reason for his death and an occurrence which was apparently inflicted as he ran. It probably had not taken bear 59 long to tear him apart and to subsequently bury parts of him nearby for later feeding. Tesinsky's skull was found in the burial mound.

No bear pictures were found on Tesinsky's camera film. Jeff Henry supposed that perhaps the fact that bear 59 wore a radio collar deterred Tesinsky from taking distant photos and encouraged him to try for a closer one, perhaps hoping for a turned-head photo wherein the radio collar would not show. Moreover, his tripod was pointed down, as if the camera were aimed at something only twelve to fifteen feet away. And Tesinsky's camera had a short lens on it rather than a long lens. "Whatever he was focusing on," says Henry, an expert photographer himself, "was very close."

Following an autopsy of the bear and of Tesinsky, a park board of inquiry concluded that Tesinsky was killed because he was trying to photograph a grizzly bear at close range, and that the bear found near his remains was the one that killed him. We will never know what happened exactly, but the team thought Tesinsky was focusing his camera on the bear only 12–15 feet away, when it charged. Tesinsky probably turned and ran toward the road, but the bear caught him from behind by the neck and killed him. Then, Jeff believes, the bear dragged Tesinsky back over the camera tripod (the bear's body or Tesinsky's thus bending one leg of the tripod) to Tesinsky's final resting place. There the bear finished its job as one of nature's consummate feeding machines.

The Tesinsky story (as do several of the bear death stories here) harks us back to the idea of the buffalo as a mythical animal. We want badly to touch these animals—for reasons of affection perhaps, or domination, or whatever. But we must not. Human philosophy, literature, feelings, all cry out for us to be more in touch with nature. But truly being in touch with nature includes knowing when *not* to touch. Tesinsky and some of the other bear victims here stepped over the line.

2 Dying to Photograph Grizzlies

BY BILL MCRAE

A friend of 40-year-old Charles Gibbs's described him as "a nice guy who had a fixation with grizzly bears." He supported efforts to save Montana's grizzly population from extinction, and as an aspiring wildlife photographer, he had an obsessive desire to photograph the bears up close. Gibbs knew quite a lot about grizzlies, but he was also a bit of a romantic: He felt that the bears would sense he meant them no harm, and wouldn't hurt him. He was wrong!

At about 5:00 p.m. on April 25, 1987, Gibbs and his wife, Glenda, were returning from a day hike in Glacier National Park when they spotted a female grizzly with three yearling cubs high on Elk Mountain. Gibbs decided to approach and photograph the animals while his wife hiked back to the trailhead. She reached their car at about 6:00 p.m., but there was no sign of her husband. At about 10:15 p.m. she contacted District Ranger Charlie Logan, who then went to the area and fired shots in a vain effort to locate Gibbs. An extensive search was launched at dawn the next day, and Gibbs's badly mauled body was found that afternoon about 1 1/2 miles from the trail.

The 40 pictures that Gibbs got with his 35mm camera (equipped with a 400mm telephoto lens) indicate that he not only approached the bears but apparently followed them when they tried to move away. His last photographs were taken at about 50 yards.

Evidence at the attack site showed that Gibbs had tried to climb a tree and was pulled down. Numerous bites and scratches on his arms, legs and head indicate that he attempted to fend off the bear while facing it. Gibbs's injuries may not have been immediately fatal, as he was found 145 feet from the attack site. The bears had not fed on the body.

A previous incident that is disturbingly similar to the Gibbs episode involved William John Tesinsky, a 38-year-old Great Falls, Montana, man who tried to photograph a grizzly bear in Yellowstone National Park on October 4, 1986. According to the pathologist's report, Tesinsky's death was "due to traumatic injuries occurring from a bear attack."

A profile of Tesinsky can be gleaned from the report of the board of inquiry that investigated his death. He was an auto mechanic, an adept woodsman and an excellent hunter, and was in good physical condition. He had a strong desire to become a professional wildlife photographer and was relying on the sale of his photos to help repay some outstanding financial obligations. Tesinsky was described as a "very determined photographer who would do anything to get a photograph," and he had recently told his brother that the only major animal in Montana that he had not photographed was the grizzly bear. None of the above says anything bad about Tesinsky; these factors did, however, set the stage for disaster.

The probable events surrounding Tesinsky's death were reconstructed as follows: Between 10:00 and 11:00 a.m. on October 4, Tesinsky was driving north toward Canyon when he spotted a grizzly feeding on vegetation in open, rolling terrain about 450 yards from the road. He hastily parked his car, grabbed his Pentax 35mm camera, an 80–200mm zoom lens and a tripod, and set out to photograph the bear. The grizzly, known to park rangers as bear No. 59, was a female that had somehow lost her two cubs a few weeks earlier (the significance of the latter is unknown).

The wind was in Tesinsky's favor, and the bear, which had moved to another feeding location nearby, out of sight of the road, was probably not aware of his approach. Due to the topography, Tesinsky would not have been able to see the bear until he topped a knoll only 40 yards from the center of the feeding site. Judging by the setting of the zoom lens (120mm), he placed his tripod 30 to 50 feet from the bear and prepared to take pictures. Unfortunately, he didn't even have time to trip the shutter.

Tesinsky was reported missing on the afternoon of October 6. On the morning of October 7 two park rangers found grizzly bear No. 59 standing over his partially consumed body, which she started to drag away as they approached. The grizzly was shot on sight.

Putting things into perspective, one should realize that attacks on humans by grizzly bears are very rare occurrences. However, studies of human/grizzly bear encounters do show that two groups of people are most apt to be involved: park employees and wildlife photographers.

I can certainly empathize with the park employees, but being a professional wildlife photographer myself, I find the incidents involving photographers most troubling, perhaps because I feel some sense of responsibility.

Having published many grizzly bear photos and magazine articles over the years, I fear that my work may have inspired other wildlife photographers—especially those starting out in the field—to adopt a cavalier attitude toward bears.

No, I'm not on a guilt trip, and I don't think that I'm taking myself too seriously. However, I hear from enough aspiring nature photographers—by letter, by phone and in person—to know that they emulate those whom they perceive to be successful. And unfortunately, established professionals haven't always been inclined to tell the truth about how grizzly bear pictures are taken. More about this later.

When I consider Gibbs and Tesinsky—and their fates—I realize that "There but for the grace of God go I." The Tesinsky incident was especially poignant because 20 years ago I did exactly the same thing in exactly the same spot. Like Tesinsky, I had seen what I took to be a lone grizzly feeding in the meadow about 400 yards from the road, and I foolishly set out to photograph it.

When I got to where the bear had been, it was gone, but since the meadow was rolling, I decided to climb a small knoll (perhaps the same one) for a better view of the area. I expected to see the animal at a distance. As I soon learned, however, it doesn't take much of a dip in the ground to hide a bear, and just as I topped the knoll, I saw the back of the grizzly about 50 feet away. If it had not had its head down feeding, it would have been looking right at me. I stood torn between taking pictures and getting the hell out of there. Suddenly a brown-colored cub that I hadn't seen stood up with its front paw on its mother's back and looked straight at me. I swallowed my heart, bent down, and as quietly as possible tiptoed away. If the cub had sounded an alarm, or if the female bear had seen me, she would probably have acted defensively and charged.

Previous to that incident, I had had other equally frightening experiences with grizzlies, and that night, as I lay alone in my tent at Madison Junction, I realized how careless I had been. I thought about my responsibility to my wife, Mary, and to our four small children, and how going home to them was far more important than getting grizzly pictures. Shortly thereafter I promised myself that I would never again stalk grizzly bears on foot, and although on several occasions I have inadvertently run into them while hiking the backcountry, I have kept that promise.

Why did I get away with a foolish stunt that was later to get Tesinsky killed? Without intending any disrespect for the deceased, I can only surmise that some fools are luckier than others.

I am still embarrassed when I think about what I did, and my only reason for mentioning the incident here is to impress upon others how dangerous it is to stalk and photograph grizzly bears in the wild.

That isn't to say that wildlife photographers don't have an inalienable right to get themselves killed—it comes with the purchase of one's first camera. However, since the bears involved in maulings are often killed, such photographers not only risk their lives but also endanger a species that has been classified as threatened under the Endangered Species Act. There are, after all, more photographers than grizzly bears.

It is to Glacier Park Superintendent Gil Lusk's credit that the grizzly that killed Gibbs was not hunted down. "She acted to protect her young after Gibbs approached them," Lusk said, "and no action will be taken against the bear." (Gibbs would have wanted it that way.)

Conversely, there was no option but to destroy the bear in Tesinsky's case: Once a grizzly has learned to regard humans as prey, it cannot be allowed to wander around in a national park.

But the adverse publicity created by such attacks is a greater threat to the survival of the species than the death of any individual bear.

Why are wildlife photographers so willing to risk their lives in order to take pictures of grizzlies? The reasons run the gamut of human emotions, ambitions and follies, and include liberal doses of machismo and egotism. Understandably, many individuals view wildlife photography as a way to escape unfulfilling 9-to-5 jobs. But they're wrong when they see "getting grizzly pictures" as a stepping-stone to achieving that goal.

Then there is that basic and pervasive desire for fame. I doubt that anyone except photographers ever reads those tiny credit lines accompanying wildlife photos, but most beginners and even some professionals don't know that.

And there's no doubt that taking pictures of animals, especially dangerous ones, has an aura of adventure about it. What's more, we wildlife photographers soon discover that it's fun to tell others about our harrowing experiences, becoming, in the process, the center of attention, especially when we start talking about encounters with grizzly bears.

So what valuable lessons can be learned from the Tesinsky and Gibbs incidents, or more precisely, what mistakes did they make?

Tesinsky shouldn't have tried to photograph the bear in the first place. To compound this error, he apparently approached very close without making the grizzly aware of his presence, which obviously startled it and provoked a defensive reaction. Clearly Tesinsky intended to get as close as possible: He had left a 1000mm telephoto lens in his vehicle and was using an 80–200mm zoom lens.

After the incident I talked with several photographers, who took some comfort in pointing out that Tesinsky wasn't a bona fide professional wildlife photographer (whatever that is), presumably because he hadn't had much work published. The logic, I suppose, was that the bear wouldn't have killed him if he had been working for *National Geographic*. That's not smart, because if you get too close to a grizzly (even the pros are always edging nearer to get better shots) and it charges, you can be sure that it isn't running up to you to ask where your credit line has appeared.

Gibbs knew from the beginning that he was dealing with a female with cubs (the most dangerous of all grizzlies), and even though the bears showed concern and tried to move away, he kept getting closer.

But Gibbs's greatest error was believing that the bears would sense his friendly intentions and reciprocate. Bizarre as that notion seems, it is commonly held by people who love animals. It may even be true for some species under certain conditions, but it doesn't apply to grizzlies. Apart from the strong bonds that exist between females and their own cubs, a grizzly bear is nobody's friend. Grizzlies literally live in a bear-eat-bear world. Add to this the fact that a female grizzly is a devoted mother who will often defend her offspring to the death—against even the largest males—and it's easy to understand how she might get the mistaken notion that a photographer plans to eat her cubs.

The greatest irony here is that those who approach grizzlies on foot seldom get good bear pictures. Most published grizzly pictures aren't taken this way. Here is how it's done: If the photos are of wild bears, they were likely taken from roads in one of three or four national parks. Some come from Yellowstone and a few from Canadian parks, but most are taken in Denali National Park in Alaska, where photographers are wisely required to work either from or near their vehicles. Most pictures of the somewhat more docile, but still dangerous, coastal (brown) grizzly bears are taken at McNeil River Falls in Alaska, where photographers work from a designated area that the bears have been conditioned to avoid.

What may come as a shock is that most of those coveted close-ups, particularly of snarling bears, are taken at zoos or game farms. Also, if a photographer has the money—and some do—he can rent a trained grizzly, complete with handler.

What should be done to prevent photographers from being killed by grizzly bears or vice versa?

Since the incidents are occurring in national parks, I'm going to presumptuously offer a couple of suggestions to the Park Service:

1. All backcountry users in grizzly-inhabited parks should be required to wear bear bells when they hike. The use of bear bells has been recommended for many years, but like seat belts, they have been steadfastly

resisted. One objection is that they spook wildlife. That's nonsense. I've used a bell for years, and it has never prevented me from approaching and photographing animals. The other objection is that the bells shatter the solitude. That is true, but isn't a little less solitude preferable to being attacked by a startled bear?

2. It should be against the law to willfully approach a grizzly bear in any of the national parks. Such is already the case in Denali Park, and it's working well to prevent bear incidents. Of course, such a rule would need to be administered with a measure of common sense, since hikers are bound to run into bears unexpectedly. But if someone with a camera is seen methodically approaching a grizzly bear, there should be no doubt about his intentions.

Defenses Against Bears

I wouldn't think of hiking or camping in grizzly country without some sort of defense. Where it is legal—usually outside the parks—I carry a 44 magnum revolver. Inside the parks (where I have grave reservations about backcountry camping in any event), I carry an aerosol spray containing capsaicin, an extract from red pepper. Despite several close encounters, in 25 years as a wildlife photographer I have never had occasion to use either defense on a grizzly bear (I did use the spray on a black bear once, with excellent results). But as pointed out earlier, I don't make a practice of stalking grizzlies.

The problem with a gun or a spray is that either can create a false sense of security. (It's worth noting that, though doing so was against park regulations, Gibbs was carrying a 45-caliber pistol, which he never got a chance to use.)

Over a century ago William Hazlitt said, "No young man ever thinks he shall die." I thought of that as I listened to a young photographer who had been stalking grizzly bears in Yellowstone Park brag of his adventures, which included being treed several times. He seemed ebullient and cocky. He had challenged death to a duel—not once, but many times—and had always won. What the young man failed to understand is that, as an adversary, death really isn't hard to beat. If you're skillful, you can defeat him again and again, almost with impunity. The problem is that death is immortal—he keeps coming back, and unlike you, he only has to win once. And when death comes riding on a charging grizzly, it's a hard way to go.

3   White Fury on the Barrens

BY BEN EAST

The weather-beaten trading schooner *Venture,* 43 feet long and aux-
iliary powered with an ancient Diesel engine, dropped anchor in
Long Island Sound on the evening of July 22, 1937.

Not the Long Island Sound you have heard about. This one is a narrow channel of the sea lying between another Long Island and the east shore of
Hudson Bay, about 35 miles north of Cape Jones, where the huge funnel of
that bay narrows into James Bay, which forms its spout.

For an Arctic trading schooner, the *Venture* carried strange cargo, including 18 humans. Nine of us were clients, sportsmen from the States, the first
such party ever to cruise up the Quebec shore of James Bay and Hudson Bay
to fish, hunt, photograph and see the country.

Lloyd Melville, from Rydal Bank, Ontario, who had organized the
trip and chartered the *Venture* for it, planned to conduct similar guided tours
into that remote and fabulously wild country each year from then on, but the
plan fell through, and ours was the last as well as the first group to undertake it.

Melville's crew consisted of three guides and a cook. The *Venture* was
owned and skippered by Jack Palmquist, the only free trader then operating on
James Bay in competition with the Hudson's Bay Company. He had a small
trading post at Old Factory, on the coast about halfway between the Eastmain
and Fort George Rivers. Married to a mission-educated Cree girl, and speaking Cree as readily as English, he had an inside track with the Indians and was
doing all right.

He had a crew of three aboard the *Venture.* Alagkok, the little Eskimo
engineer, spoke no English but understood the workings of the throbbing old
diesel as a man understands a well-loved wife—and gave it the same affection-
ate care. The deckhand was a Cree, equally innocent of English, whose name

time has erased from my memory. And because no charts existed for the treacherous island-girt passages along that coast, and no white skipper of that day would have dreamed of sailing them without a Cree pilot aboard (and probably wouldn't even today), at Eastmain we had taken on an aged and leather-faced Indian, Bosun Kagaback, as pilot.

Only the Crees knew those waters well enough, from a lifetime of canoe travel, to recall the endless landmarks along the bleak coast, follow the channels and avoid the reefs. Kagaback, who had piloted for years for the Hudson's Bay Company, saw us safely north to Fort George. There we exchanged him for Tommy Lameboy, equally weathered, who knew the coast the rest of the way.

We had left the end of steel on the T & NO Railroad at Moosonee on July 12, when the *Venture* moved down the Moose River into the open waters of James Bay and pointed her nose north. When the wind favored us, we ran under sail. When it didn't, the wheezing diesel pushed us along at a lumbering six knots.

We were headed into a region that only a handful of whites—the men of the Hudson's Bay Company, an occasional free trader, missionaries, Mounties, and now and then a roving prospector—had ever seen. Not a foot of road lay between us and the Arctic ice, not even a blazed trail save for the portages the Crees had cut around the rapids on the big rivers they traveled. If you went into that bleak Land of Midnight Twilight, you went by canoe or ship in summer, by dog team in winter.

Below decks the *Venture* carried our duffle and luggage, tents and camping equipment. Lashed to the rails were four big freight canoes that would carry us to the fishing pools of the barrenland rivers, and also would serve to ferry the clients and guides ashore each night to make camp. There was not room aboard the old 43-footer for 18 to sleep.

I have roamed the back country of this continent for almost 50 years, from the Great Smokies and the diamondback-infested flatwoods of Florida to the Aleutian Islands of Alaska, but that treeless and empty subarctic land was the most fascinating place I have ever seen.

At Moose Factory, at Eastmain and at Fort George we found big camps of the Crees, down to the posts for the summer from their trapping and hunting grounds along the big rivers of the interior, a few of them living in tents but the great majority in wigwams, as they had lived long before the first white men saw them. The wigwams were big and comfortable, and clean, too.

Consisting of a circular frame of poles, 12 to 20 feet across, they were covered with canvas, sealskins, whatever was available. The floor was carpeted deep with green spruce twigs, a ring of stones in the center contained the fire, and a small opening at the top carried the smoke out. On poles outside hung gear of all kinds, snowshoes, dog harness, frames for drying pelts, and bundles of sphagnum moss that would be used for baby diapers and sanitary napkins, the all-around absorbent cotton of the North. And tied to stakes in front of every wigwam were the gaunt, hungry sled dogs, half-wild, furtive-eyed, crafty thieves, great workers but vicious fighters, ever on the lookout for trouble. Snowshoes and every scrap of harness had to be hung beyond their reach.

On Cape Hope Island, only 125 miles north of the mouth of the Moose, we dropped anchor one morning in front of a drab and cheerless cluster of low-roofed houses, some built of logs, some of rough, unpainted lumber whipsawed by hand from driftwood. This was the home of the Cape Hope Eskimo band, the southernmost of their race on the North American continent, headed by a wise old patriarch named Weteltik.

The smell of seal oil hung over the place, rancid and all-pervading. Whale and seal harpoons were racked by the doors, canoes and boats rested on high pole frames or, if they contained no leather, were drawn up on shore, and big surly dogs ranged the camp.

We went ashore, avoiding the dogs, and were met with a welcome so friendly that I have never forgotten it. We couldn't buy anything, for money had no value there, but we gave away cigarets and traded tennis shoes and knives, soap, tea, sugar and jam, for whale harpoons, mukluks, ivory carvings and snowshoes. The trading was done through two interpreters. Weteltik understood Cree. Palmquist told him in that language what we wanted, and he passed the word on to his people in Eskimo. That morning was one I'll remember all my life.

But of that whole fascinating month, nothing stands forth in my mind more clearly than the trout fishing we found in the wonderful, tumbling rivers of the rocky moors, north of the limit of trees. (We were in that kind of country for more than a week, carrying our tent poles along from camp to camp, and combing the rocky beaches for driftwood to feed our camp and cooking fires.)

The fish were squaretails, the big speckled trout of northern Canada (we caught a few Arctic char too), but they were different in some ways from any of their kind I had ever encountered. They were untutored, uneducated and unwise.

They came of generations that had had no dealing with flies, spinners or any man-made device of treachery, save the nets the roaming Crees set at the mouths of the rivers.

They took whatever was offered, swiftly and recklessly. They rose to flies, wet or dry, they smashed at spinners or the throat latch of another trout. They were no more canny than bluegills in a millpond, and no harder to catch.

One morning, without much hope of getting a response, I tore a narrow strip from a red bandanna handkerchief, knotted it around the shank of my hook, and fed it into a chute of green water at the foot of a pool. A 16-inch fish struck like forked lightning.

The trout ran from 15 to 20 inches in length, heavy-bodied and fat. Many of them weighed three pounds, and they were as rugged in battle as any fish I have ever taken. It was no trick for three or four rods to catch in a morning all the party of 18 needed for a day. Many times two flies on a leader took doubles, and frequently we landed six or eight trout from one pool before the action slacked off. I have never seen any other fishing to match it.

In the summer camp of the Crees at the Fort George Post, where 500 Indians were living in wigwams and tents scattered over a long, level meadow below the red-and-white buildings of the Hudson's Bay Company, we were introduced in a small way to the thing I was chiefly interested in, a polar bear hunt.

One of the Crees brought three white bearskins out of his wigwam and spread them on the grass. He wanted to trade.

They were the pelts of an adult and two fair-sized cubs. When we asked him, through Palmquist, where and how he had killed them, he had quite a story to tell.

Coming down the east coast of Hudson Bay and around Cape Jones in the spring, he said, he had blundered into the sow and her yearling youngsters. He had run his canoe ashore for the night and his woman was lugging the tent and other gear up to a little hollow above the beach. The Indian himself was still fooling around the canoe when the three bears walked into sight over a low ridge only 30 or 40 yards away.

The female reared up to look things over and didn't like what she saw. She began to growl and swing her head. One of the cubs walked on a few feet, got a noseful of Cree, and squalled in alarm. That did it. The sow let go a hair-lifting bellow of rage and charged.

Luckily for the Indian, he had been watching for seals that afternoon and his rifle still lay in the bottom of the canoe, loaded and uncased. He scrambled for it while the bear was making up her mind, and when she started her rush he was ready for her. He knocked her off her feet with the first shot, finished her with the second, and then killed the cubs.

Those three pelts were the first polar bearskins I had ever seen outside a zoo. Thickly furred, ivory white and lustrous, they whetted my appetite for an ice-bear rug of my own as nothing else had done.

At the end of his recital, the Indian ventured a sentence in English. "Plenty bear this year!" he grunted.

To this day I don't know whether he meant that he had had his fill of them for the time being, or that they were abundant and our chances would be good.

There was no open hunting season for sportsmen on polar bears on that coast then. All game was kept for the natives. If an ice bear was taken by a white man, it had to be under a permit issued to a museum or scientific institution and the bear, or at least its skull, must go for scientific purposes. That did not prevent the hunter from keeping the pelt, however.

Two of us had the coveted permits, calling for two bears apiece. Howard Cooper of Kalamazoo, a friend and hunting partner of mine who died many years ago, would try to collect his bears for a museum in his home city. My permit had been issued to the Cranbrook Institute of Science at Bloomfield Hills, Michigan.

The great white bear of the north (the Eskimos call him Nanook, the Crees Wahb'-es-co) is not always an animal of sea and ice floe. In the brief arctic summer he ranges along the coast and the rocky islands of the polar sea as well, I suppose feeding on mice and lemmings, birds' eggs, berries, and fish and seals, like all bears.

The Crees and Eskimos had told us that bears summered regularly on the islands in Hudson Bay and at the northern end of James Bay, but because 20 to 40 miles of open ocean lay in their way, they rarely hunted them, although the law allowed them to kill any they could.

We found ample proof of what they said, on some of the islands, too. Bear tracks crossed the beaches, holes had been dug in gravel banks for shelter from the summer sun, grass flattened where the animals had bedded, rocks overturned, and other sign was there in abundance. One of the islands—the Crees called it Niska or Grey Goose—had been literally torn up by bears.

A few days after we saw the three pelts at Fort George and heard the Indian's story of how he took them, we reached Long Island Sound, the bleakest and most desolate region we had seen. Treeless islands, rocky shores, moss and arctic willow. We were in polar bear country at last.

The first evening Eskimos paddled out to the *Venture* to trade fresh-caught char for canned peaches. Through two interpreters, Alagkok and our skipper, they told us there were many bears on a place they called Bear Island, 15 to 30 miles offshore. It did not show on our maps, and even now I am not sure of its correct name.

Cooper and I headed for it the next morning with Palmquist and the crew, leaving the rest of the party camped on Long Island.

When we reached the island the Eskimos had talked about, it proved to be a bleak, rolling tabletop of rock and moss, some two miles long and half as wide, rising steeply in a series of cliffs at the southern end, sloping to the north and ending in a long reef running out into the ocean.

We came in under it in a northwest gale, with a black squall sweeping down on us, and the rocky bottom would not hold the *Venture's* anchors. We looked in vain for an opening in the ragged, surf-fringed beach, and when none appeared we ran for a smaller island a mile away.

There we found a snug little harbor, covered with a black raft of ducks. We went ashore to have a look at the bigger island with binoculars, and almost at once Howard Cooper spotted what we were hoping to see, a white bear at the foot of the cliffs, alternately lying down and pawing rocks around as if hunting for mice.

The storm and raging seas held us in that harbor for four hours. All that time the bear wandered around in plain sight, either below the cliffs or on the rocky tundra above them. At last our patience was exhausted. If we did not go after him before dark, Tommy Lameboy and Palmquist agreed, he would be likely to leave the island and take to the sea during the night.

There was no hope of crossing to Bear Island in a canoe. We'd have to run the *Venture* out in plain view and risk spooking him.

He saw or heard us as soon as we cleared our little harbor, and while we beat our slow way across the churning channel he stood near the top of the cliffs and watched us, the only living thing on all that bleak island or in the smoking sea, a bear carved from old ivory, the most unforgettable animal my eyes have ever rested on.

When we were within 300 yards of shore he climbed deliberately up the cliff and galloped off, stopping now and then to look back our way.

Lameboy had the *Venture's* wheel. At Palmquist's sharp order he ran the schooner within 50 yards of the jagged rocks where the surf was smoking, then turned parallel to the beach. A canoe was trailing at the stern. Tommy and Cooper and I tumbled into it, and somehow we got through the surf and scrambled out on shore, and dragged the freight canoe up beyond reach of the sea. Then we followed the bear up the cliff.

Cooper and I were carrying .300 Savage rifles. At the time we thought them adequate. I wouldn't think so today, not for a bear of that size. But at least we were better off than the old Cree. He had no gun at all.

The bear was out of sight behind the low backbone of the island, and we went after him at a run. But the running was wretchedly hard, over soft moss, around shallow pools and between huge rocks, and before we reached the crest of the ridge I dropped out. Sweat was streaming down my face despite the bitter ice-field wind, and I couldn't get enough air into my lungs. I'd be in no condition to shoot if we met the bear, I concluded. I swung back toward the sea cliffs, thinking he might have turned that way.

I was at the top of the cliff when I heard distant rifle fire. Whirling around, I could see Cooper almost at the far side of the island, alternately shooting and then running a few steps. Another shot thudded and to my total astonishment the slug sang above my head. It had ricocheted off a rock, and the realization hit me that the bear must be somewhere between Cooper and me, or he would not be shooting in my direction.

I swung my head, and sure enough there was the bear, out of Cooper's range now, coming straight for me at a lumbering run.

He did not know I was there. Directly behind me a ravine led down the face of the cliff to the sea, forming a natural bear trail. It was for that he was headed.

I went down on the moss to get out of sight and watched him lope toward me, and I had mixed feelings. I wanted him to come on. This was the thing I had come north for, and the hunt was all in my hands now. We'd be face to face in another minute or two. Unless I stopped him cleanly and in his tracks, there'd be a very one-sided bear-and-man fight.

He was the first game I had ever faced more dangerous than a whitetail deer. I was no expert rifleman, no crack shot, and I couldn't help some small misgivings as to whether I was up to my part of what was coming. Events were to prove I wasn't.

He went out of sight in a shallow dip, and I got to my feet and started after him, afraid he'd turn off and get away. Then he came up on my side of the hollow, and I suddenly realized that a running bear is neither slow nor clumsy. This one was covering ground like a racehorse.

I dropped to one knee, and when I thought he was close enough I threw my first shot. It had no effect and I tried again, with no better result.

The third one stopped him. He stood, whipping his head from side to side, lashing and biting at his own shoulders. When it was all over I learned that my 180-grain softnose had cut across his back under the skin and fat, just too high to break the spine or put him down. It was probably a painful wound, and it turned him into a bundle of explosive white fury, but it did nothing to disable him.

I thought he was badly wounded, and I scrambled erect to finish him. But just as I shot the next time he lurched ahead, and that one missed. Then, for the first time, he saw me.

The whole character of the hunt changed in a fraction of a second. I was no longer hunting the bear. He was hunting me. He dropped his head and came like an overgrown farm dog rushing out of a driveway at a passing car, and I did some desperately fast mental arithmetic.

I had started with five shells in the Savage. I had shot four times. I did the problem in subtraction with the speed of a computer, and did it over again. The answer was the same each time. There was one shell left in the chamber of the gun and there would be no time for reloading.

Instinct told me to drop the rifle and run, but my conscious mind knew better. Everything rested now on that single shell, and I still remember thinking I couldn't possibly kill him in time.

I cannot recall aiming or firing, but at the shot his head went down between his forelegs and he skidded to a stop, rolled up as tight as a shrimp. The bullet had struck him between the eyes, just below the bulge of the forehead, and had expanded so effectively that there was not a piece of unbroken bone bigger than a silver dollar left in his skull. A lightning bolt could not have killed more instantly.

I backed away while I fed five fresh hulls into the rifle. I waited two or three minutes then, feeling a whole lot better. When he did not move or twitch, I walked in with the safety off and prodded him around the head with the muzzle of the Savage. He was as lifeless as the rock he had fallen beside.

The next thing I did was walk back and find the empty cases I had levered out. From them to the bear I paced off exactly 17 steps, 51 feet.

Someone asked me long afterward whether I had actually shot at his head the last time. "Hell, no," I said. "I just shot at the bear." And I guess that was the truth.

I had my white bearskin. I also had nightmares for weeks afterward.

It happened 33 years ago. I have done much hunting since, some with a gun, some with a camera. But I have never again put myself in a situation of that kind, and as long as I live I don't intend to.

4 Sudden Encounters with Grizzlies

BY STEPHEN HERRERO

Hikers, hunters, or other persons traveling on foot in bear country may suddenly confront a grizzly. If this happens, a grizzly may attack because it perceives a threat. It follows that in these situations one should do everything possible to signal to the bear that you are not threatening. In this chapter I describe sudden encounter incidents and recommend the best course of action should you be attacked as a result of a sudden encounter. In Chapter 4 I describe the other main set of circumstances associated with grizzly bear attacks—when a grizzly is seeking human food or garbage, or, rarely, humans as food. The course of action I recommend for someone attacked under these circumstances is different.

A tragic sudden encounter occurred on the morning of July 27, 1976. Barbara Chapman, age twenty-four, was hiking in Glacier National Park, Canada, with a friend, Andrew Stepniewski, age twenty-six. They were on an old wagon road in the Cougar Valley, which the Parks Branch had allowed to revert to a trail. At the beginning of the trail there was a "Grizzly Bear" warning sign because there had been several sightings of grizzlies in the area that year, and it was known that the area had been frequented by grizzlies for years. Certainly Barbara knew this because of her work as a park naturalist. She had seen many black bears and a few grizzlies during the course of her work. Usually when she hiked she was careful to make some noise. On the morning of the attack they had been making noise repeatedly, especially by whistling.

They were about one-and-a-half miles up the trail with Andrew hiking in front. There was restricted visibility along several portions of the trail. They had just rounded a bend in the trail when they saw a grizzly bear, which was "huffing and puffing," charging toward them from less than fifty feet away. Andrew had only a second or two to notice that it was a grizzly, but not a big one, when the bear grabbed hold of him. He screamed, yelled, and resisted for a few seconds, and then realizing that resistance was futile, he relaxed and put his hands behind his head.

He thought that the attack on him lasted for only fifteen or twenty seconds and then the bear attacked Barbara. This attack lasted only a "few seconds." Andrew remembers Barbara kicking at the bear and briefly trying to resist, and then the attack was over.

Barbara Chapman was dead. Andrew Stepniewski was critically injured with head, facial, neck, and body wounds. Despite his injuries, he managed to hike out to the busy Trans-Canada Highway in an hour and a half.

Back at the site of the attack, the bear dragged Barbara's body about two-hundred feet down a steep bank into heavy alder undergrowth and began to eat it. Although it is possible that this was a predatory attack—that is, that the bear attacked to kill and eat—it is unlikely as it involved a female with cubs, encountered at close range, which abandoned Andrew once he played dead. I believe that the suddenness of the encounter triggered a defensive attack by the mother bear. Once dead, Barbara's inert body may have elicited scavenging by the bear.

Only a few hours after the attack, a grizzly bear female and her three cubs were killed by park wardens near the attack site. Evidence confirmed that the female was the bear involved in the attack. The subsequent investigation showed that the bear family had been digging for food at the side of the trail just before the attack.

Barbara Chapman is the only person who was hiking in a national park prior to being killed by a grizzly bear. In this incident I believe that, despite Barbara's whistling, the mother grizzly first became aware of Barbara and Andrew only when they were very close. I categorize this incident as a "sudden encounter" in which the bear was surprised to find people very near her and her cubs. The bear acted very aggressively, and the attack was probably triggered by the mother bear's instinct to defend her young.

We will never know if the bear heard Barbara's whistling before it attacked. I have watched grizzly bears that were so intent on feeding that they did not respond to my voice conveyed in a normal tone from 150 feet away (I was up in a tree at the time). Perhaps if Barbara and Andrew had been loudly making noise, such as by shouting or singing, the bear might have fled before they were too close. Once the attack occurred, both Barbara and Andrew seem to have actively resisted for a while. The data on what has happened during other similar attacks suggests that, if possible, both of them should have played dead when the attack began. Once Andrew did this, the bear left him and attacked Barbara. Whether or not passive resistance by Barbara might have prevented her death is unknown.

It is possible (although no specific evidence exists) that the bear that killed Barbara Chapman and injured Andrew Stepniewski was the same bear that injured three people in two separate incidents five years earlier, in 1971, on the Balu Pass Trail, only three miles away. The bear could have been involved in all three incidents because it was fourteen when autopsied in 1976. Grizzly bear adult females use the same home range year after year, and all of the attacks were probably within one adult female's home range. Consistent with this possibility was the highly aggressive nature of the female involved in one of the 1971 incidents and in the 1976 incident.

In my opinion the warden service was justified in killing the entire bear family. This may sound like an overreaction, but I consider it probable that aggressive behavior in bears has a significant degree of genetic predisposition. This bear could have attacked again, or her cubs might have grown up to have this tendency. Larry Kaniut, in *Alaska Bear Tales,* a book about bear attacks and bear lore in Alaska, suggests that once a bear has killed a person, it is likely to injure or kill other people. Larry cites three grizzly (brown) bear-inflicted fatalities in which a bear that was thought to have killed one person subsequently went after others.

While only one attack preceded by a sudden encounter between people and a grizzly in a national park has led to death, many have resulted in major injuries. In the Introduction I mention an incident that occurred in June 1977 in which Dr. Barrie Gilbert was seriously injured by a grizzly bear in Yellowstone National Park. Barrie, and his assistant, Bruce Hastings, had begun field work in early June on a study of grizzly bear behavior. The aim of the study was to understand grizzly bear behavior better and thus help prevent bear attacks.

The day before the attack occurred, Barrie and Bruce used binoculars to observe a single grizzly bear, thought to have been a male, and a female grizzly accompanied by three cubs of the year (i.e., cubs born the preceding winter). The bears were probably unaware of the researchers. The next morning they saw all of the bears again in a "grassy expanse" where they were feeding. At 6:15 in the morning, the bear thought to have been a male stood and looked toward the female and then ran off, apparently being chased by the female. Barrie and Bruce watched the female and cubs feed for two more hours. At about 8:30 a.m., the researchers left their base camp and tried to move along and behind a ridge to a knoll, which they hoped would be a good vantage point. They assumed that the grizzly bear family group would remain where it was, but at 10:30 they saw the bear, thought to be an adult male, back feeding in the area where he had been seen before. They did not see the mother or her cubs. Barrie and Bruce continued hiking along the ridge until, at about 10:45 a.m., Bruce dropped his pack and stayed behind for a few min-utes. Barrie was about to use his binoculars to look at a distant meadow to see if the female and her cubs were there when he heard a low "woof" and saw a "ball of fur, low to the ground" coming his way.

Barrie told what happened next in a narrative he dictated about a week later in the hospital.

"(I) could not estimate distance or identify the bear. My first thought was that I had miscalculated our location and thus had stumbled onto the sow. Knowing that I could not bluff a sow I felt the only solution was to give her as much room as possible. I turned and ran toward a small tree with bushes around its base. The bear caught me before I got to the tree and I went down in the bushes. The bear started biting me on the back of the head, which felt like a pick-axe scraping along my skull bones. In defense I turned over to kick and push the bear off but then she/he bit my face. I recall a deep bite which crushed the bones under my left eye—which was also lost. The face biting continued. . . . I cried out during the attack . . . but the bear kept biting. I lifted my legs up to try to kick him away but was unsuccessful. This was the time I got bitten on the leg. . . ."

When the attack on Barrie began, Bruce heard sounds that "weren't right" but also were not clearly identifiable because high winds were rushing through the branches. Bruce stepped back to his pack and about fifty feet ahead he could see the grizzly bear. Although he could not see Barrie he real-ized that the bear must be mauling him. Bruce stepped toward a shrubby clump of trees and emitted a loud and low "Ha!" The bear lifted its head and bolted off. Although neither man saw any cubs, both felt that it was probably the female that had attacked.

Bruce went to Barrie's side, where he could see that he had suffered se-vere injuries. Bleeding was extensive. Barrie told Bruce to take the VHF radio and call for a helicopter. Bruce administered first aid. Both men kept calm.

A helicopter soon arrived with paramedics. They did an excellent job, but Barrie remembers one of them saying something like, "If it will make you feel any better the park killed dozens of bears in the last ten years." Barrie replied that he did not want the bear killed because it had been an accident.

It took over 1440 hours in the hospital and more than a year, as well as many bouts of plastic surgery, for Barrie to be repaired. His strength came back fast, and within three weeks of release from the hospital he was riding his bicy-cle to Utah State University where he worked. The trauma of the attack and a missing left eye will be with Barrie all his life.

It appears probable that the bear that attacked Barrie was the grizzly bear mother with three cubs of the year. If it was the mother bear, then the earlier interaction that she had with the other single grizzly bear may have left her agitated or at least left her alert to potential threats to her family.

Barrie first became aware of the attacking bear when it was very close and was "woofing" and running toward him. Because Barrie and Bruce were hiking quietly in the high wind on the ridge, this suggests that the bear may have suddenly discovered Barrie nearby, felt threatened, and charged, probably leaving her cubs behind. If he and Bruce had been making loud noise, this might have alerted the bear to them when they were still distant. However, Barrie said the wind was so strong on the ridge top that he felt sound wouldn't carry.

It was probably a mistake for Barrie to try to run from the bear and to fight back once he was attacked.

The bear's fleeing in response to Bruce's emitting of a low pitched, loud sound during the attack was unusual. I know of no other attack where this sound has been tried to repel a bear. Loud shouting has occurred during several incidents, but this usually has served to redirect an attack to the person shouting.

The Chapman and Gilbert incidents are typical of sudden injurious encounters between grizzly bears and hikers. Hiking prior to being attacked was the most common circumstance associated with injury (50 percent, or 68 out of 135 incidents in which the party's activity prior to injury was known). In injurious encounters preceded by hiking, the persons injured were seldom aware of the bear until within fifty-five yards or less (83 percent, or 29 out of 35 incidents in which data exist regarding the distance at which a person first became aware of the bear that injured them). I assume that the surprise was mutual in most of these cases since grizzlies normally flee, or at least avoid contact, when a person approaches. Therefore, I describe these incidents as being "sudden encounters," although it is possible that in some of these incidents the bear had either stalked the person injured or heard the person coming from a distance and waited or approached.

In only 15 percent of the injurious incidents (10 out of 68) preceded by hiking did a party report making noise prior to being attacked. Evidence suggests that making noise may help to alert grizzly bears to your travel, therefore lessening the chances of sudden encounters. This idea should be tested experimentally before being accepted. Rarely did a traveling grizzly appear to have blundered onto a person who was resting or camping, apparently not becoming aware of the person until at close range.

Sudden encounters leading to human injury usually did not last long. Good data on the duration of such attacks were only available for thirteen incidents. All of these ended in less than ten minutes, and 54 percent (7 out of 13) were over in less than two minutes. The short duration of these encounters is consistent with my view that grizzlies attacking under these circumstances are responding to a perceived threat and, when they have dealt with it, they leave.

Grizzly bear mothers were responsible for 74 percent (20 out of 27) of all incidents that I regarded as sudden encounters and where records existed of the age/sex class of the bear. I regard this as a minimum figure because sometimes cubs remain hidden and a female with young is mistaken to be a single bear. Older cubs may charge people with their mothers, but it is the mothers that injure people. Mother grizzlies that injure people who suddenly confront them appear to be acting to protect their cubs in a sort of "defense reaction." Grizzly bear females with cubs of the year are probably more dangerous than are mothers with cubs more than a year old, although data adequate to test this contention weren't available.

The defense reaction is so much a part of some mother grizzlies that they a have been known to charge small groups of people and even trucks: I well remember a mother grizzly running flat out toward David Hamer and me while we, protected within my panel truck, sped up and swerved to avoid being caught. She had good reason to charge us; we had one of her cubs in a trap.

Hikers who find themselves close to a grizzly bear may discern some signs of the bear's intentions. A grizzly bear rearing onto its hind legs, a common stance, is trying to sense what is happening. Normally this is not an aggressive posture. On its hind legs the bear sniffs, listens and looks, trying to discover what kind of animal stands before it. Standing on its four legs a grizzly may show agitation by swaying its head from side to side, making huffing noises, or by opening and closing its mouth and making clacking noises with its teeth. Running and circling, usually to get downwind, may follow to get into a better position to sense (especially smell) the strange object. If the bear feels threatened, fleeing or a charge may follow. The seriousness of a grizzly's charge is usually indicated by the position of its ears. Like wolves and dogs, grizzly and black bears use the position of their ears as an indication of aggressive intent. Generally speaking, the farther back the ears are, and the more they are flattened to the neck, the more the grizzly is aroused. In combination with this, the hair may be raised on the back of the neck and on the front portions of the back.

In encounters where grizzly bears act aggressively for several minutes, but haven't attacked a person, I think that attack can usually be avoided by proper response. In Chapter 6 I give detailed recommendations regarding what a person should do during encounters with a grizzly.

Case histories of hiker–bear injurious encounters suggest that there are few aggressive displays preceding an attack and that contact most often occurs during the first charge. Available information is inadequate to test this impression scientifically.

There are data documenting that a loud growl or deep gurgling was the noise that most often accompanied charges that led to injury. People injured by a grizzly bear described this sound in fifteen incidents. In nine incidents the attacking bear was reported to have made an explosive sound such as a snort or a woof. During aggressive encounters that did not lead to injury, the relative frequency of these two sounds was reversed. In these incidents, grizzlies were reported to have growled or gurgled only ten times and to have snorted or woofed twenty-three times.

Because of the difficulties in getting accurate records about sounds emitted during encounters I would only tentatively suggest that, during aggressive encounters between people and grizzly bears, the growl is more likely to be associated with injury than is the snort. The snort may serve more as a warning sound. This seems to be the case in encounters between bears. Some sudden encounters between grizzlies and people that resulted in major injury were not preceded by any sound.

If you are attacked while hiking in the backcountry, or if, during the day, a female grizzly with cubs wanders into your camp, discovers you, and charges, you can assume that the bear is responding to the sudden encounter. Such attacks usually occur when there is sufficient daylight for a person to see. They are normally preceded by a charge, not by slow approaches or by walking later followed by a charge.

If you are attacked by a grizzly bear following a sudden encounter, I recommend that you passively resist by playing dead. I have chosen two of many similar incidents to illustrate this point.

June 4, 1976, was clear and crisp in the treeless alpine zone of Spatsizi Wilderness Park in northern British Columbia. An acquaintance of mine, Judith Donaldson, a wildlife biologist, and her companion, Mike Sather, also a wildlife biologist, were traversing a sidehill as part of their work. Neither Judy nor Mike was making any noise and neither was specifically watching for bears. At 4:00 p.m. Mike said to Judy, "Don't move." Above and upwind from them, Mike noticed a blond grizzly bear accompanied by two older blond cubs. The bears were close together in a small depression on the hillside, about fifty feet from Mike and eighty feet from Judy. The cubs noticed the biologists first and then the mother bear saw them. The adult bear waited about two seconds and then charged, roaring as she came at Mike and Judy. Mike stood and faced the female until she was about ten feet away. He then dropped to his knees, face to the ground, hands behind his head. The grizzly mother attacked Mike first. She straddled him and began biting and "batting him around like a Ping-Pong ball." Mike did not fight back and remained curled up as best he could.

As soon as Mike saw the bears and spoke to Judy she continued walking down the hill, away from the bears. A cub ran toward her and continued on down the hill. Judy stopped and watched the cub as he ran. She saw that the mother bear was mauling Mike. The attack on Mike seemed to have lasted about fifteen seconds when the bear looked up and noticed Judy, who turned and continued walking down the hill. The mother bear waited another two seconds and then charged Judy.

As Judy wrote to me:

> She got me (standing) from behind, knocked my snugly fitting hat off and my light nylon day pack, and bit me. The upper teeth entered my right shoulder, the lower teeth my ribs about ten inches lower. . . . She knocked me about eight feet down the hill. I hit the ground, curled into the same position as Mike, hands behind my neck, arms protecting my head, but on my right side facing into the hill. She could not have bitten me once I hit the ground, as my only wounds were on my right side on which I was lying. I did not lift my head or move until Mike called saying the bear had gone. We both had remained silent throughout the encounter.

Mike's injuries kept him hospitalized for a day. They included a cracked shoulder blade, puncture wounds from bites, and a C-shaped cut on his head, which required twelve stitches. Judy, who had torn puncture wounds on her shoulder and back, was treated at the hospital emergency room and released.

Given the circumstances of suddenly confronting an aggressive grizzly bear mother with her cubs, both biologists received relatively minor injuries. The attack on Mike lasted only about fifteen seconds, and the attack on Judy was probably briefer. Had either biologist actively resisted by fighting or screaming, I suspect that the attack would have lasted longer and would have resulted in more severe injuries.

This encounter could possibly have been prevented if Mike and Judy had spotted the bears sooner and had not approached the family. Since the biologists were hiking into a brisk wind, the bears probably didn't get the biologists' scent and were probably completely unaware of them until they spotted Mike only fifty feet away from the family group. Had Mike and Judy made loud noises while hiking, the bears might have been given advance notice, and the mother bear might have chosen to flee rather than attack. Such a choice by a bear is dependent on many factors such as the personality of the bear, its family status, and the specific circumstances of the encounter.

In late June 1960 Dr. Ian Stirling and a companion were working in the Verendrye Creek Basin of Kootenay National Park, British Columbia. Ian, a research biologist with the Canadian Wildlife Service who is well known for his research on polar bears, showed significant calm and carefully thought-out action during a very frightening encounter.

At the time of the incident, Ian was a summer student working for the warden service of Kootenay Park. He and his partner's job for the day was to clear deadfall from the trail in Verendrye Creek Basin. Ian was a short distance off the trail and was standing by the roots of a large spruce tree that had fallen over. He heard "sporadic puffing" coming from the direction of the trail. He peered through a hole in the roots and saw a grizzly bear. He next saw the bear "lift its nose, test the wind," and then it came running toward him. Ian and the bear next did two-and-a-half laps around the roots of the tree with Ian staying ahead of the bear. Ian saw an opportunity to sneak away to a big tree that he wanted to climb. Ian's letter to me tells what happened next.

I had only moved maybe twenty feet when she [Ian states elsewhere that he never was sure of the sex] saw me, let out a most electrifying vocalization that I could only call a "roar," and she bolted after me. I can still see her clearing the log in as much detail as if it were yesterday. I began to run for the heavy timber but, after a few steps, realized it was futile. The choice was then to get knocked down or lie down myself and play dead. I dove head first into the edge of a thick clump of alders so that my head and neck and part of my shoulders were in between some of the thin trunks. I was lying on my stomach, [and I] crossed my heels and clasped my fingers together over the back of my neck. I lay absolutely still. At the time, I fully expected to be mauled or at the least bitten a couple of times. I also knew quite well I might be killed. I was terrified at my circumstance but calm in that I knew what I was trying to do. The difficulty was going to be to carry it out if things started to get painful. I was concentrating as hard as I could on trying to be motionless and to endure whatever happened next to the best of my ability. . . . I can still remember rather clearly how annoyed I was with my heart. Here was I, trying to lie still and be quiet while my heart seemed to be thumping like the pistons of a locomotive. It felt as if it was bouncing me off the ground and it seemed the bear could surely hear it.

The bear ran up and stopped by my left leg and stood there for a moment. Then it nosed my left leg and I tried to brace myself mentally for the beginning of a mauling. Nothing happened. It nosed me a second time, not hard but about like you might tap someone's shoulder to get their attention. Then it stood still beside me. There was no sound in the basin except for the heavy breathing of the bear. I could hear the saliva bubbling in his mouth as he breathed. I lay still, face down, eyes closed, while my heart threatened to leap out of my rib cage.

I don't know how long the bear stood there, probably only a few minutes although it seemed like an eternity. Then I heard it move and readied myself mentally again but suddenly realized it was moving slowly away. . . .

The bear left without further incident. When Ian tried to stand, his knees were so shaky that he fell to the ground. He soon regained his coordination and walked to the trail, where he met his partner who was up a tree during Ian's encounter with the grizzly. Ian's partner casually said something like, "Hey! Did you see the bear?"

Not everyone would have the mental toughness to play dead under such circumstances. Given the choices of running, getting ready to fight the bear, and playing dead, I feel that Ian did the right thing. Although he could have been mauled, he played the odds and won.

The table below presents the data on which I base my recommendation regarding what to do if attacked during a sudden encounter. Passively resisting the attack by remaining as motionless and soundless as possible—playing dead—seems to have decreased the intensity of injury in this type of incident. This is a probability statement, which means that usually, but not always, playing dead decreases the intensity of such attacks. Trying to fight an attacking grizzly during a sudden encounter can't be ruled out as a strategy based on the data in the table. Because of the difficulty in quantifying these situations I have not used statistics to test for significance. My recommendation for playing dead under such circumstances is therefore based mainly on my impressions from examining similar incidents, and my understanding of bear behavior.

Response of attacking grizzly bear* to a person playing dead or fighting back

Intensity of Attack	Increase	Decrease	No Change
Play dead/passively resist	2	16	8
Fight back/actively resist	3	7	3

*The circumstance precipitating attack was in all cases judged to be defense of young, responding to sudden surprise, or responding to harassment.

After being attacked in a sudden encounter, or perhaps when a charging grizzly is just about to contact you, a person should assume a position that will minimize exposure of vital areas and parts of the body where such attacks normally focus. I recommend the position of hands behind the neck, fingers interlocked, with the forearms and elbows protecting the face as best as possible. A bear's bite can break or crush the face or neck, but its jaws won't open wide enough to crush the skull of an adult. The knees should be drawn up to the face—the fetal position. Hands interlocked around the knees with the face, especially the eyes, buried in the knees, would also be a good position except that this doesn't protect the neck. Lying flat on the ground, face down, with your hands locked behind your neck is another possibility. Leave your pack on if you have one and didn't drop it to distract the bear. The pack should help to protect your body.

During sudden encounter attacks, the face and skull commonly receive injury. I noted this in my data, and Kaniut also mentions many cases of facial and skull or scalp injuries. Attacks are usually directed to the head probably because during aggressive encounters between grizzly bears they frequently bite each other's faces and heads, trying to grab the opponent's jaws in order to disable their primary weapon.

Historical records also suggest playing dead during sudden encounters. On July 14, 1806, Simon Fraser, an explorer in western Canada, wrote of an Indian and his wife who were walking along a riverbank and surprised a large grizzly with two cubs. The Indian fired at the mother bear and wounded her. In return she attacked his wife, "and she instantly laid down flat upon the ground and did not stir, in consequence of (which) the bear deserted (her) and ran after her husband. . . ." The same response to sudden encounters with a grizzly was also recommended by a California pioneer: "If the man lies still, with his face down, the bear will usually content himself with biting . . . for a while about the arms and legs, and will then go off a few steps and watch . . . the bear will believe him dead, and will soon . . . go away. But let the man move, and the bear is upon him again; let him fight, and he will be in imminent danger of being torn to pieces."

You should not play dead before you are attacked unless a charging grizzly is extremely close and you feel certain that attack is imminent. While standing, you have options such as dodging to avoid attack. I know of several cases in which people have successfully dodged attack by dropping an object, such as a camera, to distract the bear and give themselves time to climb a tree, or by using clothing to redirect the attack away from the body, or by keeping trees between themselves and an attacking bear.

The active person in a group typically draws the brunt of an attack after a sudden encounter. This suggests that if a companion were being severely mauled you might shout or wave your arms to draw the attack to yourself, and then play dead after being attacked. This tactic frequently has worked.

A few minutes after an attack, or after playing dead, you should cautiously raise your head to see if the bear or bear family is still around. Normally a grizzly will leave within a few minutes after a sudden encounter. If it has not left, continue to be passive. Once the bear has left, determine the extent of injury to yourself or others and begin first aid. As soon as the victim is stable and the bear seems to have left, leave for help. Remember the location of the victim. If the bear attacks again (which is very rare), then play dead again.

Instead of playing dead after a sudden encounter, some people have chosen to try to fight a bear using fists, knives, or whatever weapon they might have. In exceptional cases people have stunned such attacking grizzly bears by hitting them with a club, or just their fists or knees, or by sticking their fingers in a grizzly's large nostrils, and the bear has left. Because grizzlies are stronger and have superior natural weapons, it is usually the human being who takes the worst punishment in a fight with an attacking bear.

I do not want to leave the impression that suddenly meeting a grizzly bear just about guarantees injury. Such is not the case. In the first place, most grizzlies are tolerant of people. Each year hundreds of thousands of people visit grizzly country and few injuries occur. Even when suddenly confronted at close range, most grizzlies flee without any aggressive action.

Dick Knight, who has been studying grizzly bears in the Yellowstone ecosystem for more than ten years, describes the behavior of twenty-nine radio-instrumented grizzly bears that he knew were in close proximity to people at one time or another. Only five of the twenty-nine grizzlies were ever reported to have acted aggressively toward people, and none had ever injured a person. As part of his research he deliberately approached a number of grizzlies, usually to distances of less than three-hundred feet, before they sensed his presence. He noted eight instances of bears fleeing in response to such provocation and four instances in which the grizzly acted aggressively, usually charging a short distance before fleeing.

In Waterton Lakes National Park, Canada, David Hamer, Keith Brady, and I recorded thirteen instances during 1981 in which a radio-collared female grizzly with two cubs of the year was located 110 yards or less from people. This grizzly bear mother did not act aggressively in any of these instances. In two cases she slowly approached people, causing them to slowly retreat; seven times she appeared to ignore people; and four times she moved away.

Research shows that most grizzly bears are normally tolerant of people under a great variety of circumstances. However, one of the most common situations that sometimes leads to a breakdown of this tolerance is when a person suddenly gets too close to a grizzly.

One of the most dangerous situations in which to come nose to nose with a grizzly is when it is feeding on or is near a carcass. Any grizzly bear near a carcass is potential dynamite that may explode in the direction of any animal that the bear thinks is competing with it for the food. Crows, ravens, magpies, jays, and other scavenging birds often dart in and out trying to get their share. A grizzly bear will swat and bite at these competitors. Other bears, wolves, coyotes, foxes, wolverines, and other scavenging mammals often try to approach as well. A grizzly will usually be aggressive toward such animals. To avoid having parts of a carcass taken, grizzlies will sometimes completely cover a carcass with vegetation and dirt and then sleep on top or nearby. Prudent people do everything possible to avoid suddenly confronting a grizzly bear that is near a carcass.

On Sunday morning, September 18, 1983, Trevor and Patricia Janz, both in their twenties, were backpacking on the Crypt Lake trail, in Waterton Lakes National Park, Canada. They were returning from camping overnight and it was snowing lightly, but not enough to obscure their vision. Patricia remembers the wind blowing into their faces before they were attacked by a grizzly bear. Trevor was 100 to 130 feet ahead of Patricia and was singing softly when he suddenly saw the head of a bear below the trail about fifty feet to his left. He had no way of knowing that eighty feet away there was a partly consumed bighorn sheep carcass on which the bear, a female grizzly, and her two yearling cubs had been feeding.

Later in the hospital, Trevor told me, "It was coming toward me when I saw it." He recalls that the bear ran faster as it came closer, but he does not think that it made any noise. The bear grabbed Trevor by the front of the leg and he fell to the ground. Trevor had on a large pack containing his gear and part of Patricia's gear, and when he fell to the ground the pack covered his back, neck, and the back of his head. The pack and his heavy clothing seem to have helped protect him. Trevor's face was toward the ground, and his hands were underneath his body. He stressed that he did not fight the bear but tried to keep his head down. He thinks he was mauled this time for approximately one to one-and-a-half minutes. He remembers grunting and low growling sounds between the bites. Although he was injured more severely during a second attack, Trevor thinks that his jaw was broken on the right side during the first attack.

Just before the bear left, it nosed the ground around Trevor and made low growling sounds for about fifteen seconds. Trevor thinks he then lay there for about ten minutes, during which time he heard Patricia scream twice.

Patricia had seen the bear charging Trevor until they both disappeared behind some trees. She was spared a clear view of Trevor's mauling. She was, however, aware that Trevor was being mauled and took two steps back on the trail. Then she took her pack off almost automatically, having recalled that this was a good diversion for a bear, and she picked out and began climbing a tree. She was part way up the tree (her hands were about sixteen feet above the ground according to measurements I and the park warden made) when she paused momentarily from what seemed like a firm stance in the tree. She looked down the trail and made eye contact with the bear, which was about eighty feet away. The bear immediately charged her or may have already been charging her when she made eye contact. The bear continued the charge without hesitation up the tree, and at the ten-foot level it broke a branch that formed one of Patricia's footholds. This caused Patricia to fall out of the tree, and she remembers screaming "No!"

While she was on the ground being attacked by the bear, Patricia held her hands on the side of her head and tried to keep her head down on the trail. Patricia was uncertain but she thought that the bear had tried to turn her over. The attack continued, still violently, despite the fact that Patricia offered little if any resistance. At one point Patricia got mad, and seeing the bear's nose she "tweaked" it. The bear snorted and jumped back as though surprised. It made a few woofs and then left.

Patricia felt that "her head was in pieces." She stated, "I tried to find out if I was dead or alive." She last saw the bear about twenty-five to thirty-five feet away "just kind of standing there woofing." Sometime after this, the bear returned to maul Trevor a second time.

Meanwhile, Trevor, being a medical student, tried to assess his condition. He counted his heart rate to figure his blood loss. He later stated that he was not thinking too well and got up, loosened his pack straps, and started to climb a tree, getting about five feet off the ground. The bear returned and pulled Trevor to the ground. This time the pack did not cover his entire back and head but was across his body, exposing his neck, head, and face. This time he felt that the bear inflicted worse injuries, especially to his face. He stated in retrospect that he "was happy there was just crunching and not crunching and ripping." He thought that his heavy, layered clothing helped to protect him in the arm and shoulder regions. During the second mauling he stated that he wasn't protecting his head as well as the first time because he was weaker and generally less focused. He said he thought about dying quickly. He had impressions of "the smell of blood, bear, and of his bones cracking."

Finally the bear left Trevor, and within about eight to ten minutes two hikers arrived. The hikers took Trevor and Patricia down the trail, and they were soon rushed to a hospital where their conditions were stabilized but still critical. A short while later they were moved to major medical facilities in Calgary, Alberta.

Both Trevor and Patricia had only seen one bear during the attack. They didn't know that the bear that had attacked them was a mother with cubs and that a carcass had been involved. Because these details were unknown at the time, the incident sounded to park wardens as though it might have been an unprovoked attack. Because of this, the wardens went to the mauling site hours after the attack and set snares to catch the bear. Darkness fell before they searched the area thoroughly, and they still didn't know that a female with young and a carcass were involved.

The next morning four armed wardens and I approached the mauling site. We checked the snares, discovering that one of them had been sprung. Tracks in the snow showed that at least three grizzlies were around. During the initial check of the trap site one of the wardens heard snorting noises from a bear estimated to be about 110 yards above the trail. Nothing further happened then.

We continued searching the mauling site and the surrounding area for clues that might further explain the attack. Just below the trail, we found a sheep carcass on which the grizzly bear family had recently fed. We remained cautious even though we assumed that the bears had accepted our presence because we had been near the carcass for the better part of five hours.

We left the carcass and returned to the mauling site. We radioed our findings back to Max Winkler, the chief warden, and Bernie Lieff, the park superintendent, and awaited their instructions. Because a female with young and a carcass were involved, we considered pulling the snares and closing the area for the rest of the season. The mother bear had acted very aggressively, but defensively.

We were walking from the tree that Patricia had climbed toward the site where Trevor was mauled when Keith Brady, the lead warden, saw the bear family approaching the carcass only 150 feet away. Keith quickly told two of the other wardens to back up and moved back about three feet himself. The mother bear charged almost as soon as she saw us. Keith shouted at her to warn and deter her, but she didn't break stride as she charged through the trees. Keith thought to himself, "Oh my God, no," when he was aware she probably wouldn't stop. I was about a hundred feet or so behind Keith and two other wardens, and I stood my ground and glanced at a tree that looked good to climb if the situation allowed. I also thought of playing dead if I was among the first to be attacked.

Keith had his rifle at his shoulder as the bear lurched toward us, dodging around trees. Here was a man, mature and experienced with bears and firearms, who hated to kill any bear but had cautioned other wardens in the event of necessity to wait, never take their eyes off a charging bear, and make the first shot count. Keith shot her when she was only eight or nine paces away. The first shot from his .338 Magnum hit her in the neck and shoulder region and stopped her. Several more shots killed her. At the distance she was shot, she could have reached Keith in less than half a second. The whole incident, from when we first saw her to when she was first shot, had taken three or four seconds.

The bear lay still. Her cubs had run off, never charging. In the silence after the shots I could hear my heart pounding. In examining the situation after we calmed down, we judged that Keith was standing within about ten feet of where Trevor Janz was mauled. Given the personality of this bear and the circumstances, it seemed unlikely that she would have stopped the charge without attacking us.

Both Trevor and Patricia had extensive hiking and general mountain experience before the attack. After the incident Trevor told me that "we usually avoid areas that have posted bear warnings" and that "we usually keep our heads up and watch around corners . . . and usually make noise." Sometimes such encounters at carcasses can be anticipated and avoided, but this time there were no good clues to suggest the possibility of a carcass or an attack. Fortunately such incidents are very rare. My records had ten similar cases. There were a few things that Trevor and Patricia might have done differently. They could have been making more noise prior to the attack, which might have warned the bears of their presence at a greater distance and caused them to retreat. In this particular circumstance I doubt that this would have occurred. Patricia, when she began climbing the tree, should not have stopped until she was at least thirty-three feet off of the ground. (The highest a grizzly is known to have climbed during an attack is slightly less than thirty-three feet.) The tree was a good one to climb, but whether she could have made it this far or whether the bear could have climbed higher than the ten-foot height where Patricia fell from the tree, is unknown. Autopsy suggested that the female grizzly was physically normal and healthy. Tooth sectioning put her age at fifteen or sixteen years. She probably lived for most of this time, and raised several litters, having hikers within her home range. But on September 18, 1983, a combination of circumstances—a dead bighorn sheep nearby a trail, the presence of cubs, and approaching hikers, led to attack and injury for the Janz's and the death of the bear.

Carcasses which have been claimed by a grizzly may lead to encounters if people suddenly come upon them. A carcass left overnight by hunters may also be claimed by a grizzly. Both black and grizzly bears are efficient scavengers with an acute sense of smell. Hunters should try to hoist a carcass high into the air using ropes and pulleys. This will probably save the meat, but will disperse the odor, which may attract a bear to the area. If a carcass must be left on the ground, it should be put in an open area where a scavenging bear could be seen at a distance. Many grizzly bears have been shot unnecessarily and at least six hunters have been injured as a result of approaches to carcasses left overnight.

If a carcass is left overnight in grizzly country, it should be approached the next day with the assumption that a grizzly has discovered it. Come in on horseback or by vehicle if possible. Make lots of noise from a safe distance before approaching. A grizzly may have dragged the carcass a short distance or buried it. The bear will probably be close by. If the situation looks suspicious, it is safest to abandon the kill.

I investigated one such carcass-related incident that had occurred near Grand Cache, Alberta, in mid-September 1968. Mr. Kelly Joakim, a guide, and his two American clients had been moose hunting. The day before the incident occurred the party had shot two moose, gutted them, and dragged them to a nearby seismic line. The moose were left together on top of a small hill.

Kelly, an Indian, had lived in grizzly country most of his life. When I interviewed him in the Hinton hospital, he said that he had shot one grizzly bear before at close range, but then he had his dogs with him, which helped to keep the bear at bay. He said that his grandfather had shot and killed grizzlies by hitting them in the ear with .22 long rifle bullets.

On the day of the mauling Kelly was unarmed as he and the hunters approached the moose carcasses at about eight o'clock in the morning without thinking about grizzly bears. They were at the bottom of the hill where the carcasses lay when they saw a grizzly charging from about thirty-five feet away.

When he first saw the grizzly Kelly was about ten feet in front of the hunters. As the bear charged, Kelly immediately turned and ran. In the interval, the hunters shot the bear twice but it still caught the fleeing Kelly. He felt the grizzly sink its teeth into the back of his thigh as the bear stood on top of him, biting and pinning him to the ground. The hunters waited for opportuni-

ties to shoot the bear without wounding Kelly. Four more shots from their
.307 Magnums and the bear was dead. Kelly told me that each time the bear
was shot it bit yet harder on his leg.

Examination of the moose carcasses revealed that both had been partly
dismembered and buried with sticks, earth, grass, and detritus. Obviously, the
bear had been scavenging. Had the hunting party taken precautions, this attack—and Kelly's injuries—could have been avoided.

Another carcass-related incident, described by Larry Kaniut, suggests
that under these circumstances fighting without weapons is usually futile and
most likely increases the severity of an attack. In September 1955, Forest H.
Young, Jr., and his partner, Marty Cordes, had killed a moose on the Chilkat
River, Alaska, and over several days packed most of the meat to camp. All that
was left at the kill site were the gut piles and the hide. Forest decided to make a
last trip for the hide.

When he arrived, weaponless, at the kill site, Young found that bears
had taken over—they had covered the remaining gut piles with sticks and
moss. Forest went to the tree and began to retrieve the hide when he noticed
two bears a hundred yards away. He figured they were grizzlies but wasn't concerned, his bear experience convinced him they wouldn't bother him.

Instantly one of the animals charged him. Still unalarmed, he waved
his arms and shouted, normal procedures in such a situation. But this bear
wasn't going to be bluffed. Forest jumped for a low branch on a tree and had
hardly climbed half a dozen feet when the grizzly cleared the brush and
clamped down on his right leg, ripping him from the tree.

When he landed, the bear held him down with one paw and chomped
on his thigh with its teeth, ripping out a mass of flesh. Forest pounded the
brute in the face with his fists—tantamount to a mouse chasing a cat. Their
faces were only a foot apart as the bear ripped flesh and clothing. Forest broke
his hand pounding on the bear's face, and the beast continued to shred his
lower limbs.

Young determined to play dead and fell to his side. The bear stopped
immediately and may have left, but Forest groaned in spite of himself. The bear
bit him in the side exposing his bladder.

The pain was excruciating; but Forest did not move. The bear took a
few more bites, ripping three ribs loose from the spine and opening up the
chest cavity. Forest remained silent and motionless. The bear left.

Young tried to relax and tell himself the bear was gone, but the bear
roared back two or three times to inspect his victim. The ground trembled
under him, and he lay there expecting the bear to rip him apart any moment.

After a while it became necessary for the man to turn his face to facilitate breathing and to allow fluids to drain.

It was too much to hope for. Here came the bear again! He must have sensed the man's different position because he lit into Forest anew, spanning his buttocks with its jaws and biting to the bone, picking him up and shaking him. Forest thought his head would pop off, and he feared his spine would snap. The bear then dropped him and left.

It was some time later that Marty called from a distance. He was aghast when he discovered his partner. Marty wanted to carry Forest back to camp, but the pain was unbearable for the injured man. Marty went to camp to retrieve a sleeping bag, air mattress, some food, water, gas lantern, a shotgun and shells. He took them back to Young, made him comfortable and then headed for Haines and help.

During the next $14^1/2$ hours Forest hung on to the thin thread of life. The bear returned a few more times and was frightened away by shotgun blasts. Late that night Marty returned with help, but the brute was reluctant to give up his victim for he followed them all the way back to the cabin, roaring in the distance.

The next morning a helicopter picked Forest up and took him to Juneau where Dr. Cass Carter worked on him. Young suffered a severe mauling, which included having a rib ripped out by the bear. The extent of his injuries was so critical that Dr. Carter gave little hope of survival unless the victim had received medical attention within six hours. But Forest Young, Jr., did survive.

I want to bring grizzly bear–inflicted injuries back into perspective. During the five years of our research on grizzly bears in Banff Park, I was more concerned about accidents while driving to and from the park or during my occasional helicopter flights than I was about bear attack, even though I spent far more time in the grizzly's home than on the highway or in the air. My second main concern was the crossings that we had to make across a river that even in midsummer is cold enough to numb legs and feet within seconds. Only third was I concerned about grizzlies.

My colleagues and I faced all three hazards without injury. We put in more than ten thousand hours working with the densest population of grizzly bears in Banff National Park. Eighty percent of the time we were on foot, visiting areas where grizzly bears had recently been active. We worked unarmed except when visiting carcasses where grizzlies might be nearby or when checking traps set for grizzlies. If grizzlies wanted to attack us they had ample opportunity.

The Craighead brothers reported the same absence of injury during their research on grizzly bears in Yellowstone Park. This was despite the fact that they individually color-marked 256 grizzlies and handled 524 during an eleven-year period of study. They instrumented forty-eight grizzlies with radio transmitters and tracked these animals in the backcountry for over 29,000 hours. They estimated that they hiked about 162,000 miles during the course of their work.

Another perspective on the danger posed by grizzly bears is to compare all known sources of death in a national park such as Glacier Park, Montana, which has had more grizzly bear-inflicted deaths than any other park. Even here only six of the 150 fatalities (4 percent) in the park through 1980 were caused by grizzly bears. Most deaths resulted from falls, automobile accidents, drownings, and hypothermia. Grizzly bears also kill far fewer people in the United States (two deaths in 1976; none in 1977) than does lightning (81 deaths in 1976; 116 in 1977) or the bites or stings of venomous animals (53 deaths in 1976; 55 in 1977). Grizzly attacks occur infrequently enough that most people, including even the injured, support maintaining grizzlies in the national parks and wilderness areas where they are still found. Land and wildlife managers throughout North America must take all possible steps to help people avoid injury—but should stop short of destroying the grizzly.

5   Grizzly Attacks

BY ROBERT BUSCH

"I could just hear the bones go crunch, crunch, crunch, crunch."
—Attack victim Sonja Crowley, 1998

For me, one of the most awesome aspects of the grizzly's nature is its sheer power. This animal can kill you. As grizzly biologist Bruce McLellan says, "It's a challenge to study an animal that could kill you instantly if it wanted" (Turbak, 1984).

In the early 1800s, explorer Meriwether Lewis wrote in his expedition journals that he would "rather fight two Indians than one bear." However, even when provoked, the great bear usually shows a placid nature. Although explorer Henry Kelsey declared in 1691 that "He is man's food and he makes food of man," grizzly attacks on humans are rare.

According to veteran grizzly biologist Stephen Herrero, "studies have shown that, even where grizzly bears have been shot and wounded, about three-quarters of the time they just try to get out of the way or go into cover" (Hummel, 1991).

Biologist Derek Stonorov, who has studied the coastal bears of Alaska for many years, says that "bears do not have a sinister personality . . . they aren't even particularly aggressive" (Walker, 1993).

During three years of intensive grizzly study in the Khutzeymateen valley of British Columbia, biologists learned to respect the restraint shown by the great bear. As the head biologist wrote, "Close encounters were common during the Khutzeymateen study (30 to 40 over three years) because of the nature of the work, but in no situation was a firearm essential" (MacHutchon et al., 1993).

Statistically, the chance of a grizzly attacking a human is very small. Grizzly researcher Steven French says that in terms of pure numbers, the number of grizzly attacks that kill humans "rank right up there with spontaneous human combustion" (Read, 1995).

47

In the last hundred years, less than 50 people in North America have lost their lives from grizzly attacks. About 150 attacks have been deemed serious in nature.

In the lower 48 states, only 14 people have died from grizzly attacks since 1900. Alaska, despite a grizzly population of over 30,000 bears, has recorded only 24 fatalities from bear attacks since the turn of the century. Almost half were hunters in remote parts of the state. As author Doug Peacock notes, "more people die of bad egg salad in a year than from grizzly attacks in a century" (Peacock, 1990).

Statistics do underline, however, the greater power of the grizzly compared to the black bear. In Stephen Herrero's recent study of bear injuries in British Columbia between 1960 and 1997, he found that although there are 120,000 to 160,000 black bears in that province compared to 10,000 to 13,000 grizzlies, grizzlies inflicted about three times as many serious injuries and the same number of fatal injuries (Herrero and Higgins, in press). Naturalist Andy Russell put it a bit more colorfully in his book Grizzly Country. Comparing the two bears, he said, is like "standing a case of dynamite beside a sack of goose feathers."

When one considers that over a hundred people die *every day* in car accidents in North America, the number of bear kills should fade into proper perspective.

But it doesn't. Each bear attack spawns a mass of sensational media coverage, which only magnifies the grizzly's already bad press. You never hear about the thousands of dog bites each year, or the hundreds of people stung by bees, but let one grizzly attack occur, and it's front page news.

The paranoia that accompanies a bear attack is both amazing and appalling. When one resident of Naknek, Alaska, was mauled by a female grizzly protecting her two cubs, furious townsfolk killed over a dozen innocent grizzlies in revenge.

One of the worst problems in grizzly country today is the sloppy security around most rural garbage dumps. Grizzlies feed at the dumps, learn to love the food, and learn not to fear the humans that bring additional goodies to their smelly buffet. Stephen Herrero, in his classic Bear Attacks: Their Causes and Avoidance, stated, "Up to 1970, I calculated that inside the national parks, habituated, food-conditioned grizzlies were responsible for approximately two-thirds of all injuries inflicted on people."

The key phrase here is "food-conditioned." Two decades of experience at McNeil River State Game Sanctuary in Alaska have shown that grizzlies and humans can tolerate each other very well, if the grizzlies have not learned to associate humans with easy food. Despite hundreds of human-bear encounters as close as 8 feet (3 meters), not one person has ever been seriously harmed by a bear at McNeil River.

The problem comes when the territorial instinct in grizzlies breaks down in the face of excessive food left by sloppy humans. Unusual numbers of bears can be attracted to a single dump if the dump is not fenced or if it does not use bear-proof containers. At the old Lake Louise dump in Alberta, I have counted as many as 17 of the great bears. The most famous of all garbage-eating grizzlies, though, were those at the Yellowstone National Park dumps.

Adolph Murie, writing in *A Naturalist in Alaska* in 1961, stated: "in a garbage dump in Yellowstone Park I have seen 30 grizzlies wallowing together with bodies practically touching." Add one brain-dead tourist, and the combination spells bear attack.

For decades, tourists flocked to Yellowstone's garbage dumps to watch and photograph the bears. Park rangers actually encouraged the feeding. A.S. Johnson, writing in the February 1972 issue of *National Parks and Conservation,* recounted, "Bleacher seats were built; lights were furnished; garbage was even sorted for bears. One retired park employee recalls the distribution of edible garbage on 'tables,' that visitors might have a better view of the bears as they fed." One of the best-documented of grizzly attacks occurred in 1996 north of Yellowstone National Park.

On November 8, hunting guide Joe Heimer took client Sonja Crowley on a trip to hunt trophy bull elk. Walking down a remote dirt road, they suddenly stumbled upon a sow grizzly with three cubs, a dangerous situation under any circumstances. The two backed up about 50 feet (15 meters), but not soon enough.

The mother bear charged, running low to the ground, rattling her teeth and hissing. As the bear got close, Heimer raised his rifle and shot. He missed.

The bear hit him head on, knocking him on his back and sending his rifle flying. The angry sow bit into his right knee and then went for the left leg. Heimer grabbed the bear's upper lip in his fingers, shoving her back and squeezing as hard as he could.

Meanwhile, Crowley had moved toward the rifle, attracting the bear's attention. The sow dropped Heimer and took after Crowley, hitting her in the back and pushing her face into the snow. Then the sow sank her teeth into Crowley's head. The bear's bottom teeth went into the left side of Crowley's face, destroying part of her eye. The bear shook her and then started dragging her away. During all this time, Crowley was alive and lucid. "I could hear all the bones breaking as she bit down," she says. "I could hear every bone just go crunch, crunch, crunch, crunch" (McMillan, 1998).

Heimer grabbed the rifle but couldn't take a shot for fear of hitting Crowley. Suddenly the bear remembered her cubs, dropped Crowley, and sprinted back to her little ones. Reassured that they were all right, she then wheeled and charged again.

One more time, Heimer took careful aim and shot. The bear went down, but struggled to its feet. Heimer shot again, this time at point-blank range. The bear finally fell dead at his feet and the horror was over.

The bear turned out to be bear Number 79, a 22-year-old matriarch well-known to Yellowstone biologists. Whenever natural foods became too hard to find, bear Number 79 would amble into the civilized areas around the town of Gardiner and raid apple trees. First captured in 1981, bear Number 79 was repeatedly lured into culvert traps and relocated deep within the park. She hadn't hurt anyone, but little by little, her fear of humans was decreasing. As a result, she paid the ultimate price.

Heimer was stitched up later that night and was back to guiding within a week. Crowley wasn't so lucky. She spent eight days in hospital, lost most of her vision in one eye, and today has six steel plates holding her skull together. But she did survive.

However rare, grizzly attacks on humans do occur. You might accidentally come between a mother and her cub, happen upon a grizzly lying beside its kill, or you might just stumble on a bear napping in its day bed. You just don't know.

A grizzly's reaction in most of these situations is defensive in nature; actual intentional predation by grizzlies upon humans is extremely rare. The opposite is true for the black bear; most serious human injuries or deaths caused by black bears have been the result of predation.

Some grizzlies will charge; some will not. Frank Dufresne, a former director of the Alaska Game Commission, believed that only 1 grizzly in 25 will charge. British Columbia bear hunter James Gary Shelton has had about 50 close encounters with grizzlies; half of the bears ran away, and half acted aggressively.

Experience shows, however, that most grizzlies do not begin to lick their chops when they spot human intruders in their territory. Most bears will flee; in fact, most are long gone by the time the unsuspecting hiker or hunter blunders into their range.

Many early books on grizzlies declared that it was the unpredictable nature of the grizzly that made it a force to be reckoned with in the woods. Today, however, that attitude is changing. Jim Faro, a biologist with the Alaska Department of Fish and Game, says, "The term 'unpredictable' only means our knowledge is incomplete" (quoted in Walker, 1993).

The average person's knowledge about grizzlies used to be based on hunting lore and fireside stories. Today, those fables and exaggerations are being replaced by fact, and more knowledge is emerging about how to act in grizzly country.

One of the most dangrous situations in bear country is the surprise close-range encounter, especially if the bear has cubs or is at a kill site. Steve Herrero, who reviewed bear attacks in British Columbia that occurred between 1960 and 1967, found that "of the serious or fatal grizzly bear incidents where the bear's motivation could be inferred, 62 percent were categorized as involving a bear being startled at close range" (Herrero and Higgins, *in press*).

A few simple rules are in order. It is important to be alert in bear country; watch for bear tracks, scat, day beds, diggings, overturned boulders, scratched trees, or rubbed trees. Any fresh signs should send up a red flag that it might be wise to back off. And if you smell rotting meat, do not investigate further; grizzlies defend their kills quickly and viciously. Watch for crows, ravens, and other birds congregating in one spot as a result of a kill site on the ground below.

Hikers should be careful to avoid high-risk areas such as game trails in thick brush or beside salmon streams. Other areas to avoid are avalanche chutes in spring and early summer and burned-over areas, all of which are favorite grizzly feeding areas.

In many cases, the decision the bear makes on attacking or not attacking depends on distance; the closer you are, the worse your chances. One of the best defenses, therefore, if you spot a grizzly before it spots you is to back off and increase the distance between you.

Should a grizzly spot you in its territory, it is important not to run and to stay calm. Doug Peacock recommends the following procedure: "once he sees you, you had better stand dead still. Let him be dominant. Look off to one side and avoid eye contact" (Peacock, 1990).

However, a bear posturing with a lowered head, with ears flattened back and chomping its jaws or slobbering is clearly saying *Get out of my life*. A slow retreat might be in order before the bear charges. Never look the bear straight in the eyes.

Luckily, most charges are bluffs, moves intended to drive the intruder out of a bear's territory. Sadly, many hunters panic when charged, and many grizzlies needlessly are shot as a result. In fact, one recent book on bear attacks (written by a bear hunter) even recommends always shooting grizzlies when they are closer than 82 feet (25 meters)—heavy-handed advice indeed.

If your worst nightmare comes true and you are attacked, do not try to run. If a strong tree is close by, you can try climbing it, but get as high as possible, for the bear will likely try to follow.

Opinions are mixed about dropping your backpack while you back off. Some think it may give the grizzly something to attract its attention, while others insist that you should keep the pack on, for it may protect your back if you are mauled.

Once the bear is on top of you, playing dead seems to be the most recommended move. Cover your head with your arms and then either roll into a ball or try to keep your stomach flat to the ground. Then try to stay still. The less you look like struggling prey, the better.

This factor was recognized as early as 1806, when explorer Simon Fraser wrote of a native attacked by a grizzly: "she instantly laid down flat upon the ground and did not stir, in consequence of [which] the bear deserted [her]."

More recent corroboration of this advice comes from a tragic attack in 1976 in Glacier National Park. When a grizzly attacked one hiker, he resisted for a while and then played dead, placing his hands behind his head. Only then did the bear drop him and attack a second hiker, who resisted and was killed.

The exception to the rule of playing dead comes if you are attacked while sleeping outdoors. These attacks are not the result of a bear being surprised on the trail, defending cubs, or defending prey. Rather, this type of attack is the result of predation—often involving a bear that is looking for something to eat in a campground full of food smells. Some biologists believe that the flat-lying appearance of sleeping campers reminds the bear of wounded or dead prey lying on the ground.

If you are attacked by a grizzly while you are lying on the ground or sleeping, you should fight back. As Stephen Herrero (1985) recommends, "Shout at the bear. Throw things at or near it so you can escape. Use ever possible weapon or repellent you might have." Often the bear will get the message and will leave you with little more than a ripped tent and torn sleeping bag.

Opinions are mixed about the hot-pepper sprays currently available on the market as bear repellents. As Montana bear spray researcher Martin Smith (quoted in Turbak, 1984) says, "there will never be a repellent that will work with all the bears all the time."

Others are worried that the sprays might give some hikers a sense of false security, causing them to forget common sense in bear country. National park warden Hal Morrison warns that "it's just a tool to help," and is worried that some hikers may get the attitude that " 'I can whip any bear that I see.' . . . It's no substitute for common sense" (Andreef, 1996). Morrison himself has used the spray on a charging grizzly he encountered in Larch Valley near Banff, Alberta, a popular hiking area. "Most of it missed him but . . . the loud aerosol hiss deterred him," he says.

American hikers should note that it is illegal to bring sprays with mace as the main ingredient, or sprays also intended for use on humans, into Canada.

The active ingredient in most bear sprays is not mace but capsicum, which is derived from red peppers. This substance irritates the eyes and nasal passages of a bear, incapacitating it for about five minutes if it receives a direct blast. Bears get rid of the substance by rolling in wet grass or in water, and it causes no permanent damage.

Bear sprays were first developed in 1980 by American inventor Bill Pounds. They reached the market in 1986, under such macho names as *Standoff, Counter Assault, Assault Guard, Bear Guard, Bear Scare* and many others.

Chuck Jonkel, an American bear biologist, knows of 15 incidents in which a bear spray may have prevented a serious black bear or grizzly attack. John Eisenhauer, a biologist involved in the development of *Standoff*, hopes that the spray may help condition problem bears to avoid humans.

In some cases, though, the opposite seems to be happening. Jim Hart, a conservation officer in Fort Nelson, British Columbia, has reported that some of the nuisance black bears in his area have been sprayed many times and have become partially resistant to the spray.

Many people are concerned about the potential misuse of bear sprays. Wildlife photographer Michael Francis echoes the feelings of many: "People must be very careful with this spray and not push their luck in getting too close to bears just because they have the spray with them."

It is also important to remember that bear sprays can be used only at close quarters and can be blown away by wind. Many of the cans carry suggestions that you make sure the bear is downwind before spraying it, but few people have the time or presence of mind for such maneuvering in an attack situation.

It is not recommended to test the can after purchasing it; there are many reports of cans slowly losing their pressure after such tests. And the spray cans have a limited volume, usually containing only enough spray for five or six two-second bursts. Many people now suggest carrying two cans so that one can be used in each hand.

Opinions are also mixed on the use of flares against a charging grizzly. In some cases they have worked and in others, they haven't. In many cases, their use has resulted in accidental grass fires; as a result, in some areas, flares are banned.

The supposed advantages of bear bells are a little more encouraging. In one study in Glacier National Park, only one hiker in four was found to be wearing bear bells, but of all the hikers charged by grizzlies, not one was carrying a bell. However, in dense brush, or near rushing water, the delicate sounds of bells may not be loud enough. Stephen Herrero loudly yodels in bear country, adding a "short, explosive high-pitched sound at the end" (Herrero, 1985). Other people have even carried airhorns into bear country, especially when they have expected thick brush conditions.

Hikers should note that a single high-pitched whistle is not recommended in alpine areas, as this sound is very similar to the call of the marmot and often attracts grizzlies. Unfortunately, many Canadian parks brochures still recommend using a sharp whistle, although the potential problems have been pointed out many times.

Some outdoorsmen now suggest that all yodels or yells in bear country be repeated at least once, as many animals wait for a second sound before fleeing.

It is also recommended that hikers never go alone into grizzly country; larger groups of people make more noise, and there is safety in numbers; in the case of an attack, your companions may be able to drive off a bear or summon help.

It is a good idea to avoid hiking at dusk or dawn, as these are times when bears actively feed.

Most authorities recommend that dogs never be taken into grizzly country on the basis that a dog being chased by a bear might bring it right back to the dog's owner. However, I know of two cases in which dogs have driven off attacking grizzlies and I have heard of other cases in which just the sound of a barking dog was enough to scare off an inquisitive bear. Perhaps the best advice is to keep a dog on a leash if you wish, but don't let it run loose. Aside from keeping the dog out of bear trouble, a leash will also keep a dog from chasing or killing other wildlife.

If an aggressive bear or a bear that shows absolutely no fear of humans is encountered, report it as soon as possible to the nearest park warden or ranger. Most park officials take such reports very seriously, and will close hiking trails or campsites to prevent potential problems.

Besides making sure that bears know you're around, it is also wise to take simple precautions when camping in grizzly country.

Avoid bringing strong-smelling meat such as bacon or fish into grizzly country. Try powdered or dried foods instead. Even the strong smell of wet socks can attract bears. I once had a young black bear crawl into my tent, attracted by the pungent aroma of wet socks drying near a propane heater.

A clean camp means a bear-free camp; if you leave frozen bacon out to thaw overnight or forget to do the camp dishes, you might just have a very large visitor. All food and garbage should be kept in tight air-proof containers and suspended above a bear's reach. If your vehicle is nearby, lock the food in the trunk.

Don't sleep in clothes that you've cooked in; to a bear, you'll smell like a giant hot dog in some strange kind of bun. It's also a good idea to sleep as far away from your cooking site as possible.

When you leave your campsite, burn all the garbage and then pack all of it out; burying it isn't good enough in bear country. Grizzlies have a tremendous sense of smell and the last thing you want is to get a bear used to eating human garbage.

It is also a good idea to always sleep in a tent in grizzly country. There is some evidence that bears are more likely to attack a person sleeping out in the open.

Hunters must also take special care in grizzly country. Fresh meat should be suspended at least 10 feet (3 meters) off the ground. One Wyoming outfitter thoughtlessly left his meat in saddlebags packed onto his horse, which was tied to a tree. Both the meat and the horse were taken by a hungry grizzly.

Sleeping tents should be located well away from the meat.

Gut piles should be burned, placed in airtight containers, and packed out. And hunters shouldn't hang around after a kill; fresh meat should be hauled out of grizzly country quickly as the smell will attract bears from miles around. In 1995, two hunters were mauled by a sow grizzly and her two cubs when they found the men field dressing an elk they had shot near Albert River, British Columbia. Both men died.

Hunters should be alert when hiking out with the meat; to a hungry grizzly, a hunter with a backpack full of meat is just an appetizing entrée on two legs.

Which are the most dangerous grizzlies? Studies show that females with cubs are probably at the top of the list. One research study found that in a bear population where only 17 percent of the animals were females with cubs, almost 80 percent of the human injuries caused by bears were caused by those females. In Stephen Herrero's exhaustive study of 279 grizzly-human encounterers, 74 percent involved female grizzlies with cubs. In a review of British Columbia bear attacks that occurred between 1960 and 1997, adult females were identified in 79 percent of the incidents (Herrero and Higgins, *in press*).

Subadult bears, stressed by being driven off by their mothers, and which have not yet learned to fear humans, are also often trouble bears. Like teenaged humans, they tend to be both fearless and reckless. Half of all the fatal maulings in Glacier National Park have been by subadult grizzlies.

Statistically, September seems to be the worst month for grizzly attacks. Grizzlies in the fall must eat huge volumes of food in preparation for winter and the desperate search for food seems to make bears incautious and aggressive. Half of all the fatal maulings of humans by grizzlies in Glacier National Park in the past 30 years have occurred in September.

September 1995 was a particularly bad month. In the first part of the month, a Helena, Montana, man named Lester Ashwood was mauled by a grizzly in Glacier National Park. On September 19, 18-year-old Bram Schaffer was badly mauled by a big sow grizzly about 10 miles (15 kilometers) north of Yellowstone National Park. About a week later, another big female grizzly marauded a campground at Lake Louise in Alberta, mauling six tourists.

There is some evidence that the smell of human blood, detectable by bears in menstruating women, may attract curious bears, although some grizzly biologists do not believe this has been well-documented. The smell of perfumes and colognes might similarly cause curious grizzlies to approach humans closer than they normally would. Lightning and thunder storms may also disturb bears and cause unnatural behaviour.

In August 1967, on the famous "Night of the Grizzlies," when two young women were killed by two different grizzlies in Glacier National Park, a number of these tragic factors all came into play in one terrible night.

Firstly, the summer of 1967 was unusually hot and dry, with over a hundred lightning strikes in the Park which may have agitated the bears. The hot weather resulted in a poor berry crop and the bears soon learned to steal food from fishing camps and garbage dumps.

The second major factor was alleged mismanagement on the part of park wardens. For three months prior to the fatal mauling of a young woman near Trout Lake, fishermen and hikers had lodged dozens of complaints about a very thin, unusually aggressive grizzly. Their complaints were ignored.

In the case of the young woman mauled in the Granite Park Campground on the same night, several more serious errors were made by park employees. Employees for months had been hauling garbage out to an open pit behind the Granite Park Chalet, where foraging grizzlies each night became quite a tourist attraction. This was a blatant violation of park policy, but like many rules, this one was ignored. The campground was located smack in the middle of an area frequented by grizzlies for at least ten years, and yet few people recognized the dangers. Worse yet, the Granite Park Campground was less than 200 yards (183 meters) from the garbage dump itself.

After the Granite Park Campground mauling, park wardens were dispatched into the area with orders to kill every grizzly on sight, a heavy-handed procedure which resulted in the shootings of three innocent grizzlies. Autopsies of the three bears showed that none were responsible for the mauling.

Tragically, one of the bears was a mother with two cubs. A park official tried to shoot one of the cubs and succeeded in only wounding it, blowing away part of its jaw. Unbelievably, although both orphaned cubs stayed around the area for a long time, insufficient effort was put into catching them or ending their suffering. A year later the wounded cub was spotted and seen to be in poor condition as it could not feed properly. A park ranger finally put the poor animal out of its misery. The fate of the other cub is unknown. The bear responsible for the fatal mauling at the Granite Park Campground was never positively identified.

After the two maulings, Glacier National Park officials instituted a long list of common sense measures to prevent further bear-human problems. Trails were closed down at the first report of grizzlies in the area. Open garbage dumps were closed, and rangers enforced a strict "pack in, pack out" garbage policy with hikers and fishermen. Information booklets were distributed to educate backcountry users. And all problem bears that bothered a human more than once were shot immediately.

All backcountry users would do well to heed the sage advice of grizzly expert Stephen Herrero, who wrote in *Bear Attacks: Their Causes and Avoidance,* "Your best weapon to minimize the risk of a bear attack is your brain."

6   The Predaceous Black Bear

BY STEPHEN HERRERO

Although black bears are normally tolerant, they are dangerous under certain circumstances. They can bite through live trees thicker than a man's arm. They can kill a full-grown steer with a bite to the neck. Rarely, however, do black bears use their power to injure or kill people. I have records of twenty people who were killed by black bears from 1900 through 1980. Sergeant Robert Brown of the Alaska Department of Public Safety, Anchorage, and Larry Kaniut have cursory records of an additional three deaths in Alaska. This brings the total to a minimum of twenty three. Which is about half the number of recorded grizzly bear-inflicted deaths during the same period.

Most black bear-inflicted deaths and serious injuries fit into a pattern that is different from the pattern of major injuries inflicted by grizzly bears. Only one of twenty black bear-inflicted deaths that I studied occurred within a national park, where food conditioning and habituation are most common. In contrast, food-conditioned and habituated grizzly bears killed at least ten people in national parks. Clearly most black bears can become accustomed to people and their foods without endangering human lives.

Another feature of major injuries inflicted by black bears was that predation appeared to be the motive for eighteen of the twenty (90 percent) black bear-inflicted deaths. In these incidents the bears treated the people as prey. In the fifteen black bear-inflicted deaths for which data were available on the time of day of the attack, I discovered that fourteen (93 percent) of the fatal attacks took place during the day. This too contrasts with incidents of grizzly bear predation which typically occurred at night.

In one of the predatory instances, protection of young by a female may have also been a contributing factor. Another death was due to a person falling out of a tree while being attacked by a black bear. In another case I could not ascertain the circumstances.

Of the twenty people killed by black bears, ten (50 percent) of the victims were age eighteen or under. Five were younger than ten years old, suggesting that young people may be more subject to fatal black bear attacks. Of the other victims killed by black bears, nine were adult males, and so it is clear that on occasion they will attack a full-grown man.

Three of the fatal attacks involved young children who were playing out-of-doors. Typical of these rare incidents was the death of three-year-old Carol Ann Pomranky, near Sault Sainte Marie, Michigan, on July 7, 1948. Carol Ann lived with her parents and her brother, Allan, in a cabin at Mission Hill. The cabin was in the woods and was owned by the Forest Service for which Carol Ann's father worked. July 7 was hot and Carol Ann was playing outside in the yard. The account of Carol Ann's mother, Mrs. Arthur Pomranky, as given to a forest ranger and published by S. C. Whitlock, tells what happened:

On July 7, 1948, at approximately 2:30 p.m., I was in the kitchen of our cabin at Mission Hill in company with Mrs. Merlin Summers, a friend. I was sitting about four feet from the back door with my back to the south wall of the kitchen, and Mrs. Summers was in the middle of the kitchen ironing clothes. Mrs. Summers was facing south or to the rear of the room, and in line with the back windows, although from her position, could not see the rear yard. My son, Allan, was playing in the basement which is directly under the kitchen, but which has an outside entrance. My daughter, Carol Ann, was playing in the back yard, and had been for most of the time she was outside, in the close vicinity of the back porch. My first indication that anything was wrong was when I heard Carol Ann utter a cry of alarm. I ran to the back door, which was open with the screen door closed.

Carol Ann, when I reached the door, was on her hands and knees on the porch with one hand touching the screen in the door, and a bear was about mid point of the three steps of the back porch. The bear growled showing his teeth and grabbed Carol Ann with his mouth and pulled her off the porch onto the ground where he picked her up by the arm with his mouth. At this point, Mrs. Summers pulled me from the door and shut the inside door.

I ran for my husband's pistol, a 32-20 Colt revolver, but in my excitement could not load the pistol. I ran to the door, but the bear and child had disappeared into the bushes. I did not see in which direction the bear went. I ran to the telephone, and called the Ranger Station at Raco, and told Mr. Elliott what had happened. They went into the woods to look for the bear as soon as they arrived.

Further details of the case are gruesome but offer strong evidence that the bear treated Carol Ann as prey. Soon after Carol Ann was dragged away by the bear, Mrs. Pomranky called her husband and he quickly organized a search party. The party was headed by Alex Van Luven, a former state trapper, widely recognized as a competent woodsman. A selection from Van Luven's account describes the search and the condition of the victim when she was found:

I drove to my home in Brimley, a distance of nine miles, to get my dog, Tower. No one except three men had as yet gone into the woods as the searchers who had assembled in my absence were instructed by Alex Goldade and Deputy Sheriff Randolph Wilson to wait until I had returned with the dog. I took four men from the group, instructing the men to stay behind me and the dog and instructed the balance of the men to stay out of the woods until I sent word to them as to what to do. I traveled in a westerly direction from the cabin, as no one at the cabin could definitely say as to which direction the bear had gone. At a point approximately 100 yards west of the cabin the dog apparently scented the bear, and almost simultaneously one of the three men who had preceded me into the woods shouted from a distance of about sixty yards, and in a southerly direction. I went to where the men were and discovered blood spots, one of the child's shoes, and noticed that the leaves had been disarranged at that spot. The dog at this point pulled strongly in a northwesterly direction and I followed the dog about one hundred fifty feet and discovered the child's body. The body lay face upward, with the head reclining against the foot of an 8-inch scrub oak. Part of the clothing remained, a shirt still worn, but rolled down on the arms from the top, and rolled up from the bottom to form a ring around the child's chest. The child still wore pants, but they were pulled down about the ankles. Neither article of clothing was badly torn. The abdomen was completely removed as well as the stomach and intestines, and the front part of both legs eaten away to the knees, also the left calf. No blood was in evidence and leg bones were clean and visible. One length of intestine about eight feet long was caught on a piece of brush near the body, but was disconnected from the body. Numerous deep gashes appeared about the head and neck; however, little damage had been inflicted on the face. One tooth mark appeared about an inch behind and in line with the left eye and had an appearance of depth sufficient to reach the brain.

A short while later a 125-pound black bear was shot nearby. Autopsy revealed fragments of human flesh and bone in the bear's stomach. Microscopic sections of the bear's brain and spinal cord revealed no abnormalities.

The bear was, however, "very thin," and no fat was found in any of the normal places. Considering the time of year this was not unusual, but it does suggest a hungry bear. The blueberry season, when bears in that area begin to fatten, was said to be still a few weeks away.

The woods came within forty feet of the house. The bear may have used this cover to get close to the Pomranky's house. Once there, the evidence suggests that the bear sensed Carol Ann and attacked and killed her as if she were prey, such as deer. The disembowelment of the girl is something typically done by bears to prey. After making a kill bears often will begin feeding on the contents of the digestive system.

I don't know if it would have been possible, but had Carol Ann's mother immediately attacked the bear, she might have caused the bear to drop her daughter. One need not be a prizefighter to deter a black bear.

On September 1, 1976, a ten-year-old girl was attacked and injured by a black bear about forty miles northeast of Williams Lake, British Columbia. A British Columbia Fish and Wildlife memorandum regarding the attack tells what happened:

> The attack occurred when the girl was carrying a water bucket back to a lonely hut from a nearby creek. When the bear approached her she dropped the bucket and grabbing an axe laying nearby on the ground, hit the bear twice, then ran for the house. The bear followed and swatted the child knocking her down. She managed to reach the door of the cabin. The bear attempted to follow her inside. With a good presence of mind and in spite of her injuries she managed to reach and throw a pot of boiling water into the face of the bear. The bear fled.

This young girl did everything right once she was attacked by the bear, which was probably attempting to prey on her. She fought the bear with the nearest available weapon, an axe. She then headed for nearby shelter, where despite her injuries (she suffered broken ribs) she continued to fight the bear by throwing water into its face. She caused the bear to flee and probably saved her own life.

While black bears have had countless opportunities to kill people in national parks, only one death has been recorded since 1872. Again a child was the victim. On August 12, 1958, seven-year-old Barbara Coates was playing with her sister outside their cabin at Sunwapta Bungalows in Jasper National Park, Alberta. A black bear walked into the area where the girls were playing. Barbara, startled by the bear, grabbed a small tablecloth and some cookies and ran to the cabin steps. The bear chased and caught her on the steps. Two teenaged girls who worked at the bungalows heard yelling and ran to the site. They hit the bear with branches until it dropped Barbara. The girl died of her injuries shortly thereafter.

The bear was a young female believed to have been a "highway bum," accustomed to receiving handouts. It had no history of aggressive action.

When the girl ran, a predatory response may have been triggered in this bear. The cookies, or past experience, may have attracted the bear onto the site. This was one of two incidents in which human foods and habituation were known to have been associated with a black bear-inflicted death.

The other incident was the only such case involving a camper who was asleep prior to attack. During the night of July 25, 1971, John Richardson and Linda Moore were sleeping in a mountain tent near the Holzworth Ranch steak-fry area of Colorado (now part of Rocky Mountain National Park). At about 1:55 a.m. a bear attacked them. Linda Moore was bitten on her right buttock, and John Richardson was dragged 150 feet. Gus Wedell, who was sleeping nearby in a motor home with his family, was awakened by Linda Moore. Gus grabbed a frying pan, ran to Richardson, and beat the bear with the pan, causing it to flee. Richardson was dead.

The bear responsible for the attack was hunted and killed. Autopsy showed an apparently healthy, large, male black bear, weighing 306 pounds. The contents of the bear's stomach was entirely garbage. The bear's teeth were worn, indicating an old animal.

This type of incident, in which a bear apparently accustomed to feeding on human foods or garbage attacks and kills a person in the middle of the night, occurred often enough with grizzly bears to confirm the danger of this situation. Since this is the only incident of its type that I have found regarding black bears, the odds of a person being killed by a black bear under these circumstances are slight. The fact that the bear ran off after Gus Wedell hit it with a frying pan further demonstrates the value of human aggression with whatever weapons are at hand.

A terrible encounter seemingly involving attempted predation happened in Alaska on August 13, 1977. During the summer of 1977, Cynthia Dusel-Bacon was participating in her third summer of geologic field mapping in the Yukon-Tanana Upland of Alaska. All five geologists in her group, after being helicoptered to an area, usually worked alone. Cynthia was concerned about the added risk of working alone, but she enjoyed the work and the solitude in wilderness areas.

She had encountered bears during her previous field work. In 1975 she had seen five black bears and managed to avoid them all. She doesn't think that any saw her. In 1976 she saw a black bear forty feet away on the trail. The bear ran off. Earlier in 1977 she had seen two grizzlies. During her work she tried to remain aware of bears. She looked ahead for them while traveling and regularly clapped and yelled to warn or scare off bears. She relied on these techniques instead of carrying a firearm.

In having reviewed two accounts written by her of her attack, I concluded that there is no doubt that Cynthia Dusel-Bacon is a very level-headed, intelligent professional. As events showed, she is also very brave. I quote extensively from her account (as given to Larry Kaniut) because it clearly depicts the nature of what I consider to be an act of attempted predation by a black bear.

During the morning of August 13 she was let off by helicopter pilot Ed Spencer near the top of a rocky, brush-covered ridge about sixty miles southeast of Fairbanks.

I descended the ridge slowly for several hundred yards, moving from one outcrop of rock to another, breaking off samples and putting them in my pack. I stopped at one large outcrop to break off an interesting piece and examine it. A sudden loud crash in the undergrowth below startled me and I looked around just in time to see a black bear rise up out of the brush about 10 feet away.

My first thought was, "Oh, no! A bear. I'd better do the right thing." My next thought was one of relief: "It's only a black bear, and a rather small one at that." Nevertheless, I decided to get the upper hand immediately and scare it away.

I shouted at it, face to face, in my most commanding tone of voice. "Shoo! Get out of here, bear! Go on! Get away!" The bear remained motionless and glared back at me. I clapped my hands and yelled even louder. But even that had no effect. Instead of turning and running away into the brush, the bear began slowly walking, climbing toward my level, watching me steadily. I waved my arms, clapped and yelled even more wildly. I began banging the outcrop with my hammer, making all the noise I could to intimidate the bear.

I took a step back, managing to elevate myself another foot or so in an attempt to reach a more dominant position. By this time the bear had reached the trail I was on and was slightly uphill from me. It slowly looked up the hill in the direction from which I had come and then stared back at me again. I knew that in this moment the bear was trying to decide whether it should retreat from me or attack. Suddenly the bear darted around behind the outcrop and behind me. My next sensation was that of being struck a staggering blow from behind. I felt myself being thrown forward, and I landed face down on the ground, with my arms outstretched.

I froze, not instinctively but deliberately, remembering that playing dead was supposed to cause an attacking bear to lose interest and go away. Instead of hearing the bear crashing off through the brush, though, I felt the sudden piercing pain of the bear's teeth biting deep into my right shoulder. I felt myself being shaken with tremendous, irresistible power by teeth deep in my shoulder. After playing dead for several minutes, I came to the horrible realization that the bear had no intention of abandoning its prey.

"I've got to get my radio in the pack. I've got to get a call out," I thought.

My left arm was free, so I tried to reach behind myself to the left outside pocket of my rucksack to get at the walkie-talkie. My heart sank as I discovered that the buckled flap on the pocket prevented me from getting out my radio. My movement caused the bear to start a new flurry of biting and tearing at the flesh of my upper right arm again. I was completely conscious of feeling my flesh torn, teeth against bone, but the sensation was more of numb horror at what was happening to me than of specific reaction to each bite. I remember thinking, "Now I'm never going to be able to call for help. I'm dead unless this bear decides to leave me alone."

The bear had no intention of leaving me alone. After chewing on my right shoulder, arm, and side repeatedly, the bear began to bite my head and tear at my scalp. As I heard the horrible crunching sound of the bear's teeth biting into my skull, I realized it was all too hopeless. I remember thinking, "This has got to be the worst way to go." I knew it would be a slow death because my vital signs were all still strong. My fate was to bleed to death. I thought, "Maybe I should just shake my head and get the bear to do me in quickly."

All of a sudden, the bear clamped its jaws into me and began dragging me by the right arm down the slope through the brush. I was dragged about 20 feet or so before the bear stopped to rest, panting in my ear. It began licking at the blood that was now running out of a large wound under my right arm. Again the bear pulled me along the ground, over rocks and through brush. Now it walked about four feet away and sat down to rest, still watching me intently.

Here, I thought, might be a chance to save myself yet—if only I could get at that radio. Slowly I moved my left arm, which was on the side away from the bear, and which was still undamaged, behind me to get at that pack buckle. But this time the pocket, instead of being latched tight, was wide open—the buckle probably was torn off by the bear's clawing or from being dragged over the rocks. I managed to reach down into the pocket and pull out the radio. Since my right arm was now completely numb and useless, I used my left hand to stealthily snap on the radio switch, pull up two of the three segments of the antenna, and push in the button activating the transmitter. Holding the radio close to my mouth, I said as loudly as I dared,

"Ed, this is Cynthia. Come quick, I'm being eaten by a bear." I said "eaten" because I was convinced that the bear wasn't just mauling me or playing with me, but was planning to consume me. I was its prey, and it had no intention of letting me escape.

I repeated my message and then started to call out some more information. "Ed, I'm just down the hill from where you left me off this morning . . ." but I got no further. By this time the bear had risen to its feet; it bounced quickly over to me and savagely attacked my left arm, knocking the radio out of my hand. I screamed in pain as I felt my good arm being torn and mangled by claws and teeth. [When found she had no flesh on her left arm for about five inches between her shoulder and elbow.]

It was then I realized I had done all I could do to save my life. I had no way of knowing whether anyone had even heard my calls. I really doubted it, since no static or answering sound from anyone trying to call had come back over the receiver. I knew I hadn't taken time to extend the antenna completely. I knew I was down in a ravine, with many ridges between me and a receiving set. I knew there was really no chance for me. I was doomed. So I screamed as the bear tore at my arm, figuring that it was going to eat me anyway and there was no longer any reason to try to control my natural reactions. I remember that the bear then began sniffing around my body, down my calves, up my thighs. I could read the bear's mind as it tried to decide whether it should open up new wounds or continue on the old ones.

I didn't dare look around at what was happening—my eyes were fixed upon the dirt and leaves on the ground only inches below my face. Then I felt a tearing at the pack on my back, and heard the bear begin crunching cans in its teeth—cans I had brought for my lunch. This seemed to occupy its attention for a while; at least it let my arms alone and gave me a few moments to focus my mind on my predicament. "Is this how I'm going to go?" I remember marveling at how clear my mind was, how keen my senses were. All I could think of as I lay there on my stomach, with my face down in the dry grass and dirt and that merciless, bloodthirsty animal holding me down, was how much I wanted to live and how much I wanted to come back to Charlie, my husband of five months, and how tragic it would be to end it all three days before I turned thirty-one.

It was about ten minutes, I think, before I heard the faint sound of a helicopter in the distance. It came closer and then seemed to circle, as if making a pass, but not directly over me. Then I heard the helicopter going away, leaving me. What had gone wrong? Was it just a routine pass to transfer one of the other geologists to a different ridge, or to go to a gas cache to refuel and not an answer to my call for help? Had no one heard my call?

The bear had not been frightened by the sound of the helicopter. Having finished with the contents of my pack, it began to tear again at the flesh under my right arm. Then I heard the helicopter coming back, circling, getting closer. Being flat on my face, with both arms now completely without feeling, I kicked my legs to show whoever was up above me that I was still alive. This time, however, I was certain that I was to be rescued because the pilot hovered directly over me. But again I heard the helicopter suddenly start away over the ridge. In a few seconds all was silent; it was an agonizing silence. I couldn't believe it. For some reason they'd left me for the second time.

Suddenly I felt, or sensed, that the bear was not beside me. The sound of the chopper had frightened it away. Again—for about ten minutes—I waited in silence. Then I heard the helicopter coming over the ridge again, fast and directly toward me. In a few seconds the deafening, beautiful sound was right over me. I kicked my legs again and heard the helicopter move up toward the crest of the ridge for what I was now sure was a landing. Finally I heard the engine shut down, then voices, and people calling out. I yelled back to direct them to where I was lying. But the birch brush was thick, and with my khaki work pants and gray pack I was probably difficult to see lying on the ground among the rocks.

Ed was the first to spot me, and he called the two women geologists down the slope to help him. Together they managed to carry me up the hill and lift me up into the back seat of the helicopter. I remember the feeling of relief and thankfulness that swept over me when I found myself in that helicopter, going up and away over the mountain. I knew that my mind was clear and my breathing was good and my insides were all intact. All I had to do was keep cool and let the doctors fix me up. Deep down, though, I knew the extent of my injuries and knew that I had been too badly hurt for my body to ever be the same again.

Cynthia survived this, and after several months of hospitalization and surgery she was able to state:

The bites on my head have healed, and my hair has grown back and covers the scars completely. My right side is covered with new skin; my left stump is strong and has good range of motion. I'm fitted with artificial arms, and I'm ready to resume my interrupted life as both wife and geologist. It will be difficult for me to operate a workable arm on my right side, where I have no stump, and to manage the use of the arm and hook on the other side, where I have no elbow. But with practice, I know that I will eventually be able to make my prosthetic devices and my feet and mouth do many of the things my hands did for me before. I plan to continue my job with the U.S. Geological Survey. Both Charlie and I have loved our work there, and our colleagues have been tremendously supportive of me throughout the ordeal. I'd like to stay with the Alaskan Geology Branch, perhaps specializing in petrography— the examination of sections of three-hundredths of a millimeter thick wafers of rock under the microscope to determine their mineral composition and texture. With only minor adaptations to the microscope, I should be able to do this work as effectively as I was able to do it before my accident.

I am determined to lead as normal a life as possible. I know that there are certain limitations I can't get around, having to rely on artificial arms. But I'm certainly going to do the best I can with all that I have left. And that's a lot.

Cynthia Dusel-Bacon's courage, level-headedness, and determination are an inspiration. Her actions during the encounter always seemed to have been guided by what she thought was the right course of action. At first she tried to intimidate the black bear and get it to flee. In 99 percent of such encounters she probably would have been successful. Where she erred, in my judgment, was in playing dead after the attack occurred and the bear began chewing on her. I don't know if by this time she still had the strength to fight back, but if she could have grabbed a stout stick or rock, she might have had some chance of deterring the bear if she could have struck it. Overall, her calm, collected presence—which helped her to reach her radio and call for help—no doubt saved her life.

There is some doubt concerning whether the bear that mauled her was shot. Fish and Game officials shot and killed a 175-pound female black bear near the scene of the incident. The bear had blueberries in its stomach and appeared to have been in good health. "Unidentified substance" was also in the stomach. This could have been parts of Cynthia or her clothing, although this was not proved. Fish and Game officials also saw a one-year-old cub in the area. Although a cub of this age should have been weaned by its mother, it possibly was still with the female that supposedly attacked Cynthia. Because of the age of the cub and the nature of the attack on Cynthia, I consider it almost certain that Cynthia was not attacked by a mother bear defending her cub. Rather, Cynthia was probably the victim of the rare situation in which a black bear decides to prey on a human being.

Not quite two years later, on July 4, 1979, another woman, Karen Austrom, was hiking in Mt. Robson Provincial Park of British Columbia and was attacked and badly mauled in a similar incident. Karen too was hiking alone during the day and was confronted at close range by a 125-pound young, male black bear. The bear showed considerable vacillation before attacking. It even climbed a tree, as if to escape. Once it attacked, Austrom played dead and repeatedly offered the bear one of her arms to protect her vital areas. When a large party arrived forty-five minutes later, the bear had mauled and eaten much of her arm but her other injuries were minor. The bear retreated into the bush. To me this is another clear case in which the victim should have used every possible means to fight and intimidate the bear.

Very rarely will a black bear kill two or even three people. During the summer of 1980, Leeson Morris, age forty-two, and Carol Marshall, age twenty-four, were working and were based at Cantex "Rig 10" near Zama in northern Alberta. Morris, the geologist for the camp, had apparently left around five in the afternoon and had not shown up for supper by seven. About this time Carol Marshall and a companion, Martin Ellis, went for a walk to look for Morris. Ellis's statement describes what happened next:

> We stopped for a smoke and had just sat down and Carol noticed a black bear about 10 feet in front of us in the bushes. We started to run a few yards and Carol stumbled. I told her to climb a tree and she sort of panicked and couldn't get up it. I climbed up a tree right beside it and got up about 6 feet and then I reached down and grabbed Carol by the arm. I still couldn't get her up so I reached down under her bum and she slipped so I had a hold of her around her waist. The bear was at the base of the trees and took a lunge and clawed Carol's bum. She then fell to the ground and the bear immediately grabbed her by the neck and shook her several times. He used his mouth and I could hear her neck break. He then immediately dragged her by the neck into the bushes. I stayed up the tree for about 10 minutes and then the bear came back. He climbed up the tree again and I kicked him in the head. He was up the tree about 13 feet. The bear then went back down the tree. He came up 2 more times but I got rid of him once by grabbing a smaller nearby tree and pushing it against him, and the other time by kicking him in the head. He then just chewed on branches like a crazy bear. . . . He went down the tree again and left for about 10 minutes. He circled around the back and came up the tree for about 5 or 6 minutes and then Reagan Whiting came walking by. I saw him and told him that the bear got Carol so he ran back to camp for help. The bear went to take a look in the direction of where Reagan was, saw nothing, then came back up the tree. He went really crazy chewing on the branches. Then Bud Whiting came and the bear headed in his direc-

tion. Bud shot him once; the bear let out a scream and headed off in the bushes. . . .

Later the body of Carol Marshall was found nearby as was the partly eaten body of Leeson Morris. Morris was apparently walking along a streambed, stopping occasionally to chip off rock with his geologist's hammer. He was attacked from behind and his chest was crushed. There were also bite marks on his neck, apparently from where he was dragged. The next day a mature male black bear, in apparent good health, was found and killed near the site of the attack. Evidence clearly linked this bear to the killings. Further investigation of the attack site revealed that every branch was removed from the two trees (one nine inches, the other five inches in diameter).

These incidents illustrate several important things. In my opinion the deaths of Leeson Morris and Carol Marshall were both clear cases of predation. The bear's behavior suggests that it would have tried to kill more people if it could have. In this regard the behavior suggests what zoologists call "surplus killing" or a killing frenzy—the killing of prey beyond the immediate needs for food. The bear's behavior in biting the tree limbs also indicates that it was very excited. Perhaps this was the result of having overcome its inborn tendency to avoid people.

The success of Martin Ellis in fighting off the bear further supports my contention that under such circumstances a person should use every inner resource and available weapon (even if it is only your foot or fist) to try to fight off a black bear. I have come across several other incidents in which people have successfully kicked black bears in the head and have knocked them out of trees, but sometimes black bears have grabbed people by the foot and pulled them out of trees. Black bears are much better tree climbers than are grizzlies. If a person climbs a tree to avoid an aggressive black bear they may have to fight the bear in the tree.

The deaths of Carol Marshall and Leeson Morris occurred about two hundred yards from the rig camp. The possibility exists that the bear had gotten some food from the camp or was otherwise familiar with people; although camp personnel felt that it had not been seen before. I consider it likely that it was a wild black bear with only a modest amount of experience with people.

This is a clear example of the general type of incident in which a black bear sees a person and decides to try to kill and eat its victim. The worst of this type of incident occurred in Algonquin Park, Ontario, on May 13, 1978. Four teenaged boys, who were off on a fishing trip, never went more than four hundred feet from their car. The oldest of the party was Richard Rhindress, age eighteen. He survived to tell the story of the deaths of the other three: his brother Billy Rhindress, age sixteen, and their friends, George and Mark Halfkenny, ages fifteen and twelve.

The youths arrived at the park entrance around four in the morning after driving from the nearby Canadian Forces Base at Petawawa where they lived. They tried fishing in several creeks. By late afternoon George Halfkenny had caught four speckled trout, which he carried in his pocket. About 5:30 p.m., at Stone Creek, George decided to fish some more. The others remained in the car while he walked a short distance along the bank of the stream. A little while later George's brother, Mark, and Billy Rhindress, decided either to also try fishing or to look for George. Richard Rhindress, the oldest boy in the group, decided to stay behind and catch up on sleep.

At about 6:30 p.m., Richard woke up and wondered where his companions were. He shouted and honked the horn, but there was no response. A bit later he drove around looking for them, thinking that perhaps they had come out elsewhere along the road. Later on he returned to where he had last seen them and explored along the creek bank. Mike Crammond, a journalist who later investigated the incident, thinks that Richard Rhindress could have been within one hundred feet of the bear and his dead companions. Finding no one, he returned to the car, drove home, and reported what had happened. A search party was soon organized.

The subsequent discovery of the boys' bodies and the killing of a 276-pound male black bear, which was positively linked to the deaths of the boys, allow the following interpretation of events: George Halfkenny, who had gone fishing alone and had four fish in his pocket, was probably the first to be killed. He seemed to have been attacked from behind, probably while intent on fishing. Generally the woods were thick enough that a bear could have stalked close to George without the boy being aware of it. George may have put up a fight, because branches were found broken at the scene of the attack. The bear dragged its victim away from the creek in a semicircle and stored the body about fifty-five yards upstream. A short while later, Mark Halfkenny and Billy Rhindress had apparently proceeded about 110 yards up the stream when they either surprised the bear, who by now had dragged George across the creek, or were ambushed by the bear while they were hiking. There were signs of a small struggle, but the boys' broken necks suggested instantaneous death. All three bodies were then dragged into the bush, 100 to 150 feet from the creek and up a low ridge. When searchers found the bodies they were partially covered with brush, and the bear appeared to be "standing guard over them."

Persons investigating the incident felt that the first boy who was killed, George Halfkenny, may have been attacked because he resembled another bear. George wore dark clothing and was black. Others suggested that the bear attacked George to get the fish he had in his pocket, although the fish were still in his pocket when found. I don't consider either of these explanations to be valid, although fish odors may have served to attract the bear in the first instance. There was also a high density of bears in the area at the time of the attack. One observer reported having seen twenty-nine bears during three hours of searching from a helicopter. This may have led to increased agitation in the bear that killed the boys.

Strong evidence suggests that this is another surplus-killing incident in which the bear treated the three boys as prey. The boys were killed, rather than injured. All were dragged to a common place, and two of the bodies had been partially eaten. There seems to have been little they could have done to avoid this tragic incident.

Since 1980, when my systematic data collection ended, I have received information concerning three additional black bear-inflicted deaths. Two of these, the deaths of Melvin Rudd and Clifford Starblanket, took place in central Saskatchewan in late May 1983. This year there was a late green-up and black bears were probably having trouble finding food.

Melvin Rudd, age fifty-five, who was fishing, was apparently stalked and killed by a black bear. The bear that killed him subsequently attacked Keith Ecklund and Larry Reimer while they too were fishing near to where Rudd's partly consumed body lay. When the bear attacked, Ecklund fought it off by kicking it in the head. A short time later it attacked Reimer when he came to help his friend. Reimer fought the bear, eventually killing it with his filleting knife. Autopsy of the bear revealed parts of Rudd's body in the bear's stomach.

The circumstances of the Starblanket attack were less clear because he was not found until about five days after his death. Starblanket, a trapper camping in the forest reserve, had a lot of garbage and hides strewn about. He was also rumored to have been feeding a bear prior to his death. When Starblanket's body was found he had multiple and severe injuries to the head and neck, most likely caused during a black bear attack. The bear was never found.

The circumstances of the third death are also vague. On July 5, 1983, David Anderson, age twelve, was part of a group camped on the shore of Lake Canimina in La Verendrye Wildlife Reserve, Quebec. The party had suspended their food between two trees about 165 feet from the site but sometime during the night a bear climbed one of the trees and broke a two-inch diameter limb, causing the food to fall to the ground. It subsequently ate some of the food. A bear, probably the same one, visited the camp three times during the night of July 5–6. On the last visit, at 3:30 a.m. the bear ripped open a tent and pulled young Anderson out. Anderson's dead body was found about one hundred feet from the tent.

My conclusions about known cases of predation and attempted predation by black bears on people are that habituation or garbage and food conditioning have only infrequently been primary contributing circumstances. In fact, the habituated black bear, found so commonly in some of the national parks, seems almost always to be involved only in incidents of minor injuries. Nor have black bears suddenly confronted by people been responsible for deaths, although this may have been a contributing factor in one case. Rather I conclude it is mainly wild black bears found in rural or remote areas—where they have had relatively little association with people—that occasionally try to kill and eat a human being. This behavior must be exceedingly rare, since I have found so few records of it, given that the population of black bears in North America has probably never been less than my estimate of $500,000 \pm 200,000$.

Warning signals of aggressive intent by black bears have seldom been reported to precede cases of apparent predation. Instead a typical predation scenario might involve the bear slowly approaching a person during the day, perhaps partly circling and then rushing toward the person, trying to knock the intended prey down and inflicting injuries with jaws or paws and claws. Multiple charges are not seen in these instances as, for example, frequently occur when a black bear suddenly encounters a person on a trail. Instead, the predaceous black bear typically charges a person only once and at the end of this charge it has caught its prey. Such attacks may be of prolonged duration because the bear usually does not leave unless it is scared away, overpowered, or injured by the person.

One final circumstance that may cause some black bears to attack and injure people is failure of natural food crops for the bears. Incidents of property damage by black bears increase during years of low production of wild berries on which the bears normally feed. This is understandable enough, since black bears are strongly motivated to secure adequate foods in order to fatten before hibernation. It would also not be surprising if, during years of food-crop failure when black bears are aggressively seeking human foods and garbage, they also were more likely to injure people. Scientific evidence of this actually happening is, however, weak.

David Hatler describes what happened in the interior of Alaska during 1963, a year when blueberries were "generally scarce." Failure of the berry crop caused black bears to concentrate in the few areas where blueberries were available. The bears also sought food from people's camps. Four people were injured and one person was killed by black bears. All injuries took place during the time when the bears would normally have been fattening on berries. The possibility of berry-crop failures being associated with increases in human injury merits research. If true, it might be possible to monitor berry production in a given area and to anticipate which years black bears will be a problem.

I have found almost no evidence that injury or infirmity are important factors predisposing black bears toward attacking people. I consider this a possible factor leading to attack. Rabies and trichinosis are two bear diseases that *might* influence attacks on humans. Many black and grizzly bears involved in attacks on people have been tested for rabies, and a few have been tested for trichinae levels. No association has been proven between either of these diseases and attacks on human beings.

Since I have discussed in detail several of the very rare fatal attacks by black bears, it is important to reestablish perspective on the chances of injury. John O'Pezio, a black bear specialist with New York State's Wildlife Resources Center, provided me with some of the best data to do this. He estimates that there is a relatively stable population of 4,100 black bears in New York State. During the period from 1960 through 1980, he was able to tally a minimum estimate of 77 million recreation days spent by people in areas occupied by black bears. During this twenty-year period only three bear-related injuries occurred. In all three cases a bite or a swipe was made through a tent while the injured party was asleep or resting. All injuries were minor. One was only a scratched toe.

What should a person do if attacked by a black bear? When discussing grizzly bear attacks, I tried to show that the response to an attack depends on the reason why the attack occurred. The same thing holds true for black bear attacks. While this may sound as if everyone visiting bear country should be a registered bear psychologist, it is not this complicated.

If a black bear attacks in a campground or alongside a road, or in any place where many bears appear to be habituated to people, then the first assumption should be that the bear is attacking because you have gotten too close to it and it wants more space, or it is trying to get at food that you have. In the first instance simply backing away and watching the bear should end the attack. In the second case, in which a black bear is trying to get at your food and injures you, it is best to give up the food. A person who is very familiar with black bear behavior might choose to act aggressively and get the bear to back down, especially before it attacks. However, a black bear that has become so habituated to people that it will actually injure someone to get at food can be very difficult to deter.

The most dangerous black bear appears to be one that attacks a person who has been hiking, walking, berry picking, fishing, or playing during the day in a rural or remote area. The bear's motivation in this unlikely event most often appears to be predation. The exceptions to this are the very rare instances of females with cubs in backcountry areas attacking to defend their offspring. In this case one should play dead or passively resist, as if a grizzly bear mother were attacking.

If predation is the motive for an attack, the attack typically continues until the bear is forced to back down, or the person gets away, or the bear gets its prey. People who run away, unless they have somewhere to go, or people who act passively or play dead, are simply inviting the bear to continue the attack. If a bear does not take just a minor bite or swipe at a person and leave but instead appears to be pressing an attack, then the unarmed person should either try to escape, for example, to a nearby hard-sided shelter, or fight back. Climbing trees is a possibility but the agile black bear climbs well. Heavy objects such as axes, stout pieces of wood, or rocks are possible weapons. They can be used to hit a bear on the head, with the hope of stunning it and causing it to leave. Other aggressive actions by a person might include kicking, hitting with a fist, yelling or shouting at the bear, or banging objects, such as pots, together in front of a bear's face. This is an action plan of last resort—in close combat, a bear has the advantage over an unarmed person. But in the rare situation in which a person might face such a black bear, fighting off the bear could save that person's life.

I know of three incidents in which black bears were likely trying to prey on people and were killed by the people they attacked. None of these people had a firearm handy. In two cases the people knifed the bear to death, and in the third case a small boulder was used to crush the bear's skull.

The situation might arise when one is attacked during the day while out hiking and the species of bear involved can't be determined. If it is a grizzly, then probably it is a response to a sudden confrontation of a female with cubs and therefore the person should play dead. If, on the other hand, it is a black bear looking for a meal, then fighting back is indicated. I suggest studying this or other books that explain how to tell a black bear from a grizzly.

7 Bears Of the Year-Long Day

BY A. E. MAXWELL AND IVAR RUUD

Editor's Note: Published by Lippincott in 1976, *The Year-Long Day* is a stunning tale of true adventure. It is the story of Ivar Ruud who, at various times over the span of five years, pitted himself against the fierce and lonely forces of Arctic cold and darkness while he hunted and trapped on remote Spitsbergen Island in the Arctic Ocean. Ruud's experiences during the different seasons make compelling reading, and his accounts of encounters with polar bears are outdoor classics. A. E. Maxwell is a pen name of a husband-wife writing team.

Now, in early December, the wind screamed in harsh, continuous cacophony around the corners and past the shuttered windows of Main Cabin on Spitsbergen Island in the Arctic Ocean. The Arctic darkness mixed with the driving white snow made a seething, slate-colored stew that obliterated all landmarks. There was neither sky nor ground, only gravity and the pealing wind.

The hurricane died while Ivar slept, but it was followed by another storm, an ordinary Arctic blizzard in which the wind never varied its direction. For three days he was shut up in the cabin, except for one bone-chilling outing to feed the huskies. He killed the crawling hours mending harness, washing clothes and laying them in the storeroom where the wash water froze and could be shattered off, whittling sticks for traps and talking to Naika. Halfway through the blizzard the wind snapped the antenna he had rigged for his radio, and he lost the one-way company of Radio Luxembourg.

He slept as much as he could, and when he became totally bored, he made a month's supply of bread, kneading the dough furiously to loosen muscles tense with inactivity.

77

The third morning was much like the first two, with the wind wailing laments to the dark absence of dawn. He lay for half an hour in his bed, then decided that he had earned another raid on his store of books. He rolled out, lighted the lamp and fire, made a big breakfast and a full pot of coffee and sat down near the fire with the book he had nibbled at, on and off through the storm. Scarlett and Rhett were locked in a mad embrace over his cooling oatmeal when he sensed that something had changed. He puzzled for a moment, then realized that the wind no longer shook the cabin.

The chair grated loudly in the silence as he pushed back from the table and went to the door. The blizzard had blown the last twilight out of Hornsund, leaving behind an unbroken expanse of darkness and snow. At the edge of visibility he saw a small heap of snow shift and then explode as Svarten lifted his nose into the dying wind and howled a long, rich, rising note. One by one other heaps of snow moved as the team roused itself.

The distinctive sound of an axe chopping into frozen seal brought the huskies yowling to the ends of their chains. They stood on their hind feet and leaned against their thick collars, dancing in anticipation of the coming meal. When he approached, arms full of two-pound chunks of seal meat, the huskies made enough noise to put a hurricane to shame. He threw the meat deftly, putting each chunk within reach of only one dog. As the meat was snatched out of the air, the noise subsided to steady gnawing punctuated by warning snarls.

The seal vanished like snowflakes in a fire.

When the huskies were finished, Ivar moved among them, ruffling cold fur and talking to those that appreciated human companionship. As always, Svarten leaned against him, ears raised to catch every nuance of tone. For once, even Surly and the stolid Norwegian bachelor brothers, Bumpsa and Grisen, seemed to welcome him for more than the food he had given them. Surly even wagged his tail twice. No wags out of Bumpsa and Grisen, though. They were strong, those two, but interested only in eating, sleeping and working. Lazy, the fifth husky, barely lifted his ears at Ivar's voice.

After eating, though, all the huskies were restive, the unbroken snow beckoned to them. He had allowed the huskies off their leads two at a time, but they had not had a real blood-singing run in front of the sled. They would be full of the devil when the time came to drag out the harness, Svarten in particular. His amber-yellow wolf's eyes watched Ivar's every move, plainly hoping that the harness would miraculously appear.

Ivar returned to the cabin and gathered up his gear—a sackful of ptarmigan heads for trap bait, a shovel to dig the frames out of the snow, the Mauser and a box of shells. And Naika, of course.

Outside the cabin he loaded the rifle. The cartridges made a full brassy ring as he slipped them into the magazine. The bolt moved smoothly, pushing a round into the chamber. At that sound, Svarten strained against his collar. He was a dog who loved the rifle; he knew its use. He danced at the end of his chain, tail high and waving, every movement a plea to be invited along. When Ivar and Naika disappeared around the cabin, Svarten put his nose to the stars and howled. The sound haunted Ivar for as long as he could hear it.

The air was absolutely still as he pushed his skis along an arc toward the Fox Valley flatlands, where he had laid out his first trapline. The fresh snow, packed by the wind, squeaked beneath his weight. Overhead, stars glinted cold and hard against the bottomless sky. For an hour at midday, the stars would be lost in a faint wash of slate light, but for the rest of the day, the stars would be there, pinholes in the shroud of Arctic night.

He skied quickly, using body and poles in a rhythm that was as natural to him as walking. Naika worked to keep up and at the same time explore the nooks and holes along the trail. In the low spots, the snow was several feet deep, packed by the relentless winds. The high areas were almost bare. An intense cold fell from the brittle sky as man and dog moved across the snow, pushing the shapeless night before them.

The first trap was close to the cabin, surrounded by snow. He could see that the frame still hung poised on its prop. He looked back to make sure that Naika had not followed before he skied over to check the trap.

The snow had built up in small mounds around the wooden square, added girth to the outer edge of each rock on the trap but left the area under the trap relatively free of new snow. The bait was untouched. He did not change the bait, although wind and cold had dried the ptarmigan head. The less he handled the bait, the better the results. Even though he took the precaution of keeping a pair of gloves in a box of ptarmigan feathers and using only those gloves when working with trap or bait, foxes were notoriously quick to pick up even the most tenuous foreign scent. The trap was highly visible, close by a well-used fox trail. And fox curiosity was great; it would be a rare fox that overlooked this intrusion into its domain. Once the ptarmigan tidbit was scented, the trap should do its work, especially now, at the beginning of the season.

The cold air ached in Ivar's throat as he moved away from the unsprung trap. As he skied toward the next trap, he could hear the sea ice crack and groan as it sagged on the outgoing tide.

He strained his eyes into the moaning darkness, but saw nothing. He was alone inside the womb of his limited senses. The polar night had swallowed up all creatures, digested them in a rumble of ice. It was one of those times when he questioned whether he himself lived or whether he was merely a flickering dream born of icy indigestion.

With a surge of impatience, he shook off the numbing sense of complete isolation; it was too soon to let sunless days get to him. He was definitely alive, and if he wanted to stay that way he had better keep his mind on his business. Experience and instinct told him that the sea ice was heavy enough to support wandering bears.

He closed his eyes and held himself perfectly still, searching for the least indication that his unnamed senses had discovered what eyes and ears had missed. Nothing. No malaise, no thin, uneasy feeling of being watched by other life.

He opened his eyes and skied to the next trap, all senses alert. He knew he was most vulnerable checking traps alone in the darkness, when Naika's ears and exceptional nose were 100 yards distant. He was on his own, dependent on human senses that were no match for those of the polar bear.

The first trapline check was a long and fruitless one. The storms had flattened some of the traps; others had drifted so full of snow that he had to dig them out and relocate them on higher ground. Twelve wearying hours of darkness and digging and digging and darkness. By the time he had completed the circular trek, he was clumsy with cold and hunger. The billion stars overhead gave small light and less comfort—it was cold enough to freeze mercury, to say nothing of blood.

He skied forward eagerly, anticipating the rewards of Arctic labor, fire and hot food and coffee laced with Scotch.

He reached the flat coastal ice foot halfway between Fox Valley and the cabin. The disappointingly empty packsack was crumpled on his back beneath the weight of his rifle. He disliked carrying the Mauser like that, but he could make no speed otherwise. And the quick tempo of his ski poles crunching into snow spoke urgently of his need to be home.

For all his haste, he was alert. His eyes strained into the darkness, scanning rocks and sea ice, seeking bear sign. No movement, no danger yet. He stared around intently. The new snow magnified starlight, giving the land an eerie blue glow.

Naika lagged behind. She had covered twice the distance he had, and she was tired. Her tail had drooped until it was level with her back. Suddenly she stopped, and her low growl curled down Ivar's spine.

Bear.

He stopped immediately, slipped the rifle off his back. He knew that the bear was close, for Naika had caught its scent on the wind. But he had no idea where or how close. As he thumbed the safety off, he spoke softly to the vague dark blur that was Naika. She moved up beside him, staring into the night, head lifted a little to fetch another scent. The bear must be out of sight, probably beyond the rocky rise 80 yards away. His eyes could not see the rise, but he had traveled this trail many times.

Naika was silent now, still sniffing the small breeze, and cocking her head from side to side, trying to locate a sound he could not hear. He stabbed his ski poles into the snow and knelt to undo the bindings on his boots. He worked with one hand, keeping the rifle ready in the other and watching the tiny circle of land he could see. No movement. Then he heard, far off, faint, the low sounds of a prowling bear. Naika answered, deep in her chest, uneasy yet excited. She loved the hunt, but she also understood its dangers.

Freed of the skis and poles, he shifted the rifle to his right hand and walked forward, calling very softly to Naika to follow. She trotted stiff-legged, head up.

Ivar circled toward the shoreward side of the rise, looking for tracks. He had to know where the bear was. Some bears avoided or ignored man, but the odds for either were not of an order to encourage carelessness. He had no desire to kill, only to know location, and if there were more than one bear. He paused, slowed his breathing, listened for another sound that would locate the bear.

Nothing.

He advanced another ten steps and stopped again. This time he could hear low shuffling bear sounds. In his mind he could see the bear somewhere on the other side of the rise, aware of life approaching, head swaying on long supple neck, testing the air, waiting.

Ivar swore silently. He had no desire to take on a thousand pounds of aggressive bear when he could not see more than 12 feet ahead. He shifted the rifle to his left hand and pried a stone from the slope at his feet. The stone arced silently over the rise. Naika exploded into eager yaps and charged forward. He called her back, but her excitement drowned whatever small noises a retreating bear might make. He held his breath, hand clamped over Naika's muzzle, listening with every sense of his body and mind.

Finally he heard the bear. He moved up the slope to hear better, but still could not be sure where the bear was. He had to know. The bear was between him and the only route to the cabin. The ice foot that was the trail was narrow, too narrow; it would be impossible either to avoid the bear or wait for it to wander off. The longer he waited, the colder he became. Soon he would not be able to depend on his body, his reflexes. His feet were numb, his bones sharp and cold with hunger.

Yet he waited, listening and hoping and motionless. The few squeaks and crunches he heard were inconclusive—the bear could be backing off or circling around or climbing the ridge. It was time to take the initiative again.

He moved as quietly as he could up the remaining ten yards to the top of the rise. When he breasted the small hill, the spot where the bear should have been was empty. He glanced right, toward the frozen fjord. Empty. A flicker of movement, no more, to his left.

He spun and faced the white bear less than 15 feet away, lunging from behind a boulder, cat-fast and deadly.

His shot was reflex. He snapped the Mauser forward at arm's length and pulled the trigger. The rifle barrel seemed to touch the point of the bear's shoulder as the muzzle flashed, and the 300-grain lead bullet slammed into bone and through the heart.

The impact of the shot lifted the bear off its right front paw and threw the animal sideways. The bear went down without a sound, rolling over and over down the unbroken snow slope.

Before the bear stopped rolling, Ivar whipped the rifle bolt and jacked in another round. The muzzle flash had blinded him for a few seconds. He held the rifle ready as his eyes began to readjust. Then he saw Naika growling and snarling around the bear that lay bonelessly against a boulder.

As the last echoes of the single shot faded, he listened to the silence. Was there another bear? Was this one dead? No sound or movement but Naika stalking, circling the bear with low growls. Naika was not certain either.

He circled 50 feet to the left to examine the bear's tracks. The bear had been alone. The first wanderers of the dark usually were, but usually was not good enough when dealing with polar bears.

He doubled back on the slope to the motionless bear. Naika was still holding her distance, worrying the bear with growls and stiff-legged charges that stopped just short of the thick white fur.

With the threat of a second attack diminished, he decided to risk the loss of his night vision. From the pocket of his parka, he produced a flashlight. Holding it in one hand, but not switching it on, he approached the bear cautiously. He circled the bear at a distance of ten feet, rifle trained on the long white neck.

Naika's growls increased as he walked up to the bear's head, partially buried by snow that had drifted in the lee of the rock. He switched on the light. The cold had sapped some of the strength from its beam, but the effect was still dazzling against the clean snow and pure white fur of the bear. The light picked up silver tones in the fur, gave it texture and depth. As he swept the beam across the bear, he spotted at once the small crimson entry wound, just forward of the massive shoulder. A fine shot, for reflexes—but then, the range had been point-blank.

The spot of light swept back up to the wedge-shaped head, where ebony eyes shone blankly. He extended the rifle barrel until it touched an unprotected eye. No movement, no flicker.

The bear was indeed dead.

For the first time since he had heard Naika's primal growl, he began to relax. Using his teeth, he pulled off a glove and touched the silvery-white gleaming fur. Beneath his chilled fingers, the long white hairs felt cool. He worked his fingers into the pelt, seeking warmth. And there was warmth, but as he touched it he could sense it dissipating into the polar night.

> Editor's Note: As this section begins, Ivar has just returned to his main cabin after a particularly arduous tour of his trapline, which involved spending the night in a snow cave to survive a powerful storm.

The last leg of the trip took three hours. He was thoroughly cold when he reached the cabin, but that was thoroughly normal. He fed the dogs, talking to them over the minor-key moan of the wind. When they finished eating, he knelt beside each one of them, rumpling their fur, assuring himself that there were no masked casualties from the fall down the riverbank.

Satisfied that the dogs were well, Ivar went to the cabin. He took a broom and swept the hoarfrost off ceiling and walls and floors before he fired the stove. To appease his growling stomach, he set about making a big, calorie-rich meal. Goose and creamy gravy, potatoes and vegetables and fruit, bread thick with jam and butter. Then coffee, steaming with warmth and sugar and Scotch.

In the morning he resumed his trapline rounds, beginning with the coastline traps, which had taken the brunt of the storm. It was dark and cold and desolate work, digging out traps that were drifted full or tripped by the wind. Lifting and replacing 80 pounds of rock at each trap. In the long, lightless days, there were treasured moments of clear skies and silver moon, but the clouds always returned, blotting out light. When he was too tired to lift more rocks, but not tired enough to sleep, he worked with his guitar, creating new songs.

But loneliness still swept over him, especially when he lay in bed trying to sleep. When the feeling of isolation threatened to suffocate him, he switched on a flashlight and played it over the walls and ceiling of the cabin. Pinup girls and photographs of friends stared back at him. Most of the time the pictures came alive as his mind played with past memories, present dreams, future possibilities. He could lie for hours composing, changing, rejecting, polishing his dreams like an artist with a three-dimensional canvas.

Yet this night, five nights after Christmas, the pictures remained merely pictures, flat and dead. He clicked off the flashlight and tried to sleep, telling himself over and over that the Arctic night was half gone.

While he slept, a huge wind swept down the fjord, scouring away the snow from the front entrance of the cabin. The next hard wind would probably cover it up again and he would have to dig yet another snow tunnel exit, but he enjoyed the bare doorstep anyway.

The wind kept him inside the cabin, working over fox pelts, scraping, turning, stretching until his fingers grew clumsy and his eyes ached. As he put the last pelt on the stretcher frame, he heard the huskies snarling above the dying wind. He pulled on his parka, grabbed the rifle out of the storage room and went cautiously outside. Although he had seen the wide, long pugmarks of bear as he worked the traplines, he had yet to see a bear. But when he went up to the dogs, they were already curling up again. Either the bear had fled or had been too far off to be of much interest.

He checked the dogs, though he had few worries about their safety. Their chains were long, their teeth sharp; any bear that tried to take on the pack would have a real fight. In four years, he had never had a husky injured by a polar bear.

After a last look around, he went to the side of the cabin and removed the window shutter. With the wind almost gone, he could once again sit and stare outside during his meals. Not that he could see much, but the cabin seemed less like a prison with the window uncovered.

He went back inside the cabin, trying not to think about time and the crawling progress of night. Tomorrow, for much of the world, a new year would begin. But not for him; his years were marked out by unyielding Arctic cycles. New Year's Day came in the second week of February, when the blood-red disk of the sun first breached the horizon.

Inside the living area, he removed his parka and went to work on ptarmigan rather than foxes. With small, deft motions he skinned two birds, basted them with butter and herbs and put them into the oven. He kicked off his boots, hesitated, then peeled off his heavy wool sweater. With an unconscious sigh, he settled back in a chair with a glass of Scotch, listening to the fire and the glacial music of compressed ice thawing in his drink.

As the Scotch drained away the tension of darkness, the warm fire and gentle lamplight made him sleepy. He pulled himself out of the chair long enough to baste the roasting birds, then sat down at the table and drowsed again.

He was lifted out of half sleep by a faint sound along the wall behind him. At first he thought it was Naika, then knew it could not be; her head was a heavy warmth on his stocking feet. Adrenalin swept away his stupor as he recognized the *snuffle, snuffle* of a polar bear scouting the wall of the cabin. The bear must have approached from downwind, for the huskies had not given alarm. Naika rumbled, then fell silent at a gesture from him.

Ivar moved across the cabin on noiseless stocking feet, his undershirt a vague white blur in the dark room. He gathered his rifle and reached the outer door just as the huskies went wild. He slapped the rifle bolt and checked the breech by feel. Loaded and ready. Forgetting that he was only half dressed, he went to the outer door, planning to surprise the bear from downwind just as the bear had surprised the dogs. Knowing that the yammering dogs would cover any sound he made, he pulled the door open.

The team had also covered bear sounds very nicely.

Even as his senses registered the bear rising out of the darkness right in front of him, the rifle snapped up and the sound of two quick shots drowned out the dogs. The bear somersaulted backward and rolled down and out of sight.

Ivar kicked the door shut and jacked a third round into the rifle chamber. Then he stood and listened, knowing that a wounded bear would make more noise than any eight teams. Two shots at point-blank range into the base of the neck should have killed the bear, but he was not going to bet his life on it. He had used up enough luck for one night.

Suddenly the night exploded into growls and massive roars and the repeated *slam-slam* of great hooked paws against the wall of the cabin. Splintering-tearing sounds as tar paper and logs gave under the immense power of an enraged polar bear.

Ivar did not stop to wonder how a bear that should have had a broken neck could be so terrifyingly alive.

He slipped across the darkened entryway and into the storeroom. There was a trapdoor in the ceiling, an emergency exit after heavy storms. He climbed the short ladder quickly. With the rifle barrel, he lifted the square trap and pushed it back. Rifle at the ready, he silently pulled himself out on the roof. It was like stepping into an ice cube, but he did not notice the cold. As he stood up, the sounds of the attack stopped. Maybe the bear had finally died.

He scanned the roof, then crept on hands and knees toward the corner that the bear had attacked. Cautiously, finger curled around the trigger, he eased his eyes over the edge of the roof, expecting to see the wounded bear directly beneath him.

Nothing.

He eased a few feet to his right looking down the other side of the cabin. There, immediately to his right and at a spot that would have been just out of sight from the entryway door, lay the bear, unmoving. He relaxed. There would be no more trouble from that bear. But it must have been extraordinarily powerful to attack the cabin like that with its dying strength.

A small stealthy sound behind him sent his back hairs up on end. He spun on his knees in time to see the head and shoulders of a white bear rise above the edge of the roof. At Ivar's movement, the bear knew the stalk was over. It leaped for the roof in a single surge of white power.

Ivar's reflexes took over, triggering a shot at the same instant the bear leaped. The shot caught the bear in the chest. The huge animal hung for a moment, defying gravity. A second shot tripped the balance. The bear tumbled backward in slow motion, landing on the drifts at the back of the cabin with a muffled thump.

He released his breath in one long, toneless whistle, took a slow breath of cold air and held it, tasting it, savoring it, aware of all its icy textures. Mechanically he slapped the bolt of the rifle, flipping the cartridges out. It rang musically on the icy roof, then rolled down and disappeared over the edge, falling noiselessly into the snow. He rammed a new cartridge home before he advanced to look over the roof where the attacking bear had disappeared.

It lay a few feet below the edge of the roof, on a snowdrift that had piled up within a yard of the eave. He waited for several long moments, straining into the darkness for any sign of movement. There was none.

He suddenly realized that he was intensely cold. His nearly bare feet had lost all sensation; his right hand, curled around rifle stock and trigger, was immovable.

He hobbled across the roof toward the trapdoor. By hooking his left arm through the ladder rungs, he prevented a headlong descent. By the time he reached the floor he was shivering violently. He stowed the rifle in its rack and made his way into the living quarters, where the heat of the stove rolled over him. Soon the stove and the shivering restored his temperature to near normal. He pulled his clothes on, retrieved the rifle and went outside for a more thorough look at the two bears.

He snapped on the flashlight and clamped it over the rifle barrel with his left hand; whatever moved within that cone of light would automatically be a target. As he approached the first bear, he saw that it was young. Fur of purest white, muzzle soft with short white hairs, no scars. Closer examination showed that the bear was average sized, perhaps a little larger, and male.

Moving silently around the cabin, he compared the position of the second bear with his rooftop memories. No change, no reflex from rifle barrel on unprotected eye. Very dead.

The second bear was female, old. Almost all of her muzzle was black and callused, the white hairs worn off from years of scraping against snow and ice. A truly ancient matron. Improbable as it seemed, the other must have been her cub, staying with her long after the usual two years. That would explain the blind savagery of her attack. A female with a cub, even a fully grown cub, was always more dangerous than an adult male.

He knelt beside her and touched the aged muzzle.

You had no choice, but I had no choice, either.

New Year's was followed by three weeks of wind and storm, trapline work and intense restlessness. The end of the long Arctic night was near, but the fact did not comfort him. Light was hanging just below the southeast horizon, two weeks to dawn. Just 14 days. Just eternity.

Because the end of darkness was so close, he had unconsciously loosened his control over his tightly held emotions. Now they were racing ahead of him like a runaway team, pulling him in every direction. Almost three months with no more light than rare, cloudless hours dotted with tiny stars, and rarest of all, a full moon in a clear sky. Pale moon, paler stars, tiny lamps and flashlights and fires. Not enough. Not nearly enough. Cold and black and alone on the edge of the world.

He struggled against his writhing loneliness, knowing that it would vanish with the first touch of sunlight.

Each noon he stood outside, scanning the southeast horizon for the faintest chalk-gray promise of dawn. Each day he worried that the predawn time would be cloudy or stormy, that the promise would not be kept. When the countdown to light reached seven days, his restlessness won.

It was time to go to Bird Mountain.

When he arrived at Bird Mountain Cabin, it showed the scars of winter, plus long scratches down the wall where a prowling bear had casually raked claws across tar paper. A recent wind had dislodged the spring cache of dog food from the roof. The seal lay uncovered in the snow near the doorway. Bear tracks were all around it; the seal hide had long gouges but was otherwise intact. Apparently the bear preferred its dinners warm.

He considered heaving the carcass back onto the roof, then decided not to. The next bear probably might not be so fussy. He would rather have bears gnawing on the seal than gnawing on the cabin, or him.

The inside of the cabin was dark, cold and coated with hoarfrost. He swept out the frost before he lit the fire. The six-foot-square living room warmed quickly.

Ivar shrugged out of his parka and put the rifle in the entryway-storeroom. The stove's heat would not penetrate that far, and the rifle would be safe from repeated cycles of heat and cold that could leave a destructive condensation of water and ice in the firing mechanism. Though he invariably cleaned his rifles at least once a week, he knew that no amount of care could compensate for alternating between fire and ice.

He warmed his fingers by the stove until they grew supple again. After he had eaten an indifferent dinner of stew and coffee, he put on his parka and went back to the storeroom. He pulled open the hinged panel in the outer door, looked out, saw nothing. He picked up a hammer and a can of nails from a nearby shelf and renailed the tar paper on the outside of the cabin and the insulation on the inside. Where wind and claws had torn the tar paper, frost had gotten underneath the insulation, forcing it away from the wall. Nothing serious, but worth repairing.

Inside again he sat in the lamplight for a few minutes, studying the 6×6-foot living space for other projects, and finally decided on a small-shelf below the window, on the wall beside the stove, opposite the bunk. It was the only section of wall that was not already in use for storage. A fine place for tobacco, Scotch, seasonings and whatever else would fit.

By the time the shelf was completed and completely full, he felt ready for sleep.

The next day he walked the Bird Mountain trapline, digging out and setting twenty traps. Even though he planned on staying only a few days, he might take a fox.

When he returned to the cabin, the wind was picking up a little, just enough to make moaning noises through rocky passes and around cabin eaves.

Shivering, he pulled his chair close to the oil-barrel stove. In spite of his work, Bird Mountain was not as snug as Main Cabin. When the fire faded to embers, the room temperature would drop like a head-shot goose. Even now a skim of ice had formed on the water bucket; by morning the water would be as solid as stone.

Ivar finally gave up and crawled into the mummy bag on the bunk, which filled one entire wall of the cabin. In spite of the cold, he slid into the down bag wearing no more than his undershirt. Any more clothes and he would wind up uncomfortably warm. Any less, and the draft from the opening of the mummy bag would stiffen his neck and shoulders. He eeled deep into the bag, reached over his head, and tied the top as tightly as he could from the inside. His fingers, already numb with cold, fumbled. The result was a knot, but he did not bother to untangle it. It would be easier in the morning, when his fingers were warm.

The strident sounds of splintering wood, screeching nails and shattering glass brought Ivar instantly awake. Only a polar bear could demolish the heavily shuttered window so quickly. And with the window gone, all the rich food smells of the cabin would pour out, spurring the bear's hunger.

Ivar thrust his hands above his head, groping for the tie cord. As he tugged at the cord, he heard the delicate, filelike sound of bear claws brushing down the nylon skin of the mummy bag. It took him less than a second to remember the knot and realize he was trapped.

A heavy weight fell on his chest and the sound of claws became less delicate. The bear had reached across the room and was testing the curious unfleshlike covering of the wriggling bag. Adrenalin swept through Ivar's body, releasing a wave of strength. His arms went rigid, then slammed out against the bag, once, twice, and the tough nylon slit away from his driving fists.

He flattened himself on the bunk, trying to avoid the bear's probing paw as he peeled the sleeping bag off his body and kicked free. He started to sit, but his head crashed into what felt like a rock. Even as he realized that the rock was the polar bear's lower jaw, he threw himself flat again and scooted down the bunk on his back.

The sudden blow, and the equally sudden appearance of Ivar's white undershirt where the dark mummy bag had been, caused the bear to pull back slightly. Ivar was so close to the animal's massive head that he saw the bear's eyes widen with surprise, smelled the mixture of carnivore breath and spilled Scotch from the shattered bottle on the new shelf, felt the quick rush of air as the bear cleared its nostrils of the astringent alcohol scent. The bear's withdrawal sent a second bottle of Scotch flying over the stove. The room reeked of steaming, stinging Scotch, and the wind poured snow through the open window.

When the bear sneezed, Ivar came off the bunk in a tumbling rush. His bare feet came down on a pile of broken glass. He felt cutting edges and heard his curses over the bear's snarls. He threw himself back on the bunk, yanked pieces of glass out of his foot and hit the floor at the far end of the bed.

The smell of blood encouraged the polar bear; its paw hissed by Ivar's body. Had he been standing, he would have been neatly gutted. He scrambled toward the door of the room without thinking, intent only on getting to his rifle in the entryway-storeroom before the bear got more than a long neck and a longer arm into the tiny cabin.

The bear pushed hard against the groaning window frame and swiped again, lower this time. Ivar heard the whistle of claws an inch above his head. He hugged the floor and squirmed on. Then there was silence broken only by the creak of the door as he pushed it open and crawled into the storeroom.

He noticed the silence but not the minus-20 cold of the outer room as he stood up. He lifted the rifle from its rack, pushed a round into the chamber and slipped to the outer door. He listened. Nothing. He held his breath. Still no sound. Slowly, he eased open the hinged panel in the upper half of the door.

The bear's head and neck burst through the opening. Ivar jumped back, narrowly avoiding the open mouth and lethal teeth. Two steps and he was flat against the closed livingroom door. The bear's hot breath bathed his stomach. No room to swing the door open and escape back into the livingroom, not even room to bring the rifle to his shoulder. The small space seemed filled with claws and teeth.

He raised the rifle over his head, wrapped his left hand around the barrel, hooked his right thumb through the trigger and slammed the muzzle down on top of the bear's weaving head. The flash of exploding powder was like a knife across his eyes and the recoil slammed him against the wall. Blind, dazed and deafened, he tripped the rifle bolt and rammed home a new shell. When his eyes recovered, the bear was gone.

Ivar edged sideways down the row of shelves. He heard nothing, which meant the bear was either dead or waiting. At such close range it seemed impossible he had missed, but it was also impossible to rip a mummy bag like wet cardboard. He oozed up to the open panel and looked out.

The bear lay motionless a few feet away.

Ivar slid outside and checked the bear's eye for reflexes. The bear was quite dead. He laid his palm on the rough warmth of the white head and drew a slow breath, relishing the icy bite of air against his throat. He felt weightless, flying, incredibly and totally alive. Under pale starlight the land was exquisite, each fine detail utterly distinct, the frost tracery over tar paper, the pewter gleam of snow crystals, the timeless strength of wind, perfect beyond dreams.

With a sort of distant shock, he realized he was getting warm and sleepy; the snow was as inviting as a down quilt.

Back inside, Superman. You're freezing faster than that bear.

With glacial reluctance, he turned his back on the flawless moment and reentered the cabin. It seemed to take forever to build up the fire. Coal kept jumping out of his hands and rattling across the cabin. After the fire was going, he pulled on his pants and parka and surveyed the damage to his feet.

He boiled a pan of water on the stove, washed the cuts, poured Scotch over them and gritted his teeth, wishing that feeling had not returned quite so quickly. The right foot bled freely now, but pressure and bandages solved that problem. He bandaged the other foot, pulled on socks and boots and crunched through the glass to find a hammer and nails. He felt very lucky; none of the cuts had required stitches. Sewing himself up was his least favorite pastime.

Outside, the night had lost its fine edge of perfection, but he did not care. The moment of exhilaration was engraved on his soul, half of the answer to why he had chosen the Arctic. The other half must wait for the dawn. But dawn was below the horizon, and a freezing wind was pouring drift snow into the cabin.

He gathered the various pieces of shutter and nailed them over the ruined window. The job was not elegant, but it stopped the wind. He went back inside, found a broom and swept the cabin clean of glass and snow. Then he picked up his skinning knives and approached the bear. Unless he wanted to haul over 800 pounds of carcass all the way to Main Cabin, he had to skin the bear here, quickly, before the flesh froze solid.

The work was less exacting than skinning a fox, for the bear's hide was tougher. But he was extremely careful with the sharp blade. If he knicked his fingers while working with bear blubber, the cuts could become infected with a strain of bacteria immune to even the modern antibiotics he had in his kit. More than one isolated hunter had discovered that the only way to halt the infection was to amputate the infected finger . . . or die very slowly.

He worked without stopping, except for occasional glances around to make sure that other bears had not been attracted by the fresh kill. His bare hands were cold, but the residual warmth of the bear's body kept his fingers from freezing. Toward the end, he had to make a deep cut and press his hands into the bear's body cavity to catch the fast fading heat of life.

When he finished, he stretched his complaining back and flexed his numbing fingers. It had taken less than two minutes to kill the bear and ninety minutes to skin him. But the work was done now. Over. He rolled the pelt carefully and dragged it into the storeroom to freeze.

With the last of his strength he thoroughly scrubbed his hands and arms and knife. Tomorrow, before the weather changed, he would shut down the trapline and return to Main Cabin, dragging the 150-pound pelt.

After six more hours of sleep, he hurried through breakfast and cabin cleanup, including nailing tar paper over the broken window. In five hours, if the clouds were not too thick, he would be able to see some light in the eastern sky. It was illogical to hurry. The clouds would either lift or not. His rushing about would make no difference. But Ivar's hunger for light was not a logical matter. His movements were electric with anticipation. He hitched himself to the heavy, frozen skin and moved down to the fjord ice.

Clouds were an invisible ceiling overhead, and the wind gusted erratically. The ice had brine slicks in some areas, slowing him down. After four hours he saw a star, then three, then hundreds scattered through rents in the cloud cover. The air was very cold and tipped with ice. Another storm in the making.

Half an hour later, just before noon, he stopped and drank from the small canteen he carried inside his parka. The water was chilly but well above freezing. As he tucked the canteen away again, he glanced overhead. The stars were very pale, almost invisible. The clouds were mounds of dark gray wool. He looked automatically over his shoulder, southeast. He blinked, fought the impulse to rub his eyes, and stared. There, unmistakably, were the twin points of Hornsund Peak, silhouetted against the faintest wash of pale, pale blue light. As he watched, the horns sharpened, then faded again into darkness and clouds.

The afterimage glowed in his mind like a first kiss from a shy and lovely woman.

He leaned on his ski poles for a long moment, wondering if he had really seen that pale light, knowing he had, but hardly daring to believe. It had been so long since he had seen the mountains across the fjord that it was almost as though they existed only in his memory. But the mountains were real. He had seen them. The long night was ending.

He straightened above his ski poles and pushed over the fjord ice with easy, powerful strides.

8 Anatomy of a Tragedy: The Yellowstone Grizzly Called "Old Fifteen"

BY THOMAS MCNAMEE

What grizzly bears do not do can be as intriguing as what they do, and their occasional refusal to do the expectable "natural" ursine thing also offers striking clues to their intellectual capability.

Recall, first, the grizzly's postglacial evolutionary heritage: indomitable monarch, climax carnivore, the biggest, the brazenest, the meanest bully in the countryside, the terror of pocket gopher and stone age man alike. Remember how when four-footed prey and beached marine carrion grew scarce in primeval California, grizzly bears would cruise into town to devour hapless tribesmen and their dogs.

Why, then, are the grizzly and her cubs digging for the starch-rich but decidedly low-calorie roots of Cous biscuitroot (*Lomatium cous*) tonight at the edge of an alpine pasture on which six tons of mutton bleat in the moonlight? The answer is probably some knowledge, perhaps not firsthand but passed along from their less law-ramparted foremothers, of the possible untoward consequences. What their innate bearhood dictates is simple and clear: meat is good; kill it if you can. And as for *can,* well, nothing could be easier. All that's needed to render a domestic sheep edible is a brief untaxing chase and a medium bop on the head. But somehow the mother bear knows that trouble would follow. Obviously such knowledge is not inborn, so where did she get it? Has she remembered her earlier cub's sudden death on the cattle ranch and extrapolated from that the thought that all livestock is to be avoided? Or did she learn from her mother to leave sheep alone, and is there then something like a cultural tradition at work?

If the latter case has played a part in her self-restraint tonight, we should consider what happens to cultural traditions when their realism wanes. Clearly, many human traditions hang on for a long time after their usefulness is lost, but it seems reasonable to assume that after a while the principle of natural selection will weed them out. Once we begin to understand the weather for example, we no longer try to make it rain by sacrificing virgins. By the same token, if genuine complete protection of grizzly bears is accomplished—if their killers actually go to jail, and sheepherders at last so truly fear the law that they no longer even shoot over the heads of grizzly bears—then wouldn't it figure that grizzlies will eventually lose their fear of killing sheep?

No big deal if so, most hard-line conservationists would say: those range-maggots have no business in the wilderness in the first place, shearing the alpine flowers down the bear dirt and robbing good forage from bighorns and grizzlies. But few of those conservationists are likely to have thought further, to the possible consequences of total grizzly protection over the long term, when more than domestic sheep may have outlasted the bear's stigmatic fear of armed retribution.

Consider the story of Number Fifteen. Old Fifteen—so monikered because in 1976 he became the fifteenth grizzly to be captured, marked, and studied by the Interagency Grizzly Bear Study Team—was a well-known bear around Yellowstone, and what both officials and biologists like to call a good bear. That is, he stayed out of trouble with people, made an honest living, and was almost eager to jump into researchers' traps. Even good bears, of course, have their occasional brushes with people, and so it was that in 1971, when still a cub-of-the-year, Fifteen was first trapped at Yellowstone Park's Pelican Creek campground. He and his mother may have been there scouting for garbage, or they may have just been innocently passing through and have been drawn to the trap by the scent of the bait. Whatever the case may have been at Pelican Creek, Fifteen was soon, like almost every other Yellowstone bear in those days, well acquainted with the pleasures of dining on garbage. The park's dumps had been closed by then, but there was still plenty of garbage to be had around the town of West Yellowstone, Montana, and Fifteen was a regular fixture there, easily recognizable because of a large bald scar on his rump. Fifteen was captured three times in 1974 in and near garbage at West Yellowstone, and after the third time he was tranquilized, bundled up, and transported clear across the park and into the remote backcountry of the Shoshone National Forest. Upper Sunlight Creek and its environs were excellent grizzly habitat, and Fifteen stayed put. He denned not far to the southeast that winter, on Rattlesnake Mountain, his den door actually within sight of the town of Cody,

Wyoming, and he was observed in the Sunlight area again in the summer of 1975, but eventually a yearning for his old home must have gotten to him, for in 1976 he was caught in the interagency team's trap near the Gallatin National Forest's Rainbow Point campground on the shore of Hebgen Lake, a good ninety-five airline miles west over several rugged mountain ranges from the point to which, two years before, he had been moved.

Even in his young adulthood it was obvious that Fifteen was going to be a really big bear. He was a superb predator, killing elk even in their midsummer prime, and the good nutrition showed. When he was trapped again in May 1977, in his first year as a full-grown adult, he already weighed four hundred pounds, and by that September, when he was captured yet again, he weighed nearly five hundred.

Through much of this period, Fifteen was wearing a radio collar and providing information for the grizzly bear study about his home range, movements, habitat use, and general way of life. He was an extraordinarily vigorous bear, always one of the last grizzlies to den up in fall and one of the first out in spring—a fact that probably reflected his exceptional predatory skill, which allowed him to obtain food when other grizzlies, more dependent on vegetation, would have to be hibernating. In 1978, for example, he had emerged from his den by the first of March, and at midmonth, when many other bears were still asleep, he was seen feeding on the carcass of a large bull elk.

Fifteen also always maintained a lively interest in garbage. His home range included several large and busy campgrounds, as well as a number of summer cabins near Hebgen Lake, and the researchers had good reason to believe that some local residents were actively feeding garbage to bears. Fifteen's day beds were often found close to the town of West Yellowstone. Nonetheless, he never got into trouble with people. Despite considerable livestock grazing within his home range, the only time Fifteen was known to have fed on domestic animals was when an algae bloom on Hebgen Lake was responsible for the deaths of many cattle and he made use of the carrion. And he had never been an aggressive bear: the study team's tests showed that when he was in the trap and so could be presumed to be under some degree of emotional stress, Fifteen's blood carried exceptionally low levels of catecholamines, the family of chemicals usually associated with aggressiveness.

He was almost friendly. Like other bears who feed on garbage but never kill livestock, Fifteen knew that he had little to fear from the hand of man—and often something to gain. In August of 1978, for instance, at a time of year when carrion is scarce and elk, in their sleek prebreeding puissance, are almost impossible for a grizzly to catch, Fifteen was caught in the study team's trap near West Yellowstone four times within eighteen days: the allure of the meat used as bait was so powerful that he had apparently lost all fear of the trap, and, because he had spent most of his life near human settlement and its nourishing refuse, man-scent, far from scaring him away, may even have acted as an additional attractant.

For the most part, however, Fifteen resolutely avoided direct encounters with people. As one of the principal study animals for Bart Schleyer's master's thesis on grizzly bear daily routine, Fifteen was often radio-tracked at close range on the ground by Schleyer and his associates, and there were occasional unavoidable meetings. On July 28, 1979, just one day after he had been captured and fitted with a new radio collar, Fifteen met Schleyer head-on in dense lodgepole forest, and the bear's reaction, in this circumstance in which many another grizzly might have reflexively charged, was to turn tail and flee. Three days later, Fifteen moseyed back to Schleyer's camp at night and slowly circled it until he was quite close. Hearing tree limbs cracking in the darkness, the biologist whistled. Fifteen replied with a deep, rolling growl, and Schleyer clambered up a tree. The bear continued to roam peacefully around the area for several hours, showing no interest whatever in the treed man, and eventually he ambled off. The next day, radio-location from the air showed that he was over ten miles away. In all, over the two years of his field work, Schleyer spent three hundred forty-eight hours tracking and observing Number Fifteen at close range, and the bear was frequently known to be near other people, unbeknownst to them—fishermen, backpackers, and so forth—and never once did Fifteen display the least hint of aggression.

Fifteen was captured again in 1980 by the interagency study team, and twice in 1981. In August of 1982, when he was trapped yet again, his weight was nearly five hundred pounds, and within *six weeks*, when he was captured once more after he had been feeding on cattle carcasses along the South fork of the Madison River, his weight was up to six hundred eight pounds. To forestall the possibility of trouble with live cows from this awesomely large grizzly—although he had never shown any inclination to kill cattle—officials moved Fifteen well into Yellowstone Park, to the Blacktail Deer Plateau. The taste of beef apparently lingered tantalizingly in his mind, however, for within two weeks he was back on the South Fork, now up to six hundred thirty-five pounds. On October 14, when he spotted Bart Schleyer and an assistant at a distance of about fifty yards, Fifteen scared the daylights out of the biologists by charging fast straight at them—already too close for them to try to scale the one tree at hand—but they quickly realized that the bear's ears were erect and tilted forward, a sure sign of strictly nonhostile curiosity, and in any case Fifteen had almost immediately (probably as soon as he had recognized them as human) executed a fast right-angle turn and was loping away. When Schleyer located the bear's day bed nearby, he found two large scats in it containing melon seeds and plastic bags. The next day, Fifteen was trapped and again shipped off to Blacktail Deer. It was the nineteenth time in his eleven years that Fifteen had been caught in a trap reeking of man. In the light of subsequent events, researchers agonized that their own activities may have contributed to Fifteen's habituation to people, but any such contribution was surely insignificant compared to that made by garbage.

In May of 1983, probably in a fight with another male over mating prerogatives, Fifteen lost his radio collar, and the study team lost contact with him. He was spotted once that spring with an elk kill along Gneiss Creek, near Yellowstone Park's western boundary, an important elk wintering ground and Fifteen's usual spring neighborhood, and the study team's pilot saw him again in the same area in June, copulating with a female grizzly. The pilot estimated his weight at about four hundred pounds—a normal weight loss, since it is in mid-June that carrion and prey availability declines sharply, fruits and other high-energy vegetable foods are not yet available, and grizzly bears are paying off the last of the metabolic deficit of the past winter's hibernation. Because it is the height of the mating season, male bears' testosterone levels are very high, and elevated testosterone is classically associated with increased appetite in all mammals. That factor combined with the decline in caloric value of his diet undoubtedly made for a very hungry and highly stressed bear. Under the circumstances, it was only to be expected that Fifteen would head toward West Yellowstone, prowling for garbage.

About five-thirty in the morning on Thursday, June 23, 1983, an enormous, rangy grizzly bear broke into an ice chest that had been left out overnight on a picnic table at the Bakers Hole campground on the Gallatin National Forest just outside the park, three miles north of West Yellowstone. The victims of the burglary reported it and were issued a citation by the Forest Service for improperly making food available to bears.

On Thursday night, at the condominium development known as Yellowstone Village—where, to officials' despair, bears have been openly fed time and time again—a bear got into some dog food.

On Friday morning, June 24, a longtime summer resident was awakened by a commotion outside her cabin near Hebgen Lake, ran out onto the porch, and saw a large bear going through the garbage can below. Fifteen stood up on his hind legs and took a violent swipe at her, but luckily the porch was some ten feet up, a height to which he could almost but not quite reach. The woman had seen many grizzlies before, but this one, she felt, was by far the most aggressive she had ever encountered.

That night about ten-thirty, at another cabin on Hebgen Lake, a large grizzly bear got into the garbage bags. The cabin's occupants had been leaving their garbage out on the porch all spring, but this, they said, was the first time they had had any problems.

About midnight, at the Rainbow Point campground, barely two hundred yards from the cabin on the lake, a camper saw a very large bear moving through the campground toward the southwest—the direction of Yellowstone Village, where, sometime the same night, the garbage dumpsters were overturned and rifled.

From about twelve-thirty to one-thirty in the morning, dogs at another cabin nearby were barking continuously. A large bear had stolen their food from the cabin porch, and had overturned an old empty refrigerator in the yard.

Earlier that evening, about eight-thirty, William Roger May, a twenty-three-year-old shipbuilder from Sturgeon Bay, Wisconsin, and his friend Ted Moore, also from Sturgeon Bay, had arrived at the Rainbow Point campground and, in the gathering darkness, had cooked a dinner of steak and corn on their charcoal grill and had a couple of beers. Then they had done the dishes and, as the Forest Service recommended, stowed all their gear in their car. They had set up their large canvas tent—a relatively new one, free of food odors—and, about eleven, they had gone to bed.

About two-thirty in the morning, the tent began to shake. They had heard shouting and an exuberant ruckus from some people nearby earlier in the evening, and Moore's first thought was that it was some kind of prank.

May had been sleeping with his head and neck pressed against the wall of the tent, and now, it is thought, something bumped against his neck. The next thing Moore heard was May screaming. The bear's first—and perfectly natural—reaction to bumping something animate with his nose was to bite it and hold it still and investigate. What he bit, through the wall of the tent, was Roger May's neck. The carotid artery was severed by that one bite, and blood gushed forth.

Whatever may have been a bear's learned reticence and caution, the immediate presence of a wounded and bleeding animal, particularly if it is struggling to escape, sets in motion an ancient genetically programed sequence of predation.

The bear, still holding Roger May by the neck through the wall of the tent, began to pull, and his strength was such that the canvas was rent, and the bear pulled May through the hole thus created. The tent collapsed.

Moore struggled out of the wreckage of the tent. The moon was full, and the sky was clear, and Moore could see May clearly on the ground about ten feet away, and the bear standing over him. Seeing Moore, the bear grabbed May by the ankle and dragged him about thirty feet away. Moore reached into the collapsed tent, took an aluminum pole, and ran at the bear, brandishing it. He threw the tent pole at the bear, and the bear withdrew into the shadows.

May could still speak, but he was obviously gravely injured. Moore returned to the tent to search for his glasses and car keys. When he emerged, his friend was gone, and the woods were silent.

The bear had carried May only about twenty feet farther away, but he had gone into shadowed brushy timber where he could not be seen, and had now begun silently to consume his prey.

A few other campers, who had heard May's brief screaming, arrived to offer help, and they and Moore wandered terrified through the campground calling, "Roger! Roger!" Someone telephoned the sheriff in West Yellowstone, and the bear's reaction to the arrival of the police car with its loud siren and flashing lights was only to drag the body a little farther into the woods. This was known because the drag marks and bear tracks across the campground's dirt road were found on top of the tracks of the police car's tires. Throughout the shouting and flashlight-shining and siren-wailing, the bear had not abandoned his kill and had continued to feed.

An investigative team began to form early that morning. Dick Knight, head of the Interagency Grizzly Bear Study Team, flew over the area to see if any of the study's radio-collared bears were around, and none was. The site of the killing was roped off, and investigators began to reconstruct the scenario. Both the Rainbow Point campground and the nearby Bakers Hole campground were evacuated, and all trails on the west side of Yellowstone Park were closed. By late afternoon, thirteen bear traps had been set, some at the campground, some along the road, and some at Yellowstone Village.

The investigative team gathered that evening at the district ranger station, and at midnight they began to check the traps. Those at Yellowstone Village and along the road were empty. Barely ten feet from the spot where Roger May's body had been found, there was a bear in the trap—a large grizzly with a bald scar on his rump. Fifteen.

They tranquilized Fifteen with a dose of Sernylan. They took scrapings from his claws and around his muzzle, clipped hairs from his paws and face, and collected about three pounds of fresh scats, in which what looked very much like human hair and skin could be seen. Dick Knight took these samples, along with the samples of the victim's hair and blood, to Bozeman, Montana, from which they were in turn flown on to Missoula, where the state crime lab was calling in (it was a Sunday) a hematologist, a hair expert, and a pathologist. Meanwhile, in Bozeman, Ken Greer, of the interagency study team, had already looked at hairs from Fifteen's scats under the microscope and was sure they were human. Soon the state lab had matched up hairs from the victim with those from the scats and confirmed that they had come from the same individual. Fifteen was injected with a massive drug overdose, and he quietly died.

Everyone's first thought was to try to find what must have driven the bear crazy enough to do such a thing. His body was sent to Bozeman, where Ken Greer performed a detailed autopsy. Fifteen's weight was down to four hundred and thirty-five pounds—from the previous autumn's six hundred plus—but that was normal for this time of year, and the bear was in perfect health. The investigation showed that Roger May and Ted Moore had followed all the rules for staying out of trouble with bears—clean camp, no food in the tent or anywhere else around camp, no provocative behavior whatever. Gradually, the plain fact had to be faced that neither Roger May nor Grizzly Bear Fifteen had done anything wrong. Tragedy to be tragedy must be avoidable; this was just a case of bad luck. Wherever there are people and grizzly bears in the same place, it can happen, and, mercifully rare as such encounters may be, they will always happen.

"The incredible thing," Chris Servheen, the federal grizzly bear recovery coordinator, later said, "is not that it happened, but that it doesn't happen more often."

And why doesn't it happen more often? What could be easier prey than a person? Certainly a backpacker is easier to catch and kill than an elk, and there are more of them too.

The answer is fear. Most grizzly bears have learned that people are not to be killed, and those few who do not learn virtually always pay with their lives. The minuscule number of grizzly-caused human fatalities have all resulted from situations where, through a disastrous confluence of circumstances, bear instinct has suddenly overwhelmed bear learning—where the basic drives governed by the brain's limbic system, such as feeding, sex, and aggression, momentarily override the inferential, synthesizing, and ultimately inhibitory activity of the cortex. Even Fifteen, if he had even a moment to think about it, never approached a human being with malign intent.

The only villains, if there must be villains, in the sad story of Roger May and Grizzly Bear Fifteen, are the people who despite years of warnings made their garbage accessible to bears. Most of them knew it was wrong, and dangerous, but they liked seeing bears. It was garbage that drew Fifteen into human precincts, and it was garbage that accustomed him to not minding being near people. Perhaps if Yellowstone Village and the summer people on Hebgen Lake had kept their garbage secure, Fifteen would never have been in the neighborhood in June of 1983. Perhaps if he had not been feeding on garbage year after year, Fifteen would have been too wary of people to have come snooping around a campground. But the area where Roger May died is good grizzly habitat irrespective of garbage, and certainly as long as there are both people and grizzly bears in the same place they will occasionally come into contact, and while careful precautions, as Yellowstone Park's great success in recent years suggests, may minimize bear-caused human injuries and deaths, we cannot hope that they will never happen.

Let us circle back now to the question that prompted this brief biography of Fifteen. Might it be that grizzly bears' reluctance to kill people is a moribund cultural tradition, surviving from the days when retribution was automatic and inevitable, when indeed innocent grizzlies were often slaughtered just for the hell of it, and every grizzly bear knew that people and firearms went together? If so, what may we expect to happen with long-term total protection? Yes, Fifteen was caught and killed, and most other man-killing grizzlies have met the same end. But suppose one got away—say a mother, who then taught predation on humans to her cubs. Suppose that, gradually, a few grizzly bears learned how easy it can be to kill and eat people. If enough of them began to do it, would there not be an immediate collision between the law, which forbids endangering a population of a threatened species, and the human outrage that would cry out for capital revenge?

This may sound like a preposterously hypothetical question. After all, you are still much safer camping out in grizzly bear country than you are driving to it in an automobile. (From 1978 through 1982, for example, of Yellowstone National Park's approximately eleven and a half million visitors, about twenty-three hundred people were injured seriously enough in various mishaps to require medical attention; there were about twenty-three hundred traffic accidents; and twenty-six people died in drownings, automobile wrecks, thermal burns, and climbing accidents. Of the twenty-six hundred personal injuries, five were caused by grizzly bears, two by black bears, and three by bears whose species was not determined. Roger May, in 1983, was the first person killed by a Yellowstone grizzly in over ten years.) Nevertheless, some bears in Yosemite and Glacier national parks seem to be learning that if you charge a backpacker, the first thing he's likely to do is drop his pack, and voilà! you have something good to eat. How big a step is it, ask, in the mind of a bear, from armed robbery to outright murder, especially when the rewards for the latter are so much greater?

Bears are obviously able to understand the distinction between acceptable and unacceptable predation, but it is equally obvious that some of them will break the rules if they can get away with it. Thus in Yellowstone we have both stock-killing grizzlies and those, like our protagonist, who spend their lives feeding peacefully alongside peacefully grazing cattle and sheep. It might be thought that the sensible Darwinian thing for *every* bear is to kill all the livestock he can get hold of, and people too: they're much better food than biscuit-root and spring beauty, and certainly such behavior would be consistent with the grizzly's evolutionary heritage of omnipotence and his genetic predisposition to carnivorism. But the fact is they don't do it. As long as they associate certain activities with the likelihood of human retribution (and it is not clear exactly how they learn this, only that they do), grizzlies are fully capable, given a moment to reflect, of making the necessary discrimination. Of course there will not always be that crucial moment to reflect, and so neither livestock nor man will ever be perfectly safe in grizzly country.

Nevertheless, as long as attractants are also minimized, a system of punishment *can* keep danger to an acceptably low level. But for such a system to work over the long haul, grizzly populations obviously must be secure enough to sacrifice the occasional miscreant. Unfortunately many are not. If there were to be some sort of epidemic of grizzly attacks in Yellowstone—which, in the case, for example, of a series of severe drought years, is not inconceivable—what people would regard as appropriate retribution could well end up killing so many bears that the population would be reduced beyond hope of recovery. To the other compelling arguments for grizzly recovery, therefore, we may add that of human safety.

How much control of delinquent bears, in the end, can we hope for? There are a number of research projects on what biologists call aversive conditioning recently completed or still under way, and the results so far have not exactly been encouraging.

Take, for example, a study by Bruce Hastings, Barrie Gilbert, and David Turner in Yosemite National Park. Yosemite's black bear problem is horrendous. The bears there have learned to open jars and to pull down food bags from specially constructed, supposedly bear-proof suspension systems, and sometimes they literally chase people out of their campsites at mealtime. So savvy have Yosemite's black bears become that they know that only a closed container is likely to hold food: uncapped bottles and backpacks with flaps and zippers open are rarely messed with. *Sixty-one percent* of Yosemite's backcountry visitors in 1979 had some kind of encounter with a bear.

The author of this book and a friend, in the summer of 1981, had barely arrived at a high-country lake in Yosemite and leaned their packs against a boulder when a good-sized black bear came sauntering out of the woods and, with barely a glance at the people, made a beeline for their packs. Shouting, arm-waving, tree-limb-brandishing bothered that bear no more than a muttering panhandler slows down a Manhattan chairman of the board. The bear wasn't aggressive; it was just as if the people weren't there. As the bear sidled ever nearer and the packs' two defenders were losing their nerve and ready to give up their goodies—which would have meant giving up their whole trip—two headbanded, no-shirted young Californians burst over the hill yelling, "There's that son of a bitch!" and hurling brick-sized rocks at the bear. This seemed perhaps excessively provocative of a dangerous animal, but the bear took it sufficiently meekly to withdraw, still none to hurriedly, to the upper limbs of a large pine tree, from which, seated upright on one branch with his chin resting photogenically on his paws on another branch, he continued a placid vigil for nearly an hour—thus denying the dust-covered and exhausted backpackers their swim in the lake. The bear finally moseyed nonchalantly off, but the night was punctuated with yells and pot-banging throughout the echoing mountains as the bear visited first one and then another and another campsite, raising perfectly fearless hell wherever he went.

So Hastings's study focused with some intensity on ways of discouraging such rampaging ursine vandals. If things ever got half this out of hand with a grizzly population, clearly it would be disastrous. To avert a bloodbath you would have to eliminate either people or grizzlies from the area altogether. (Perhaps it should be reemphasized here that one does not chuck stones at a *grizzly* bear, *ever,* even if he is on a beeline for one's pack.) Hastings first tried sticking lithium chloride pellets—an emetic—in hot dogs and leaving them around a campground, and, um, as he puts it, "No definite effect was documented."

Then he tried booby-trapped food sacks: "A plastic bag with one liter of two percent ammonium hydroxide was placed in a counterbalanced food sack 2.5 m. above the ground. A string was left dangling from the food sack for easy access by the bears. A balloon was also placed in the stuff sack for a twofold purpose, that of providing a loud noise and of producing a full appearance to the sack. . . . The bears usually avoided touching the aversion sack and exposing its contents. However . . . this did not alter the normal food-obtaining activities of the bears; there were no significant differences in bear activity, interactions, or damages after the aversion sack was used compared with the same measures before the treatment."

Next Hastings tried upping the concentration of ammonia and the number of food sacks. This time the bears occasionally touched the sacks, but only thirteen percent of the balloons were ever broken. Still, the bear activity at the particular campsites where the ammonia bags were mingled among real food bags did decrease moderately, leading Hastings to conclude, in wonderfully poker-faced biologese, "These data indicate that this technique might be employed to pressure problem bears from one campground to another."

Grizzly bears' response to such deterrents as electrically charged wire fences has been similar. Usually they will manage simply to find a way around the painful obstacle, but if they really want what's on the other side, they will virtually walk through fire to get it. "You have to understand it in terms of the history of the species," says Dick Knight, leader of the Yellowstone grizzly study. "Grizzly bears have evolved not to care very much about pain unless there's really damaging injury involved, and their hide is so tough they're very rarely injured under natural circumstances. Once they've identified a high-energy food source, they're just programed to go after it, and the only thing that will stop them is fear of being killed. If they have to go through some electric shock or chemically induced nausea or whatever you want to throw at them, that's okay. They'll do it."

It has been almost unanimous popular wisdom that keeping bears and people apart is the only real way to keep people safe from bears. But a study by Katherine McArthur Jope in Glacier National Park has found precisely the opposite: "Most hiker injuries have been inflicted after the hiker was charged by the bear . . . [and] charges occurred primarily on trails with little human use. The findings of this research together with records on human injuries in the park, suggest that habituation of grizzly bears to high numbers of hikers in their habitat may reduce the rate of injuries resulting from fear-induced aggression." The apparent contradiction, however, may be less deep than one may at first suspect. Much of Glacier Park is either extremely heavily vegetated in the forest understory or else rugged, steep, rocky, and open—the first a situation in which bears and people may easily surprise one another at extremely close range, and the second, in open alpine country, one in which grizzlies are naturally nervous and aggressive because of the lack of visual cover into which they can quickly disappear. Thus, in both situations, whatever aggression occurs is more likely to be *fear-induced* than, say, related to food. If we could leave out the food-getting issue—that is, in an ideal world where campers never littered and all garbage dumps were walled off like prison yards—then a comfortable proximity of grizzlies and people might well be manageable. But as long as food and people remain closely linked in the minds of grizzly bears, neighborly relations are bound from time to time to be strained. Moreover, as long as illegal killing remains a serious threat to grizzlies, any loss of fear of humans will expose more bears to the deadly trigger-happy few. Nevertheless, increasing grizzly habituation to people is probably inevitable as long as backcountry recreation in grizzly habitat continues to increase, and it is in dealing with this inevitability that Jope's study will doubtless prove invaluable. In showing how clearly grizzly behavior distinguishes between fear-induced aggression and that which is instrumental, or goal-oriented, it is further testimony to the subtleties of judgment grizzlies are capable of and to the wisdom of the choices they will make if, first, their innate aggression-alarms are not set off and, second, they have not been allowed to become garbage addicts. As long as they perceive people as bell-wearing, predictable, harmless, ungenerous with food, and unacceptable as prey, grizzly bears are—even at close quarters—going to leave us alone. Well, okay . . . most of the time.

Surely the romance of the grizzly would be less potent if the bear were not dangerous to us. Of the deep change in human attitudes toward nature that was at the heart of the Romantic movement, Kenneth Clark, in *Animals and Men,* wrote, "Man in his relationship to animals began to sympathize with the ferocity, the cruelty even, that he had previously dreaded and opposed."

What Clark called "this new religion of violence," as exemplified in Delacroix's savage "lion-hunt" pictures—"episodes in a war between men and animals in which for the first time in art, the outcome is uncertain"—continues albeit confusedly to inform our love of the likes of lions and tigers and grizzly bears. Perhaps the primary element that confuses our sympathy is the human overreadiness to identify animal violence with human anger. Clark's "cruelty even" puts the finger on the most vulnerable spot of the Romantic fallacy—the centrality of individual human consciousness—for the evidence is that cruelty is a distinctly human idea and would be unfamiliar to grizzly bears or indeed to any other wild beast. A truthful and truly sympathetic human membership in the community of nature would demand that we distinguish between those aspects of violence which we know we share with our fellow creatures and those which may be uniquely, tragically our own. In instrumental aggression such as predation, it may be that the concomitant elevation of such brain chemicals as epinephrine produces a subjective response in the mind of the grizzly in some way similar to the excited, hypervigilant fight-or-flight emotion that is a component of human anger, but the apparent utter placidity of the predator once his kill has been made, or even once the kill has been missed, suggests an important difference. The best candidate for an analogue of human fury is probably the aggression of mother grizzlies defending their young, but the fact that removal of the threat to the cubs seems always to result in immediate extinction of the mother's aggressive behavior does not harmonize well with the rhapsodic and somewhat self-perpetuating passion that we experience as anger. Mother grizzlies whose young have been threatened do not stalk and ambush the perpetrators as human mothers are wont to do.

As for cruelty—the idea is too uniquely human to waste much time getting animals tangled up in it. We say that nature is cruel, but what we mean is that if we behaved in such a way *we* would be acting cruelly. For a valid human ethics with respect to the wild, the distinction is crucial. Nature does not provide us with exculpatory examples of cruelty. By the same token we have no business *in*culpating nature's violence. Acts of ignorant barbarity like Yellowstone Park's slaughter of wolves in the early twentieth century no longer, thank goodness, seem even conceivable, but we still have some distance to go toward an honest recognition that there is no pattern in nature for human evil.

It is, then, in supreme innocence of us—whom she knows only as alien beings inconveniently at large in her realm, to be avoided with cool xenophobic self-possession—that the bear chooses the path she will travel, and the way she will live. What she does not do and where she does not go are determined largely by her rigorous avoidance of the two creatures capable of harming her or her young, man and the adult male grizzly bear. What she does do and where she does go are at bottom very simply decided, almost entirely by nutritional needs. At certain times there are other influential factors at work—the cubs' education, the need for cover, the regulation of her body temperature, the imperatives of the mating season—but all of these can be summarily subordinated, should the need arise, to that single-minded drive for food.

We must not, however, fall into the romantic-nostalgic trap of thinking that ultimate causation somehow "solves" the grizzly bear "puzzle." No more than infantile sexuality explains the variety of adult neurosis, no more than the selfish gene can account for the variety of lifeforms, does the ceaseless hunger of the grizzly bear give adequate meaning to the full variety of her behavior. It is essential to our understanding that we keep constantly in mind the nutrition-centeredness of her motivation, but it is far from sufficient. The wonder of her existence resides not in her most basic drives but in their expression. Occam's Razor (which holds that "entities ought not to be multiplied except from necessity") has done great service in the physical sciences, but it has also, as in the naïve behaviorism that reduced much animal study in the middle years of the twentieth century to mechanomorphic absurdity, far too often shaved biology to an impossibly fine point.

In *Animal Thought,* Stephen Walker quotes what has become known as Lloyd Morgan's Canon, the early modern behaviorist reincarnation of Occam's Razor: "In no case may we interpret an action as the outcome of the exercise of a higher psychical faculty, if it can be interpreted as the exercise of one which stands lower on the psychological scale."

To this Walker responds, "It is debatable . . . whether parsimonious explanations, especially of biological and psychological phenomena, are necessarily the best ones. Applied to human actions, the Canon would require us always to assume that people act for the most straightforward and least intellectually demanding motives. This might be a useful palliative against the urge to search for deep and dark explanations every time someone forgets a name, or misses a bus, but it would surely be unwise to assume that the simplest explanation of a politician's promise, or a child's tears, is always true. Similarly, because all animals feed, and move, and fight, it does not follow that the mechanisms which control these actions in the lowest and simplest species are the only ones at work in all the others."

Quite right. But where does this leave us? Well, humbled, for one thing. There is so much we cannot know because we cannot even think of what questions to ask. When we see the bear sitting on her haunches at the top of a cliff looking out over a sea of forest and meadow, and we ask, "What is she doing?" the only available empirical answer is "Nothing." But that seems woefully unsatisfactory. Can we say then that she is thinking? Surely her brain is not so unlike ours that her consciousness can simply be turned off when she is evidently awake and aware. But *thinking?* Thinking *what?* Can man hope ever to know?

For the moment we can only wonder, and observe. As our observations ramify and perhaps begin to interconnect, at least an external reality may gradually take shape. And must suffice.

Part Two:
Denizens of the Deep
Sharks
One Bite is Enough!

9   The Shadows Attack

BY THOMAS B. ALLEN

Down the beach he ran, an impatient young man drawn to the cool and beckoning sea. He had arrived at the resort in Beach Haven, New Jersey, scarcely minutes before. And now—Saturday, July 1, 1916—Charles Van Sant was plunging into the surf.

He was twenty-three years old, and his life stretched before him as did the sea—invitingly, excitingly, seemingly without end. On his own horizon, and on the horizon of millions of other young men, there hung a cloud of war. On the horizon of the sea around him, there was not a cloud.

Behind him, on the beach, a holiday crowd was gathering. Soon his father and two sisters would be there. He had left them still in their shorefront suite, unpacking and settling themselves. They had been too slow for him. Time had been too slow for him. He had spent ages on the hot, jammed trains that carried him across the breadth of New Jersey from the Van Sant home in Philadelphia to Long Beach Island, a narrow strip of land dotted with resorts like Beach Haven. Finally, the trip had ended. Charles rushed into the suite, hastily donned his bathing suit, threw on a robe, and rushed to the beach. As he dived in, he might have heard someone singing "By the sea, by the sea, by the beautiful sea. . . ." The sea was beautiful in Beach Haven that day.

Charles was a strong swimmer. With powerful strokes he pulled away from shore. He swam out about a hundred yards—far enough, he decided, for a first swim. Leisurely, reluctantly, he turned back toward shore, trying to prolong this serene and solitary communion with the sea. But he was not alone.

Directly behind him, knifing toward him straight and sure, was a gray shadow beneath a black fin that crested the water. They saw it from the beach. Bathers screamed, but the man did not hear their cries. Then, suddenly, they stood silent and motionless, frozen by the sight of the narrowing gap between

Van Sant and the pursuing fin. He was still swimming excruciatingly slowly, unaware that he was the hunted in a deadly chase.

He was close to shore when the water churned and red foam billowed around him. At that moment Alexander Ott, a former U.S. Olympic swimmer, dived into the sea and swam faster than he ever had before. As Ott reached the red blotch on the water, the gray shadow turned menacingly, then darted away for blue water, leaving Van Sant to the man who had come to save him.

Ott managed to get Van Sant to shore, and there, on the warm sand, Van Sant's life ebbed away. His legs had been horribly ravaged. He died that night from shock and loss of blood.

The gray shadow glided seaward, unseen and unheralded. No alarm was spread. No one could remember a shark ever having killed a swimmer before. Perhaps it had happened in the South Seas or in Australia. But never in New Jersey. And the experts said that there never had been an absolutely authenticated case of a shark attacking a swimmer anywhere in the world. Herman Oelrichs, a wealthy New York banker, had offered a $500 prize to anyone who could prove to him that any bather actually had been attacked by a shark anywhere north of Cape Hatteras. The prize had gone unclaimed for 30 years.

Only three years before, on August 26, 1913, a fisherman had caught a shark off Spring Lake, New Jersey, forty-five miles up the coast from Beach Haven. When the shark was cut open, a woman's foot wearing a knitted stocking and a tan shoe was found in its stomach. But this gruesome discovery—like similar ones attested to down the years by numerous sailors and fishermen—was explained away. Though sharks might devour bodies, never would a shark attack a live swimmer.

In Spring Lake on July 6, five days after Charles Van Sant was killed, more than five hundred people were lounging or strolling on the beach. It was after lunch; the tide had ebbed. Relatively few swimmers were in the water. Children splashed at the water's edge. A few bathers stood in knee-deep water.

Life was elegant and tranquil at Spring Lake, one of the favorite society resorts. The socially prominent of Philadelphia, New Jersey, and New York gathered there. Some lived in fabulous shore homes they liked to call cottages. Others stayed at the New Monmouth Hotel or the Essex and Sussex Hotel. Secretary of the Treasury William G. McAdoo, who was married to a daughter of President Wilson, was one of the leaders of Spring Lake society. New Jersey Governor James F. Fielder and former Governor John Franklin Fort spent most of their summers there. And hundreds of wealthy New Yorkers had fled to

Spring Lake with their children that year to escape the polio (then called infantile paralysis) epidemic in New York City. Since June 10, 165 persons had died of the disease in the city. On July 5 alone, twenty-four deaths had been reported. . . And there were rumors that the epidemic was spreading to New Jersey. So the talk on that July 6 afternoon in Spring Lake was not about the new Allied offensive against the Germans or the neutrality policy of Wilson. It was not about Wilson's chances of reelection or Charles Evans Hughes's chances of defeating him. It was not about sharks, or the death of an obscure young man at a rather unfashionable beach resort forty-five miles away five days before. Infantile paralysis dominated the conversations at Spring Lake just as it dominated the headlines in the New York City newspapers. . . .

In the egalitarian sea, a bellboy was as good as a millionaire. Perhaps that was why Charles Bruder loved the sea. Charles was a bellboy at the Essex and Sussex Hotel and, when he was not working, he could usually be found swimming. He was twenty-eight years old, personable, and well liked by hotel guests, who considered him part of Spring Lake. Even people who had been going there for much of their lives could not remember Spring Lake without him, for it was said that he had appeared there when he was eight years old and had been working at various hotels every summer since. From the tips he earned he supported himself and his only known relative, his mother, who lived in Switzerland.

Bruder had the afternoon off on July 6, and ebb tide or not, he was going swimming. He walked out through the surf, nodding and smiling at hotel guests he recognized. When the water reached his waist, he dived in and began to swim. He was soon beyond the lifelines. George White and Chris Anderson, the lifeguards on duty, did not call him back as they would have summoned most swimmers, for everybody knew that Charles Bruder was a strong swimmer.

A woman's scream shattered the air of Spring Lake. Instinctively, White and Anderson turned narrowed eyes seaward. Bruder had disappeared.

"He has upset!" the woman screamed. "The man in the red canoe is upset!"

Even as she screamed, White and Anderson were racing toward their boat. They knew that it was not the reflection of an overturned canoe they saw, as even now the red blot was spreading, and in the midst of it, for one awful moment, Bruder's agonized face appeared, and he flung up a bloodied arm. The boat reached him. White leaned from the bow and held out an oar to Bruder. Somehow he grasped it. They pulled him toward them. His face was sickeningly white and his eyes were shut. "Shark—shark got me—bit my legs off!" he gasped and, mercifully, fainted. White hauled him over the gunwale. His body was not heavy.

Mrs. George W. Childs, one of the principal envoys of Philadelphia society at Spring Lake, was standing on the private balcony outside her suite at the Essex and Sussex when she heard the screams from the beach. She turned to her maid and asked for her spyglass.

Below on the shore, she saw White and Anderson beaching their boat. She saw them hesitate to lay Bruder on the sand. From the crowd a woman darted forward and put down her linen coat, turning her eyes away as she did so. Several women fainted. Mrs. Childs, seventy-four years old and indomitable, did not faint. She went to the phone in her room, called the manager, and told him what she had seen. She also asked that her car be brought around. Three minutes later she was speeding to Deal Beach, some five miles north. Her niece took a plunge in the surf there every afternoon, and Mrs. Childs wanted to get to Deal Beach before the shark did.

Bruder was dead. The doctor called to tend him was treating the women who had fainted. At the Essex and Sussex, the telephone operator was ringing up every central switchboard from Point Pleasant to Atlantic Highlands. Within twelve minutes, swimmers were streaming ashore along 20 miles of New Jersey beaches.

But was it a shark? Was it true that man-eaters were prowling the shore of New Jersey? Hotel men, resort operators, summer colonists wanted to be told that it could not happen. They anxiously awaited the verdict of Colonel William Gray Schauffler, an eminent physician and surgeon general of the New Jersey National Guard. He had examined Bruder within 15 minutes after he had been taken from the sea.

"There is not the slightest doubt," Colonel Schauffler reported, "that a man-eating shark inflicted the injuries. Bruder's right leg was frightfully torn and the bone bitten off halfway between the knee and ankle. The left foot was missing, as well as the lower end of the tibia and fibula. The leg bone was denuded of flesh from a point halfway below the knee. There was a deep gash above the left knee, which penetrated to the bone. On the right side of the abdomen, low down, a piece of flesh as big as a man's fist was missing."

That night, while hotel residents, at Mrs. Childs's suggestion, took up a collection for Bruder's mother, motorboats equipped with searchlights slipped out to sea in a futile hunt for the shark. Colonel Schauffler called a meeting of resort owners and town officials to discuss ways to make the beaches safe from sharks. Rifle-toting boatmen were hired to patrol the beaches. Fishermen volunteered to fish for the shark with great hooks, sturdy lines, and chunks of prime mutton, reportedly the best shark bait, donated by cooperative Spring Lake meat markets. "I am certain that the bathing beaches will be made safe within two or three days," Councilman D.H. Hill announced. No shark was caught, shot, or even seen.

The day Bruder was killed, 24 people died in New York City of polio, then called infantile paralysis. Bruder's death received far greater coverage in the New York papers.

Each resort town along the New Jersey coast went its own brave way. Atlantic City was more upset by a ban on bathing suits that exposed "the nether extremities" than by sharks, although some daring souls made an adventure out of the shark scare by contemptuously swimming beyond the end of the piers. At Asbury Park, with a flourish of publicity, a motorboat shark patrol was begun and workmen were set to enclosing the bathing area with "sharkproof" wire netting. A net was not necessary, according to a sea captain interviewed as a "shark authority." Sharks scared easily, he said. "The best thing to do when a shark comes along," he advised, "is to shout as loud as you can and splash the water with your hands and feet."

The Atlantic seemed alive with sharks and tales of sharks. At Spring Lake, a lifeguard told of battling a twelve-foot shark with an oar some fifty feet offshore. At Bayonne, New Jersey, twenty boys were swimming off a yacht-club float when they saw a shark. A policeman heard their cries and emptied his revolver at an ominous black fin. The shark, he said, fled to the open sea. In shallow water off Eldred's Bar near Rockaway Point in Brooklyn, eight men digging for sandworms saw a shark driving a school of weakfish toward shore. With eel tongs, oars, spears, and spades, they said, they splashed at it and killed it. All along the coast, shark vigilantes were firing their rifles at anything that looked big and moved in the sea.

Finally, out of this hysterical war on sharks, porpoises, and any other shadows in the sea, came the sobering voice of academic authority. Dr. John Treadwell Nichols, curator of the Department of Fishes in the American Museum of Natural History in New York, and Dr. Robert Cushman Murphy, of the Brooklyn Museum, declared there was very little danger that a shark would attack anyone. Dr. Frederick A. Lucas, director of the Museum of Natural History, added his agreement. No shark, he said, could snap off a man's leg "like a carrot." A shark's jaws were simply not powerful enough to do the kind of bodily damage that Dr. Schauffler had described, Dr. Lucas insisted.

The experts had spoken. The shark scare abated somewhat. New Jersey bathers believed they could once more enter the water unafraid. But the shark panic had cost New Jersey resort owners an estimated $250,000 in lost tourist business. In some areas, bathing had fallen off more than 75 percent. Six weeks of summer still remained, and, with plenty of hard work, the resort owners as-sured each other, the loss could be made up.

"Tiger sharks will hold but little terror for bathers in the waters here-abouts within a few days," the *New York Times* reported from Asbury Park on July 10. "Today the final work was being rushed on the net protectors about the Asbury Park beaches, and in Ocean Grove the contractors who received the job of erecting steel nets began work. At Fourth Avenue, where the grounds had been enclosed by the steel nets, a record-breaking crowd of bathers enjoyed the surf."

The dispatch was not entirely optimistic, for it reported that a fishing boat had sighted four sharks eight miles off Asbury Park. Another shark had been reported two hundred yards off Bridgehampton, Long Island, by Esterbrook Carter, nephew of Charles E. Hughes, the Republican candidate for President. Carter, along with all other Republicans, was relieved to learn that Hughes had spent the day indoors, polishing his speech accepting the nomination.

Officials of the U.S. Bureau of Fisheries in Washington tried to dispel the fear of sharks en masse. A *single* shark, they theorized, was probably responsi-ble for both fatal attacks. Because of a scarcity of food fish off the New Jersey shore, they said, this renegade shark may have been driven far inshore and, mad-dened by hunger, attacked Van Sant. Then, having acquired a taste for human flesh, it continued swimming near shore until its appetite was satiated by Bruder. It was a ghastly theory. In an apparent attempt to still renewed apprehension, U.S. Commissioner of Fisheries Hugh M. Smith hastily pointed out on July 9 that "the case is extremely unusual. I don't look for it to happen again. The fact that only two out of millions of bathers have been attacked in many years is evidence of the rarity of such instances." Again, the very best assurance—from an expert.

On a map, Matawan, New Jersey, appears to be an inland town. It is eleven miles west of the Atlantic Ocean and two miles south of Raritan Bay, a body of water that blends into the Lower Bay, gateway to the great port of New York. Matawan's only link to salt water is a tenuous one, a meandering tidal creek—barely a stream at high tide—that empties into Raritan Bay.

In the summer of 1916, as in countless summers before, Matawan boys spent every minute they could in Matawan Creek. The most popular swim-ming hole was at the old Propeller Wyckoff Dock, named after the tug-sized steamer *Wyckoff*, which, years before, used to come up the creek with the tide to pick up farmers' produce and carry it to the New York market on the next tide. The dock had deteriorated into a dozen or so pilings that jutted close to one another along the edge of a dilapidated pier. Diving and jumping off the pier and the pilings were not adventurous enough for the boys who swam at

Wyckoff Dock, so they usually played tag, hopping from piling to piling in pursuit of one another.

One day in early July, 1916, Rennie (for Rensselaer) Cartan, age four-teen, was playing tag on the Wyckoff pilings. To escape an outreaching hand, Rennie dived into the creek. As his head and shoulders entered the murky water, he felt something like a strip of very coarse sandpaper grate along his stomach. He arched his body to the surface and stroked to the pier. His stom-ach was streaked with blood as he clambered up a piling and onto the dock. "Don't dive in any more!" he shouted to his companions. "There's a shark or something in there!"

No one paid much attention to Rennie, and, as a matter of fact, he ig-nored his own warning a few minutes later by diving into the creek. He was in a hurry to get home. It was much faster to swim across the creek than to walk to the nearest bridge. (More than 40 years later, the scars from the sandpaper-like burn still on his stomach, Rensselaer Cartan would stand by the creek, and, shaking his head, say to the author, "It might have been me. You know, it might have been me.")

On July 11, in Belford, on Sandy Hook Bay, a few miles east of the mouth of Matawan Creek, Herman Tarnow, a fisherman, caught a nine-foot shark 120 feet out from the low-water mark. No one paid much attention to Herman Tarnow, either.

In the late morning of July 12, Captain Thomas Cottrell, a retired sailor and part-time local fisherman, was walking along the new trolley draw-bridge that crossed Matawan Creek about a mile and a half downstream from Wyckoff Dock. Eleven days had passed since Charles Van Sant had died at Beach Haven, seventy miles as a shark would swim, from Matawan. Six days had passed since Charles Bruder had died at Spring Lake, twenty-five miles as a shark would swim, from Matawan. Now, as Captain Cottrell walked across the bridge that hot, bright morning, he saw a dark gray shadow sweeping up the creek with the incoming tide. The shadow was moving swiftly. But the captain, a man who trusted his eyes, believed what he had seen. He shouted to two workmen on the bridge. They saw the shadow, too. They ran to a telephone and called John Mulsonn, a barber who was also Matawan's chief of police. Captain Cottrell ran the half mile to Matawan center. He tried to stop a group of boys who were heading for the creek. He toured Matawan's short and busy lower Main Street, shouting his warning to merchants and their customers. Everyone laughed at the idea of a shark in the shallow creek, only thirty-five feet across at its widest point. Chief Mulsonn did not even leave his barber-shop. Captain Cottrell walked back toward the creek.

One of the shops Captain Cottrell stuck his head into during his futile trip up Main Street was Stanley Fisher's new dry-cleaning establishment. Stanley, one of Matawan's best-liked young men, had only recently started this business, which had shown no promise of making his fortune. As a sideline he was also taking orders for men's suits. He had made an unusual sale a few days before. A man had come in and bought a suit. Instead of paying cash for it, he had bought Stanley a $10,000 life insurance policy. Stanley, a blond-haired, 210-pound giant of a man, was taking a ribbing from his friends. He was, after all, only twenty-four years old—in the prime of life, they told him. What would he need with an insurance policy?

Stanley's father, Watson H. Fisher, had followed the sea most of his life and risen to commodore of the Savannah Line. Now retired and well off, he was one of Matawan's leading citizens. If he had ever wished that his son might go to sea, he had kept the wish to himself. Some people in Matawan did say, though, that it was a shame that a big, strong man like Stanley was running a dry-cleaning store instead of sailing the seas as his father had before him.

July 12 was a scorching, muggy day. The heat was nearly unbearable in Anderson's Saw Mill, where Lester Stilwell worked with his father, William Stilwell. By two o'clock, Lester had finished nailing up his last wooden box, a task he was especially good at, and, since he was only twelve years old, he was given the rest of the day off. He waved good-bye to his father, dashed out of the stifling mill, and headed for Wyckoff Dock with his pals—Johnson Cartan, Frank Clowes, Albert O'Hara, and Charles Van Brunt. Soon they were all splashing around in the creek. Most of them, like Lester, were not wearing bathing suits.

Albert O'Hara, age eleven, was near the dock, about to climb out of the water, when Lester yelled, "Watch me float, fellas!" Albert turned to look. Lester was so thin he usually had trouble floating. At that instant, something hard and slippery slammed Albert's right leg. He looked down and saw what looked like the sinuous tail of a huge fish. Charles Van Brunt, 13, still in the water, saw it too. It was the biggest, blackest fish he had ever seen, and it was streaking for Lester Stilwell. Lester screamed. Charles saw the big black fish strike, its body suddenly twisting as it hit Lester, and Charles saw that the fish was not all black, for as it rolled it exposed a stark white belly and gleaming teeth. And Charles knew, to his everlasting horror, that he had seen a shark. In an instant, it all but closed its jaws about Lester's slim body and dragged him beneath the reddening waters of Matawan Creek. Lester had neither time nor life to scream again.

Lester's pals and other boys who had been swimming nearby got out of the water as fast as they could. Some ran into Fischer's bag factory at the creek and summoned workmen to Wyckoff Dock. Others ran up the steep dirt road from the creek and raced to the center of town. Now, where Captain Cottrell had walked, there was panic, and screaming, naked boys. Boys who had seen the shark were yelling, "Shark! Shark! A shark got Lester!" Along the shore by the dock, those who knew only that Lester Stilwell had gone under were calling his name: "Lester! Lester!" Out of this tumult somehow came the report that Lester, "a boy who took fits," had been seized by an attack and was drowning. All that the townspeople knew for sure was that a boy was in trouble at the creek, and men, women, and children began running there to help him. Among them was Stanley Fisher, who had ducked into the back of his dry-cleaning shop only long enough to put on a bathing suit.

"Remember what Captain Cottrell said," Mary Anderson, a Matawan teacher, shouted at Fisher as he ran. "It may have been a shark!"

Fisher stopped for a moment. "A shark? Here?" he asked. He looked immense as he stood there, towering above Mary Anderson. "I don't care," he said, as if finally answering some inner doubt. "I'm going after that boy."

Then, turning to his errand boy, eight-year-old Johnny Smith, who was standing nearby, Fisher said, "Take care of the store until I get back." And Fisher sprinted to the creek.

The son of Commodore Fisher took command at Matawan Creek. His quarterdeck was Wyckoff Dock, and his enemy was a shark. Some 200 townspeople, including Lester Stilwell's mother and father, lined the dock and the nearer bank. Fisher soon had men in boats, poling for Lester's body. Someone brought a roll of chicken wire to the dock. Fisher ordered a couple of young men to get into a rowboat and string the chicken wire, weighed down with stones, along the bottom of the creek, downstream from the dock, where the channel was about twenty feet wide. Fisher knew there was a deep spot, off the farther bank, directly opposite the dock. There, he believed, the shark was lurking with Lester's body. Fisher's plan was to flush out the shark, driving it into shallower water downstream, where it would be trapped by the chicken-wire barrier. But the hastily strung fence only partially blocked the creek.

When this futile fence was completed, Fisher dived into the creek. Several men were in the water, diving to the bottom, feeling in the mud for Lester's body. Fisher swam along to the deep spot. Arthur Smith, fifty-one, a carpenter by trade and a hunter by avocation, was diving, too. On shore, his daughter was screaming to him: "Come back, Pa! Come back!" The task was for younger men. But Smith kept diving, defying the death that swam by him and, finally, touched him. (*A day would come when Arthur Smith, half blind and almost deaf at ninety-five, would sit hunched and feeble in an old house on the bank of Matawan Creek. Suddenly, at shouted mention of that awful day, he would spring forward in his chair and vividly re-create that moment when he felt the shark scrape his leg. At ninety-five, he would still carry the scars and show them to the author.*)

Smith saw Fisher make two "overhangs"—powerful overhand strokes—and dive down, down . . .

Arthur S. Van Buskirk, a local deputy of the Monmouth County Detectives Office, had just arrived at the creek. He was sitting on the forward deck of a small boat when he saw a thrashing in the water at the farther shore. Even as he looked, the water calmed and a rapidly widening red stain spread on the surface. Van Buskirk yelled at the other man in the boat to start the engine. While it sputtered to life, Van Buskirk sculled toward the red stain, in the midst of which Stanley Fisher had suddenly appeared.

Fisher was facing the farther bank. The silent crowd at Wyckoff Dock could see only his broad back and shoulders. He was drawn up, half crouching in waist-deep water, and he seemed to be tottering on one leg. The boat pulled up directly behind Fisher. Van Buskirk could see that Fisher was holding bloody remnants of his right leg in both hands. Just as Fisher was about to pitch forward face first into the water, Van Buskirk reached out and pulled him into his arms. He could get Fisher only halfway out of the water. The boat backed out of the shoal water and, as it turned to head toward the dock, a gasp rippled through the crowd. Now they could see Fisher, breasting the water like a macabre figurehead on the prow of the boat. Enough of him was out of the water so that his terrible wound could be seen. From groin to kneecap the flesh was gone from his right leg. Several women fainted. Little Alfreda Matz, one of the many children on the dock, tried to look. But her father threw the tail of his suit coat across her eyes and hugged her face to his side. She thought, *A crocodile bit Mr. Fisher.*

A sound like a moan went up as the boat neared the dock, for Fisher almost slipped from Van Buskirk's grasp. Staring down at Fisher's leg—it was hardly more than a bone and that bore jagged scratches running lengthwise along it—Van Buskirk saw blood pulsating from a torn artery. There was a rope on the deck beneath him, and he thought of tying a tourniquet with one hand. His own weight and that of his burden combined to prevent him from getting the rope, and he almost lost his grip on Fisher as well. Just then, hands reached out from the dock and grabbed Fisher. He was still conscious. Gently, men placed Fisher on a stretcher improvised from planks and bore him to the

Matawan railroad, about a quarter of a mile way. Each jolting step up the bank and along the track stabbed him with searing pain. Merciful unconsciousness awaited him, but he seemed to fight it off. There was something he very much wanted to say.

At the station, they placed him on a baggage car and waited for the next train. A doctor had been found. There was little he could do, other than to retard the flow of blood. Nearly three hours went by until the 5:06 train from Long Branch was flagged down. Even on the train, Fisher held onto consciousness. Not until 7:45 that night, as he was wheeled into the operating room at Monmouth Memorial Hospital, did he die. Before he died, he had said what he wanted to say: On the bottom of Matawan Creek, he had reached the body of Lester Stilwell and wrested it from the jaws of the shark.

While Fisher lay on the baggage car waiting for death and the 5:06, several men went to Asher P. Woolley's store and got dynamite to blow up the shark they believed to be still off Wyckoff Dock. The creek was cleared of boats. But moments before the charge was to be set off, a motorboat hove into view from downstream. Jacob R. Lefferts, a Matawan lawyer, was at the wheel. Lying on the bottom of the boat was a boy. His right leg was swathed in bloodied bandages. "A shark got him," Lefferts shouted, as he pulled in to shore. The boy was transferred to a car and sped to St. Peter's Hospital in New Brunswick.

At first the boy would not give his name. He was afraid his mother would be angry at him. Soon he was identified as Joseph Dunn, age fourteen. He had been swimming with his older brother, Michael, and several other boys off the dock of the New Jersey Clay Company brickyards about a half mile down Matawan Creek, near Keyport. Someone had run to the brickyards and told the boys about the shark. They were all in the water when the warning came, and they swam swiftly to the dock. Joseph Dunn, the youngest, was the last one out of the water. As he started up the ladder, something that felt like a big pair of scissors, he said, grabbed his right leg. ("I felt my leg going down the shark's throat," he said later. "I believe it would have swallowed me.")

Joseph screamed, and the older boys sprang to the ladder. Joseph kicked the water with his free leg. Michael Dunn and two others began a tug-of-war with the shark, ripping Joseph's flesh to save his life. For a moment or two, the shark hung on. Then, suddenly, Joseph was free. The shark had let go—and vanished. Its third victim in less than an hour had been snatched from death.

In St. Peter's Hospital, hope was high that Joseph Dunn's life would be saved, but saving his torn leg—slashed with tooth marks, a major tendon severed, muscles badly mangled—seemed hopeless. Dr. R.J. Faulkingham, on general surgical service at the hospital, was given the case.

All that night and into the morning, Matawan Creek was the scene of an orgy of vengeance. Blast after blast of dynamite sent geysers of water and fish skyward. Hundreds of men lined both banks, armed with scythes, pitchforks, and old harpoons taken from living-room walls. By lantern light and by the first glimmer of dawn, men fired shotguns and pistols into the creek. At low tide, men waded into the water with knives—and even hammers.

The creek was soon laced with tangles of chicken wire and fishing nets. Newspaper reporters and photographers swarmed into Matawan, and one newspaper proclaimed that it had organized a shark hunt—a boat loaded to the gunwales with men carrying rifles. Extra-large charges of dynamite were set off for the benefit of newsreel cameras. Stores in Matawan and Keyport ran out of explosives and ammunition. A special order was sent to Perth Amboy, New Jersey, for more.

"We've got a shark!" a man shouted here . . . then there. Reports came in with the tide: One shark, two sharks, three sharks, four sharks were trapped in Matawan Creek. With the outgoing tide went reports that shark after shark had escaped from Matawan Creek.

The only respite from the frenzy at the creek came when Matawan buried its dead. The boys who had been the last to see Lester Stilwell alive carried him to his grave. At the First Methodist Church on Main Street, Stanley Fisher's voice was missing from the choir. But his memory would live on in the church. With the money from the new insurance policy he had so strangely acquired, Stanley's parents purchased a stained-glass window—a landscape of Bethlehem. In the years to come, the rays of the setting sun would filter through the window as day's end came to the little town of Matawan.

At St. Peter's Hospital, Dr. Faulkingham was quietly, skillfully tending the wounds of Joseph Dunn. Newspapers had already reported that Joseph's leg would undoubtedly have to be amputated. But Dr. Faulkingham didn't have time to read the newspapers. He had sutured Joseph's severed tendon and ripped muscles, and a slow, uncertain recovery began. It would be fifty-nine days before Joseph Dunn would walk out of St. Peter's Hospital, but walk he would, on two strong legs.

Six days after the attack, a shark was finally caught in Matawan Creek—by none other than Captain Cottrell. He was coming up the creek in his motorboat *Skud* with his son-in-law, Richard Lee, when, about 400 yards from the bay, not far from the bridge where he had first seen that lethal shadow, he saw a dorsal fin rise out of the water, then disappear. Swiftly, he and Lee let out several yards of gill net, weighted with lead at the bottom and strung with corks on the top. The net billowed out as the outgoing tide carried it down creek. Both ends of the net were secured in the boat. By deft maneuvering, the captain trapped the shark between boat and net. The shark struggled furiously, but foot by foot, the two men hauled in the net, which was to be the shark's shroud.

Using the hull of his boat as an anvil, Cottrell smashed the shark on the head again and again with a large mallet. When he was convinced the shark was dead, Cottrell hauled it ashore. It weighed 230 pounds and was almost exactly seven feet long. He put it on exhibition in his fish shed, and nearly everyone in Matawan and Keyport lined up to see it as it lay on ice. They paid ten cents each to view the "Terror of Matawan Creek."

In Bridgehampton, Long Island, the scene of another shark scare, a fisherman caught a shark, rented a zinc-lined coffin from a local undertaker, and exhibited *his* shark for five cents a look.

Actually, the killer of Matawan Creek may have been caught two days after the attack. Michael Schleisser, a New Yorker who was one of the many shark hunters prowling the local waters on July 14, was dragging a drift net behind his boat in hope of snagging a shark. He was in Raritan Bay, off South Amboy, New Jersey, less than four miles northwest of the mouth of Matawan Creek, when a large shark charged the net. Though quickly enmeshed, the 8½-foot shark fought savagely, snapping a jaw in which row upon row of teeth glistened menacingly. Schleisser, unaware that he had caught a shark of the most feared species in the sea, strained to haul the net closer to the boat, and clubbed the shark again and again. Although many other sharks were being hauled in and displayed by fishermen, Schleisser's shark *was* a killer. Had Schleisser slipped and tumbled into the net, he might have become another victim. For, when he finally subdued the shark, towed it into South Amboy, and ripped it open, he found 15 pounds of flesh and bones in its belly. One of the bones, eleven inches long, was identified as the shinbone of a boy. Another fragment appeared to be part of a human rib. There was no doubt that the shark had probably attacked and certainly eaten at least one human being.

Dr. Lucas, of the Museum of Natural History, skeptical about local shark attacks only a few days before, personally identified the remains as human.

The shark itself was identified, too. It was a great white shark (*Carcharodon carcharias*), feared as a man-eater in tropical waters but, until the period dealt with here, unreported along beaches as far north as New Jersey. Dr. Nichols, an expert who had joined the Doctors Murphy and Lucas in mini-mizing the possibility of shark attacks after the first two New Jersey killings, now joined with them in conceding the existence of dangerous sharks in northern Atlantic waters. They granted at least one man-eating shark, for Nichols and Murphy concluded that Schleisser's *Carcharodon carcharias* was probably responsible for all five attacks. Whether or not this conservative esti-mate was accurate, it is possible that there were many of these dangerous sharks in the waters at the time.

Schleisser, who had had some training as a taxidermist, mounted his shark and placed it on exhibit in a New York newspaper office. Later, "The Jaws of the New Jersey Man-Eater" wound up in the window of a Broadway fish shop.

The capture of the apparent killer did not stop the stories that were sweeping the eastern seaboard. From Florida to Rhode Island came reports of sharks. Virtually every ship that came into New York carried a cargo of shark stories. Several hundred sharks were reported off Fire Island, Long Island, and posses were formed to track them down.

Theories abounded, too. One was that heavy cannonading in the North Sea had driven sharks across the Atlantic to more tranquil seas. Another theory held that sharks were feeding on swimmers because they had been de-prived of their usual diet of refuse from passenger liners, whose sailings were being curtailed by another kind of shark, the U-boat. The European war also spawned the idea that sharks had been feasting so well on war dead floating down rivers into the sea that they had undergone a change of dietary habits. One *New York Times* letter writer gravely calculated the figures: More than 12,500 war casualties had been gobbled up by sharks, he claimed.

By stoking their imaginations a little more, some of the theorists con-cluded that the ghoul sharks of European waters had deserted their bountiful feeding grounds in the war zone for the far less ample larder offered by New Jersey bathing beaches.

Logic and reason fell victims to the shark scare. A neighbor of Teddy Roosevelt's said he saw a shark off the beach in Oyster Bay, Long Island, and called upon him to do something about it. A long-distance swimmer an-nounced that he would brave the terrors of the Lower Bay of New York Har-bor in a round-trip from the Battery to Sandy Hook—in a wire basket. In the *New York Times,* America's leading woman swimmer, Annette Kellerman, ad-vised bathers to dive under an onrushing shark. "As he is coming at you upside down," she explained, "you have a chance to get away, if the distance to shore or safety is not too far." A chorus girl rushed into print with the exciting news that she had escaped a shark by frightening it off with an impromptu ballet of splashes and kicks. Human sharks profiteered from "special swimming courses" to teach bathers how to outwit sharks. Arguments broke out over whether the shark attacks weren't rather the doings of giant turtles!

After losses estimated at $1,000,000 in canceled reservations, the mayors of ten New Jersey resort towns met at Beach Haven, where the first shark attack had occurred, and pleaded for an end to the panic. They asked newspapers to refrain from publishing stories that "cause the public to believe the New Jersey seacoast is infested with sharks, whereas there are no more than in any other summer." The resort men thus went on record with the news that there *were* sharks in their water *every* summer!

The mayors' plea went unheard. Shark stories continued for a few more days to push news of the war and the infantile paralysis epidemic to secondary positions on newspaper front pages.

"Sharks are the undisputed masters of the Atlantic coast," one New York newspaper exclaimed. "The federal government yesterday abandoned its proposed campaign of extermination along the New Jersey beaches. The enemy was too numerous for the Coast Guard to tackle, it was said."

There was some truth in the story of the government's so-called surrender. The federal government had indeed declared war on sharks. A Coast Guard cutter had been dispatched to New Jersey to fight them. A congressman, predictably from New Jersey, had risen in Congress and asked for a $5,000 appropriation to launch a federal crusade against the shark.

And ultimately the strategy of the shark war was discussed at the highest possible level. At a time when presidential worries included Pancho Villa's raids, a national election campaign, and possible U.S. participation in the world war, the president's cabinet actually placed the subject of sharks on its agenda. After this cabinet meeting, Secretary of the Treasury McAdoo announced that the Coast Guard had been ordered to do what it could, which eventually turned out to be nothing. Secretary of Commerce William C. Redfield stated that his Bureau of Fisheries had not yet discovered why the sharks had appeared. Later, the Bureau of Fisheries officially warned bathers to stay in shallow water, because there was no known way to get rid of sharks.

But already, as unexpectedly and as unpredictably as they had appeared, the sharks had disappeared and become, once more, merely shadows in the sea.

Why?

Why was the New Jersey coast the fateful rendezvous for four deaths by shark bite? Why had five shark attacks occurred in twelve days in an area where none had occurred before?

Why? (And why is the New Jersey coast still one of the most shark-ridden coasts in the northern latitudes?)

After the panicmongers and the tale spinners had left the stage, taking with them their bizarre theories, the scientific experts stepped forward to explain the 1916 attacks. The experts looked a bit embarrassed.

In April 1916, three months before the attacks in New Jersey, Doctors Nichols, Murphy, and Lucas (the three shark experts) had collaborated on an article on sharks in Long Island waters. Their paper, published in the highly respected *Brooklyn Museum Quarterly,* all but dismissed the possibility of a shark attack on a "living man."

"Probably few swimmers have actually met in him their fate," Nichols and Murphy wrote, "but doubtless many a poor drowned sailor has there found his final resting place." And in a separate postscript, Lucas added his voice of authority:

"Cases of shark bite do now and then occur," Lucas conceded, "but there is a great difference between being attacked by a shark and being bitten by one, and the cases of shark bite are usually found to have been due to someone incautiously approaching a shark impounded or tangled in a net, or gasping on the shore. And, under such circumstances, almost any creature will bite."

Recalling the unclaimed $500 reward Herman Oelrichs had offered for proof of a shark attack north of Cape Hatteras, Lucas concluded: "That this reward was never claimed shows that there is practically no danger of any attack from a shark about our coasts."

In October 1916 Nichols and Murphy were back in print again. In a cautious understatement, they noted that "the New Jersey accidents of July 1916" had brought "the whole shark question before us in a new phase." After making the concession that four "living men" had indeed been killed by sharks, they wrote: "It must be admitted that deaths from shark bite within a short radius of New York City would seem to be one of those unaccountable happenings that take place from time to time to the confounding of savants and the justification of the wildest tradition."

After investigating the attacks and searching for clues to explain them, Lucas, Nichols, and Murphy confirmed that an unusual number of sharks had summered in New York/New Jersey waters. "The nearest I can come to accounting for the sudden preying of these fish," Lucas said, "is to say that this is a 'shark year.'" In line with this theory, Nichols and Murphy wrote:

"It is not impossible that this summer sharks really are with us in unprecedented force, and that we are experiencing an extraordinary shark migration, a movement comparable with the sporadic abundance during certain years of army worms, or jellyfishes, or even western grasshoppers, or northern lemmings—movements that all have their source in overproduction and other little understood natural agencies."

Further indication that 1916 was a "shark year" comes from the records of a remarkable shark-watcher, Edwin Thorne, a member of the board of Managers of the Zoological Society. Thorne's hobby was not only shark-watching but also shark catching. Between the years 1911 and 1927, Thorne spent a total of 302 days looking for sharks in Long Island's Great South Bay, then and now a popular bathing and boating area. Great South Bay was also popular with sharks, Thorne discovered: In those seventeen years, he sighted 1,799 sharks and killed 305 of them.

In 1916 he saw 277 sharks and killed 102. *In no other year did he see or kill as many.*

Nearly all the sharks Thorne killed were female brown sharks (*Eulamia milberti,* formerly *Carcharinus milberti*), which had entered Great South Bay to spawn their litters of six to thirteen young. (Like many species of shark, the brown shark brings forth its young alive.) Great South Bay was—and is—a "shark nursery," a sheltered spot where newborn sharks can begin their lives in relative tranquillity. This is one of many such nurseries that have been found all over the world and that are used by various species of sharks.

No brown shark has ever been convicted of attacking a bather. An increase in the number of brown sharks in New York waters would have had no direct connection with the New Jersey attacks. The indication, however, that more brown sharks than usual were around in 1916 did raise the question of whether a population explosion in indigenous sharks somehow had brought about the appearance of a dangerous stranger, such as a great white shark.

Besides the "shark-year" theory, there was some speculation that hunger had driven sharks closer to shore. Because of unexplained shortages of normal food at sea, the sharks were said to be prowling the coasts, seeking new prey; and five times—or so the theory went—that had been a human being. This theory, of course, did not square with the assumption that a single shark had been responsible for all five attacks. But even though human remains had been found in the great white shark caught on July 14, this was not irrefutable proof that the great white had been the only one of its kind—or the only large and potentially dangerous shark—in New Jersey waters during that particular summer.

On a hot August afternoon in 1960, 44 summers after the New Jersey shark attacks of 1916, John Brodeur, a 24-year-old accountant, and Jean Filoramo, his 22-year-old fiancée, walked hand in hand into the surf off a beach at

Sea Girt, New Jersey, barely two miles from Spring Lake, where Charles Bruder had been killed by a shark so long before.

In waist-deep water, John and Jean waited for a breaker that would carry them to shore. A glistening, frothing breaker bore down on them. Brodeur let it pass; he wanted a bigger one. As the breaker rolled past him, he thought he saw something black within it. He wondered idly for a moment what that something was.

Then, something—*that black something*—struck him from behind and seized his right leg. Brodeur kicked his left leg at the thing that was clamping an ever-tightening grip about his other leg. His left leg struck something hard and coarse. He twisted and hit a black body with his left hand. So rough was the surface of what he hit that it badly cut two of his fingers. The sea around him was red and he saw, floating to the surface, bits of red flesh torn from his leg.

Submerged by the next breaker, Brodeur lost consciousness. Miss Filoramo pulled him to the surface and screamed for help. Three men dashed into the surf and helped her carry him to the beach. Norman Porter, a former Marine major, ran to where Brodeur was being placed on the beach, grabbed a leather belt from a lifeguard, and wrapped it around Brodeur's thigh as a tourniquet.

The calf of his leg was hanging by a few shreds of flesh and muscle. One leg bone was crushed; the other was deeply gouged. By the time he reached a hospital, only a few minutes after he was carried to shore, he had lost an estimated eight pints of blood. Eight days after he entered the hospital, Brodeur's mangled right leg was amputated at the knee. But he was lucky. He had survived a shark attack.

The sharks were off the New Jersey coast in the summer of 1962, just as they were every year. But when, one pleasant Sunday in August, a bather stumbled, bleeding, out of the water at the beach in Manasquan, the resort-minded police stubbornly insisted that "a big fish," not a s—k, had done the job.

The bather, Michael Roman, age 24, was taken to Point Pleasant Hospital. The physician who stitched up Roman's left hand and left thigh said that an outline of teeth, forming an incomplete oval of 7½ by 9½ inches, was clearly visible on Roman's leg. Still, the official report persisted: "a big fish."

On Monday, Kendall H. Lee, city manager of Asbury Park, a popular resort a few miles north of Manasquan, sent telegrams to newspapers in the area: PLEASE BE ADVISED OUR BATHING BEACHES ARE AND HAVE BEEN IN FULL OPERATION AND HAVE NOT BEEN SHUT DOWN AT ANY TIME . . . ASBURY PARK IS PROUD OF ITS LONG AND OUTSTANDING SAFETY RECORD.

Finally, on Tuesday, State Conservation Commissioner H. Mat Adams courageously faced the fact emblazoned on Michael Roman's left thigh. What had attacked Michael Roman, the commissioner solemnly announced, was a shark. It was a very special kind of shark, however, because, Adams pointed out, it had not engaged in a "vicious attack." He said that the shark had not closed its jaws. Rather, Roman had unknowingly put his arm into the shark's mouth up to his elbow. It almost seemed as if Roman was being blamed for attacking the shark!

What happened to John Brodeur that day in 1960; what happened to Charles Van Sant, to Charles Bruder, to Lester Stilwell, to Stanley Fisher, to Joseph Dunn; what happened down the years to so many—and yet, proportionately, to so few—bathers could happen on any warm day in any year at any beach on the East Coast, West Coast, or Gulf Coast of the continental United States. It could happen, too, on any day or night in any warm or temperate sea on earth, for the shark lives in them all. And there are many rivers and at least one freshwater lake where it could happen!

Rarely does it happen. The chances of being attacked by a shark, it is often said, are about as great as being struck by lightning. Australia is regarded as one of the most shark-infested countries in the world. At one Australian beach, even after three attacks took place, it was calculated that for each bather attacked by a shark, about 30 million bathers had suffered no more than sunburn. Of the swimmers who have enjoyed Florida waters in modern times, only about one in every 5 million has been attacked in any way by a shark.

But statistics cannot still the fear evoked by the sight of a dark dorsal fin or just an ominous shadow beneath the surface—or the panic loosed on beaches when an attack does occur.

Brodeur was attacked on August 21, 1960, and a mild panic began. Police of several New Jersey shore towns ordered the beaches closed. Lifeguards at New York City's teeming beaches were ordered to use "extreme alertness and caution" in watching not only for sharks but also for panic caused by baseless shark reports. (A New York Park Department spokesman explained that in past shark scares children had been trampled during the stampede out of the water.)

On August 24, a man in 4½ feet of water 75 yards offshore in Bridgeport, Connecticut, was nipped on the left arm by a shark. The panic increased. Sharks were being reported—and, occasionally, caught—off beaches from Boston to Florida. Beach after beach was closed. In New York City, policemen armed with submachine guns manned six police launches, which, along with two helicopters, were assigned to special shark-patrol duty.

On August 30, still in 1960, a man swimming two miles from shore at Ocean City, New Jersey—about forty miles south of the scene of the Brodeur attack—was savaged by two or more sharks. His right leg was severely torn and his body slashed, but he managed to swim ashore. Eventually, he recovered without losing his leg.

The panic was really on now: Some 25,000 bathers were ordered out of the water after a shark was reported off New York City's Orchard Beach. (There were no reports of children being trampled.) Coney Island bathers scrambled ashore when policemen, firing rifles and submachine guns for the benefit of cameramen, inadvertently triggered a shark scare.

It was like 1916, with modern touches. Besides the submachine guns and the helicopters, a Navy blimp was put on shark-spotting duty, and Coast Guard cutters scoured the sea, directed to reported shark packs by radio.

The anxieties of bathers presumably were put to rest by the knowledge that nearly every modern weapon was being used against the shark. But few realized what a senseless war it was. The seas abound in sharks. They menace popular bathing, boating, and water-sports areas all over the world—from the beaches of Australia, South Africa, and California to the sun worshipers' meccas of Florida and the shores of Long Island. And with the ever-growing number of people diving, swimming, sailing, and kayaking in the oceans, the number of shark attacks has sharply increased in recent years.

Information on the density of shark populations is haphazard. Usually, no one counts sharks until a shark attacks a human being. Then there is a flurry of activity and a new set of statistics that will remain until the next shark attack leads to the next reaction.

Undoubtedly inspired by the Brodeur attack of 1960, a shark census was conducted between August 13 and October 13, 1961, off the New Jersey and the Long Island coasts by agents of the U.S. Fish and Wildlife Service. The census was described as a very limited study of predators of game fishes. The agents caught a total of 310 sharks. According to Dr. Lionel A. Walford, director of Sandy Hook Marine Laboratory at Highlands, New Jersey, the census study included six great white sharks (*Carcharodon carcharias*), ranging in weight from 151 to 285 pounds.*

---

*Other species caught in the Fish and Wildlife survey: 124 Sandbars (*Eulamia milberti*), weighing 8 to 348 pounds; 77 Duskys (*Carcharhinus obscurus*), 12 to 590 pounds; 52 Smooth Dogfish (*Mustelus canis*), 1½ to 18 pounds; 29 Tigers (*Galeocerdo cuvieri*), 29 to 1,100 pounds; 9 Hammerheads (*Sphyrna zygaena* and *Sphyrna diplana*), 24 to 225 pounds; 6 Makos (*Isurus oxyrinchus*), 220 to 320 pounds; 1 Sand (*Carcharias taurus*), 250 pounds, and a 650-pound Thresher (*Alopias vulpinus*). Six sharks were lost before they could be positively identified.

Florida, with its 1,277 miles of coastline, has at least forty species of sharks within its waters. Bathers have been scraped, maimed, or killed by small sharks, big sharks, and such bizarre shark relatives as the sawfish, whose long snout is studded with thick and massive teeth, and the stingray, whose tail is a whip that bears one or more venomous spines. It is impossible to classify precisely some sharks as harmless and some sharks as dangerous.

But there is one shark that ranks above all others as a killer, and that is the great white shark. Even after the attacks in 1916, when the great white was captured off New Jersey, U.S. Commissioner of Fisheries Hugh M. Smith said, "It must be regarded as comparatively inoffensive in our waters." The great white was then thought to be a tropical shark. We know today, though, that it often cruises as far north as Nova Scotia. The great white is also described as a pelagic (oceanic) shark, but it makes excursions into bathing areas. And monstrous specimens have been taken not far from such areas. A 3,000-pound, sixteen-foot great white, for instance, was harpooned a few miles off Amagansett Beach on Long Island in 1960. In August 1986 Donnie Braddick, fishing off Montauk, Long Island, with Frank Mundus, the famed shark fisherman, caught what was described as "the largest fish ever taken on rod and reel"—a great white seventeen feet long weighing 3,427 pounds. (Because a whale carcass was used to attract the shark, the catch was disqualified as a record fish by the International Game Fish Association.)

In 1950, the California Bureau of Marine Fisheries published a guide to sharks found in that state's waters. The guide said that the great white was "uncommon at best in our waters, and, since it rarely comes inshore, it is a negligible hazard to California swimmers." Five years later a shark appeared near two skin divers swimming not far from shore off La Jolla, California. The divers were not attacked, and the incident probably would not have been investigated except for a quirk of geography. The shark had chosen to appear right off the pier at the Scripps Institution of Oceanography—and an ichthyology student was there to identify it as a great white shark. The next day, a Scripps specialist in sharks, Arthur O. Flechsig, was at the pier. He baited a hook and caught the shark. It got away before Flechsig and his two companions could land it. But it had attacked their boat not far from the pier and left behind proof of identification as reliable as a fingerprint: two teeth embedded in the gouged bottom of the skiff. One of the most positive means of identifying a shark is by its teeth. There was no doubt that the teeth in Flechsig's boat belonged to a great white.

Within two weeks, nine great whites had been caught in the area.

Shark attacks had been rare in California coastal waters up to 1955, when the great whites suddenly appeared. Besides two cases of swimmers being brushed by sharks, there were on record only three known attacks, one of which in Monterey Bay, on December 7, 1952, was fatal. But in 1955, California's shark-attack pattern changed drastically: two reports of minor injuries from encounters with sharks off Venice Beach . . . a grapple between a surfboarder and a shark off Santa Monica . . . a vicious attack upon a scuba diver by a 3-foot shark . . . the astonishing escape of a spear fisherman who had been seized by a shark but suffered only a scratched foot. The spear fisherman had been diving in Monterey Bay. He wore a black rubber diving suit and rubber swim fins. The shark grabbed him by the ankles, ripped both "ankles" off the diver's rubber suit, tore off his right swim fin and a heavy wool sock, and bit through his left swim fin. The fisherman identified the shark as a great white.

There was one report of a nonfatal attack in California in 1956. Then in 1957 one eerie encounter with a shark was reported. Peter Savino and Daniel Hogan were swimming beyond the breakers of Morro Bay, near San Luis Obispo. Savino became tired and Hogan began towing him toward shore. A shark appeared, nudged Savino, and slashed his arm, apparently by rubbing him with its sandpaper hide. "I have blood on my arms! We'd better get out of here!" Savino yelled to Hogan. They began swimming separately. Hogan turned a moment later to see whether Savino was all right. Savino had disappeared, without an outcry, and was never seen again.

In 1959, California again experienced a Year of the Shark. On May 7, a swimmer was killed by a shark practically within the shadow of Golden Gate Bridge. And on June 14 there almost certainly was another great white shark off La Jolla, but this time the shark was not caught. Instead, it caught a man.

Robert Pamperin, a husky thirty-three-year-old aircraft engineer, was diving for abalone about fifty yards off La Jolla with another skin diver, Tom Lehrer. Suddenly, Pamperin rose high out of the water. His skin-diver faceplate had been torn off. He screamed once.

"I was swimming about fifteen feet from Bob," Lehrer said later. "I heard him calling, 'Help me! Help me!'

"I swam over to him. He was thrashing in the water, and I could tell he was fighting something underneath. . . ."

In the next instant, Pamperin went under. Lehrer peered underwater through his faceplate. The water, though bloodied, was remarkably clear, and he saw his friend's body in the jaws of a shark.

"It had a white belly and I could see its jaws and jagged teeth," Lehrer said. "I wasn't able to do anything more. So I swam to shore to warn the other swimmers."

Before 1959 ended, there were three more attacks in California—a spear fisherman whose left leg was slashed by a hammerhead shark 300 yards from where Pamperin had been devoured; a swimmer whose left arm was raked from wrist to elbow by a shark off Malibu; and a skin diver who lived to tell how (what he presumed to be) a great white shark bit down on one of his rubber fins, "shook me like a dog shakes a bone," and then released him, unharmed.

Public officials in California talked of somehow finding a way to stop the sharks. Swimmers and skin divers sought an explanation for the attacks and the presence of great whites in California waters. Oceanographers said that there had been a rise in water temperatures off the coast of California in recent years. But no one really knew why the sharks had come, why the bathers had been attacked—or knew how many had been attacked: When a man goes for a long ocean swim and never returns, or when men go out fishing in a small boat and only the boat is found—what was their fate? Captain Charles Hardy, chief of San Diego lifeguards, remarked after Pamperin's death that three people had disappeared in the area during the previous three months, and that their bodies had never been found. Were they, too, victims of sharks?

Eight days after Pamperin was killed, a 12½-foot shark was caught off Catalina Island, about sixty miles north of La Jolla. In its belly was found a man's watch, too badly deteriorated to be identified. It could not have been Pamperin's, for he wore no jewelry when he went on his last abalone hunt. But whose watch was it? Had a man lost it at sea and, as it fell to the bottom, had its gleam lured a curious shark? Or had a man been wearing it?

Questions about sharks arose again in the 1990s along the California coast, the East Coast, and in Hawaii. Why, suddenly, were the sharks back again? Why were surfers the victims?

Between 1926 and 1993 there were sixty-nine attacks by great white sharks along the northern California coast, seven of them fatal. But it was in 1989 that the latest wave began: four in 1989, five in 1990, three in 1991, two in 1992, three in 1993.

Surfer publications called 1992 the Year of the Shark. But the first of the attacks came in July 1991, when thirty-two-year-old surfer Eric Larsen was enjoying the waves about fifteen miles north of Monterey Bay, California. Then, out of the sea came a great white shark. It clamped its jaws around

Larsen's left leg and pulled him down. Larsen tried to pry the jaws from around his leg. The shark let go of his leg and bit down on his arms. Larsen managed to extract one arm, ripping it to the bone as he dragged it through the shark's razor-sharp teeth. He pounded his bloody fist on the shark, and as suddenly as it appeared the great white vanished.

Larsen miraculously managed to paddle to shore. Just as miraculously, he survived after losing half the blood in his body. It took 400 stitches to sew up his wounds.

Eighteen-year-old Aaron Romento was not so lucky. He was body-board surfing on the leeward coast of Oahu, in water four feet deep when a tiger shark bit him on the thigh. Romento bled to death on the shore.

Between 1982 and 1987 there had been twenty shark attacks in California and Hawaii. Between 1987 and 1993 there were thirty-three—and the overwhelming number of victims were surfers.

Along the East Coast, attacks also increased. In November 1990, a surfer in three feet of water off Boca Raton, Florida, fell off his board. He felt pain and instinctively swung at what had stabbed him. He pulled away a hand covered with blood. He had been bitten on the shoulder; his hand had grazed the shark's teeth. The surfer stumbled to shore and survived. He was one of the statistics that Florida shark scientists began collecting: twenty-two attacks in 1994; twenty-eight between January and October 1995. The suspected attackers were not great whites but three- or four-foot black-tip sharks.

In September 1994 a woman swimming in chest-deep water near Hilton Head Island, South Carolina, was bitten by a shark, which left an eighteen-inch wound that ran diagonally from thigh to chest. She survived. It was the first attack since 1988, when a man was bitten on the arm by a shark about three miles from where the woman was attacked. There were seven other attacks in North and South Carolina and one in Georgia. None of them was fatal.

Surfer Magazine in March 1993 reported a sharp increase in shark attacks on surfers off favored beaches in California, Florida, Australia, and Oregon (where there were ten nonfatal attacks on surfers between 1976 and 1991). The fundamental reason for the increase is simply the increase in surfers. In the early 1950s, when surfing was beginning to become popular around Santa Cruz, California's "Surf City," there were perhaps 1,500 surfers. Today, along the entire West Cost, there are an estimated 500,000. Also, the surfers' habits happen to coincide with the sharks' habits: Both favor dusk and dawn, the surfers for surfing, the sharks for eating. And surfers often hunt for the perfect wave in areas where sharks hunt for food. To a shark, a surfer in a shiny black wet suit may look like an elephant seal or sea lion—the favored prey of great white sharks.

Surfers also may look like a school of mullet, George Burgess, of the Florida Museum of Natural History, told *Surfer Magazine*. "Here in Florida," he said, "the soles of the feet and palms of the hands tend to be much lighter than the rest of the surfer's tanned skin. Black-tip sharks, who are very good at distinguishing contrast, naturally perceive the flashing white as fish bellies."

The Marine Mammal Protection Act, passed in 1972, saved the pinnipeds and at the same time probably imperiled more surfers and divers. This theory holds that a substantial increase in sea lions attracted pelagic great whites to hunting areas closer to shore, where the humans were.

In Hawaii, the surfers' story in 1992 was much the same. In February 1992, surfer Bryan Adona disappeared after heading out on his board at Leftovers, a surfers' spot near Waimea Bay, on the north shore of Oahu. His board was found the next day, bearing what appeared to be the teeth marks of a tiger shark. A few months before, Martha Morell, swimming near her home on Maui, was attacked and killed by a twelve-foot tiger shark about a hundred yards off-shore.

On October 22, surfer Rick Gruzinsky, in the waves off the north shore of Oahu, felt a jolt under his surfboard. Out of the sea came a shark, which twisted its head and clamped down on the surfboard, biting with a typical twisting motion. While Gruzinsky held onto one end of the board, the shark bit off the other. Gruzinsky, untouched, lived to tell the tale. Two weeks later, off the island's west shore, a shark bit a surfer in the leg. He bled to death. In December another shark off the north shore bit a chunk out of a surfer's board. There had also been a fatal shark attack in 1992 in the waters of Maui.

People wondered in the 1990s in Hawaii, as they had wondered in New Jersey in 1916, whether sharks had developed a taste for human food. "If tigers considered people a food source," a shark expert said, "they'd be attracted to areas of human use, like Waikiki." Attacks are very rare, he noted, adding that "the shark usually takes a single bite. It almost seems as though the shark realizes it has made a mistake."

A Year of the Shark came to Australia when the southern summer began in November 1961. Fishermen and bathers started reporting the sighting of more offshore sharks than had been seen in recent memory. This time, there was no mystery about what had lured the shark packs. Heavy rains and floods had swept countless fish down the river and into the sea along much of Australia's coast.

At many beach resorts, shark patrols were doubled, and swimmers were continually warned against swimming alone or venturing out too far. Along the coast of Victoria and New South Wales, at least fifteen gray nurse and white pointer sharks were killed.

But in mid-December, a 22-year-old man was attacked off the Queensland coast. His left leg was mauled, and he died within a week. Then, on December 29, an eighteen-year-old woman and her 24-year-old boyfriend went swimming at Mackay, Queensland. They were standing in about $2\frac{1}{2}$ feet of water about twelve feet from shore when a shark knocked down the girl. In three savage attacks, the shark ripped off one of the girl's arms and part of the other and slashed her right thigh. Her companion desperately beat the shark with his fists. His right hand suddenly gushed blood. By this time, a third bather came to their aid, and the shark disappeared. Forty-eight hours later, the girl died.

Other horrors came year after year. As in California and Oregon, the sharks were back in Australia in the 1980s and 1990s. In 1985 a woman was bitten in two by a great white while she was snorkeling in water about seven feet deep. The shark ate half of her in the first pass and then made a second pass and took the rest of the woman.

In June 1993 John Ford, a thirty-one-year-old scuba diver on his honeymoon, was diving near Byron Bay, 400 miles north of Sydney, Australia, with his twenty-nine-year-old bride, Deborah, when a shark attacked them, swimming off with Ford in its jaws. A short time later fishermen caught a sixteen-foot great white shark, which rammed their boat, spat out human remains, and swam away.

Snorkeler, scuba diver, surfer. What was happening? Was there basis for the theory that an attack on a human being is merely a matter of mistaken identity?

John McCosker, of the Steinhart Museum in San Francisco, tested the surfer-as-seal theory off Dangerous Reef in Australia in 1985. A mannequin was placed on a surfboard and put in water where animal blood had been dumped. Lured by the blood, a great white shark saw the surfboard and attacked—although there was neither blood nor meat on the board or the wetsuited dummy. Sixty feet below, a dummy in a scuba suit was not attacked until McCosker attached a fish to it—divers sometimes tie a speared fish to a line about the waist. That did attract a shark.

"I think you're much better off underwater than at the surface," McCosker told an interviewer. "In fact, I'm convinced you're better off, and I think the experiment proves it."

Part Three:
Simba!
The African Lion
What Waits Downwind!

10   The Man-Eaters of Tsavo

BY LT. COL. J. H. PATTERSON, D. S. O.

Editor's Note: When assigned to help supervise the building of a Uganda Railroad bridge over the Tsavo River in east Africa in March, 1898, Lt. Col. J. H. Patterson, D. S. O., had little idea of the magnitude of the adventure upon which he was embarking. The site of the bridge, which is today a part of Kenya, became the scene of savage attacks by man-eating lions preying on the workers. Col. Patterson's stirring book, "The Man-Eaters of Tsavo," remains in print to this day. The drama was also captured quite well in the film, "The Ghost and the Darkness," starring Val Kilmer and Michael Douglas.

The First Appearance of the Man-Eaters

Unfortunately this happy state of affairs did not continue for long, and our work was soon interrupted in a rude and startling manner. Two most voracious and insatiable man-eating lions appeared upon the scene, and for over nine months waged an intermittent warfare against the railway and all those connected with it in the vicinity of Tsavo. This culminated in a perfect reign of terror in December, 1898, when they actually succeeded in bringing the railway works to a complete standstill for about three weeks. At first they were not always successful in their efforts to carry off a victim, but as time went on they stopped at nothing and indeed braved any danger in order to obtain their favourite food. Their methods then became so uncanny, and their man-stalking so well-timed and so certain of success, that the workmen firmly believed that they were not real animals at all, but devils in lions' shape. Many a time the coolies solemnly assured me that it was absolutely useless to attempt to shoot them. They were quite convinced that the angry spirits of two departed native chiefs had taken this form in order to protect against a railway being made through their country, and by stopping its progress to avenge the insult thus shown to them.

I had only been a few days at Tsavo when I first heard that these brutes had been seen in the neighbourhood. Shortly afterwards one or two coolies mysteriously disappeared, and I was told that they had been carried off by night from their tents and devoured by lions. At the time I did not credit this story, and was more inclined to believe that the unfortunate men had been the victims of foul play at the hands of some of their comrades. They were, as it happened, very good workmen, and had each saved a fair number of rupees, so I thought it quite likely that some scoundrels from the gangs had murdered them for the sake of their money. This suspicion, however, was very soon dispelled. About three weeks after my arrival, I was roused one morning about daybreak and told that one of my *jemadars,* a fine powerful Sikh named Ungan Singh, had been seized in his tent during the night, and dragged off and eaten.

Naturally I lost no time in making an examination of the place, and was soon convinced that the man had indeed been carried off by a lion, and its "pug" marks were plainly visible in the sand, while the furrows made by the heels of the victim showed the direction in which he had been dragged away. Moreover, the *jemadar* shared his tent with half a dozen other workmen, and one of his bedfellows had actually witnessed the occurrence. He graphically described how, at about midnight, the lion suddenly put its head in at the open tent door and seized Ungan Singh—who happened to be nearest the opening—by the throat. The unfortunate fellow cried out *"Choro"* ("Let go"), and threw his arms up round the lion's neck. The next moment he was gone, and his panic-stricken companions lay helpless, forced to listen to the terrible struggle which took place outside. Poor Ungan Singh must have died hard; but what chance had he? As a coolie gravely remarked, "Was he not fighting with a lion?"

On hearing this dreadful story I at once set out to try to track the animal, and was accompanied by Captain Haslem, who happened to be staying at Tsavo at the time, and who, poor fellow, himself met with a tragic fate very shortly afterwards. We found it an easy matter to follow the route taken by the lion, as he appeared to have stopped several times before beginning his meal. Pools of blood marked these halting-places, where he doubtless indulged in the man-eaters' habit of licking the skin off so as to get at the fresh blood. (I have been led to believe that this is their custom from the appearance of two half-eaten bodies which I subsequently rescued: the skin was gone in places, and the flesh looked dry, as if it had been sucked.) On reaching the spot where the body had been devoured, a dreadful spectacle presented itself. The ground all round was covered with blood and morsels of flesh and bones, but the unfortunate *jemadar's* head had been left intact, save for the holes made by the lion's tusks on seizing him, and lay a short distance away from the other remains, the eyes staring wide open with a startled, horrified look in them. The place was considerably cut up, and on closer examination we found that two lions had been there and had probably struggled for possession of the body. It was the most gruesome sight I had ever seen. We collected the remains as well as we could and heaped stones on them, the head with its fixed, terrified stare seeming to watch us all the time, for it we did not bury, but took back to camp for identification before the Medical Officer.

Thus occurred my first experience of man-eating lions, and I vowed there and then that I would spare no pains to rid the neighbourhood of the brutes. I little knew the trouble that was in store for me, or how narrow were to be my own escapes from sharing poor Ungan Singh's fate.

That same night I sat up in a tree close to the late *jemadar's* tent, hoping that the lions would return to it for another victim. I was followed to my perch by a few of the more terrified coolies, who begged to be allowed to sit up in the tree with me; all the other workmen remained in their tents, but no more doors were left open. I had with me my .303 and 12-bore shot gun, one barrel loaded with ball and the other with slug. Shortly after settling down to my vigil, my hopes of bagging one of the brutes were raised by the sound of their ominous roaring coming closer and closer. Presently this ceased, and quiet reigned for an hour or two, as lions always stalk their prey in complete silence. All at once, however, we heard a great uproar and frenzied cries coming from another camp about half a mile away; we knew then that the lions had seized a victim there, and that we should see or hear nothing further of them that night.

Next morning I found that one of the brutes had broken into a tent at Railhead Camp—whence we had heard the commotion during the night—and had made off with a poor wretch who was lying there asleep. After a night's rest, therefore, I took up my position in a suitable tree near this tent. I did not at all like the idea of walking the half-mile to the place after dark, but all the same I felt fairly safe, as one of my men carried a bright lamp close behind me. He in his turn was followed by another leading a goat, which I tied under my tree in the hope that the lion might be tempted to seize it instead of a coolie. A steady drizzle commenced shortly after I had settled down to my night of watching, and I was soon thoroughly chilled and wet. I stuck to my uncomfortable post, however, hoping to get a shot, but I well remember the feeling of impotent disappointment I experienced when about midnight I heard screams and cries and a heartrending shriek, which told me that the man-eaters had again eluded me and had claimed another victim elsewhere.

At this time the various camps for the workmen were very scattered, so that the lions had a range of some eight miles on either side of Tsavo to work upon; and as their tactics seemed to be to break into a different camp each night, it was most difficult to forestall them. They almost appeared, too, to have an extraordinary and uncanny faculty of finding out our plans beforehand, so that no matter in how likely or how tempting a spot we lay in wait for them, they invariably avoided that particular place and seized their victim for the night from some other camp. Hunting them by day moreover, in such a dense wilderness as surrounded us, was an exceedingly tiring and really foolhardy undertaking. In a thick jungle of the kind round Tsavo the hunted animal has every chance against the hunter, as however careful the latter may be, a dead twig or something of the sort is sure to crackle just at the critical moment and so give the alarm. Still I never gave up hope of some day finding their lair, and accordingly continued to devote all my spare time to crawling about through the undergrowth. Many a time when attempting to force my way through this bewildering tangle I had to be released by my gun-bearer from the fast clutches of the "wait-a-bit"; and often with immense pains I succeeded in tracing the lions to the river after they had seized a victim, only to lose the trail from there onwards, owing to the rocky nature of the ground which they seemed to be careful to choose in retreating to their den.

At this early stage of the struggle, I am glad to say, the lions were not always successful in their efforts to capture a human being for their nightly meal, and one or two amusing incidents occurred to relieve the tension from which our nerves were beginning to suffer. On one occasion an enterprising *bunniah* (Indian trader) was riding along on his donkey late one night, when suddenly a lion sprang out on him knocking over both man and beast. The donkey was badly wounded, and the lion was just about to seize the trader, when in some way or other his claws became entangled in a rope by which two empty oil tins were strung across the donkey's neck. The rattle and clatter made by these as he dragged them after him gave him such a fright that he turned tail and bolted off into the jungle, to the intense relief of the terrified *bunniah,* who quickly made his way up the nearest tree and remained there, shivering with fear, for the rest of the night.

Shortly after this episode, a Greek contractor named Themistocles Pappadimitrini had an equally marvellous escape. He was sleeping peacefully in his tent one night, when a lion broke in, and seized and made off with the mattress on which he was lying. Though rudely awakened, the Greek was quite unhurt and suffered from nothing worse than a bad fright. This same man, however, met with a melancholy fate not long afterwards. He had been to the Kilima N'jaro district to buy cattle, and on the return journey attempted to take a short cut across country to the railway, but perished miserably of thirst on the way.

On another occasion fourteen coolies who slept together in a large tent were one night awakened by a lion suddenly jumping on to the tent and breaking through it. The brute landed with one claw on a coolie's shoulder, which was badly torn; but instead of seizing the man himself, in his hurry he grabbed a large bag of rice which happened to be lying in the tent, and made off with it, dropping it in disgust some little distance away when he realised his mistake.

These, however, were only the earlier efforts of the man-eaters. Later on, as will be seen, nothing flurried or frightened them in the least, and except as food they showed a complete contempt for human beings. Having once marked down a victim, they would allow nothing to deter them from securing him, whether he were protected by a thick fence, or inside a closed tent, or sitting round a brightly burning fire. Shots, shouting and firebrands they alike held in derision.

The Attack on the Goods-Wagon

All this time my own tent was pitched in an open clearing, unprotected by a fence of any kind round it. One night when the medical officer, Dr. Rose, was staying with me, we were awakened about midnight by hearing something tumbling about among the tent ropes, but on going out with a lantern we could discover nothing. Daylight, however, plainly revealed the "pug" marks of a lion, so that on that occasion I fancy one or other of us had a narrow escape. Warned by this experience, I at once arranged to move my quarters, and went to join forces with Dr. Brock, who had just arrived at Tsavo to take medical charge of the district. We shared a hut of palm leaves and boughs, which we had constructed on the eastern side of the river, close to the old caravan route leading to Uganda; and we had it surrounded by a circular *boma,* or thorn fence, about seventy yards in diameter, well made and thick and high. Our personal servants also lived within the enclosure, and a bright fire was always kept up throughout the night. For the sake of coolness, Brock and I used to sit out under the verandah of this hut in the evenings; but it was rather trying to our nerves to attempt to read or write there, as we never knew when a lion might spring over the *boma,* and be on us before we were aware. We therefore kept our rifles within easy reach, and cast many an anxious glance out into the inky darkness beyond the circle of the firelight. On one or two occasions, we found in the morning that the lions had come quite close to the fence; but fortunately they never succeeded in getting through.

By this time, too, the camps of the workmen had also been surrounded by thorn fences; nevertheless the lions managed to jump over or to break through some one or other of these, and regularly every few nights a man was carried off, the reports of the disappearance of this or that workman coming in to me with painful frequency. So long, however, as Railhead Camp—with its two or three thousand men, scattered over a wide area—remained at Tsavo, the coolies appeared not to take much notice of the dreadful deaths of their comrades. Each man felt, I suppose, that as the man-eaters had such a large number of victims to choose from, the chances of their selecting him in particular were very small. But when the large camp moved ahead with the railway, matters altered considerably. I was then left with only some few hundred men to complete the permanent works; and as all the remaining workmen were naturally camped together the attentions of the lions became more apparent and made a deeper impression. A regular panic consequently ensued, and it required all my powers of persuasion to induce the men to stay on. In fact, I succeeded in doing so only by allowing them to knock off all regular work until they had built exceptionally thick and high *bomas* round each camp. Within these enclosures fires were kept burning all night, and it was also the duty of the night-watchman to keep clattering half a dozen empty oil tins suspended from a convenient tree. These he manipulated by means of a long rope, while sitting in the hopes of terrifying away the man-eaters. In spite of all these precautions, however, the lions would not be denied, and men continued to disappear.

When the railhead workmen moved on, their hospital camp was left behind. It stood rather apart from the other camps, in a clearing about three-quarters of a mile from my hut, but was protected by a good thick fence and to all appearance was quite secure. It seemed, however, as if barriers were of no avail against the "demons", for before very long one of them found a weak spot in the *boma* and broke through. On this occasion the Hospital Assistant had a marvellous escape. Hearing a noise outside, he opened the door of his tent and was horrified to see a great lion standing a few yards away looking at him. The beast made a spring towards him, which gave the Assistant such a fright that he jumped backwards, and in doing so luckily upset a box containing medical stores. This crashed down with such a loud clatter of breaking glass that the lion was startled for the moment and made off to another part of the enclosure. Here, unfortunately, he was more successful, as he jumped on to and broke through a tent in which eight patients were lying. Two of them were badly wounded by his spring, while a third poor wretch was seized and dragged off bodily through the thorn fence. The two wounded coolies were left where they lay; a piece of torn tent having fallen over them; and in this position the doctor and I found them on our arrival soon after dawn next morning. We at once decided to move the hospital closer to the main camp; a fresh site was prepared, a stout hedge built round the enclosure, and all the patients were moved in before nightfall.

As I had heard that lions generally visit recently deserted camps, I decided to sit up all night in the vacated *boma* in the hope of getting an opportunity of bagging one of them; but in the middle of my lonely vigil I had the mortification of hearing shrieks and cries coming from the direction of the new hospital, telling me only too plainly that our dreaded foes had once more eluded me. Hurrying to the place at daylight I found that one of the lions had jumped over the newly erected fence and had carried off the hospital *bhisti* (water-carrier), and that several other coolies had been unwilling witnesses of the terrible scene which took place within the circle of light given by the big camp fire. The *bhisti,* it appears, had been lying on the floor, with his head towards the centre of the tent and his feet nearly touching the side. The lion managed to get its head in below the canvas, seized him by the foot and pulled him out. In desperation the unfortunate water-carrier clutched hold of a heavy box in a vain attempt to prevent himself being carried off, and dragged it with him until he was forced to let go by its being stopped by the side of the tent. He then caught hold of a tent rope, and clung tightly to it until it broke. As soon as the lion managed to get him clear of the tent, he sprang at his throat and after a few vicious shakes the poor *bhisti*'s agonising cries were silenced for ever. The brute then seized him in his mouth, like a huge cat with a mouse, and ran up and down the *boma* looking for a weak spot to break through. This he presently found and plunged into, dragging his victim with him and leaving shreds of torn cloth and flesh as ghastly evidences of his passage through the thorns. Dr. Brock and I were easily able to follow his track, and soon found the remains about four hundred yards away in the bush. There was the usual horrible sight. Very little was left of the unfortunate *bhisti*—only the skull, the jaws, a few of the larger bones and a portion of the palm with one or two fingers attached. On one of these was a silver ring, and this, with the teeth (a relic much prized by certain castes), was sent to the man's widow in India.

Again it was decided to move the hospital; and again, before nightfall, the work was completed, including a still stronger and thicker *boma*. When the patients had been moved, I had a covered goods-wagon placed in a favourable position on a siding which ran close to the site which had just been abandoned, and in this Brock and I arranged to sit up that night. We left a couple of tents still standing within the enclosure, and also tied up a few cattle in it as bait for the lions, who had been seen in no less than three different places in the neighbourhood during the afternoon (April 23). Four miles from Tsavo they had attempted to seize a coolie who was walking along the line. Fortunately, however, he had just time to escape up a tree, where he remained, more dead than alive, until he was rescued by the Traffic Manager, who caught sight of him from a passing train. They next appeared close to Tsavo Station, and a couple of hours later some workmen saw one of the lions stalking Dr. Brock as he was returning about dusk from the hospital.

In accordance with our plan, the doctor and I set out after dinner for the goods-wagon, which was about a mile away from our hut. In the light of subsequent events, we did a very foolish thing in taking up our position so late; nevertheless, we reached our destination in safety, and settled down to our watch about ten o'clock. We had the lower half of the door of the wagon closed, while the upper half was left wide open for observation: and we faced, of course, in the direction of the abandoned *boma,* which, however, we were unable to see in the inky darkness. For an hour or two everything was quiet, and the deadly silence was becoming very monotonous and oppressive, when suddenly, to our right, a dry twig snapped, and we knew that an animal of some sort was about. Soon afterwards we heard a dull thud, as if some heavy body had jumped over the *boma.* The cattle, too, became very uneasy, and we could hear them moving about restlessly. Then again came dead silence. At this juncture I proposed to my companion that I should get out of the wagon and lie on the ground close to it, as I could see better in that position should the lion come in our direction with his prey. Brock, however, persuaded me to remain where I was; and a few seconds afterwards I was heartily glad that I had taken his advice, for at that very moment one of the man-eaters—although we did not know it—was quietly stalking us, and was even then almost within springing distance. Orders had been given for the entrance to the *boma* to be blocked up, and accordingly we were listening in the expectation of hearing the lion force his way out through the bushes with his prey. As a matter of fact, however, the doorway had not been properly closed, and while we were wondering what the lion could be doing inside the *boma* for so long, he was outside all the time, silently reconnoitring our position.

Presently I fancied I saw something coming very stealthily towards us. I feared however, to trust to my eyes, which by that time were strained by prolonged staring through the darkness, so under my breath I asked Brock whether he saw anything, at the same time covering the dark object as well as I could with my rifle. Brock did not answer; he told me afterwards that he, too, thought he had seen something move, but was afraid to say so lest I should fire and it turn out to be nothing after all. After this there was intense silence again for a second or two, then with a sudden bound a huge body sprang at us. "The lion!" I shouted, and we both fired almost simultaneously—not a moment too soon, for in another second the brute would assuredly have landed inside the wagon. As it was, he must have swerved off in his spring, probably blinded by the flash and frightened by the noise of the double report which was increased a hundredfold by the reverberation of the hollow iron roof of the truck. Had we not been very much on the alert, he would undoubtedly have got one of us, and we realised that we had had a very lucky and very narrow escape. The next morning we found Brock's bullet embedded in the sand close to a foot-print; it could not have missed the lion by more than an inch or two. Mine was nowhere to be found.

Thus ended my first direct encounter with one of the man-eaters.

The Reign of Terror

The lions seemed to have got a bad fright the night Brock and I sat up in wait for them in the goods-wagon, for they kept away from Tsavo and did not mo-lest us in any way for some considerable time—not, in fact, until long after Brock had left me and gone on *safari* (a caravan journey) to Uganda. In this breathing space which they vouchsafed us, it occurred to me that should they renew their attacks, a trap would perhaps offer the best chance of getting at them, and that if I could construct one in which a couple of coolies might be used as bait without being subjected to any danger, the lions would be quite daring enough to enter it in search of them and thus be caught. I accordingly set to work at once, and in a short time managed to make a sufficiently strong trap out of wooden sleepers, tram-rails, pieces of telegraph wire, and a length of heavy chain. It was divided into two compartments—one for the men and one for the lion. A sliding door at one end admitted the former, and once in-side this compartment they were perfectly safe, as between them and the lion, if he entered the other, ran a cross wall of iron rails only three inches apart, and embedded both top and bottom in heavy wooden sleepers. The door which was to admit the lion was, of course, at the opposite end of the structure, but otherwise the whole thing was very much on the principle of the ordinary rat-trap, except that it was not necessary for the lion to seize the bait in order to send the door clattering down. This part of the contrivance was arranged in the following manner. A heavy chain was secured along the top part of the lion's doorway, the ends hanging down to the ground on either side of the opening; and to these were fastened, strongly secured by stout wire, short lengths of rails placed about six inches apart. This made a sort of flexible door which could be packed into a small space when not in use, and which abutted against the top of the doorway when lifted up. The door was held in this position by a lever made of a piece of rail, which in turn was kept in its place by a wire fastened to one end and passing down to a spring concealed in the ground inside the cage. As soon as the lion entered sufficiently far into the trap, he would be bound to tread on the spring; his weight on this would release the wire, and in an instant down would come the door behind him; and he could not push it out in any way, as it fell into a groove between two rails firmly embedded in the ground.

In making this trap, which cost us a lot of work, we were rather at a loss for want of tools to bore holes in the rails for the doorway, so as to enable them to be fastened by the wire to the chain. It occurred to me, however, that a hard-nosed bullet from my .303 would penetrate the iron, and on making the experiment I was glad to find that a hole was made as cleanly as if it had been punched out.

When the trap was ready I pitched a tent over it in order further to deceive the lions, and built an exceedingly strong *boma* round it. One small entrance was made at the back of the enclosure for the men, which they were to close on going in by pulling a bush after them; and another entrance just in front of the door of the cage was left open for the lions. The wiseacres to whom I showed my invention were generally of the opinion that the man-eaters would be too cunning to walk into my parlour; but, as will be seen later, their predictions proved false. For the first few nights I baited the trap myself, but nothing happened except that I had a very sleepless and uncomfortable time, and was badly bitten by mosquitoes.

As a matter of fact, it was some months before the lions attacked us again, though from time to time we heard of their depredations in other quarters. Not long after our night in the goods-wagon, two men were carried off from railhead, while another was taken from a place called Engomani, about ten miles away. Within a very short time, this latter place was again visited by the brutes, two more men being seized, one of whom was killed and eaten, and the other so badly mauled that he died within a few days. As I have said, however, we at Tsavo enjoyed complete immunity from attack, and the coolies, believing that their dreaded foes had permanently deserted the district, resumed all their usual habits and occupations, and life in the camps returned to its normal routine.

At last we were suddenly startled out of this feeling of security. One dark night the familiar terror-stricken cries and screams awoke the camps, and we knew that the "demons" had returned and had commenced a new list of victims. On this occasion a number of men had been sleeping outside their tents for the sake of coolness, thinking, of course, that the lions had gone for good, when suddenly in the middle of the night one of the brutes was discovered forcing its way through the *boma*. The alarm was at once given, and sticks, stones and firebrands were hurled in the direction of the intruder. All was of no avail, however, for the lion burst into the midst of the terrified group, seized an unfortunate wretch amid the cries and shrieks of his companions, and dragged him off through the thick thorn fence. He was joined outside by the second lion, and so daring had the two brutes become that they did not trouble to carry their victim any further away, but devoured him within thirty yards of the tent where he had been seized. Although several shots were fired in their direction by the *jemadar* of the gang to which the coolie belonged, they took no notice of these and did not attempt to move until their horrible meal was finished. The few scattered fragments that remained of the body I would not allow to be buried at once, hoping that the lions would return to the spot the following night; and on the chance of this I took up my station at nightfall in a convenient tree. Nothing occurred to break the monotony of my watch, however, except that I had a visit from a hyena, and the next morning I learned that the lions had attacked another camp about two miles from Tsavo—for by this time the camps were again scattered, as I had works in progress all up and down the line. There the man-eaters had been successful in obtaining a victim, whom, as in the previous instance, they devoured quite close to the camp. How they forced their way through the *boma*s without making a noise was, and still is, a mystery to me; I should have thought that it was next to impossible for an animal to get through at all. Yet they continually did so, and without a sound being heard.

After this occurrence, I sat up every night for over a week near likely camps, but all in vain. Either the lions saw me and then went elsewhere, or else I was unlucky, for they took man after man from different places without ever once giving me a chance of a shot at them. This constant night watching was most dreary and fatiguing work, but I felt that it was a duty that had to be undertaken, as the men naturally looked to me for protection. In the whole of my life I have never experienced anything more nerve-shaking than to hear the deep roars of these dreadful monsters growing gradually nearer and nearer, and to know that some one or other of us was doomed to be their victim before morning dawned. Once they reached the vicinity of the camps, the roars completely ceased, and we knew that they were stalking for their prey. Shouts would then pass from camp to camp, *"Khabar dar, bhaieon, shaitan ata"* ("Beware, brothers, the devil is coming"), but the warning cries would prove of no avail, and sooner or later agonising shrieks would break the silence and another man would be missing from roll-call next morning.

I was naturally very disheartened at being foiled in this way night after night, and was soon at my wits' end to know what to do; it seemed as if the lions were really "devils" after all and bore a charmed life. As I have said before, tracking them through the jungle was a hopeless task; but as something had to be done to keep up the men's spirits, I spent many a wry day crawling on my hands and knees through the dense undergrowth of the exasperating wilderness around us. As a matter of fact, if I had come up with the lions on any of these expeditions, it was much more likely that they would have added me to their list of victims than that I should have succeeded in killing either of them, as everything would have been in their favour. About this time, too, I had many helpers, and several officers—civil, naval and military—came to Tsavo from the coast and sat up night after night in order to get a shot at our daring foes. All of us, however, met with the same lack of success, and the lions always seemed capable of avoiding the watchers, while succeeding at the same time in obtaining a victim.

I have a very vivid recollection of one particular night when the brutes seized a man from the railway station and brought him close to my camp to devour. I could plainly hear them crunching the bones, and the sound of their dreadful purring filled the air and rang in my ears for days afterwards. The terrible thing was to feel so helpless; it was useless to attempt to go out, as of course the poor fellow was dead, and in addition it was so pitch dark as to make it impossible to see anything. Some half a dozen workmen, who lived in a small enclosure close to mine, became so terrified on hearing the lions at their meal that they shouted and implored me to allow them to come inside my *boma*. This I willingly did, but soon afterwards I remembered that one man had been lying ill in their camp, and on making enquiry I found that they had callously left him behind alone. I immediately took some men with me to bring him to my *boma,* but on entering his tent I saw by the light of the lantern that the poor fellow was beyond need of safety. He had died of shock at being deserted by his companions.

From this time matters gradually became worse and worse. Hitherto, as a rule, only one of the man-eaters had made the attack and had done the foraging, while the other waited outside in the bush; but now they began to change their tactics, entering the *boma*s together and each seizing a victim. In this way two Swahili porters were killed during the last week of November, one being immediately carried off and devoured. The other was heard moaning for a long time, and when his terrified companions at last summoned up sufficient courage to go to his assistance, they found him stuck fast in the bushes of the *boma* through which for once the lion had apparently been unable to drag him. He was still alive when I saw him next morning, but so terribly mauled that he died before he could be got to the hospital.

Within a few days of this the two brutes made a most ferocious attack on the largest camp in the section, which for safety's sake was situated within a stone's throw of Tsavo Station and close to a Permanent Way Inspector's iron hut. Suddenly in the dead of night the two man-eaters burst in among the terrified workmen, and even from my *boma,* some distance away, I could plainly hear the panic-stricken shrieking of the coolies. Then followed cries of "They've taken him; they've taken him," as the brutes carried off their unfortunate victim and began their horrible feast close beside the camp. The Inspector, Mr. Dalgairns, fired over fifty shots in the direction in which he heard the lions, but they were not to be frightened and calmly lay there until their meal was finished. After examining the spot in the morning, we at once set out to follow the brutes, Mr. Dalgairns feeling confident that he had wounded one of them, as there was a trail on the sand like that of the toes of a broken limb. After some careful stalking, we suddenly found ourselves in the vicinity of the lions, and were greeted with ominous growlings. Cautiously advancing and pushing the bushes aside, we saw in the gloom what we at first took to be a lion cub; closer inspection, however, showed it to be the remains of the unfortunate coolie, which the man-eaters had evidently abandoned at our approach. The legs, one arm and half the body had been eaten, and it was the stiff fingers of the other arm trailing along the sand which had left the marks we had taken to be the trail of a wounded lion. By this time the beasts had retired far into the thick jungle where it was impossible to follow them, so we had the remains of the coolie buried and once more returned home disappointed.

Now the bravest men in the world, much less the ordinary Indian coolie, will not stand constant terrors of this sort indefinitely. The whole district was by this time thoroughly panic-stricken, and I was not at all surprised, therefore, to find on my return to camp that same afternoon (December 1) that the men had all struck work and were waiting to speak to me. When I sent for them, they flocked to my *boma* in a body and stated that they would not remain at Tsavo any longer for anything or anybody; they had come from India on an agreement to work for the government, not to supply food for either lions or "devils." No sooner had they delivered this ultimatum than a regular stampede took place. Some hundreds of them stopped the first passing train by throwing themselves on the rails in front of the engine, and then, swarming on to the trucks and throwing in their possessions anyhow, they fled from the accursed spot.

After this the railway works were completely stopped; and for the next three weeks practically nothing was done but build "lion-proof" huts for those workmen who had had sufficient courage to remain. It was a strange and amusing sight to see these shelters perched on the top of water-tanks, roofs and girders—anywhere for safety—while some even went so far as to dig pits inside their tents, into which they descended at night, covering the top over with heavy logs of wood. Every good-sized tree in the camp had as many beds lashed on to it as its branches would bear—and sometimes more. I remember that one night when the camp was attacked, so many men swarmed on to one particular tree that down it came with a crash, hurling its terror-stricken load of shrieking coolies close to the very lions they were trying to avoid. Fortunately for them, a victim had already been secured, and the brutes were too busy devouring him to pay attention to anything else.

The District Officer's Narrow Escape

Some little time before the flight of the workmen, I had written to Mr. Whitehead, the District Officer, asking him to come up and assist me in my campaign against the lions, and to bring with him any of his *askaris* (native soldiers) that he could spare. He replied accepting the invitation, and told me to expect him about dinner-time on December 2, which turned out to be the day after the exodus. His train was due at Tsavo about six o'clock in the evening, so I sent my "boy" up to the station to meet him and to help in carrying his baggage to the camp. In a very short time, however, the "boy" rushed back trembling with terror, and informed me that there was no sign of the train or of the railway staff, but that an enormous lion was standing on the station platform. This extraordinary story I did not believe in the least, as by this time the coolies—never remarkable for bravery—were in such a state of fright that if they caught sight of a hyena, or a baboon, or even a dog, in the bush, they were sure to imagine it was a lion; but I found out next day that it was an actual fact, and that both stationmaster and signalman had been obliged to take refuge from one of the man-eaters by locking themselves in the station building.

I waited some little time for Mr. Whitehead, but eventually, as he did not put in an appearance, I concluded that he must have postponed his journey until the next day, and so had my dinner in my customary solitary state. During the meal I heard a couple of shots, but paid no attention to them, as rifles were constantly being fired off in the neighbourhood of the camp. Later in the evening, I went out as usual to watch for our elusive foes, and took up my position in a crib made of sleepers which I had built on a big girder close to a camp which I thought was likely to be attacked. Soon after settling down at my post, I was surprised to hear the man-eaters growling and purring and crunching up bones about seventy yards from the crib. I could not understand what they had found to eat, as I had heard no commotion in the camps, and I knew by bitter experience that every meal the brutes obtained from us was announced by shrieks and uproar. The only conclusion I could come to was that they had pounced upon some poor unsuspecting native traveller. After a time I was able to make out their eyes glowing in the darkness, and I took as careful aim as was possible in the circumstances and fired; but the only notice they paid to the shot was to carry off whatever they were devouring and to retire quietly over a slight rise, which prevented me from seeing them. There they finished their meal at their ease.

As soon as it was daylight, I got out of my crib and went towards the place where I had last heard them. On the way, whom should I meet but my missing guest, Mr. Whitehead, looking very pale and ill, and generally dishevelled.

"Where on earth have you come from?" I exclaimed. "Why didn't you turn up to dinner last night?"

"A nice reception you give a fellow when you invite him to dinner," was his only reply.

"Why, what's up?" I asked.

"That infernal lion of yours nearly did for me last night," said Whitehead.

"Nonsense, you must have dreamed it!" I cried in astonishment.

For answer he turned round and showed me his back. "That's not much of a dream, is it?" he asked.

His clothing was rent by one huge tear from the nape of the neck downwards, and on the flesh there were four great claw marks, showing red and angry through the torn cloth. Without further parley, I hurried him off to my tent, and bathed and dressed his wounds; and when I had made him considerably more comfortable, I got from him the whole story of the events of the night.

It appeared that his train was very late, so that it was quite dark when he arrived at Tsavo Station, from which the track to my camp lay through a small cutting. He was accompanied by Abdullah, his sergeant of *askaris*, who walked close behind him carrying a lighted lamp. All went well until they were about half-way through the gloomy cutting, when one of the lions suddenly jumped down upon them from the high bank, knocking Whitehead over like a ninepin, and tearing his back in the manner I had seen. Fortunately, however, he had his carbine with him, and instantly fired. The flash and the loud report must have dazed the lion for a second or two, enabling Whitehead to disengage himself; but the next instant the brute pounced like lightning on the unfortunate Abdullah, with whom he at once made off. All that the poor fellow could say was: *"Eh, Bwana, simba"* ("Oh, Master, a lion"). As the lion was dragging him over the bank, Whitehead fired again, but without effect, and the brute quickly disappeared into the darkness with his prey. It was, of course, this unfortunate man whom I had heard the lions devouring during the night. Whitehead himself had a marvellous escape; his wounds were happily not very deep, and caused him little or no inconvenience afterwards.

On the same day, December 3, the forces arrayed against the lions were further strengthened. Mr. Farquhar, the Superintendent of Police, arrived from the coast with a score of sepoys to assist in hunting down the man-eaters, whose fame had by this time spread far and wide, and the most elaborate precautions were taken, his men being posted on the most convenient trees near every camp. Several other officials had also come up on leave to join in the chase, and each of these guarded a likely spot in the same way, Mr. Whitehead sharing my post inside the crib on the girder. Further, in spite of some chaff, my lion trap was put in thorough working order, and two of the sepoys were installed as bait.

Our preparations were quite complete by nightfall, and we all took up our appointed positions. Nothing happened until about nine o'clock, when to my great satisfaction the intense stillness was suddenly broken by the noise of the door of the trap clattering down. "At last," I thought, "one at least of the brutes is done for." But the sequel was an ignominious one.

The bait-sepoys had a lamp burning inside their part of the cage, and were each armed with a Martini rifle, with plenty of ammunition. They had also been given strict orders to shoot at once if a lion should enter the trap. Instead of doing so, however, they were so terrified when he rushed in and began to lash himself madly against the bars of the cage, that they completely lost their heads and were actually too unnerved to fire. Not for some minutes—not, indeed, until Mr. Farquhar, whose post was close by, shouted at them and cheered them on— did they at all recover themselves. Then when at last they did begin to fire, they fired with a vengeance—anywhere, anyhow. Whitehead and I were at right angles to the direction in which they should have shot, and yet their bullets came whizzing all round us. Altogether they fired over a score of shots, and in the end succeeded only in blowing away one of the bars of the door, thus allowing our prize to make good his escape. How they failed to kill him several times over is, and always will be, a complete mystery to me, as they could have put the muzzles of their rifles absolutely touching his body. There was, indeed, some blood scattered about the trap, but it was small consolation to know that the brute, whose capture and death seemed so certain, had only been slightly wounded.

Still we were not unduly dejected, and when morning came, a hunt was at once arranged. Accordingly we spent the greater part of the day on our hands and knees following the lions through the dense thickets of thorny jungle, but though we heard their growls from time to time, we never succeeded in actually coming up with them. Of the whole party, only Farquhar managed to catch a momentary glimpse of one as it bounded over a bush. Two days more were spent in the same manner, and with equal unsuccess; and then Farquhar and his sepoys were obliged to return to the coast. Mr. Whitehead also departed for his district, and once again I was left alone with the man-eaters.

The Death of the First Man-Eater

A day or two after the departure of my allies, as I was leaving my *boma* soon after dawn on December 9, I saw a Swahili running excitedly towards me, shouting out *"Simba! Simba!"* ("Lion! Lion!"), and every now and again looking behind him as he ran. On questioning him I found that the lions had tried to snatch a man from the camp by the river, but being foiled in this had seized and killed one of the donkeys, and were at that moment busy devouring it not far off. Now was my chance.

I rushed for the heavy rifle which Farquhar had kindly left with me for use in case an opportunity such as this should arise, and, led by the Swahili, I started most carefully to stalk the lions, who, I devoutly hoped, were confining their attention strictly to their meal. I was getting on splendidly, and could just make out the outline of one of them through the dense bush, when unfortunately my guide snapped a rotten branch. The wily beast heard the noise, growled his defiance, and disappeared in a moment into a patch of even thicker jungle close by. In desperation at the thought of his escaping me once again, I crept hurriedly back to the camp, summoned the available workmen and told them to bring all the tom-toms, tin cans and other noisy instruments of any kind that could be found. As quickly as possible I posted them in a half-circle round the thicket, and gave the head *jemadar* instructions to start a simultaneous beating of the tom-toms and cans as soon as he judged that I had had time to get round to the other side. I then crept round by myself and soon found a good position and one which the lion was most likely to retreat past, as it was in the middle of a broad animal path leading straight from the place where he was concealed. I lay down behind a small ant hill, and waited expectantly. Very soon I heard a tremendous din being raised by the advancing line of coolies, and almost immediately, to my intense joy, out into the open path stepped a huge maneless lion. It was the first occasion during all these trying months upon which I had had a fair chance at one of these brutes, and my satisfaction at the prospect of bagging him was unbounded.

Slowly he advanced along the path, stopping every few seconds to look round. I was only partially concealed from view, and if his attention had not been so fully occupied by the noise behind him, he must have observed me. As he was oblivious to my presence, however, I let him approach to within about fifteen yards of me, and then covered him with my rifle. The moment I moved to do this, he caught sight of me, and seemed much astonished at my sudden appearance, for he stuck his forefeet into the ground, threw himself back on his haunches and growled savagely. As I covered his brain with my rifle, I felt that at last I had him absolutely at my mercy, but . . . never trust an untried weapon! I pulled the trigger, and to my horror heard the dull snap that tells of a misfire.

Worse was to follow. I was so taken aback and disconcerted by this untoward accident that I entirely forgot to fire the left barrel, and lowered the rifle from my shoulder with the intention of reloading—if I should be given time. Fortunately for me, the lion was so distracted by the terrific din and uproar of the coolies behind him that instead of springing on me, as might have been expected, he bounded aside into the jungle again. By this time I had collected my wits, and just as he jumped I let him have the left barrel. An answering angry growl told me that he had been hit; but nevertheless he succeeded once more in getting clear away, for although I tracked him for some little distance, I eventually lost his trail in a rocky patch of ground.

Bitterly did I anathematise the hour in which I had relied on a borrowed weapon, and in my disappointment and vexation I abused owner, maker, and rifle with fine impartiality. On extracting the unexploded cartridge, I found that the needle had not struck home, the cap being only slightly dented; so that the whole fault did indeed lie with the rifle, which I later returned to Farquhar with polite compliments. Seriously, however, my continued ill-luck was most exasperating; and the result was that the Indians were more than ever confirmed in their belief that the lions were really evil spirits, proof against mortal weapons. Certainly, they did seem to bear charmed lives.

After this dismal failure there was, of course, nothing to do but to return to camp. Before doing so, however, I proceeded to view the dead donkey, which I found to have been only slightly devoured at the quarters. It is a curious fact that lions always begin at the tail of their prey and eat upwards towards the head. As their meal had thus been interrupted evidently at the very beginning, I felt pretty sure that one or other of the brutes would return to the carcase at nightfall. Accordingly, as there was no tree of any kind close at hand, I had a staging erected some ten feet away from the body. This *machan* was about twelve feet high and was composed of four poles stuck into the ground and inclined toward each other at the top, where a plank was lashed to serve as a seat. Further, as the nights were still pitch dark, I had the donkey's carcase secured by strong wires to a neighbouring stump, so that the lions might not be able to drag it away before I could get a shot at them.

At sundown, therefore, I took up my position on my airy perch, and much to the disgust of my gun-bearer, Mahina, I decided to go alone. I would gladly have taken him with me, indeed, but he had a bad cough, and I was afraid lest he should make any involuntary noise or movement which might spoil all. Darkness fell almost immediately, and everything became extraordinarily still. The silence of an African jungle on a dark night needs to be experienced to be realised; it is most impressive, especially when one is absolutely alone and isolated from one's fellow creatures, as I was then. The solitude and stillness, and the purpose of my vigil, all had their effect on me, and from a condition of strained expectancy I gradually fell into a dreamy mood which harmonised well with my surroundings. Suddenly I was startled out of my reverie by the snapping of a twig; and, straining my ears for a further sound, I fancied I could hear the rustling of a large body forcing its way through the bush. "The man-eater," I thought to myself; "surely to-night my luck will change and I shall bag one of the brutes." Profound silence again succeeded; I sat on my eyrie like a statue, every nerve tense with excitement. Very soon, however, all doubts as to the presence of the lion was dispelled. A deep long-drawn sigh—sure sign of hunger—came up from the bushes, and the rustling commenced again as he cautiously advanced. In a moment or two a sudden stop, followed by an angry growl, told me that my presence had been noticed; and I began to fear that disappointment awaited me once more.

But no; matters quickly took an unexpected turn. The hunter became the hunted; and instead of either making off or coming for the bait prepared for him, the lion began stealthily to stalk *me!* For about two hours he horrified me by slowly creeping round and round my crazy structure, gradually edging his way nearer and nearer. Every moment I expected him to rush it; and the staging had not been constructed with an eye to such a possibility. If one of the rather flimsy poles should break, or if the lion could spring the twelve feet which separated me from the ground . . . the thought was scarcely a pleasant one. I began to feel distinctly "creepy," and heartily repented my folly in having placed myself in such a dangerous position. I kept perfectly still, however, hardly daring even to blink my eyes: but the long continued strain was telling on my nerves, and my feelings may be better imagined than described when about midnight suddenly something came flop and struck me on the back of the head. For a moment I was so terrified that I nearly fell off the plank, as I thought that the lion had sprung on me from behind. Regaining my senses in a second or two, I realised that I had been hit by nothing more formidable than an owl, which had doubtless mistaken me for the branch of a tree—not a very alarming thing to happen in ordinary circumstances, I admit, but coming at the time it did, it almost paralysed me. The involuntary start which I could not help giving was immediately answered by a sinister growl from below.

After this I again kept as still as I could, though absolutely trembling with excitement; and in a short while I heard the lion begin to creep stealthily towards me. I could barely make out his form as he crouched among the whitish undergrowth; but I saw enough for my purpose and before he could come any nearer, I took careful aim and pulled the trigger. The sound of the shot was at once followed by a most terrific roar, and then I could hear him leaping about in all directions. I was no longer able to see him, however, as his first bound had taken him into the thick bush; but to make assurance doubly sure, I kept blazing away in the direction in which I heard him plunging about. At length came a series of mighty groans, gradually subsiding into deep sighs, and finally ceasing altogether; and I felt convinced that one of the "devils" who had so long harried us would trouble us no more.

As soon as I ceased firing, a tumult of inquiring voices was borne across the dark jungle from the men in camp about a quarter of a mile away. I shouted back that I was safe and sound, and that one of the lions was dead: whereupon such a mighty cheer went up from all the camps as must have astonished the denizens of the jungle for miles around. Shortly I saw scores of lights twinkling through the bushes: every man in camp turned out, and with tom-toms beating and horns blowing came running to the scene. They surrounded my eyrie, and to my amazement prostrated themselves on the ground before me, saluting me with cries of *"Mabarak! Mabarak!"* which I believe means "blessed one" or "saviour." All the same, I refused to allow any search to be made that night for the body of the lion, in case his companion might be close by; besides, it was possible that he might be still alive, and capable of making a last spring. Accordingly we all returned in triumph to the camp, where great rejoicings were kept up for the remainder of the night, the Swahili and other African natives celebrating the occasion by an especially wild and savage dance.

For my part, I anxiously awaited the dawn; and even before it was thoroughly light I was on my way to the eventful spot, as I could not completely persuade myself that even yet the "devil" might not have eluded me in some uncanny and mysterious way. Happily my fears proved groundless, and I was relieved to find that my luck—after playing me so many exasperating tricks—had really turned at last. I had scarcely traced the blood for more than a few paces when, on rounding a bush, I was startled to see a huge lion right in front of me, seemingly alive and crouching for a spring. On looking closer, however, I satisfied myself that he was really and truly stone-dead, whereupon my followers crowded round, laughed and danced and shouted with joy like children, and bore me in triumph shoulder-high round the dead body. These thanksgiving ceremonies being over, I examined the body and found that two bullets had taken effect—one close behind the left shoulder, evidently penetrating the heart, and the other in the off hind leg. The prize was indeed one to be proud of; his length from tip of nose to tip of tail was nine feet eight inches, he stood three feet nine inches high, and it took eight men to carry him back to camp. The only blemish was that the skin was much scored by the *boma* thorns through which he had so often forced his way in carrying off his victims.

The news of the death of one of the notorious man-eaters soon spread far and wide over the country: telegrams of congratulations came pouring in, and scores of people flocked from up and down the railway to see the skin for themselves.

The Death of the Second Man-Eater

It must not be imagined that with the death of this lion our troubles at Tsavo were at an end; his companion was still at large, and very soon began to make us unpleasantly aware of the fact. Only a few nights elapsed before he made an attempt to get at the Permanent Way Inspector, climbing up the steps of his bungalow and prowling round the verandah. The Inspector, hearing the noise and thinking it was a drunken coolie, shouted angrily "Go away!" but, fortunately for him, did not attempt to come out or to open the door. Thus disappointed in his attempt to obtain a meal of human flesh, the lion seized a couple of the Inspector's goats and devoured them there and then.

On hearing of this occurrence, I determined to sit up the next night near the Inspector's bungalow. Fortunately there was a vacant iron shanty close at hand, with a convenient loophole in it for firing from; and outside this I placed three full-grown goats as bait, tying them to a half-length of rail, weighing about 250 lbs. The night passed uneventfully until just before daybreak, when at last the lion turned up, pounced on one of the goats and made off with it, at the same time dragging away the others, rail and all. I fired several shots in his direction, but it was pitch dark and quite impossible to see anything, so I only succeeded in hitting one of the goats. I often longed for a flashlight on such occasions.

Next morning I started off in pursuit and was joined by some others from the camp. I found that the trail of the goats and rail was easily followed, and we soon came up, about a quarter of a mile away, to where the lion was still busy at his meal. He was concealed in some thick bush and growled angrily on hearing our approach; finally, as we got closer, he suddenly made a charge, rushing through the bushes at a great pace. In an instant, every man of the party scrambled hastily up the nearest tree, with the exception of one of my assistants, Mr. Winkler, who stood steadily by me throughout. The brute, however, did not press his charge home: and on throwing stones into the bushes where we had last seen him, we guessed by the silence that he had slunk off. We therefore advanced cautiously, and on getting up to the place discovered that he had indeed escaped us, leaving two of the goats scarcely touched.

Thinking that in all probability the lion would return as usual to finish his meal, I had a very strong scaffolding put up a few feet away from the dead goats, and took up my position on it before dark. On this occasion I brought my gun-bearer, Mashina, to take a turn at watching, as I was by this time worn out for want of sleep, having spent so many nights on the look-out. I was just dozing off comfortably when suddenly I felt my arm seized, and on looking up saw Mahina pointing in the direction of the goats. *"Sher!"* ("Lion!") was all he whispered. I grasped my double smooth-bore, which I had charged with slug, and waited patiently. In a few moments I was rewarded, for as I watched the spot where I expected the lion to appear, there was a rustling among the bushes and I saw him stealthily emerge into the open and pass almost directly beneath us. I fired both barrels practically together into his shoulder, and to my joy could see him go down under the force of the blow. Quickly I reached for the magazine rifle, but before I could use it, he was out of sight among the bushes, and I had to fire after him quite at random. Nevertheless I was confident of getting him in the morning, and accordingly set out as soon as it was light. For over a mile there was no difficulty in following the blood-trail, and as he had rested several times I felt sure that he had been badly wounded. In the end, however, my hunt proved fruitless, for after a time the traces of blood ceased and the surface of the ground became rocky, so that I was no longer able to follow the spoor.

About this time Sir Guilford Molesworth, K. C. I. E., late Consulting Engineer to the Government of India for State Railways, passed through Tsavo on a tour of inspection on behalf of the Foreign Office. After examining the bridge and other works and expressing his satisfaction, he took a number of photographs, one or two of which he has kindly allowed me to reproduce in this book. He thoroughly sympathised with us in all the trials we had endured from the man-eaters, and was delighted that one at least was dead. When he asked me if I expected to get the second lion soon, I well remember his half-doubting smile as I rather too confidently asserted that I hoped to bag him also in the course of a few days.

As it happened, there was no sign of our enemy for about ten days after this, and we began to hope that he had died of his wounds in the bush. All the same we still took every precaution at night, and it was fortunate that we did so, as otherwise at least one more victim would have been added to the list. For on the night of December 27, I was suddenly aroused by terrified shouts from my trolley men, who slept in a tree close outside my *boma* to the effect that a lion was trying to get at them. It would have been madness to have gone out, as the moon was hidden by dense clouds and it was absolutely impossible to see anything more than a yard in front of one; so all I could do was to fire off a few rounds just to frighten the brute away. This apparently had the desired effect, for the men were not further molested that night; but the man-eater had evidently prowled about for some time, for we found in the morning that he had gone right into every one of their tents, and round the tree was a regular ring of his footmarks.

The following evening I took up my position in this same tree, in the hope that he would make another attempt. The night began badly, as while climbing up to my perch I very nearly put my hand on a venomous snake which was lying coiled round one of the branches. As may be imagined, I came down again very quickly, but one of my men managed to despatch it with a long pole. Fortunately the night was clear and cloudless, and the moon made every thing almost as bright as day. I kept watch until about 2 a.m., when I roused Mahina to take his turn. For about an hour I slept peacefully with my back to the tree, and then woke suddenly with an uncanny feeling that something was wrong. Mahina, however, was on the alert, and had seen nothing; and although I looked carefully round us on all sides, I too could discover nothing unusual. Only half satisfied, I was about to lie back again, when I fancied I saw something move a little way off among the low bushes. On gazing intently at the spot for a few seconds, I found I was not mistaken. It was the man-eater, cautiously stalking us.

The ground was fairly open round our tree, with only a small bush every here and there; and from our position it was a most fascinating sight to watch this great brute stealing stealthily round us, taking advantage of every bit of cover as he came. His skill showed that he was an old hand at the terrible game of man-hunting: so I determined to run no undue risk of losing him this time. I accordingly waited until he got quite close—about twenty yards away—and then fired my .303 at his chest. I heard the bullet strike him, but unfortunately it had no knockdown effect, for with a fierce growl he turned and made off with great long bounds. Before he disappeared from sight, however, I managed to have three more shots at him from the magazine rifle, and another growl told me that the last of these had also taken effect.

We awaited daylight with impatience, and at the first glimmer of dawn we set out to hunt him down. I took a native tracker with me, so that I was free to keep a good look-out, while Mahina followed immediately behind with a Martini carbine. Splashes of blood being plentiful, we were able to get along quickly; and we had not proceeded more than a quarter of a mile through the jungle when suddenly a fierce warning growl was heard right in front of us. Looking cautiously through the bushes, I could see the man-eater glaring out in our direction, and showing his tusks in an angry snarl. I at once took careful aim and fired. Instantly he sprang out and made a most determined charge down on us. I fired again and knocked him over; but in a second he was up once more and coming for me as fast as he could in his crippled condition. A third shot had no apparent effect, so I put out my hand for the Martini, hoping to stop him with it. To my dismay, however, it was not there. The terror of the sudden charge had proved too much for Mahina, and both he and the carbine were by this time well on their way up a tree. In the circumstances there was nothing to do but follow suit, which I did without loss of time: and but for the fact that one of my shots had broken a hind leg, the brute would most certainly have had me. Even as it was, I had barely time to swing myself up out of his reach before he arrived at the foot of the tree.

When the lion found he was too late, he started to limp back to the thicket; but by this time I had seized the carbine from Mahina, and the first shot I fired from it seemed to give him his quietus, for he fell over and lay motionless. Rather foolishly, I at once scrambled down from the tree and walked up towards him. To my surprise and no little alarm he jumped up and attempted another charge. This time, however, a Martini bullet in the chest and another in the head finished him for good and all; he dropped in his tracks not five yards away from me, and died gamely, biting savagely at a branch which had fallen to the ground.

By this time all the workmen in camp, attracted by the sound of the firing, had arrived on the scene, and so great was their resentment against the brute who had killed such numbers of their comrades that it was only with the greatest difficulty that I could restrain them from tearing the dead body to pieces. Eventually, amid the wild rejoicings of the natives and coolies, I had the lion carried to my *boma,* which was close at hand. On examination we found no less than six bullet holes in the body, and embedded only a little way in the flesh of the back was the slug which I had fired into him from the scaffolding about ten days previously. He measured nine feet six inches from tip of nose to tip of tail, and stood three feet eleven and a half inches high; but, as in the case of his companion, the skin was disfigured by being deeply scored all over by the *boma* thorns.

The news of the death of the second "devil" soon spread far and wide over the country, and natives actually travelled from up and down the line to have a look at my trophies and at the "devil-killer," as they called me. Best of all, the coolies who had absconded came flocking back to Tsavo, and much to my relief work was resumed and we were never again troubled by man-eaters. It was amusing, indeed, to notice the change which took place in the attitude of the workmen towards me after I had killed the two lions. Instead of wishing to murder me, as they once did, they could not now do enough for me, and as a token of their gratitude they presented me with a beautiful silver bowl, as well as with a long poem written in Hindustani describing all our trials and my ultimate victory. As the poem relates our troubles in somewhat quaint and biblical language, I have given a translation of it in the appendix. The bowl I shall always consider my most highly prized and hardest won trophy. The inscription on it reads as follows:—

Sir,—We, your Overseer, Timekeepers, *Mistaris* and Workmen, present you with this bowl as a token of our gratitude to you for your bravery in killing two man-eating lions at great risk to your own life, thereby saving us from the fate of being devoured by these terrible monsters who nightly broke into our tents and took our fellow-workers from our side. In presenting you with this bowl, we all add our prayers for your long life, happiness and prosperity. We shall ever remain, Sir, Your grateful servants,

Baboo Purshotam Hurjee Purmar, *Overseer and Clerk of the Works, on behalf of*
your Workmen.
Dated at Tsavo, *January* 30, 1899.

Before I leave the subject of "the man-eaters of Tsavo," it may be of interest to mention that these two lions possess the distinction, probably unique among wild animals, of having been specifically referred to in the House of Lords by the Prime Minister of the day. Speaking of the difficulties which had been encountered in the construction of the Uganda Railway, the late Lord Salisbury said:—

"The whole of the works were put a stop to for three weeks because a party of man-eating lions appeared in the locality and conceived a most unfortunate taste for our porters. At last the labourers entirely declined to go on unless they were guarded by an iron entrenchment. Of course it is difficult to work a railway under these conditions, and until we found an enthusiastic sportsman to get rid of these lions, our enterprise was seriously hindered."

Also, *The Spectator* of March 3, 1900, had an article entitled "The Lions that Stopped the Railway," from which the following extracts are taken:—

"The parallel to the story of the lions which stopped the rebuilding of Samaria must occur to everyone, and if the Samaritans had quarter as good cause for their fears as had the railway coolies, their wish to propitiate the local deities is easily understood. If the whole body of lion anecdote, from the days of the Assyrian Kings till the last year of the nineteenth century, were collated and brought together, it would not equal in tragedy or atrocity, in savageness or in sheer insolent contempt for man, armed or unarmed, white or black, the story of these two beasts. . . .

"To what a distance the whole story carries us back, and how impossible it becomes to account for the survival of primitive man against this kind of foe! For fire—which has hitherto been regarded as his main safeguard against the carnivora—these cared nothing. It is curious that the Tsavo lions were not killed by poison, for strychnine is easily used, and with effect.★ Poison may have been used early in the history of man, for its powers are employed with strange skill by the men in the tropical forest, both in American and West Central Africa. But there is no evidence that the old inhabitants of Europe, or of Assyria or Asia Minor, ever killed lions or wolves by this means. They looked to the King or chief, or some champion, to kill these monsters for them. It was not the sport but the duty of Kings, and was in itself a title to be a ruler of men. Theseus, who cleared the roads of beasts and robbers; Hercules, the lion killer; St. George, the dragon-slayer, and all the rest of their class owed to this their everlasting fame. From the story of the Tsavo River we can appreciate their services to man even at this distance of time. When the jungle twinkled with hundreds of lamps, as the shout went on from camp to camp that the first lion was dead, as the hurrying crowds fell prostrate in the midnight forest, laying their heads on his feet, and the Africans danced savage and ceremonial dances of thanksgiving, Mr. Patterson must have realised in no common way what it was to have been a hero and de-liverer in the days when man was not yet undisputed lord of the creation, and might pass at any moment under the savage dominion of the beasts."

(★I may mention that poison *was* tried, but without effect. The poi-soned carcases of transport animals which had died from the bite of the tsetse fly were placed in likely spots, but the wily man-eaters would not touch them, and much preferred live men to dead donkeys.)

Well had the two man-eaters earned all this fame; they had devoured between them no less than twenty-eight Indian coolies, in addition to scores of unfortunate African natives of whom no official record was kept.

11   Man–Eaters

BY C. J. P. IONIDES

One of the most serious problems I had to cope with as a Game Ranger was that of man-eating lions. The reason for this was of course the dearth of the carnivore's natural prey, a situation for which man has only himself to blame. He himself has created the problem, and looking at it solely as a conservationist I must admit to a sneaking sympathy for the man-eater. He is, as it were, the instrument of poetic justice, exacting dire retribution for the indiscriminate slaughter of the great herds of beautiful creatures which once animated the whole of this lush and variegated Southern Province, or Region as it is now designated.

The lion, though adaptable to change, had begun to feel the pinch about ten years before I came to be responsible for the wild life in those parts. They lived mainly on pig and wart hog, and to a lesser degree on the smaller forest animals, all of which during the rainy seasons are very alert besides being dispersed and difficult to find.

The young lion in his third year, barely full grown though with a full set of teeth—having lost his milk teeth at two—has a particularly difficult job to maintain himself. He may try to go after pig, but more usually he settles for ground birds, such as guinea-fowl and rodents, as well as any carrion he can find.

The terrain along the coastal belt, as I have already mentioned, is dense thicket dotted here and there with villages where you find *shambas* or gardens with crops and big leafy mango trees. There is very little grazing.

The beginning of a man-eater is often a combination of several circumstances. In December and January the mangoes ripen and fall from the trees. In the middle of the night some villager will feel peckish and, despite grim warnings, go outside to pick up some of the fruit. But pigs also like mangoes and a lion may be waiting for a pig. It is a lot to expect of a hungry lion not to try it on. If he is immature he might make a hash of it by grabbing the villager by the arm or leg, and get the fright of his life with all the yelling and noise and people rushing out of huts with knives and firebrands. He may never go near man again, though the odds seem to be that he will and this time, probably being a more experienced killer, he does a proper job. He goes straight for the back of the neck where his large fangs meet; he is as quick as a humane killer, and he discovers how easy it is.

At this point he may follow one of two courses. He may just go through life taking the odd man when he can, if he must—from the number of cases of casual man-eating recorded in the coastal districts, it is safe to say that every lion born there is a potential man-eater. On the other hand, he may be a particularly bold animal. He knows he is taking a risk but being a lion he is lazy, so he tries it again and again, realising each time how vulnerable man is and how little he really needs to worry. It is a short step to the next stage when he actually starts hunting down people. By that time the DC has heard of him and is demanding 'immediate effective action' by the Game Department.

A lion is an intelligent animal, therefore it is vital to get a man-eater quickly; indeed to make a nonsense of hunting him in the early stage is to create a menace that possibly might never be accounted for. In one region a man-eater has been terrorising a district for the past ten years. Little wonder that a lion of this calibre is often credited with being a magic animal. He will not be driven off by a line of beaters, having learned that it is a bluff. He will not return to an un-finished meal, knowing that a hunter might be waiting. He has found out all about traps and avoids them with uncanny instinct. Poison is out of the question as he will not return to a kill. Worst of all he keeps moving, ranging far and wide.

Nothing seems to deter these ferocious beasts. They will crash down the doors of huts or claw their way through mud walls and thatched roofs to get at people inside. Fire will not keep them away. One man-eater entered among blazing fires inside which Bill Harvey was sleeping on a bed surrounded by his staff and porters. The lion got his fore paw into the crutch of one of the porters and flipped him out of the circle as a kitten would a ball of wool.

Man-eaters develop their own favourite techniques. One I had to deal with used to stalk up to a village, rush the women as they sat outside cooking the evening meal and pick off one of them. Another, a lioness, would lie up behind a hut at night, waiting to grab the first person who came out to uri-nate. Another lay up in clumps of bamboo where the inhabitants of a village used to come to tap *ulanzi* or bamboo wine from the young shoots. Another habitually ambushed footpaths.

There was no man-eater control policy when I first joined the Game Department. The work was generally left to African game scouts using gangs of beaters but, although they were occasionally successful, as far as I could judge more people were killed in these drives than lions. The entire population of a village would turn out and make a field day of it. Perhaps a man-eater would be isolated in a patch of bush and a game scout or two, supported by possibly twenty men armed with muzzle-loaders, would then start blazing away into the undergrowth while parts of it were cut away to reduce the area of cover, and a mob of several hundred people milled around yelling and banging sticks and tins. Eventually the lion charged, clawing a path through the mob and usually got away scot free leaving a number of people shot to death in the fusillade that greeted the charge.

Gun-traps, too, were a danger to human life and limb, since it was necessary to lay them on paths where any notice you might put up warning people off seemed about as intelligible to them as they were to a lion. Poison was sometimes used. Strychnine was inserted into cuts made in a carcass in the hope the lion would not get the intensely bitter taste as he tore off and swallowed chunks of the meat. But too much poison made him vomit, while too little, one assumes, merely gave him a bellyache, as the death caused by a correct dose is an extremely painful one. For my part I flatly refused to use the stuff; in doing so perhaps I neglected my duty, but frankly I considered it indecent, and from what I have read in his books on hunting man-eating tigers in India I believe Jim Corbett felt the same way. To me a poison such as strychnine is morally unjustifiable, as are traps and any other method employed to destroy a pest if the method is likely to cause suffering, even in the case of a man-eater.

In addition to these difficulties there was that of making contact with the proscribed lion. It was an extremely frustrating business. You would hear that a man-eater had started somewhere. You got to the place as quickly as possible only to find the lion had gone. You waited perhaps a fortnight. Not a sign of the animal. You had work elsewhere and off you went. Then a few days later back he would come and pick off another victim.

In the end, in desperation, I devised a system of my own. The next time news came of a man-eater—it was in Lindi district, I went to a point within a ten-mile radius of its activities, where I camped. From here I spread out my game scouts, each with a local guide and a man with a drum. They were to comb the area for fresh spoor of the lion. The moment this was found by a party the drummer was to start sounding the lion warning. This was a local drum call known as the *ngula mtwe* (literally 'A man is eaten'), two short beats and a long one repeated. Meanwhile the game scout would be hurrying on his way to my camp in case I did not hear the call. Speed was important. In the dry weather tracking is difficult, but I reckoned that if I heard the *ngula mtwe* early enough in the morning I could get to the spoor possibly before the trail of dew brushed off leaves and grass would have gone, thus making the tracking of the animal immeasurably easier.

The lion was fairly notorious. It had started man-eating part-time about two years before, but had been getting steadily more audacious, and on this occasion it had timed its arrival on the scene so opportunely that the entire village were convinced it was acting under orders.

What had happened was that an elderly, well-to-do farmer had gone away from his home on a short business trip, leaving behind a flighty young wife. The same evening she was visited by her lover who took her into an open, shed-like construction with a grass roof but no walls. They were actually copulating when the lion suddenly appeared, picked the man off the woman, and dragged him into the bushes and ate him. The woman had been mauled a bit and had to be taken to hospital, and of course, in consequence, the husband was credited with being a very bad wizard who had the lion for a slave.

Next morning I heard the drum call. With my tracker and one of my gun-bearers, a man named Hemedi Ngoe, I hurried across country towards the sound, being met on the way by the game scout in charge of the party which had found the fresh spoor. He immediately led us to the spot where we arrived to find the drummer, who had been deserted by the guide, almost beside himself with fear. The belief was that the slave lion did not like having his movements spied upon and generally ate people who had the temerity to betray its whereabouts to the Game Ranger. It must have been a very frightening experience for the poor man, knowing the lion could hear the drum call and, being diabolically cunning, would realise what it was all about. It was a most satisfying deduction, therefore, that the drummer was even more afraid of the Game Ranger!

We began following up the spoor, and discovered after a while that the lion was actually walking ahead of us at very close range. Then a honey guide made its appearance. A honey guide is an African phenomenon, a shrike-like bird about the size of a starling with a thickish bill. There are nine species in Africa, all sombrely coloured in grey with black markings. By constantly twittering and nagging till you follow, a honey guide will lead you to a beehive. It wants you to get rid of the bees and open the hive, being interested in the grubs and honey. It is usual to leave some of the honey for the bird, and there is a belief among Africans that if this is not done it will lead the next man it sees to a lion or a snake. There is evidence of the truth of this behaviour—though not of the bird's motive—because I have on three occasions been led by it to things other than honey, and this was one of them. It would fly to us twittering insistently, then go over to the man-eater: it was fairly open country and we could follow the passage of our quarry by the birds suddenly getting up from bushes as it passed under. We came upon several places where the lion had tried to lie down for a rest, but had got up and moved on because of the racket this infernal bird was making. This performance went on for quite a long time, till the lion suddenly bolted away, probably in an attempt to shake off the pest.

Twice again in the next four days we found spoor and followed the lion but each time we lost him. Then early on the fifth day word came from a village that the lion had killed a pig. Our informant had heard the pig squealing in the bushes. He showed us the spoor when we arrived at the place, and we went into a very dense patch of undergrowth, where I made the tracker get behind me as it seemed we were very close to the lion. I was crawling on hands and knees when I suddenly saw the bushes moving just ahead, and going on a few yards came across the carcass of the pig. The lion had been there but had seen us and gone. We followed him for a little way, finding from time to time where he had stopped and waited to see if he was being followed, then had spotted us and carried on. To the surprise of my Africans I called off the hunt and went back to camp for breakfast.

After breakfast I opened a book and read till lunch. Then at about two, and to the intense relief of Hemedi, I said, 'Now we will hunt that mother-seducer. We will get him while he is having his afternoon sleep.'

For the next two hours we followed the suspicious course the man-eater had taken through the undergrowth as he made a wide detour back near the village. Then at last, in a very dense patch, we found the impression of his body where he had been lying on the ground till just a few moments before—it was still warm. He had just got up and walked on: later I observed it was fairly usual with lions to move from one place to another; we must have missed this one by just a few seconds.

We were on hands and knees, edging our way forward with the greatest possible caution, when I stopped for some reason. Glancing round I saw Hemedi suddenly stiffen with his eyes fixed on something just ahead. Then I smelt the lion and, moving slowly forward again, I saw at point blank range a whitish patch of fur in a gap in the undergrowth. The difficulty was to raise my rifle to my shoulder in that tangle of brambles and creepers. In the end all I could manage was to twist my shoulder down to the butt, contorting my neck so as to get my head under a branch and my eye to the sights. My right forefinger was septic at the time, so I got the middle finger on the trigger of my .470. I fired and there was a tremendous roar so loud and near I nearly jumped out of my skin. We heard the lion crashing off for a few yards, then silence.

We waited, remaining absolutely still. Then a groan came to us from where the movement had stopped. It was followed by another groan. Then there was the low moaning of a lion's death song, a sound which has never failed me as an indication of the approaching end. Suddenly it broke off in a gurgling roar and we heard nothing more. The man-eater was dead.

After that whenever conditions made it possible I hunted man-eaters during their siesta hours, and killed several in particularly dense cover where presumably they had imagined themselves pretty secure. If we could get on the spoor early enough in the morning the dew helped in showing us where the animal had gone for his lie-up. We would wait till the sun rose and it got really hot. Then we would go in with the greatest possible care, gently moving aside overhanging branches and twigs before passing under, most of the time on hands and knees, stopping every few minutes and remaining dead still to listen. By doing this we were quite often able to locate a lion's position in thick bush some time before actually coming up with it. Lions are at times rather noisy when they sleep. You may hear periodic grunts, the occasional growl, even moans. I remember one man-eater, a large male, who had devoured the whole of a fat woman, then finished the meal with a snack of a wart hog. When I finally came up with him he was having a nightmare, lying on his back with his legs in the air and uttering a series of gruff groans and little cries. He never knew what hit him.

When you start getting really close to a lion you are after, you come across places where he has tried to make himself comfortable but moved on to a better spot, perhaps with a little more shade. He seldom moves far at this stage, but will change his position possibly six or seven times before finally settling down and going to sleep. He may even change direction so that on occasions I have actually found my quarry behind me.

The bullet, I found, was the only clean and positive way of dealing with man-eaters, but it did involve some rather doubtful risks. I recall a lioness which had only just started man-eating. She and a young male lived in a dank, overgrown, swampy place near a village, but she was the villain in the piece. She had taken three people, each time getting bolder. She had the makings of becoming a real menace.

When I got to the scene of the crime it was too late to hunt, so I decided to camp for the night and gave orders for 'roaring sticks' to be put out on the ground: each time the lions roared in the night a stick was to be placed pointing in the direction of the roar. The last roar would thus provide a rough idea of where to look when I set out to hunt the female in the morning. When man-eaters were in an area I always made my Africans sleep in huts in a village, but as I personally do not like noise my tent would be pitched some distance away. I usually slept very lightly when hunting these lions, and with my rifle beside my bed I felt reasonably secure. In fact that night I slept heavily.

Next morning, on waking early, I went out to urinate and noticed lion spoor all round my tent. My servant then asked me where my ground sheet was. My bath tub on safari was a simple affair. A shallow hole would be dug in the ground and a canvas ground sheet was placed over the depression, which was then filled with warm water. When not in use the ground sheet was kept rolled up at the foot of my bed.

We found it some fifty yards away. What had obviously happened was that the lioness had come into my tent, grabbed the ground sheet and rushed off no doubt thinking it was me; fortunately she was inexperienced at the game. Then on discovering her mistake she had really gone sour because the canvas had been torn to shreds. I was furious.

'I am going to make her pay for it,' I told my men.

The spoor took us down into a dark, tangled gully, a most unpleasant place, though tracking was fairly easy. In half an hour we were up to her, and I fired at a range of twenty yards at no more than a patch of skin which was all I could see. There was a loud roar, and a moment later I saw a movement in the undergrowth streaking towards me. I could not see her to fire again; at that range in a charge you have got to make your bullet count. Then just as she was very close, though still difficult to see, she was brought to a stop by a very tough creeper across her chest, and she had to pause for a moment to bite her way through. Then she came out obliquely, and I dropped her at three paces as she swung round. My first shot had been in her lunch. I could not help thinking that but for her mistake the night before that lunch would have been me.

That animal was skin and bone, which meant that she had obviously embarked on her man-eating career out of sheer necessity. That was in Kilwa district where the food situation for lions was particularly bad. I recall in the same district a pride of six man-eaters, of which I killed four adults one after another—the remaining two were juveniles but just old enough to fend for themselves so were reprieved. During the period I hunted this pride, fourteen days, I am practically certain none of its members ate anything at all.

One of them, a lioness, I will never forget as she gave me the fright of my life. I had wounded her and was running towards a clump of grass where she had disappeared. I had not stopped to reload, as there was a cartridge in the second barrel of my .470, and I thought that all I had to do now was finish her off. Suddenly with a roar she rose out of the grass ten paces from me where she stood snarling, her tail swishing from side to side. I aimed at the chest and pressed the trigger. Instead of the expected bang and recoil all I felt was the sickening sense of a misfire. I put my hand behind me for more ammunition, but the gun-bearer had brought none. He was a game scout recruit who was

standing in, both my regular men being away on sick leave. Through carelessness I had omitted to instruct him before the hunt on what he should bring.
So I opened the breech and moved the round to the other barrel. Very often a
dud will go off the second time you try. Another click.

I was watching the animal's tail, always an indication of a lion's intentions. If it went straight up like a rod she would almost certainly charge.

'Don't run,' I warned the stand-in. 'I am going to step slowly backwards. Move as I move.'

Without taking my eyes off the lioness I stepped back one pace. Immediately the tail twitched and she took one pace forward. I stopped and she
stopped. I took another step, she took another step. I paused, she paused. I was
beginning to wonder whether I had really hit her seriously when to my relief I
saw her stagger. Then she turned and went into a bush. It was now our chance
to pull out, which we did. On getting more ammunition I was able to go back
after her and finish the job.

It was sad to see fine animals reduced to desperate straits for food. I like
lions. Given a decent chance in life I think they would behave fairly respectably. In
fact they sometimes show to my mind quite remarkable restraint. One man-eater,
on finding a man lying drunk outside a hut, merely nipped a chunk out of his behind, rather as you might take a passing bite from an apple and leave the rest.

Lions are playful creatures. The man-eating pride I have mentioned
would occasionally have a game of football in a village with baskets and cooking pots, while the terrified inhabitants shivered in their huts. I once saw a lion
tear open a sack of mealies and scatter the contents just for the heck of it. I saw
another try a melon. They are quite unpredictable, but it is their curiosity
which makes them always potentially a source of danger, even in areas where
their normal diet is plentiful.

There was a case not long ago of a party of men on their way through
the Selous Game Reserve. They were camped for the night near a small water-
course when one of the men was bitten in the abdomen by a passing lion. It is
unlikely that the animal was a man-eater, or for that matter even recognized
the man for what he was: in that vast uninhabited area human beings are far
more rare than any of the other species which share the habitat. My theory is
that the lion was just curious about the strange, unfamiliar thing it saw lying on
the ground covered up with a cloth of some kind, rather like the lion I have
mentioned that had a go at the melon. The sad part of it is that the unfortunate
man had half his insides taken away and died shortly after.

In my twenty-three years in the Game Department I shot over forty
lions, the majority of which were man-eaters, while the remainder were either

on their way to becoming man-eaters or were stock-raiders. The hunts I enjoyed, but the work was seldom accompanied by any sense of satisfaction, despite the good one was doing for people by ridding the countryside of a menace.

For some reason almost every hunt seemed bedevilled by complications and unpleasantness. Efforts were often deliberately frustrated by the very villagers you were trying to help. One headman was actually caught covering up the fresh spoor of a man-eater to prevent my going after it, although it had already taken several people of his village. He, I can assure you, was suitably dealt with. The trouble of course was the African's belief in witchcraft. The man-eater was not so much a lion as one animated by the spirit of some deceased person who had returned to life in this form to pay off old scores. It might even be a magic animal, impervious to bullets, possessing a satanic intelligence, a black heart and a monstrous appetite. Either way it resented being informed upon, as I have explained before, and to do so was only to invite its most determined attention—a belief no doubt fostered by the trouble some man-eaters take to select certain often difficult victims after ignoring the more obvious and accessible ones.

In 1950 my assistant, a young man of twenty named Brian Nicholson had a porter taken one night from his camp on the edge of the Selous Reserve. Two lions entered the camp, twice circled Nicholson's tent with the flaps wide open and the walls rolled up, passing within two feet of where he was sleeping under a mosquito net. They then went to where a number of porters were sleeping in the open, stepped in and out between the men. Still not satisfied, they then carried on to where two men were sleeping inside a grass hut. Instead of using the open doorway, one of the man-eaters, a female, clawed her way through the grass wall and stepped on the man lying next to it to get at the second man whom she killed and carried off. The man she had stepped on had woken up and thrown his arms round her neck, but had let go in a hurry when the answer he got was a growl. His yells woke the camp.

Flashing his torch Nicholson saw the two lions with the man's body just outside his tent. They bounded off into long grass, taking the corpse with them. Nicholson with his gun-bearer followed the drag mark with the aid of the torch, came upon the lions feeding a little distance away and shot them both.

There are several other cases on record of man-eaters making remarkably persistent attempts to take a particular individual. The only reason I can suggest for this behaviour is that the lion is attracted by the individual's smell. I personally doubt if taste has anything to do with it because a lion when feeding tears off great chunks of flesh which it swallows whole. It may be some comfort to white men when they camp in lion country that, apart from one or two isolated cases of Europeans being eaten in Kenya, the man-eating lion has so far confined its attention to Africans.

One of the worst man-eaters I had to deal with was a so-called devil lion. It had begun, as far as I could make out, as a *simba malaika,* a sort of guardian angel lion. This is usually a powerful male which has mating fights with other males—the local villagers think he is driving off the man-eaters and protecting them. He also keeps the pigs down and thus does the village a deal of good. But in this case the *simba malaika* had become too old to catch pig. After doubtless a lean time, during which he had survived probably by digging for mice and stalking birds, he had become hungry enough to risk taking a man and suddenly realised that here at last was the answer to his food problem—the slowest, thinnest skinned, most vulnerable and plentiful prey to be found. Having lived for years in the vicinity of people, he knew all about their habits. The game scouts sent to deal with him had made a hash of several attempts, and after that he had become a nightmare. He would make a kill and feed, then instead of lying up in the usual way he would travel perhaps twenty miles. I hunted him off and on for many months while he ate more than ninety people within an area of some 2,500 square miles.

In the end it was decided to placate a certain wizard who was believed to be the lion's master. A fee was paid and doubtless some mumbo jumbo was recited. I certainly do not subscribe to any belief in the paranormal or wish to encourage credulity, but the odd thing is that a few days later a young man of nineteen saw a lion in some bushes near his village. He shot it with a muzzle-loader, and mysteriously the killings stopped. Had the wizard dispensed with his slave, or was it a coincidence that the lion shot by the young man was the man-eater? I for one would not like to hazard an answer.

What I disliked about the whole business, apart from the frustrations mentioned, was having to take shots which would have been altogether inexcusable in ordinary regulated hunting. I refer to firing when one is not absolutely certain of delivering a fatal blow. I am not yet convinced that doubtful shots are justified even in the case of a man-eater, but I took the view that it would not have been right to pass up any opportunity given me of ridding the community of a danger, although it was possibly contravening the ethics of hunting. In addition to this consideration is the harm that chance shooting often creates.

Though in my experience it is easy enough to kill a lion with a well placed bullet, a wounded lion, drawing upon enormous reserves of resistance, can take an astonishing amount of punishment and still come on. There was a magnificent male on the Public Enemy list which I was summoned by drum call to deal with. He had killed and left a girl of seventeen outside a hut, and one of my scouts had waited in the hut, hoping to shoot the lion when it returned to the kill. Instead, the lion had nearly got the scout. It had tried to climb into the hut under the eaves, the structure had collapsed and the man had spent the rest of the night buried under a pile of mud, sticks and thatch.

The spoor took me to some youngish grass and bushes between two thickets. Suddenly the man-eater stood up just ahead and bounded off. I managed to get a shot just before he disappeared, wounding him in the side.

Before going on I think it would be a help if I mentioned a few important points on the follow up of a wounded animal. I personally found it necessary to rest or pause from time to time in order to maintain my maximum concentration. You are afraid, of course. You go in following his tracks, perhaps a blood spoor, knowing he is not far ahead and wondering how badly he has been hit. You begin the right way, making good use of every scrap of cover, every bush, every tree. A bird getting up makes you start, your hair stands on end and you break out in a sweat. But if you are not careful you soon wake up to find yourself behaving in a most casual manner. The reason for this is nervous exhaustion; you are not getting braver; it is just that your nerves have become too tired to keep you alert. It is therefore necessary to use every opportunity to rest.

You must frequently stop and sit down, and while resting listen carefully. If it is a lion you may hear a bird chattering at him. If it is a buffalo it will have been circling and zig-zagging to throw you off its track. During this deployment the hunter may pass very near where it is lying up, and if he listens carefully he may hear the animal breathing. A wounded lion is more likely to charge than a wounded buffalo, but if you have been on the latter's tracks long enough to make him desperate he will in the end charge, possibly from behind. You need all your alertness and concentration because it may come any moment, and in the case of a buffalo there may be a pile of undergrowth caught on its horns like a great bush being hurled at you and it is difficult to know just where to place your shot.

Fear is nature's gift to enable us to safeguard ourselves. But of course the moment the animal chases you lose all sense of fear or nervousness. You have too much to do at the time. The reaction comes later, if you have had a bad turn; you have been strung up and now it is all over. You feel very tired. You may even feel a great repentance for having killed the animal. You may then throw all caution to the winds and do something quite ridiculous, like the Afrikaans hunter I knew who, instead of making sure a wounded lioness he had shot was really dead, walked up to where the tail was sticking out of a bush and pulled it. The lioness was not dead and he went to hospital for the next six weeks.

As I said, it takes a lot to kill a wounded animal, but to continue with my man-eater. The follow up was through particularly dense thorn bush and creeper in which it would have been difficult to handle a rifle in an emergency. The essence of correct hunting is not to permit yourself to get into a situation over which you have no control, but we all do it. A wounded lion usually charges when followed, so I was intensely relieved when I came out into a glade where I could see for a good sixty yards.

Suddenly there was a grunt, the bushes just opposite parted and next thing the lion was coming at me, very smoothly and very fast, a tawny mane sticking out round a set of large teeth getting larger. Usually I prefer to sit or kneel, to get on the same level as the target, and it was best to aim for the chest; the head is always a tricky shot, but here, on account of some intervening scrub, it was Hobson's choice. I had to wait till the animal was clear of it, which meant he was very near when I fired my first barrel. I was using a .470 with, as was my practice in those days when hunting lion, a soft nosed bullet. That bullet glanced off the cheek bone into the chest, and he came on without the slightest sign of being touched.

By the time I was ready with my second barrel he was up to a slender sapling, measured later at eight paces from where I stood. He swung round it. Then he fell over, presumably from the effects of the bullet. He was up again though, almost immediately, and it was in his final rush, when I was practically looking down his throat that I fired the second shot. He dropped close to my feet. After that experience I changed to hard-nosed bullets for lion.

When following lion in undergrowth I have on occasions observed that my quarry has gone round in a complete circle on his tracks, so that he has wound up actually following me. I do not think that in such circumstances there is any immediate need to worry. Normally when you are hunting an animal he is not likely to be simultaneously hunting you, though he may be keeping an eye on your movements. The danger is when you give up the hunt. If you have left it late for your return home he might then turn the tables on you. This actually happened to Bill Harvey with one of the worst man-eaters I have yet heard of in our part of the country.

The circumstances are as follows. Harvey was out after this man-eater, which had been terrorising much of Masasi district for some time. Being a particularly bold animal it had acquired a sinister reputation with all the usual overtures of magic and witchcraft which multiplied the effect.

That day Harvey had spent the afternoon spooring it through an area of scrub, till his tracker noticed they had gone round in a complete circle. They were back on their own tracks with a second set of the lion's spoor superimposed upon theirs. It was now 5:30, and as they were a good two hours journey from camp, Harvey immediately called off the hunt and they started heading back. By 6:30 it was nearly dark, and by 7 it was pitch black, a clouded, moonless night without, it seemed to Harvey, any vestige of light.

However Africans as a rule possess wonderful night vision, and he was able to make his way by staying close behind the man immediately in front of him in a single file of five consisting of a local guide, the tracker carrying a shotgun—(Harvey was a very fine ornithologist and was making a collection of the birds of Tanganyika), then Harvey, then an armed game scout, and finally Harvey's gun-bearer carrying his heavy rifle.

It was from Harvey himself that I got this account. He told me they had got fairly near the camp, which was at a village. A little distance from the village the country there is cut across by a deep gully. Harvey said that as they went down into this gully he suddenly heard a scuffle, followed by a shot.

'What is it?' he called, and the game scout behind him replied that the lion had taken the tracker and he had fired at it.

Harvey recovered the shotgun which had been dropped. He went back up the path down which they had entered the gully. At the top the heard a sound ahead of him, and, bending down so as to get a silhouette against the skyline, saw what he thought looked like the crouching figure of a lion. He immediately fired, and there was a roar as the animal bounded away. Then, going on a few paces, Harvey found the tracker dead.

The party were then deliberating as to what they should do about the corpse, when the lion suddenly came back, and made off with it, Harvey being unable to shoot as they had no light of any kind. Then, since the tracker was dead and in any case there was nothing further he could do that night, Harvey decided they should carry on back to camp. Next day all they found were a few cracked bones of the victim.

That lion, after continuing its man-eating career for several more weeks over a very wide area, completely lost all fear of humans. In broad daylight it would attack a village and take and eat its victim in the open just outside. In the end, I believe two game scouts decided upon drastic indirect action. They got hold of a wizard, who was credited with being in control of the lion, and beat up the man till he agreed to call it off. There followed the usual type of ceremony, and various incantations were uttered, after which the game scouts, fortified with this counter-magic, went out to brave the lion sitting on a hill in a patch of open bush.

The game scouts were supported by a mob with knives and spears. The lion merely got up, charged and took one of the mob. It was finally killed on the next sortee by one of the game scouts, who went back alone and shot it. That should have closed the case, but as it happened the wizard was thought to have failed in his magic because of the casualty from among the mob, and the man was so persecuted he finally went out and hanged himself.

I, too, lost one of my best men to a man-eater. He was none other than Hemedi Ngoe, my companion on many a hunt. The trouble with Hemedi was his excessive fondness for women. He had eight wives, yet on one occasion when we got to a village called Tunduru on a search for a very dangerous and elusive man-eater he spotted some sloe-eyed local beauty and decided he wanted her too.

I was very annoyed when he came to me asking for leave to take the female back to Liwale, which by then had become my headquarters and, therefore, the place where he lived.

'All right,' I said. 'You realise you are putting me to great inconvenience, but if you must go, go. When you have completed all your arrangements for your new bride, come out and join me wherever I happen to be.'

The next I heard of Hemedi was that he had been eaten by the very lion I was hunting.

Apparently he and his wife had made their way towards Liwale, and the second day had arrived at a village where they intended to spend the night. Unknown to them the lion had come along the identical path they had used, though it was not possible to tell from the spoor whether it was actually following them or merely travelling in the same direction. The inhabitants of this village had been living in terror of the lion. Theirs was a small place, just a few houses, and for safety at night they used to congregate in one large hut. Hemedi was warned of the danger, but being an obstinate man and quite fearless he refused to sleep in the communal hut. Instead the newly-weds slept on a string bed on the verandah. The night passed uneventfully.

Next morning Hemedi woke with a mild go of malaria, so he decided to stay a second night in the village, and again he and his young wife went to bed on the verandah. I subsequently went to the village and got the whole story of what happened from the people on the spot. It seems that about 10 p.m. those inside the hut heard a thud as of someone falling. They called out and the wife presently replied that her husband was not with her. 'He must have gone to urinate,' she said. She had been asleep and had heard nothing of the thud. The villagers however were not satisfied. Taking torches lit from the fire, they went out to investigate and found blood on the bed and on the ground. There was nothing more they could do, being unarmed, so they brought the woman inside the hut and made the door fast. A good thing too, because from what they were able to tell later the lion had been watching them from under a tree not fifteen yards away, with the body of Hemedi lying nearby in the grass. Next morning all that remained of my gun-bearer was his head.

However, after all the difficulty that lion had caused, his end came surprisingly quickly. Two days later he was seen on the carcass of an elephant that had been shot on control near the village. He was stalked by three game scouts who came up through long grass and shot him in a barrage of gunfire. I saw the skin afterwards. It was that of a young adult of about four years old, in prime condition, with a fine glossy coat and a good set of teeth. There appeared to be no good reason for his man-eating, except that he had got into bad habits. Hemedi was his forty-fifth recorded victim.

Part Four:
Croc!
The Crocodile
Dundee Won't Save You!

The Crocodile

"Consider the chief of the beasts, the crocodile
Who devours cattle as if they were grass.
What strength is in his loins.
What power in the muscles of his belly.
His tail is rigid as a cedar,
The sinews of his flanks are closely knit.
His bones are like tubes of bronze.
And his limbs like bars of iron.
He is the chief of God's works,
Made to be a tyrant over his peers,
For he takes the animals of the hills for his prey
And in his jaws he crushes all wild beasts.
There under the lotus plants he lies
Hidden in the reeds and the marsh
The lotus flower conceals him in its shadow . . ."

—The Book of Job, Old Testament

12   Fatal Encounters

BY HUGH EDWARDS

There are statistics available on crocodile attacks on humans in Australia. One set, compiled from official records, states that there have been some 60 attacks, with 27 deaths, since 1876. This makes an interesting comparison with the list of 185 shark attacks, and 93 fatalities—or it would if either list were accurate.

Unfortunately the documentation of both shark and crocodile attacks through the years has been so haphazard that the figures are almost meaningless.

Officially there are supposed to have been only two crocodile-caused deaths in Western Australia. Paul Flanagan at Wyndham in 1980 and Ginger Meadows at the Prince Regent in 1987. But I know of at least three others and there are certainly more than that still undocumented.

One of the pathetic unrecorded stories I found accidentally in the graveyard of the abandoned Benedictine mission at Pago, on Vansittart Bay near Kalumburu in the Kimberleys.

A large stone cross stood in a corner of the cemetery overgrown by shrubs and creepers. The legend on the face of the cross was spelled out clearly in brass lettering, in marked contrast to the graves of forgotten monks and brothers who had died in the work of the Lord, far, far from their native Europe. These last resting places were indicated only by uninscribed boulders of local stone. The graves themselves were so overgrown by jungle that they were hardly recognisable.

I was told that the Navy had built the cross, and in Royal Australian Navy tradition the materials used were designed to last forever. The grave contained the incomplete remains of Gunner H. Davies, Royal Australian Navy, who had come to Vansittart Bay in HMAS *Geranium* in September 1920.

Poor Gunner Davies was in high spirits when *Geranium* dropped her anchors with a splash and a rattle of chain out in the bay. When the ship reached Fremantle he was going to be married. His fiancée was already on the high seas, sailing on a passenger liner to meet him there.

Boats were lowered over the side and officers and men were allowed ashore for rest and relaxation. Some took fishing lines, others books. Gunner Davies, in an adventurous mood, set out to explore the surrounding country.

By nightfall he was lost.

In his eagerness to examine the new land he had not taken sufficient care to remember the way he had come. The rugged Kimberley country is treacherously deceptive. Even bushmen are careful to keep landmarks in sight, and it is all too easy for the inexperienced to lose their way.

Davies panicked. Began to run.

But as darkness set in there was still no sign of anything familiar. He spent a wretched night, and in the morning began walking again. By the end of the day he was suffering tortures from thirst, and his boots had worn through so that as he dragged his weary feet the marks of his blistered and blood-stained toes showed clearly through the patches of sand.

A creek barred his way at a place the Aborigines called Njana. For a moment he was overjoyed. It must lead to the sea. At last he thought he had his bearings. The ship would not be far away. What a relief! Grateful for the coolness of the water he began to swim. As he neared the far bank the crocodile surged forward. There was a flash of jaws and a swirl . . .

The diary kept at Kalumburu Mission records the sad progress of events. "On 28 September 1920 the distressed captain of the HMAS *Geranium*, Lieutenant Commander W.M. Vaughan Lewish, called for assistance. The officers and crew of his ship had gone ashore in Vansittart Bay for relaxation and in the evening one had failed to return. Could the missionaries—or rather the Aborigine trackers of the mission—help to find the missing man?"

The remarkable tracking skills of the tribal Aborigines pieced the story together as one scrap of evidence after another was found. They discovered the tracks and saw the pitiful evidence of the worn boots and the dragging footmarks. They found that the tracks went down into the creek but they did not reappear on the other side.

On 9 October there was an ominous entry. "M-yuron and Puntji arrived with the belt of the missing man. At Njana Matjeri had found one leg."

15 October: "We came with the mission lugger *Voladora* in front of Njana where Matjeri and Maramen were waiting for us with the body, minus head, arms and one foot." They said they had found the skull and arms. But they had been buried in sand and could not be found again.

16 October: "We buried the remains in the mission at Pago."

Captain Vaughan Lewish called again several times in HMAS *Geranium* and eventually brought the stone cross which was carried ashore and erected with a service by Davies' shipmates. It still stands in the corner of the now-abandoned graveyard.

It was a story of life brought abruptly to a halt, of a wedding which never took place. That was the end of it all for Gunner H. Davies, 67 years ago. Now all that is left is the cross over his grave.

Two other fatalities which are not recorded on official lists involved the superintendent of a mission, taken in Walcott Inlet, north of Derby, and a young policeman lost at Derby in the 1890s. The policeman was fond of fishing. He liked to sit on a lower landing on the town wharf and dangle a line, unaware, like Val Plumwood, that crocodiles could jump.

He went regularly to the same spot and sometimes the enormous tides that rise and fall 25 feet at Wyndham came very close to the landing. One day he did not return from fishing. When a large crocodile was caught some time later, his uniform buttons were found in its stomach.

One of the problems in recording crocodile attacks is to know that they happened at all. Witnesses almost always say the same thing. "It happened so quickly . . . there was just a great swirl of water . . . No scream. Not a sound . . ."

This is in cases where there are witnesses. Where someone sees the crocodile take the victim.

In other instances where people are missing in crocodile areas portions of the torn body are occasionally found, or sometimes remains are recovered from inside a caught crocodile.

But in many cases of disappearance people are simply presumed drowned. At Wyndham, in 1987, not long before we called through in the vessel *Kimberley Explorer,* three Aboriginal men had tried to cross crocodile-infested Cambridge Gulf in an overloaded dinghy on their way back to the Kalumburu district.

Some time later the overturned craft drifted ashore on the far side of the gulf. Two bodies were found—one minus a foot. But no trace was ever found of the third man.

Aborigines were convinced that he had been taken by a crocodile, but there was no proof and the Coroner's verdict was death by drowning.

In another instance at Wyndham, a British refrigeration engineer, John Thompson, disappeared from a freighter tied up at the wharf in 1948. The nearby meatworks was discharging blood and offal into the gulf, and in the red waters of the 'drain' at the mouth of the discharge pipe there was the greatest congregation of saltwater crocodiles to be seen in Australia at that time.

Because of the huge tides at Wyndham, ramps moving with the rise and fall were used for access from ships to the jetty. On the night Thompson disappeared, after a few drinks, a temporary ramp without rails was in place. He had evidently walked straight over the edge in the darkness and no one heard his cry as he splashed down into the black Gulf waters.

"They searched for him for a week and never found a body," Tex Boneham, a crocodile shooter, recalls. "Then I caught this real big fellow of a croc. He must have been 18 feet long. Inside him was a gold signet ring with the initials J.T. on it. The ring was sent to Britain and it turned out that John Thompson had been wearing it on the night he died."

Did Thompson drown? Or was he taken by the crocodile as he struggled in the tidal water?

In the absence of any evidence the Coroner decided that death was by drowning. But the question about whether he was taken by a crocodile remains open. It seems most likely that he was, for the reason that crocodiles like to kill their own prey. Once they have done so they will revisit a 'stored' carcass again and again, and they will also attack prey killed by other crocodiles. But it is a curious fact that the bodies of humans who drown in crocodile waters (like the two Aborigines from the Wyndham dinghy accident) are usually recovered.

One of the ironies of the Beryl Wruck case in the Daintree in North Queensland was missed by the press in the drama following her crocodile attack. On the day after she was taken, an Aborigine, Ned Fisher, suffered a fatal heart attack while rowing his dinghy. He fell overboard and his body drifted up and down the Daintree with the tide for a day and a half before he was found. Despite the concentration of crocodiles in the area and Beryl's tragic death— which might have been thought to stir the crocodiles in the way that sharks become excited—no crocodile touched Ned Fisher.

There must have been many instances through Australian history in the north of Australia where people on their own in lonely places succumbed to crocodile attack without anyone ever knowing what happened to them. Val Plumwood would have been one if she had not survived to tell the story.

But even if the toll ran into two or even three hundred victims, it is still insignificant compared with the annual road toll. In 1987 three people were officially killed by crocodiles in Australia; 2,572 died in road accidents; 23,000 had their lives terminated by smoking-related diseases. The road casualty list on any one weekend exceeded the total number of known crocodile deaths for the past 10 years.

As crocodile numbers continue to rise in the north, and more and more tourists flock to the Kimberleys, there must necessarily be more crocodile-human contact. It seems logical to expect more attacks in the future, though theoretically increased public awareness as a result of publicity from attacks like those of 1987 should induce more public caution.

But there will probably still be the occasional tragedy, like the one which befell Kerry McLoughlin at Cahill's Crossing on the East Alligator River, Kakadu, in March 1987.

McLoughlin was a 40-year-old storeman who worked at Jabiru. He had been in the Territory 20 years or more and knew the East Alligator well. Perhaps too well. Familiarity created the unlucky situation which led to his death.

To understand what happened it is necessary to have a mental picture of the location.

Cahill's Crossing—named after the old King of the Territory buffalo shooters, Paddy Cahill—traverses the East Alligator river bed at the Oenpelli side and Aboriginal Arnhem Land.

It is a concrete driveway set over big, rounded river boulders and used at low water. At high tide it is flooded. The actual crossing is about 150 metres long and is comparatively narrow—14 feet wide, or not much more than the width of a truck. At low tide, when it is exposed, it is plain to see. But when the tide rises above the level of the crossing it becomes invisible under the muddy waters. The concrete also becomes dangerously slippery. There are crocodile warning signs at each end, and these used to raise a smile from knowledgeable locals.

McLoughlin had gone to the crossing with his 17-year-old son on 17 March 1987 to go fishing. The crossing was a favourite fishing platform with local fishermen. The prized fish was barramundi—the fish everyone in the north wants to bring home—and a good time to catch them was on the rising tide when the water began to swirl back over the crossing from the sea. At weekends there would be a row of waving fiberglass rods as anglers cast their lines and wound in their reels hoping to hook into a fine fat 'barra.'

There were also crocodiles. They had a habit of congregating downstream from the crossing at low tide. On the rising tide some of them cruised up river.

Local fishermen knew about the crocodiles. They kept an eye on them but did not regard them as a problem. Tourists were sometimes alarmed by the sight of the crocodile visible only a little way downstream from rod fishermen up to their knees in water. The anglers thought this a bit of a joke.

The locals would laugh when concerned tourists shouted warnings. "We know all these crocs by their first names," they would reply.

On 17 March 1987, a crocodile came who was a stranger. A big animal more than 16 feet long. McLoughlin was unaware that it was a newcomer. He was regarded as a typical tough Territorian. A man who would dive to unsnag a barramundi lure from a sunken branch without a second thought, and who regarded crocodiles with a confident grin. He was also a friendly soul and when he saw the big crocodile passing upstream he told some visiting American tourists about it. He knew they would like to photograph the large reptile.

When he saw some friends across the river he had what turned out to be a fatal impulse. He waded over to say 'g'day' with his fishing rod in one hand and a stubby of beer in the other. It was a normal enough thing to do, except that maybe he had left it a little late.

Once on the Oenpelli side, McLoughlin did not stay a long time, and he did not have a lot to drink. They pointed out to him what he already knew—that the tide was rising fairly rapidly over the crossing.

So with a few parting cheery remarks he began wading back again. As he reached the centre of the crossing he found that the tide was higher and was running more strongly than he had thought. But at that point he saw it as an inconvenience rather than a danger.

Then—with a curse—he missed his footing and slipped over the edge of the concrete roadway. Now he was in a different situation. He was stumbling amongst the big rounded river boulders, difficult to walk through even at low tide. With the tide now swirling between waist and chest deep (the concrete was raised half a metre above the ordinary river-bed level), McLoughlin realised that he was in difficulties.

The tourists on the bank he was making for had started yelling. From his point of view it didn't help. He knew he had a problem, and he was furiously aware that he was making a spectacle of himself.

He tried hard to return to the crossing and regain his footing. But the surging tide pushed him farther away. There was nothing for it now but to head for the bank, wet and bedraggled. Bloody nuisance! What were all those idiots on the bank yelling about?

The group of elderly American tourists he had spoken to earlier on the bank saw McLoughlin in the water. Having no local knowledge they couldn't understand why he was there at all. They had photographed the crocodile and knew how big it was. They could not comprehend the lack of concern of the local fishermen who said, "The crocs are always there. Don't worry, mate. They're OK."

But for once, it wasn't OK. The big crocodile, who had been causing some disturbances—'humbugging' the Aborigines called it—with the smaller crocodiles below the crossing, was new to the East Alligator system. Rangers later believed that he had been driven out from somewhere else and was looking to establish himself in a new territory. He was in a cranky mood.

As McLoughlin struggled, waist-deep, toward the bank the large crocodile became alert, attracted by the splashing. It began to cruise upstream to investigate the source of the sound.

Now even the locals became concerned.

The tourists began to frantically throw sticks and stones at the crocodile. As the crocodile passed McLoughlin, people screamed and yelled. It went a little way past him, assessing the situation, then turned back purposefully towards him.

Now it became a race.

McLoughlin by this time had heard the shouts of "crocodile!" and understood the danger. As he splashed toward the bank, a man trying too hard and out of breath, it seemed to the horrified watchers to be a tragedy happening in slow motion.

"It was all so needless," said Everett Galbraith, a 63-year-old American tourist. "We saw the crocodile and yelled to the man to get out of the water. But he didn't."

In fact, McLoughlin was doing his best. But with his wet clothes, the current drag and the rough bottom, it was hard to make progress.

The crocodile submerged. In what some people saw as a final gesture of defiance—but which may also have been an intelligent attempt to distract his tormentor—the hunted man hurled his stubby of beer at the spot where the crocodile had gone down.

Then, probably knowing how hopeless it was, he tried again to reach the shore. To the huge relief of the watchers he actually reached the bank by some rocks ahead of the crocodile and some distance above the crossing. Gasping for breath he began to pull himself up and out of the water by a branch.

But just when it seemed he might be saved the crocodile leaped, bursting through the surface. The tourists, who had been throwing stones and branches, stopped and stood appalled as the huge jaws flashed and closed across McLoughlin's head and shoulders.

"There was a hard slap," Galbraith said. "Then there was nothing. It was all quite still."

With that first bite and roll the crocodile tore his head off and decapitated McLoughlin. Then it seized the twitching body in the bloodstained water and swam away upstream to be lost to view around the bend.

The watchers (who included McLoughlin's 17-year-old son Michael, frozen with a can of soft drink in his hand) stood numbed in horror.

"It was all so fast," Galbraith said. "And yet so slow. I could just visualise what was going to happen. I had a three-metre stick and tried to get to him. But he was too far away and it all happened so fast.

"Afterwards, after all the yelling and shouting, it went quite still. Just nothing, as people realised what had happened. It was bizarre."

The rangers at the nearby Kakadu National Parks and Wildlife were called at once and a boat was launched at a ramp just south of the crossing and sent out after the crocodile.

It was found in the mangroves a little distance upstream, still with McLoughlin's limp body clutched triumphantly in its jaws.

The rangers fired and scored a definite hit, the animal convulsed, dropped the body and disappeared.

"Unfortunately we were never able to tell whether we killed it or just wounded it," said ranger superintendent Clive Cook. "It was disappointing.

"Usually, if they're wounded they go up on the bank and stay out of the water. If they're dead they float after four or five days. This one was different. We kept boat patrols out, but we never saw him again.

"You couldn't blame the crocodile. But we felt it was necessary to preempt local vigilante groups taking the law into their own hands as happened in Queensland. It wasn't a crocodile that had been seen in the area before, and if it survived it hasn't been seen since.

"Our main role in Kakadu," he said, "is to manage the people. The crocodiles look after themselves quite well. McLoughlin was a local. He'd been in the area a long time and had become accustomed to a prior situation where crocodiles were comparatively rare and there wasn't the kind of danger we have today.

"He was unfortunate. He was caught by a number of related minor things which went wrong and suddenly found himself in a situation he hadn't expected. Also he was obviously very, very unlucky that there was a big crocodile strange to the area which was hungry at that moment. Most times he would have got away with it."

Queensland has had the most recorded crocodile attacks on humans in Australia. This is not because it has the most crocodiles, but because there were more people in crocodile areas in the past, resulting in more interaction than in the Northern Territory or Western Australia.

The Beryl Wruck tragedy occupied national headlines at Christmas 1985, and in the early part of 1986. In February, eight weeks after her death, there were new headlines.

An attractive woman fisherman had been taken at the Staaten River in Queensland's Gulf Country.

It was another story of bad luck. Kate McQuarrie, a 31-year-old first hand on the barramundi fishing boat *Kiama,* had gone up the river in a dinghy with the skipper Bob McNeil to set barramundi nets.

The outboard motor refused to start for the return trip. They were forced to walk 15 kilometres along the river bank in steamy, hot conditions, back to where the *Kiama* lay at anchor. Then they had to swim out to the boat. They were aware of crocodiles—what barramundi fisherman wasn't? But they had no choice. Exhausted after the walk, lathered in sweat, there was no other way to reach the boat. The choice was to stay with the sandflies on the river bank or to swim out to the boat which was also their home. A place where there was a shower to clean off the mud, food and a cool drink. A cool drink . . .

So they said, "Here goes . . ." and swam side by side, with steady strokes, until they reached the *Kiama*. There was no indication that anything was wrong. The side of the boat was steep and Kate was exhausted after the long walk and the swim. Bob McNeil swung himself up and over the rail and turned to help Kate on board.

To his horror he saw a huge crocodile head appear behind her. The jaws opened. "It just grabbed her in a second. There was a huge swirl and she was gone . . ."

He ran to the cabin to grab a rifle but in the few seconds it took him to find it and get back on deck Kate and the crocodile had disappeared. "It was a monster," McNeil told his base at Karumba, 150 kilometres away, by radio. "At least 5.5 metres long."

Police came from Karumba with heavy-calibre weapons to search for the crocodile and at dawn next day, a fisherman sighted the crocodile with Kate McQuarrie's mutilated body in Vaon Rook Creek, a tributary of the Staaten River.

A group including Bob McNeil trapped the crocodile, blocking off its escape with barramundi nets. McNeil shot the crocodile, which sank.

Kate McQuarrie's mutilated torso was recovered. But the fishermen were never able to secure the dead crocodile, though they waited for several days for the huge body to float.

Kate's heartbroken parents at their farm in Murwillumbah, in northern New South Wales, said that she had discussed the danger of crocodiles with them only a month before she was taken. "It must have been an absolute last resort for her to go into the water," her Scottish-born father Archie McQuarrie told reporters. "She told us she would never swim in any North Queensland creek or river for fear of crocodiles. She was afraid of them," he said.

If Kate McQuarrie was taken despite her fear, or premonition, of crocodile attack, Paul Flanagan was at the other end of the scale.

Flanagan, a 26-year-old truck driver from Midland in Western Australia, arrived at the northern port of Wyndham, driving a big truck rig on 24 November 1980.

Wyndham had the highest temperature in the State that day—a searing 41 degrees Celsius. Paul Flanagan and another truck driver arrived about 9:30 p.m. and parked their big trucks outside the hotel. Then they settled down to slake some of the enormous thirst they had generated on the hot and dusty road north.

At closing time they said they were going to roll out their swags on the beach to try to catch a cool breeze.

"Don't do it," the locals warned. "This is crocodile country."

Flanagan and his mate laughed. The more seriously the locals tried to dissuade them, the more determined they became.

Wyndham was famous for its meatworks and its crocodiles. The two went together. Cattle from the Kimberley hinterland were brought in to be slaughtered during the cool months, and the blood drained out into Cambridge gulf near the town wharf.

Where the blood reached the water at a point known as 'the drain', crocodiles lay row on row.

Killing had stopped at the meatworks for the hot weather period three weeks before Flanagan's arrival. But the crocodiles were still about and hungry because of the cessation of the blood which brought fish and birds as prey for them to catch.

A narrow belt of mangroves separated the beach on the Gulf, and the town dinghy ramp, from the town streets and the nearest backyards. Goats and dogs were sometimes taken by crocodiles in the mangroves. Wyndham people were always cautious using the dinghy ramp.

Flanagan and his mate took a carton of beer and their swags down to the ramp with some other drinks for some companions they had acquired. They were Aboriginal ladies who seemed happy to share a good time with the truck drivers celebrating reaching the end of the State's longest road haul— more than 2,000 kilometres from Perth.

Midnight came and went. In a spirit of bravado Flanagan announced that he was going for a swim "to cool off." The Aboriginal ladies begged him not to. That was all the extra encouragement he needed.

He splashed around happily, a beer in his hand, calling for the crocodiles to come and get him. Fortune sometimes favours the foolhardy. He staggered out of the water, dripping and triumphant, and exclaiming loudly that the Wyndham crocodiles were "all bullshit."

Half an hour later he went into the water again. This time, instead of splashing on the edge, he set off for a swim about 30 metres offshore.

"There's a croc behind you!" one of the women screamed, seeing a vee of ripples on the dark shining water. Flanagan took no notice. Perhaps he thought they were joking.

Suddenly there was a huge swirl, familiar in most descriptions of crocodile attacks. Flanagan disappeared without a sound—no scream or shout. Not even a splash.

Constable Kevin Doy and Constable A. Mettam at the Wyndham Police Station, only a short distance from the landing, received an incoherent call from Flanagan's new friends at 1:20 a.m., and they and the district wildlife officer set off at once in a Fisheries Department launch to search the area.

Two hours later, at first light, they found Flanagan's body 800 metres from where he was attacked, dragged up on a mud bank. Two crocodiles lay beside it, one on each side.

The bigger crocodile, which was nearly four metres, was shot so that the body could be recovered, and the smaller one—not much more than two metres—slithered away and escaped.

The dead crocodile was well known to Aborigines in Wyndham. It had an injured leg, giving it a limping gait on land and a distinctive track. It had taken a dog in the mangroves not long before.

Another attack where alcohol impaired judgement occurred at the remote Northern Territory Gulf town of Borroloola, on 9 September 1986.

Rusty Wherrett (39), of Mareeba, Queensland, who had been working locally on fencing contracts, had been on a Saturday night drinking spree with his mate Dennis Vowken. They were accustomed to moving around. Police said Wherrett travelled under at least four different names and in all news reports he was referred to as "Lee McLeod." The two decided to sleep out in the open. "Starlight Hotel," the old swagmen called sleeping under the stars. The spot they chose was 500 metres from the pub on the river bank at the Rocky Creek landing, a popular fishing spot near the town, on the McArthur River. Before turning in they had a few more drinks.

When the mate woke on the bank next morning—considerably the worse for wear after the night's heavy drinking—Wherrett was nowhere to be seen. His shirt was still there. But there was no sign of Wherrett. Feeling hung-over, disoriented and reluctant to approach the police, Vowken did nothing for the best part of Sunday. He said later he thought Wherrett might have "gone for a walk."

But by nightfall he reluctantly reported Wherrett missing. Constables Rex Grass and Mal Jensen began a search believing him drowned. But they changed their minds when they made the grisly discovery of two severed human legs 100 yards upstream from the boat ramp.

Inspector Maurie Burke, of the Northern Territory Police, later described the body search in a graphic article in the *Australian Police Journal*, edited by Phil Peters.

The dismembered legs immediately identified a crocodile attack and the prime suspect was a large local crocodile called 'Gus' who had taken up territory in that part of the river.

Wildlife officers who went out in a boat to search for Gus located him in an unusual way.

"It was highly likely that he was the culprit," Inspector Burke wrote. "And this was partially confirmed by the particularly putrid stench from his breath. Whilst patrolling for him the officers, whether they could see him or not, were aware of his presence by the stench of his breath.

"Even submerged the bubbles expelled were putrid enough to cause near-vomiting by officers if they were caught unaware leaning from the boat and having the bubbles burst in their faces.

"It appears that this is peculiar to the crocodile, especially if it has taken a human. Apparently the contents of a croc's stomach virtually ferment in a cocktail of powerful gastric juices and acids, giving rise to the crocodile's particularly foetid breath."

The officers from the Northern Territory Conservation Commission Bryan Walsh, Phil Hauser, Bill Binns and Ross Bryam, harpooned and finally shot Gus on the Thursday night, five days after the attack.

An examination of his stomach contents proved that Gus was indeed the killer. He was a large crocodile. The end of his tail had earlier been bitten off either by a shark or in territorial conflict. But his estimated normal length was 16 feet (5.1 metres).

The remains of the unfortunate victim were found inside the crocodile. Inspector Burke reported: "The digestive juices had already reduced bone matter to the consistency of rubbery gristle, flesh to a jelly-like substance and skin bleached and rubbery in texture.

"From the bruising sustained to the hands and arms it was evident that McLeod/Wherrett was alive when taken. It would appear that he was taken from behind, crushed through the middle by the immense power of the jaws. Whilst struggling to escape his arms and hands were lacerated and punctured by the crocodile's teeth.

"He was carried upstream for 100 metres before the final 'death-roll' and flailing of the now-lifeless body severed the arms and legs, one of the legs being flicked high onto the river bank."

The pelvic bone was rendered vertically through. "The awesome power of the crocodile being evident in the fact that it was the flailing action which literally tore the arms and legs from the torso."

Identification was made by police forensic specialists. Senior Constable Dave Prowse of the Territory Police took skin tissue sloughed off in the stomach. This was washed, dried and dusted with black powder. When the powder was wiped off with methylated spirits the residue in the ridges of the skin showed the whorls and lines. Constable Prowse was able to place a thumbprint under a microscope. It matched perfectly police records for 'McLeod' (one of Wherrett's aliases) supplied from Queensland, and completed one of the most bizarre and unusual identifications in Australian police records.

Ironically, crocodile warning signs had been placed at the landing only days before Wherrett and Vowken arrived there on that fatal Saturday night.

The luckiest man in Borroloola was a local who five months earlier had attempted to cross the river carrying a carton of beer. The crocodile grabbed him and then 'spat him out.' He was taken to Darwin for treatment for bruising and a severely lacerated right arm and shoulder. He also lost the carton of beer!

Inspector Burke's final summing up was: "It was a little sad that that chance meeting of man and beast resulted in a horrific exodus from this world by Wherrett and the final destruction of one of nature's relics of prehistoric times.

"Had Wherrett's judgement not been clouded by alcohol there would have been no cause to write this account."

There was a theory, for a time, that crocodiles did not attack divers. It was dispelled when Trevor Gaghan, a 28-year-old skin-diving enthusiast on holidays from Melbourne, went diving at Nhulunbuy, a mining settlement on the Gove Peninsula in the Northern Territory. With a Nhulunbuy friend Max Cumming, on 8 October 1979 he went to a spot called Rainbow Cliffs to dive for crayfish. While the two men were out in the water, Trevor's wife Christine sunned herself on the beach.

She watched their fins going up in the air and the disappearing underwater as they searched under rocks and ledges for crayfish. The hunt for the tropical 'painted' crays seemed to be going well.

Suddenly, there was a scream. Christine Gaghan looked up and was horrified to see that a large crocodile had appeared and seized her husband by his arm.

He shouted desperately for help but was dragged under in a boil of water. Christine, incoherent with shock, drove into Nhulunbuy to call the police. But when they returned to the Rainbow Cliffs with a four-wheel-drive vehicle, there was no sign of the crocodile or the diver.

"That night we used searchlights to go up into the creek," Constable Dave Benson said. "Soon after, Trevor Gaghan's body surfaced faced down in the middle. He had a broken arm and had been bitten and badly bruised across the torso. But the thick wetsuit protected him from the teeth to an extent."

However, the wetsuit did not save his life.

Wildlife officers flew from Darwin. The body and the crocodile were located in a small creek about a kilometre away from the scene of the attack.

Rangers waited for the crocodile and eventually harpooned and shot the 3.5-metre animal responsible.

The carcass was put on show in the main park and in the school at Nhulunbuy.

"This was done to quieten local residents who were talking wildly about shooting all crocodiles in the area," Constable Benson said. "After the Rainbow Cliffs killing, people were talking about shooting them willy-nilly. We didn't want to see a lot of people running about recklessly with high-powered weapons."

Several days later Christine Gaghan, who had witnessed her husband's tragic death, was still being treated for shock in Nhulunbuy hospital.

Wildlife officers said that it was unlikely that Trevor Gaghan's bag of crayfish had attracted the crocodile. It had established a territory in the nearby creek. It dominated the area and it would have been attracted by any activity in the water.

In February of the following year another visitor to Nhulunbuy disappeared in mysterious circumstances while swimming in a local waterhole. On 1 July 1980 there was a confirmed fatality when a 30-year-old Aboriginal woman, Bukarra Number One Munyarrwun of Nhulunbuy outstation, was taken near where the Cato River joins Arnhem Bay, a place where there is an old wartime airstrip near the river.

She was a mother of two children living in a tribal situation, subsisting largely on bush tucker. She had been fishing waist-deep in the billabong of the isolated Dhalinbuy settlement, 50 kilometres from Nhulunbuy. Friends heard her scream and saw a crocodile, which they estimated to be five metres long, seize her and drag her under the surface of the billabong.

Police were called by radio and came bumping by four-wheel-drive down the dusty track from Nhulunbuy. Later Bukarra's torso, minus the severed lower half of her body, was found 500 metres away by Police Sergeant Bob Haydon. Her pitiful remains were taken to the mortuary of Nhulunbuy hospital with all the possessions she had—a shredded remnant of a cotton dress.

The Aborigines of her tribe said that all of them, Bukarra included, had known that the big crocodile was there. They called him 'Baru' and he was a religious totem, a 'grandfather,' not only of their tribe but also eight other Aboriginal areas nearby.

Police and Northern Territory wildlife officers had intended to shoot the crocodile after Bukarra's death. Sergeant Haydon believed that the crocodile Baru had also been responsible for the disappearance of an old man and a boy near the settlement in previous months.

Tribal elders had at first agreed reluctantly that the crocodile could be shot. But then they changed their minds and vehemently shook their heads. Baru must not be harmed.

"Out there it is sometimes difficult to know what happens," Sergeant Haydon told a reporter from the Perth *Sunday Independent* newspaper when he was questioned about the missing people.

"The billabong is that crocodile's territory and he will stay around. But they told us that he's their religious totem. So that's it. Now he's safe."

The Aborigines' own answer was a series of 'sorry' ceremonies. Corroborees to appease Bukarra's spirit, and to persuade the crocodile, as an ancestor spirit from The Dreaming, not to attack again. The ceremonies went on for a fortnight after the death. Then what was left of Bukarra was flown back from Nhulunbuy for burial by the settlement with further mournful corroborees.

With five possible crocodile-caused deaths in the area, two of them confirmed and all of them occurring within 12 months of each other, it was natural that people in the mining town of Nhulunbuy became alarmed. With a population of 4,500 people, including 1700 children, they had reason to be concerned. A number of townsfolk called for an end to the protection of 'sacred' crocodiles.

"Who will be the next victim?" the town newspaper queried in an article which demanded a 16-kilometre 'crocodile-free zone' around the town.

But as years went by the people of Nhulunbuy learned to live with crocodiles.

Perhaps the ceremonies of Bukarra's people were effective after all. In the 17 years since, there has not been another crocodile attack in the area.

The list of northern crocodile victims goes on.

In April 1975, Peter Reimer, aged 32, a plant operator for Comalco in Weipa, North Queensland, and formerly of Perth, was killed by an enormous crocodile in water that was little more than knee deep.

He had been on a hunting and fishing trip with two friends. After a pig hunt he had gone to cool off in a lagoon in the Mission River, in the Gulf country, 32 kilometres east of Weipa.

His two friends, Rodney Kirby and Douglas Goelener, both Comalco aluminum plant operators in Weipa, had decided to go fishing when they arrived at the river about 3 o'clock on a Friday afternoon. Reimer went off on his own pig shooting.

When he had not returned to camp with the vehicle by nightfall they became worried. They searched until they found their vehicle parked by a swamp not far from camp but there was still no sign of Reimer.

They spent all night lighting fires and firing shots in the belief that he was lost. But soon after daylight on the Saturday they found Reimer's hat, belt, rifle, watch, ammunition and clothing near a tree on the bank of the lagoon, and saw the ominous signs. Reimer's footprints led down to the water and nearby was the track of a huge crocodile.

Thoroughly alarmed by now, they called the Weipa police. "We saw the marks where the crocodile slid down the bank to get him," Sergeant Ron Rooks said. "The water was only 45 centimetres deep."

The police, Kirby and Goelener took up vantage points around the lagoon and sighted bubbles coming up to the surface where the crocodile was submerged. They blew it to the surface with a charge of gelignite and shot it while it was stunned.

When they dragged it ashore they found Reimer's body inside the crocodile which had swallowed him whole. It was an enormous beast—19 feet in length.

It was the largest crocodile of any involved in the fatal attacks. Most of the man-killers that were measured were over 11 feet 6 inches (3.5 metres) and most were in the 13 feet to 16 feet-plus (4 to 5 metres) size range.

The victims were usually taken by surprise. One or two had time to scream. But most often the attack was swift and soundless, culminating in the swirl of water which was the last of the victim.

Though there were sometimes witnesses, the recorded attacks usually were completed so quickly that there was nothing which could have been done to help the victims.

One of the most remarkable escapes was that of Mrs. Platner Chudualla, a 54-year-old Aboriginal woman from Kalumburu Mission, in north-western Australia.

On 8 May 1976, she was at a fishing spot about eight kilometres from the mission when she was seized by the arm by a five-metre crocodile and dragged into deep water. The bite crushed her forearm and shattered the bones.

Then the crocodile changed its grip. Taking her by the right thigh it swam off, dragging her below the surface for more than 50 metres.

Then, as she was sure that she would die, the crocodile—astoundingly—let her go. Bleeding and terrified she swam back to the bank. Later she was flown to the Derby hospital where she recovered after a series of operations to rebuild her smashed forearm.

The final fatal attack for 1987 was at the tip of Cape York Peninsula. Torres Strait Islander Cornwall Mooka of Mabuiag Island left his dinghy to walk to Cornwall Creek on 27 June. Later, leg bones and clothing were washed up on the beach. A week later an 11-foot (3.3-metre) crocodile was shot by National Parks officers and human remains were found inside it.

In most cases the people taken by crocodiles were in the water when the attack took place. Exceptions to this were Val Plumwood, who was trying to climb a tree from water level, and Kerry McLoughlin, who had just dragged himself out of the water by a fallen tree at Cahill's Crossing on the East Alligator.

In all instances the unfortunate people killed were intruders in crocodile territory. But for every attack there must have been hundreds, perhaps thousands, of people who had been in a situation where they might have been attacked but who got away with it. Either there were no crocodiles at that point, or if there were they weren't hungry or weren't interested. The fact is that while some crocodiles, like sharks, attack humans, the majority do not. Statistically, those who became victims were desperately unlucky. The most remarkable thing is not how often crocodiles attack people but rather the reverse. It is surprising that with all the chances offered by humans, crocodiles attack so seldom. Nonetheless, for safety, it has to be assumed that any large crocodile may be attracted to human prey in certain circumstances.

When the attacks do occur they earn a nationwide notoriety for crocodiles which often seems to be out of logical proportion to the actual threat. The death of American Ginger Meadows at the Prince Regent, in 1987, for instance, became an international incident.

The instinct to protect—looking after our own—is strong in the human race. It is a desirable trait and one reason why *Homo sapiens* is the most successful animal alive.

But it does make for a difficulty in our relationship with other animals. We tend to see things only from one side.

The dislike of crocodiles as a creature which can eat people is understandable. We sometimes take this to an extreme where the fear of a man-eating predator amounts to a national phobia, as it does in the case of sharks and crocodiles. Perhaps it goes back to the misty shadow memories of our ancestors. A time when "things which went bump in the night" were no joke, but deadly and life-threatening. A time when the red eyes of hungry predators glowed in the darkness beyond the protective fire at the mouth of the cave. A reason, also, why a log fire still makes us feel so cosy and safe.

Human survival in the face of so many natural enemies must have been desperate indeed. Today there are few creatures left which eat people and confrontations with terror are no longer a part of daily existence.

But when an attack does occur, as in the case of Ginger Meadows, it revives all those ancient horrors. Perhaps this is why we react so dramatically.

Our thinking on the subject is more emotional than logical. While crocodiles may have killed somewhere between 50 and 150 people in Australia in the past 100 years, the numbers are a pinprick compared with our decimation of the crocodile population. Some 113,000 skins were shipped out of the Northern Territory in the 1950s and '60s, with other consignments from Queensland and Western Australia.

Similarly we call sharks 'man-eaters' regardless of species, and every shark caught and killed by 'sportsmen' is a death justified on that account. But hundreds of thousands of sharks are caught off Australian coasts each year in nets and set-lines, most of them to be eaten by humans as fish and chips.

In any such comparison it is man who is the major predator. A killer so technically efficient, that we have pushed whole species of animals to extermination. And while crocodiles and sharks kill simply to eat, humans have killed large numbers of animals large and small for amusement. For 'sport.'

Both sharks and crocodiles are interesting creatures. If we regard them merely as objects of irrational horror, we are depriving ourselves of an understanding of animals which evolved to a balance in the environment long before we came on the scene.

As Val Plumwood put it, a crocodile is not a creature you could come to love. Only another crocodile of the opposite sex could do that—and they do it very well.

But our tendency is to look at animals simply in terms of their use to humans. 'Good' animals are dogs which protect and love us, cats which eat mice and purr affectionately, hens which lay eggs, cows which provide milk and meat. 'Bad' animals are foxes which eat the hens, wolves which eat the sheep. Particularly 'evil' animals are those which have the temerity to eat people.

Crocodiles may one day become 'useful' to us in an industrial sense. When they are raised in artificial situations in farms or crocodile ranches they can provide skins for a lucrative world market. They have the potential to be a major tourist attraction and tourism has rapidly become one of Australia's most important industries.

Though they will never make cuddly pets, and would always definitely be of doubtful value for giving rides at a children's party, crocodiles have their own unique qualities and they were, after all, around long before man.

At Gantheaume Point, at Broome, the pearling port of Western Australia, there are a set of three-toed dinosaur footprints indented in the red rock by the sea.

The creature which made them, an individual of the species *Megalosaurus,* had a two-metre stride and passed that way 70 million years ago when the rock was mud.

At that time there were crocodilians in the ocean and in the swamps. Today the dinosaur is long extinct and remembered only by the impressions left by its feet. The crocodilians are still with us. Alive.

13   African Attacks

BY PETER HATHAWAY CAPSTICK

W hat's with the birdcage?" asked Paul Mason over his scrambled egg and impala liver breakfast. I glanced across the hard-packed earth of the safari camp to the slender figure of the young woman padding softly through the early light of the nearby lagoon.

"Fish trap, actually," I told him, ambushing a sausage from the platter Martin was passing. The woman disappeared into the bush, the cone-shaped cage of woven cane balanced lightly on her shaven head. "The women wade out into the lagoons along the river when they're low like this in the dry season and just slam the wide end of the trap into the bottom ahead of their feet. The bream and catfish are so thick when the water drops, they always get a few in the trap, then they just stick their hands through the open top and grab them."

Paul grunted, then spoke over his shoulder. "Martin! *Buisa maquanda futi!*" I was surprised that he even had the proper Q-click in the word for eggs. The old waiter, once the batman of a colonel of Kenya's crack regiment, the King's African Rifles, came to attention smartly, then trotted off to the kitchen for more scrambles. Mason grinned, proud of the Fanagalo he had picked up on his first two weeks of safari in the Luangwa. Even if it wasn't the formal language of the country, Chenyanja, the Tongue of the Lakes, Fanagalo did the same job for central and southern Africa as KiSwahili served on the east coast. And, a hell of a two weeks it had been. Still in his thirties Mason was fit and tough enough to hunt really hard, tracking twenty miles a day with nothing but an occasional breather, the kind of hunting that can produce the quality trophies he had taken. The third day out he'd busted a lunker lion from spitting distance with a better black mane than Victor Mature's and had built on that with a forty-eight-inch buffalo and a kudu that would necessitate an addition on his house if he planned to hang it on the wall. From the reports brought in by Silent, things looked pretty fair in the leopard department, too. The number three bait had been taken by a kitty that left a track like it was wearing snowshoes. Mason was one of the really good ones, a humble man who never thumped his chest, a fine shot and a better companion, a genuine pleasure to bwana for.

"What say we just screw around with some *Zinyoni* today, then hit the leopard blind about four?" I asked. "There's any amount of francolin and guinea fowl over by the Chifungwe Plains, and we could shoot the water holes on the way down for ducks and geese. Always the chance of picking up a decent elephant spoor in that area, too."

"You just purchased yourself a boy," he answered. "But, how's about we pot another impala? This liver's out of this world."

"Sure," I told him, "you've got two left on your license and the camp is getting kind of low on meat. That kudu filet's about finished and . . ."

The scream was low at first, more a cry of surprise than alarm, then crescendoed into a piercing shriek of pure animal terror echoing hollowly through the *mukwa* hardwoods, up from the lagoon. Again it cut the cool morning air, even higher, a throbbing razor-edged wail that lifted my hackles and sent a shiver scampering up my spine like a small, furry animal. We both froze for an instant, Mason with a piece of toast halfway to his open mouth, his eyes wide in surprise. Reacting, I snatched the .375 H. & H. from where it leaned against the log rack on the low wall of the dining hut and loaded from the cartridge belt as I ran toward the lagoon. I heard Mason trip and curse behind me, then regain his feet and run, stuffing rounds into the magazine of his .404 Mauser action. My heart felt like a hot billiard ball in my throat as I bulled through the light bush along the 150 yards to the low banks of the lagoon, a reedy, dry-season lake that would join the Munyamadzi River 100 yards away at the first flooding rains. Bursting into the open, I could see a flurry of bloody foam fifty yards from shore, a slender, ebony arm flailing the surface at the end of a great, sleek form that cut the water with the ease of a cruiser. I raised the rifle. Should I shoot? What if I hit the woman? Like a mallet blow, I realized that even if I did hit her it would be a blessing, far better than being dragged inexorably, helplessly down by the huge crocodile. I lined up the sights and carefully squeezed off a 300-grain Silvertip, which threw a column of water just over the top of the croc's head, then whined off to rattle through the trees at the far side of the lagoon. A second later Paul fired, the big .404 slug meeting empty water where the croc had been an instant before, the giant saurian submerging like a U-boat blowing positive. Slow ripples rolled across the calm surface, waving the dark, green reeds until they lapped the low banks. Once again, the lagoon was silent. We stood helplessly, shocked into muteness, thinking of the woman. We could almost feel the tent-peg teeth deep in her midriff, the rough scaliness of the croc's horny head under her hands as she used the last of her strength to try to break loose before her lungs could stand no more and she would breathe dark death.

"Jesus Christ," said Paul in a hoarse whisper. It didn't sound like a curse. Silent, my gunbearer, Martin, and Stomach, a skinner, came running up. A glance at the floating fish trap and at the woman's sandals on the bank told them what had happened. Wading to his knees, Silent retrieved the cane trap and placed the other effects inside. He started a slow trot that would carry him to the woman's village, a miserable huddle of mud and dung huts called Kangani. Slowly we turned back to camp, the shock of witnessing the most horrible death in Africa leaving us numb. I took the rifles and unloaded them, placing a cartridge bullet-first into the muzzle of each to prevent mud wasps from starting nests in the bores, a bit of Africana that had cost hunters their sight and even lives when they forgot it. Martin came over to us and spoke quietly in Fanagalo. "There is nothing for it, Bwana," he intoned with the exaggerated fatalism of the bush African. "It has always been so. Always has *Ngwenya* been waiting; always will he wait."

Ngwenya, the crocodile, has been waiting a very long time. For 170 million years he has been lurking, patient and powerful, in the warmer fresh and salt waters of this planet. Virtually unchanged from his earliest fossil remains, he demonstrates with deadly efficiency the value of simplicity in design. The crocodile is the master assassin, the African Ice Man, combining the ideal qualities of cunning with ruthlessness and cold voracity matched with a reptilian intelligence far greater than his small brain would indicate. He is little more than teeth, jaws, and stomach propelled by the most powerful tail in nature. He will eat anything he can catch and digest almost anything he can eat. Someday, if you spend enough time around the watery haunts of *Ngwenya*, that may include you or—Lord forbid—me.

In these days of moon landings and lasers, it can be difficult to fathom the fact that crocodiles are still a very substantial threat to human life in Africa. Most Americans, were you to conduct a poll, would probably offer some vague impression that crocodiles are teetering on the brink of extinction in Africa today, hardly any threat to man. I've got some big news. By the most conservative estimates of professional researchers, something approximating ten human beings are dragged off to a death horrible beyond description *each day* in modern Africa. The figure may even be considerably higher since successful croc attacks, unless witnessed, normally leave no trace whatever of the victim, who may have died by any of the methods Africa has developed to make evolution a working proposition. The facts boil down to this: *Crocodylus niloticus* is the one man-killer who, if he's big enough and you're available enough, will eat you every time he gets a chance.

I was taught in Sunday School, I dimly remember, that it's not nice to hate anything. Nonetheless, I do hate crocs, an opinion shared rather vocally by such ne'er-do-wells as Winston Churchill and Theodore Roosevelt. I do not believe in their being driven to extinction, heavens no, because we find to our infinite wonder that everything in nature has its place. On the other hand, I have not an ounce of regret at having been in on the killing of about a hundred of them, all legally shot, I might add, and not for their hides. I have often wondered what stand the ultrapreservationists would take if we were to stock a few hundred crocs in New York's Central Park, where their philosophizing might become more than the armchair variety next time they walked their poodles. I'm sure it would lower the crime rate, if nothing else.

As with snakes there has been a great deal of exaggeration as to the length crocodiles may attain and at the same time a lack of appreciation of the weights they may reach. Adventure books are full of vivid reports of twenty-five and even thirty footers, but few realize how truly immense even a twelve-footer is. The Luangwa Valley of Zambia probably has the largest population of crocodiles in Africa, perhaps the world. Never having been hunted for their hides in this area, they have flourished in untold thousands. In a normal afternoon of hunting along the banks of the Luangwa and Munyamadzi Rivers, it is not unusual to see hundreds sunning themselves on the sand bars and banks, their mouths agape in sleep, oxpeckers and tickbirds hopping around their jaws with impunity. Yet of all the thousands I have seen, I must conclude that a twelve-footer is big and one of thirteen feet edging up to huge. The biggest croc I have ever seen, besides the one who killed the woman in the lagoon, went about fifteen feet with three feet of tail missing, fairly common for some reason in very big crocs. That would make him roughly eighteen feet, which is one hell of a lot of crocodile. I've owned cars shorter than that! He crawled out to sun himself on a small island 150 yards from my camp one hot afternoon when I was between safari clients. I watched him for about a half-hour, out of film for my camera, of course, and God, but he was immense. He looked like a big, scaly subway car with teeth, that could have taken a buffalo and three wart hogs with one gulp. To tell you the honest truth, I came very close to killing him. Crocs that big are very often man-eaters, learning the habits of native women until they try a couple and find they're a lot easier to handle than trying to pull a rhino in by his nose. But, I didn't have a license and knew that the locals would turn me in for the reward offered for violators, so I reluctantly let him go. At least they can't take away your white hunter's ticket for what you're thinking. When the next clients arrived two days later, he was never to be seen.

One famous hunter, shooting years ago in Kenya's Lake Rudolph, which has some Godzilla-league crocs in it, swatted over one hundred, of which only three beat fifteen feet, and those only by a whisker. The largest crocodile "officially" recorded was killed by the Uganda Game Department in the Semliki River along the Congo border in 1953. It was only three inches short of twenty feet. I have seen a mounted croc in a museum that tapes sixteen feet, and he stands higher than my waist, so you can imagine how colossal that nineteen-footer was. When crocs get over twelve feet or so, they gain tremendously in weight for each inch they grow. You could practically shoplift an eight-footer, but you had best have three strong friends along if you want to even roll over a twelve-footer. I have never weighed a big croc, but I'll bet you a hangover that a fifteen-foot *Ngwewnya* will outweigh a big buffalo, well over a ton. A croc this size will stand about four feet when walking and have a girth of about eight feet.

Crocodiles never stop growing their whole lives, so the age of an immense one must be very impressive. Consider that one Asian specimen, a saltwater crocodile, has been living in an American zoo for over thirty years and has grown only about four feet since his capture. Conceivably, a brute like the Semliki nineteen-footer may have seen two centuries turn over.

As much, if not more than, the lion, the history of African exploration is written around the crocodile. In fact, there is hardly an explorer or a missionary that doesn't mention a few squeaks with *Ngwenya, Mamba, Nkwena,* or whatever his local name may be, often with fatal results. By way of example, let's look at just one passage of the writings of Sir Samuel Baker on a military expedition in the great papyrus Sudd of southern Sudan:

"Among the accidents that occurred to my expedition, one man had his arm bitten off at the elbow, being seized while collecting aquatic vegetation from the bank. He was saved from utter loss by his comrades who held him while his arm was in the jaws of the crocodile. The man was brought to me in dreadful agony, and the stump was immediately amputated above the fracture. Another man was seized by the leg while assisting to push a vessel off a sand bank. He also was saved by a crowd of soldiers who were with him engaged in the same work; this man lost his leg. The captain of No. 10 tug was drowned [by a croc] in the dock vacated by the 108-ton steamer, which had been floated into the river by a small canal cut from the basin for that purpose. The channel was 30 yards in length and three feet deep. No person ever suspected that a crocodile would take possession of the dock, and it was considered the safest place for the troops to bathe. One evening the captain was absent and as it was known a short time previously that he had gone down to walk at the basin, he was searched for at the place. A pile of clothes and his red fez were upon the bank, but no person was visible. A number of men jumped into the water and felt the bottom in every portion of the dock, with the result that in a few minutes, his body was discovered; one leg was broken in several places, being severely mangled by the numerous teeth of the crocodile. There can be little doubt that the creature, having drowned its victim, had intended to return."

Several months later, sitting in the cool of the evening with Lady Baker and Commander Julian Baker, RN, Sir Samuel was accosted by one of his men, panicked almost into incoherency. To let Baker tell it:

"The man gasped out, 'Said, Said is gone! Taken away from my side by a crocodile, now, this minute!'

"'Said! What Said?' I asked: 'There are many Saids!'

"'Said of the No. 10 steamer, the man you liked, he is gone. We were wading together across the canal by the dock where Reis Mahomet was killed. The water is only waist deep, but a tremendous crocodile rushed like a steamer from the river, seized Said by the waist and disappeared. He's dragged into the river and I've run here to tell you the bad news.'

"We immediately hurried to the spot. The surface of the river was calm and unruffled in the stillness of a fine night. The canal was quiet and appeared as though it had never been disturbed. The man who had lost his companion sat down and sniffled aloud. Said, who was one of my best men, was indeed gone forever."

One can only hope that those of Baker's men working the No. 10 steamer got hazardous duty pay.

Arthur Neumann, the same chap who got the fifteen-minute battering from a bull elephant referred to earlier, was the horrified witness to a classic croc attack on New Year's Day, 1896, on a river near Lake Rudolph in modern Kenya:

"Late in the afternoon, I went down for another bathe, with Shebane (my servant) as usual carrying my chair, towels, etc., and did the same thing again. It is a large river and deep, with a smooth surface and rather sluggish current; its water dark-coloured and opaque, though hardly to be called muddy, deepens rapidly, so that a step or two in is sufficient at this point to bring it up to one's middle, while the bottom is black, slimy mud.

"Having bathed and dried myself, I was sitting on my chair, after putting on my clothes, by the water's edge, lacing up my boots. The sun was just about to set behind the high bank across the river, its level rays shining full upon us, rendering us conspicuous from the river while preventing our seeing in that direction. Shebane had just gone a little way off (perhaps a dozen yards) along the brink and taken off his clothes to wash himself, a thing I had never known him to do before when with me; but my attention being taken up with what I was doing, I took no notice of him. I was still looking down when I heard a cry of alarm, and, raising my head, got a glimpse of the most ghastly sight I have ever witnessed. There was the head of a huge crocodile out of the water, just swinging over towards the deep with my poor Swahili boy in its awful jaws, held across the middle of the body like a fish in the beak of a heron. He had ceased to cry out, and with one horrible wriggle, a swirl and a splash all disappeared. One could do nothing. It was over; Shebane was gone. . . A melancholy New Year's Day indeed!"

Because there are far more blacks than whites in the range of the Nile Crocodile, it follows that the preponderance of victims are black. Most are women, the traditional duty of that sex being to draw water from the river bank where they are most vulnerable. However, crocs are equally partial to white meat, as the grisly case of William K. Olson, a Cornell graduate and Peace Corps volunteer attests. Olson was recovered in large chunks from the stomach of a thirteen-foot one-inch croc who killed and ate him while he was swimming—despite warnings—in the Baro River near Gambella, Ethiopia, on April 13, 1966. The croc was shot the next day by a Colonel Dow, a safari client of my friend, Karl Luthy, a Swiss white hunter operating in Sidamo Province. I have seen the photos taken by Luthy of removing the body from the croc's stomach, and if you are interested to see what Olson looked like after twenty hours in a croc's paunch, you may see one of them reproduced on page 200 of Alistair Graham's and Peter Beard's book, *Eyelids of Morning* (New York Graphic Society, 1973). I don't recommend it, however, unless you considered *The Exorcist* light comedy.

The inside of a croc's stomach is sort of an African junkyard. I have found everything from human jewelry to whole wart hogs to Fanta bottles and three-pound rocks inside them. One ten footer I shot in Ethiopia even had a four-foot brother tucked in his belly. According to a reliable writer-hunter, one east African man-eater contained the following horribilia: several long porcupine quills, eleven heavy brass arm rings, three wire armlets, an assortment of wire anklets, one necklace, fourteen human arm and leg bones, three human spinal columns, a length of fiber used for tying firewood, and eighteen stones. I wasn't there, but that sounds just a touch exaggerated if only for the simple amount of the inventory. Stones are commonly found in the stomach of crocs, but whether they are picked up accidentally when the croc lunged for a fish or whether they are meant as an aid to the digestive process like the grit in a bird's crop is unknown. Maybe they're used for ballast.

The collections of indigestible items found in the stomachs of crocodiles points out their fantastic digestive powers. I have found good-size antelope leg bones that were almost dissolved; they would have to be since they were far too large to be passed through the normal process. The arm bracelets are worn by African women very tightly on the bicep, and the only way for them to be found free would be for the arm to have been digested.

The Nile crocodile holds the unquestioned title as the most accomplished of Africa's man-eaters. Some individual crocs have been credited with hundreds of human victims and since the species is more or less limited to water, there is only one factor that makes this possible—the incredible sense of fatality that the African holds toward the crocodile.

There are innumerable cases of scores of women being taken by crocs at the *same spot* every few days as they draw water for their families. Crocs easily learn where to wait and, apparently, the fate of the last person who filled her jug from a particular place has no effect whatever on the next one who may have even been present when the last victim was taken. I have lived with Africans in the bush for many years, but I have found it impossible to understand their total indifference to horrible death. I have seen this phenomenon from Ethiopia to South Africa, so it is not a matter of one particular tribe but a continent-wide indifference that defies explanation. Ask a woman why she takes her water from the same place where her sister was killed the week before and she will just shrug. It's weird.

I was once crossing a river in Mozambique by cable pontoon, which is a raft drawn across the stream by cables operated by government personnel. One man jumped off near shore to unfoul a line and was immediately taken by a croc in a swirl of bloody water and never seen again. Yet when I returned the following day, the surviving raft operators were happily splashing and washing not twenty yards from where their fellow worker was killed!

Crocodiles are considered "saurians" by science (as in dinosaur) and are available in a wide variety of flavors. Among these are their cousins, the alligators, gavials, and caimans. With the exception of the African or Nile crocodile (the same animal, even though found nowhere near the Nile) and the saltwater crocodile of the warm Asian islands, most of the clan is relatively inoffensive. Of course, the American alligator has caused some deaths and injuries, including a fully documented fatal attack that took place in Sarasota, Florida, in August 1973. A sixteen-year-old girl was taken by an eleven-foot gator and, despite efforts of onlookers to prevent it, partially eaten. Between 1948 and 1971 there were an additional seven unprovoked attacks, which produced various injuries but no fatalities. Although rare, there is an American crocodile reputedly as dangerous as the African breed.

The salt-water crocs of Asia are lumped under several types, including the marsh or mugger crocodile and estuarine types, all considered very dangerous. In fact, one of the greatest clashes between man and croc took place during World War II. At the time that Burma was being retaken by the Allies, about 1,000 Japanese infantrymen became caught between the open seas and the island of Ramree, deep in mangrove swamps crawling with crocs, expecting to be evacuated by ships that never arrived. Trying to retreat, they found themselves cut off by the British Royal Navy in such position that they could not regain the mainland. When night came, so did the crocodiles. Witnesses on the British ships have told of the horror of the mass attack on the men, of the terrible screaming that continued until dawn when only 20 men out of 1,000 were left alive. Certainly, some were killed by enemy fire and others by drowning, but all evidence points up that most were slaughtered by the big salt-water crocs.

Any animal as obviously dangerous as the crocodile is bound to have a thick layer of legend wrapped around its reputation. Of course, a lot of it is *marfi,* a polite term for droppings. Time and again tales are heard of people who have had an arm or leg removed, "snapped off in one bite," by crocs. Not so. One look at a croc's dentures point out that, because of their spacing and rounded design, they are intended for catching and holding rather than cutting. If you have ever tried to carve a London broil with a tent peg, you've got the idea. Anything a croc can get down his gullet at one try he will swallow whole, tilting his head back so the morsel falls to the back of his throat. Anything bigger, he must wait for decay to set in and soften the meat so that he can grip it and spin his body, ripping off a healthy chunk in the same way that a Frenchman tears off a piece of bread.

Another myth about the croc is his supposed ability to knock animals into his jaws by using his powerful tail, even from elevated river banks. No way. I have seen at least twenty animals taken by crocs, both on banks and in the water. All were caught with pure speed and surprise. No animal of the size and bulk of a croc cold possibly jump in such a way as to get his tail behind his meal and flip it toward him. Yet crocs have been reported as accomplishing this with animals on river banks six feet over them!

I had a good lesson in the speed a croc may generate late one afternoon when I was sitting in a leopard blind along the river. My client and I were watching a small troop of impala wander idly down a path to the water to drink, pausing thirty-one feet, by later measurement, from the river's edge. Instantly, a twelve-foot crocodile erupted from the water like a Polaris missile, crossing the ground to the nearest impala, a ewe, like a green blur. As she spun to escape, he was on her, grabbing her right rear haunch and effortlessly dragging her to the dark river. In less than a minute there wasn't even a ripple to mark where she had disappeared. Considering that the impala is one of the fastest of the African antelopes, the speed a croc can crank out over a short rush must be well over thirty-five miles per hour. I can tell you I didn't walk as close to the river after the demonstration.

The awesome power of big croc has been demonstrated on large game many times. In a Tanzanian (Tanganyikan) game park in the late 1950s, a party of tourists were photographing a black rhino cow as she drank at a water hole. She was fair sized for a female, probably shading 4,000 pounds. As she stuck her odd, prehensile nose into the scummy water, the water exploded and a big croc clamped down on her muzzle. There followed an amazing test of strength between the two armored monsters, the croc trying to pull the rhino into the water and the rhino trying to pull the croc out of it. After an hour of straining, with neither gaining more than a foot, the rhino was actually inched toward the water. Thirty minutes later, her head was held under and, after a final flurry, she rolled over, drowned. The croc was estimated as about fourteen feet by the ranger driving the tour car.

The crocodile is a cold-blooded creature in more ways than one. Like most nonmammals, his ability to hang onto the last shreds of life would make a vampire wild with envy. So tough is the croc that there is an old hide hunters' maxim quite as valid today as it ever was: A croc ain't dead until the hide's salted, and even then don't count on it! Besides the fact that really large crocs—twelve feet and over—are sneaky as revenuers, the felony is compounded by their anatomy offering only the smallest of targets for a fatal shot. I have heard other professionals claim that a lung-shot *Ngwenya* will leave the water before he drowns, although I have never witnessed this. But then, to be fair, I have never shot a croc in the lungs. For my money the only way to anchor a crocodile where he lies and thus prevent his certain escape to the river where he will be lost or eaten by his pals is to separate him from his brain. Smaller than your fist, it's located just behind the eyes, an angle that can almost never be made from dead on or astern without at least 30 degrees of elevation above the croc. The brain is encased in some very impressive bone (I once broke a steel spearhead in two trying to drive it through the skull) and just can't be reached from a flat angle. The only reliable position for the brain shot is from the side, where your target will be about two inches high by three inches wide. Joe Joubert, a fine professional hunter who had a camp near mine in Zambia, was once shot in the face by a ricocheting .22 bullet when an ex-cited client bounced it off the skull of a big croc in an attempted *coup de grace.*

Just how much pummeling a crocodile can absorb came to my definite attention during a safari in Botswana's Okavango Swamps, which had been pretty well picked over by professional hide hunters years before. Yet, after the market shooting was stopped, the crocs had come back strongly, if warily. I spotted one of a dozen feet sunning himself half out of the water on the base of an old termite heap. He was a good 400 yards out, and open water prevented stalking any closer. But, the croc was a good one for Okavango, and I knew my client to be an excellent shot with his "toy," a .257 Weatherby Magnum with a variable power telescopic sight, a flat-shooting iron too light for most game but perfect for a long shot like this.

We hunched along through the light *mswaki* scrub at the edge of a sand flat, the tsetse flies absolutely mobbing us. I have never seen them in greater numbers or more savage. Ignoring the saber-toothed mauling he was getting, my client rested the rifle across his hand on a broken wrist of branch, lined up with plenty of holdover, took his shooting breath, and sent one off Air Mail Special. I was amazed to see the little slug lash out and strike right on the money, a light mist of bone chips and brain matter erupting from the skull. Typical of a brain-shot croc, his prehistoric nervous system jammed in flank speed, his powerful tail whipping the water like a paddle wheeler gone aground.

As I watched through my binoculars, I could see the growing pink cloud in the water and the tail slowed to a stop. My gunbearers and skinners, who very wisely share a common sentiment of loathing anything to do with crocs, dead or alive, decided that they just weren't getting paid enough to help me drag that one back through open water. I stoked up the .470 with soft-points, removed my wallet, and, in the best Stewart Granger tradition, started wading. The water was only to my waist, and I wasn't nearly as worried about crocs as I was leery of the small herd of hippos who were eyeing me with some annoyance from seventy yards away. After a few minutes, however, the herd leader finally decided that I wasn't there to rape any of the ladies fair, and he ponderously ignored me. The big crocodile was lying mostly in the water, just his shattered head on the ant hill, so I was able to work him out into deeper water despite his bulk, which was largely negated by his buoyancy. With the end of his tail across my shoulder, I began to drag him back like a small ant with a dung beetle. I had made about forty yards when I noticed a tiny quiver through his body and began to reflect seriously on the prudence of my position. I didn't have much time to think about it because, with a tremendous wrench, he flattened me. The fist-sized crater in his head where his brain used to be had lulled me to the hasty conclusion that he was dead, a status he was clearly contesting.

I came up spitting muddy water, trying to get the double rifle free from where it was slung around my neck. He hit me again with his body, and I went back down, stumbling and thrashing to keep way from the jaws. I managed to break the rifle, pour the water out of the barrels and present the croc with 1,000 grains of high velocity tranquilizer right behind the smile. When the little pieces of the rest of his head stopped falling out of the sky, I grabbed him again and completed towing him back to shore. Polaroids appeared as if by witchcraft, and the client and I squatted down in the hero position and opened the jaws, the teeth gleaming like a nest of bloody *punji* sticks. Just as the camera clicked, there was a sound like an iron maiden being slammed, and people became very scarce. We jumped back as the croc began to thrash around, snapping his jaws and actually growling, a sound I have never heard one make before or since. My client belted him twice more with a .300 Magnum, his head looking like a jam jar somebody had stuck a grenade into. That calmed him down considerably. We finished the pictures and three of my men had to sit on the battered body to hold it down from nervous reaction as the belly skin was taken. Hunting back past the spot a few hours later, I was surprised to see the corpse surrounded by a ring of vultures, odd because normally they would have swarmed him and finished him up in short order. As we got closer, they flew off and I noticed something: a dead vulture was clamped tightly between the "dead" croc's jaws. That boy wasn't about to quit!

Paul Mason and I began to hunt the man-eater the same afternoon as the attack on the woman. I hadn't had much of a look at him beyond his obvious bulk, but that was so exceptional it would give him away if we ever saw him again. From the size of his head and the wake he was throwing, he had to be better than fifteen feet, and there just weren't many of that size anywhere. I decided to abandon the rule that the professional only shoots in case of a charge or imminent escape of dangerous game and split us into two groups on either side of the big lagoon, which was separated from the Munyamadzi by a sandy umbilical a hundred yards wide. We sat, rifles ready, through the long afternoon, watching the water until our temples throbbed for some sign of the huge croc, but not a ripple betrayed his presence. Crocodiles can hold their breath by only showing the tiniest tip of nostrils. As the last of the light disappeared, we pushed aching, cramped joints into action and returned to camp.

We ate early that night, not saying very much, and after a few belts of man's best friend went off to bed. It was still full dark when tea arrived and we shrugged off blankets in the chill morning air. Well before dawn, we were picking our way to the lagoon. Even in the growing half-light, I could see that we were too late. Across the sand spit lay a spoor like a half-track; a deep, wide belly mark flanked by huge tracks showed where the killer croc had crossed from the lagoon and entered the river. I said a bad word. We had a good chance of finding him in the limits of the lagoon, but now, in the expanse of river, where he could move at will, things looked much dimmer. Still, I thought, given enough time, hard work and a fifty-five-gallon drum of pure, Grade A, vitamin-enriched luck. . . .

Paul and I retraced our steps and wolfed down a fast breakfast of the remaining kudu steaks and plenty of sweet, black tea. Before heading for another long day on the river, I thought it best we check the "zero" of our rifles, having decided to switch from the heavier .375 and .404 to Paul's .25-06 Remington and my .275 Rigby Rimless, reasoning that any shot we might get would probably be a long one requiring the precision of the lighter rifles over the power of the heavier. My .275 didn't have the velocity of Paul's superhot Remington, but I had put so many rounds through it that holdover and windage were as indelibly ingrained in my subconscious as Raquel Welch's bustline. Satisfied that any misses could not be blamed on Messrs. Rigby or Remington, we headed back to the river.

In view of the fact that, considering the size of the area the croc could be in, our best approach would be a saturation campaign, I called all my staff together. There were twenty-six of them, a mixture of Sengas, Awizas, Baila, and even a couple of BaTonkas up from the Zambezi. There were cooks, waiters, skinners, trackers, gunbearers, water boys, laundry boys, *chimbuzi* boys, and firewood gatherers, all my bush family. Leaving only Martin to watch things around camp, I split them up into pairs with instructions to watch for the big croc at various vantage points on the river. If seen, one would stay while the other would come to fetch us. My strategy wasn't entirely hit or miss: it had been a cold night, and since crocodiles must regulate their body temperatures by alternate sunning and wetting, I was pretty sure that the man-eater would show somewhere within three miles in either direction of my camp. Therefore, I had somebody watching nearly every convenient sand bar.

The sun was an incandescent, white cueball on a blue felt sky when I saw the first smoke a half-mile downriver. Someone had seen the crocodile! I sent Silent to bring Paul, 300 yards upriver from me, and, when he arrived, breathless from running, we started off toward the tendril of smoke. On the way I met Chenjirani, partnered with Invisible, sent to fetch us if we did not notice the smoke. From a bend in the river, I climbed a small bluff and turned the binoculars on the shimmering water. Eight hundred yards away, the dark, water-wet form of a gigantic croc smothered the tip of a sand bar. It looked like we had him. I mentally marked a tree on the bank that was opposite the croc, deciding to use it as a firing point. I motioned to Paul that we should sweep in a large half-circle through the heavy brush so there would be no chance of the croc or his tickbird sentinals spotting us, and we came out at a point a few yards from the grass-skirted tree trunk.

It was a perfect stalk, the soft ground giving no warning that our tip-toe approach would set up vibrations that the animal could feel through the dense medium of water. The tree loomed nearer above the towering elephant grass until we were up to it. Ever so slowly, Mason moved up, slipping into firing position with the .25-06 clenched by the pistol grip ahead of him. We could see the edge of the upper part of the bar through the fringe of grass as I worked closer to Paul, ready for a backup shot if necessary. The croc should be only thirty yards away, sleeping in oblivion, a shot a blind man could make. I slid my hand forward to push the grass away from Paul's muzzle and we both popped up to find . . . *nothing. Nowhere. Empty.*

I was absolutely baffled. What in bloody hell could have spooked him? He must have just changed his mind about the sunbath during the ten minutes it had taken us to make the stalk. Or, maybe he had gotten to grow so big by realizing that to expose himself for any amount of time could mean the hot whiplash of a bullet. Whatever the reason, he simply was not there.

Two days later, our knees raw as minute steaks from crawling along the brushy banks looking for the croc, he still hadn't tipped his hand. I increasingly feared that, like many of his brethren who had achieved great age and size, he had figured out that safety lies in darkness.

"Paul," I said that night after dinner, pouring him something to dispel his mood, "we're gonna have to bait that croc to have any chance at him at all. I'm convinced he just isn't active during daylight or we would have seen him more than just once."

"Whatcha got in mind, Bwana?" he asked. "Want me to go fish trapping in the river?"

"Not 'til you pay your safari bill, I don't," I grinned back. "I think that big lizard has been hunted before. Shot at. Maybe he came all the way up from the Zambezi. After five months in this camp I've never seen him before or even cut tracks that big." I took a flaming splinter from the fire and lit the tip of a Rhodesian Matinee from the thirty-pack in my breast pocket. "Maybe he's not even in this section of river anymore, but I doubt that."

We ghosted the banks of the Munyamadzi the next morning until the sun was high in the cloudless, dry-season sky. September dust-devils swirled black grass ash thousands of feet up to rain back on us in a fine, grassy film until Silent joked that we were now dark enough that he might adopt us. Scores of crocs were basking on sand bars and small beaches, but nothing approaching the size of the man-eater. Then, as I swept the glasses across a stretch of calm water at the head of a pool, I caught two dark lumps that protruded oddly above the slick surface. As I stared, they disappeared without a ripple, as if they felt my stare. From the distance between the knobs, I knew they were the eyes of a monster crocodile, and I would take all bets that he was our boy. I crawled back from the bank and got Paul. We drove the hunting car quietly upriver a half-mile where a hippo herd lay in the tail of the current. Paul wedged himself into the sitting position and slammed a 400-grain .404 slug through the brain of a big, scarred bull, who collapsed without a twitch and disappeared into the black depths.

"How long, Silent?" I asked the spindle-shanked old gunbearer. He knelt down and felt the temperature of the water and glanced at the sun, calculating for a moment. A great poacher in his youth, Silent was never fifteen minutes off in predicting how long it would take a hippo's body to bloat and leave the bottom. Finally, he pointed to an empty piece of western sky where the sun would be when the hippo would rise to the surface. At five, we were back with the crew just in time to see the carcass balloon up and drift into a quiet eddy where we were able to rope it. After a long struggle we wrestled his tons into position where the Rover could winch him over in stages. When we were finished, he lay at the edge of a shallow bar beneath our ambush point, a low, riverine bluff thirty yards away and twenty feet high. Powerful ropes of his own hide held him to stakes driven deeply into the mud to prevent the crocs from pulling and tugging him into the current.

I showed Paul the big, wedge-shaped bits in the hide, tooth marks of crocs testing the degree of decomposition of the body. Usually, they would have to wait several days before the hide had rotted enough to be torn away, exposing the meat beneath, but this hippo would be table-ready. Already the skinners were busy struggling to slash away huge patches of the thick skin so the crocs could feed immediately. I suppose I should be able to tell you how crocodiles locate carrion, but I'm not really sure. I believe that they hunt living prey by both sight and sound of water disturbance, but I couldn't say how good their sense of smell is. Judging by the short time it takes a large number of crocs to find a decomposing carcass, though, they must have fairly decent noses, although whether they discern the odor from airborne scent or from tainted water evades me. Stomach brought over the corrugated ivory arcs of the fighting tusks and the smoother, amber rods of the interior teeth and presented them to Mason. Nearly dark, we drove back to camp and a couple of sun-downers followed by an excellent stroganoff of hippo filet. We were both dead to the world before ten o'clock.

"*Vuka,* Bwana, *tiye!*" I tried to drag myself back from deep sleep, the hissing glare of Martin's pressure lamp searing through my eyelids. I forced them open, taking the big tea mug and pouring the sweet, strong brew down in a few hot swallows. Martin laid out clean bush shorts and jacket for me, then refilled the mug.

"*Yini lo skati?*" I asked him, blearily squinting at my watch in the shadows.

"*Skati ka fo busuku,* Bwana," he answered. Jesus! Four a.m. I had better get moving if we were to be in position before first light. I shivered into the shorts and bush jacket and stepped into the sockless shoes, almost bumping into Mason on his way to the *chimbuzi.* He muttered something sleepily about idiots and disappeared into the toilet hut. I had finished my third tea and, while he swilled some coffee, I checked the rifles, deciding to go back to the big guns. If we got a shot this morning, it would be barndoor stuff and the .375 and .404, with their express sights, would be better over the dimly lit short range. If necessary, their big slugs would also penetrate water better.

Leaving the hunting car a full half-mile back on the track, I led the way toward the bluff in the velvety darkness, our bare legs and shoes soaked by the dew-wet grass before we had walked ten yards. A trio of waterbuck clattered off, caught in the slender beam of the electric torch, and an elephant could be heard ripping tender branches from a grove a hundred yards to our right. Somewhere in the night a hyena snickered and was taunted by the yapping of a black-backed jackal. Eyes sharp for the reflected sapphire of snakes' eyes, we sneaked closer until we were only fifty yards from the bluff. I kept the beam well covered even though I realized that the crocs on the carcass were deep in the hill's defilade and could not see it. After another twenty feet, I eased it off completely, slipping slowly forward in complete silence, the sugary river sand hissing beneath the soles of our shoes. Dully, from ahead, came the disgusting, watery sounds of crocs feeding on the hippo—the tearing rip of meat, the muffled clash of teeth, the hollow, retching, gagging sound of swallowing the big, bloody lumps of flesh. Ten feet from where I guessed the lip of the bluff was, Paul and I squatted and froze in the darkness awaiting enough light to slip up for a shot if the man-eater was there. If.

With maddening slowness, like a low fire heating the inside of a heavy steel barrel, the gun-metal sky began to blush. As we waited, cramped, listening to the crocs, the light swelled from mango to cherry to carmine tinged with thick veins of wavy gold and teal-wing blue. My outstretched hand began to take shape before my face. I nudged Paul to move with me to the edge of the overhang. The river was still black, but after a few seconds the darker blob of the hippo carcass loomed dimly, pale feathers of water visible as dozens of crocs swirled and fought over the meat. Behind a light screen of grass on the lip, I got Paul into a sitting position, his rifle eased up to his shoulder. Seconds oozed by like cold caramel as the dawn strengthened, the bulk of the hippo more discernible. I thanked our luck that we were on the west bank and would not be skylined by the growing light.

As I stared through the felt-gray shadows toward the water, smaller dark shapes began to take form and outline; then I saw one, partially behind the hippo, that was much larger than the others. I felt a thrill of triumph as I realized that our plan had worked. He was *there,* just thirty yards away, unaware that in a few seconds lightning was going to strike. A few more seconds and Paul could kill him. My stomach tightened as the giant length moved, then again. God, no! He was returning to the water with the dawn. The loglike outline moved again, two feet closer to deep water and safety, his head already in the river. Couldn't Paul see him? Didn't he understand that in a few seconds he'd be gone forever? Frustration coursed through me. I could not risk whispering. A tiny sound snicked through the half-blackness, and I realized it was the safety of the .404. Shoot, I willed him. Shoot now! He's still moving! He's going to . . . A yard of orange flame roared from Paul's muzzle, a brilliant stab of lightning that blinded me as the thunderclap of the shot washed over my arms and face. I was deafened, great, bright spots exploding wherever I focused.

"I think I got him," Paul yelled over the ringing of my ears. Twice more, the big bore rifle fired as Mason opened up on the spot where the croc had been. Slowly, my vision began to clear with growing dawn, the orange blossoms of light fading. I stared down at the dead hippo, my hope welling up as I saw the tremendous, dark shape beside it, half in the water. The great tail waved feebly as a shudder passed through the killer, then all was still. Paul knelt and put his last shot through the man-eater's skull. It was over.

Pounding each other's back in congratulations, we half-fell down the sandy bank and walked across the sand bar to the bodies, the odor of the dead hippo already sickly in our nostrils. Behind us came Silent and Stomach, their hands covering their open mouths in polite astonishment, muttering the usual, "Eeehhh, eeehhh," over and over. When two more men arrived, we were able to roll him onto dry land and examine him with mounting awe. Paul's first shot had been perfect, taking out the rear half of the brain as he faced away and below us. The rest hadn't mattered. One thing was for sure; he was the biggest croc I had ever seen up close, let alone killed. I put the tape on the two pegs we ran between snout and tail-tip, even though we couldn't get the tail all the way straightened out. The third unrolling of my six-foot measure totaled fifteen feet, two and one-half inches! We all guessed him at over a ton, perhaps quite a bit more. Crocs are very dense and heavy for their size.

After almost an hour had passed, the entire village of Kangani arrived to revile the dead reptile by spitting on him and kicking him in impotent frustration for the death of the woman. When Silent made two long incisions in the side and cut the stomach wall, we all gagged. From the slimy mass of hippo meat and crushed bones, slid the putrefacted arm of a woman, a copper bangle still tightly in place, gleaming dully from the croc's stomach acid.

Mason and I sat, smoking slowly in the warm sun, watching the men skin the man-eater and place what they could find of the woman in a plastic bag. Her head and one arm and shoulder were missing, as best I could tell. Somehow, the killing of the crocodile had felt anticlimactic, and I wondered if there wasn't something more to the episode than a woman being eaten and a croc being killed. No, I finally decided, it was exactly that simple. It had been going on for a million years and would continue as long as there were people, crocodiles, and water. But, at least, I thought on the walk back to camp, that's one *Ngwenya* who won't be waiting.

Part Five:
Death Wears Stripes and Spots
Tigers, Leopards, Panthers
The Track of the Cat!

14 In the Jaws of a Tiger

BY JESSE FOWLER SMITH

Allll my varied experiences of the last thirty years have not obliterated the record of one experience in the jungles of Burma. Today I can turn back memory's pages and see again that tropical landscape of meadow, field and forest, where, by all the laws of logic, my grave should be found. The faces of my companions of that day readily come back to me, and I hear again the very tones of Mr. Geis' voice as his pent-up feelings found expression in words.

The end of March, 1902, which was the beginning of my "hot-season" vacation, found me, with my wife and baby daughter, the guest of Rev. George J. Geis and his family in the Mission bungalow at Myitkyina, Burma, northern terminus of the Burma Railway. We had been there about a week when failure of the meat supply in the village market induced my host to plan a hunting trip in the hope of replenishing the larder with venison. Officers from the British regiment posted at Myitkyina had reported deer plentiful at a place about twelve miles down the railway, where, not long before, the soldiers had camped for a week for field maneuvers. We decided to bring back our venison from that region.

Our party also included three members of the border tribe known as Kachins: namely, Ning Krawng, a teacher in the Mission School; one of his pupils, who was to be our cook; and an older Kachin, an escaped slave from a neighboring valley who bore, as a mark of his servitude, a scar where his left ear had been lopped off by his master. The ex-slave carried a *dah,* a sort of glorified butcher knife, the only tool and weapon of the Kachins. Ning Krawng and I were armed with double-barreled shotguns loaded for deer; Mr. Geis had a rifle.

From the station-master permission had been obtained to occupy as our camp the railway bungalow which, with water tank and the huts of the "pumpers," made up all there was of the railway station nearest to Myitkyina.

Except when a railway official or his guests occupied the bungalow, four native "pumpers" were the sole inhabitants of this station.

With provisions for twenty-four hours we set out by the one daily train from Myitkyina. At nine o'clock, about an hour after our departure, we detrained at the station. It was several weeks before I saw another train on this railway. When the return train passed about four o'clock that day, I was five miles back in the jungle, Ning Krawng my sole companion.

Having left the cook in charge of our folding cots, bedding and food, we took our weapons and left the bungalow to look over the ground where, later in the day, we hoped to discover herds of grazing deer. Our course led down a sharp slope to an extensive meadow. A quarter of a mile by a narrow, winding path through elephant-grass that reached five feet above our heads brought us to a wooded ravine.

As we crossed this meadow, Mr. Geis said: "Here we must be on the lookout for sleeping tigers. They like to crawl into this tall grass during the day."

However, we roused no sleeping tigers. We descended the ravine, at the bottom of which trickled a dry-season stream, climbed the opposite bank and emerged from the fringe of trees, which bordered the ravine, into a large grassy plain, much like an American prairie. Through the trees above us leaped a small troop of chattering monkeys. In other trees flocks of noisy parrots were feeding on several varieties of wild fruit.

No other signs of animal life were discernible, for before us, instead of a field of lush grass that would furnish forage to scores of deer, we looked out over several hundred acres of desolation, beyond which, some two miles away, was the edge of a deep forest. A devastating fire, traceable to the soldiers, whose former camp ground we had reached, had destroyed every vestige of food for bird as well as beast.

Disappointed, we returned to the bungalow to eat our rice and curry, enjoy a siesta, and plan a campaign for deer "in the cool of the day."

Between three and four o'clock we started once more over the same route to the hunting ground. Upon reaching the ravine, we laid our plans for obtaining a good bag despite the fire-blackened feeding grounds. We decided to look for deer in the fringe of trees that marked the courses of the ravines which seemed to encircle the open plateau.

We separated into two parties. Mr. Geis and the Kachin freed-man followed the border to the right, while Ning Krawng and I took the border on the left. It was agreed that both parties should continue until we met on the far side of the open area. It was also agreed that, in case of trouble, three shots fired at distinct and regular intervals would be a call for help. So we parted.

Long-legged, barefooted Ning Krawng stalked ahead at such a pace that I could hardly do more than trail him. In a short time he disappeared from view altogether among the brush and trees. With the conviction that my safety depended upon keeping him in sight, I began to run, but before I gained sight of him his gun rang out, followed almost instantaneously by the loud crashing of some animal through the brush. My first thought was that he had shot an elephant, for it seemed to me that nothing smaller could make so much noise tearing through the undergrowth.

On reaching Ning Krawng, I found him a new man. The lust of the killer was in his blazing eyes as he told me by means of a few Burmese words and much use of pantomime that he had shot a tiger—"a big one, wounded in the shoulder." Excitedly he showed me the pool of blood at his feet; breathlessly he pointed to the trail of blood leading off into the underbrush. Assured that I understood his words and signs, he waited not a second, but strode off along the crimson trail. With only a moment's hesitation, but with a question in my mind as to the wisdom of this procedure, I followed him, for I reasoned that, dangerous as this course might be, it was better than being left alone in a tiger-infested wilderness.

On the green carpet beneath the trees the bright red line of blood was easy to follow. For some distance ahead the undergrowth was not dense and the trees were small and scattered. No tiger was in sight. We would be alert and quick on the trigger at the first intimation of his being in range. Moreover, both of us were impressed by the amount of blood that the tiger had spilled along the way. Ning Krawng, with many ejaculations, repeatedly pointed to the crimson pools which showed so plainly the effectiveness of his aim. And with each ejaculation he bounded ahead on the trail. At intervals I paused to listen. In my ignorance I expected to hear the death groans of the animal that was losing his life-blood in such quantities.

After a few minutes we came to a steep but narrow gully athwart the trail. To the bottom of this the tiger had plunged headlong, then clambered up the opposite slope, leaving at the bottom a bucketful of gore. We, too, leaped into the gully and climbed breathlessly to the other side, expecting to find our quarry so weakened from loss of blood that one more well-aimed shot would make him ours. At the top of the gully, the trail of blood led into a tangle of bushes and bamboos that was too thick for our eyes to penetrate.

We looked at each other. We shook our heads. Ning Krawng turned to the right and took a few steps toward the open field. I turned to follow, but before I had taken two steps there came an angry roar from the bamboo thicket. I looked to see, not thirty feet away, the black and tawny stripes of an enormous tiger some ten feet in the air, headed straight for me. One thought flashed through my mind: "If you're going to use your gun, now is the time."

I raised my gun to take aim. As the stock pressed my shoulder I drew back my right foot to brace myself for the shot. My heel caught a trailing root, and I was thrown flat on my back so suddenly that, when the infuriated tiger landed, his right forepaw came down on my left breast, his huge body covered me completely, and his fiery eyes looked into mine for one split second.

Instinctively I turned my face away. My cork helmet fell over my features; the left side of my head alone was exposed to the tiger's fangs. With a snarling bite his jaws closed on my skull. I heard his teeth crunch through my scalp, but I felt nothing. A silent prayer went up from my heart for my wife and child, to whom I had said good-by that morning. I breathed one plea for forgiveness for my folly, as I was sure that this was the end of my earthly career.

But the monster's jaws were not fatal. He had taken his bite, and I was still alive and conscious. I said to myself, "He didn't open his mouth wide enough. He'll do a better job next time." A second time he clamped his jaws upon my head; a second time I heard the crunch but felt no pain; a second time I realized that a tiger's bite had not ended my life.

My uninjured brain worked fast. "Once more," I thought. "A third time, he'll try it and complete the job." A third time, indeed, he crunched into my scalp, causing no pain.

Then, hardly realizing what had happened, I opened my eyes, raised myself on my elbow, and saw the brute's tail disappearing into the same thicket from which, but a few seconds before, I had seen him spring. I sat up and turned my face toward Ning Krawng, who was standing like one in a trance only a few paces away.

Forgetting his ignorance of the English language, I blurted out, "Well, I'm alive, but he's got my ear." I thought that his last bite had taken my ear clean off.

As soon as he saw me get up and heard me speak, Ning Krawng cried out in Burmese, "Run! Run!" and he proceeded to climb the nearest tree. In my confusion I could see no other tree; so I tried to climb after him. My exertions caused my wounds to bleed; the smell of the blood, now trickling down my face, nauseated me. Furthermore, when I attempted to pull myself up to the branch on which Ning Krawng sat, I found that my left arm was useless. Unable either to climb the tree or to get Ning Krawng to pull me to safety, with blanched face and a feeling of faintness I began to slide down the tree, murmuring: "It's no use. I can't make it."

Then Ning Krawng became alarmed for me. He descended, fired in quick succession both barrels of his gun, and with two more hurried shots emptied mine. Thus he had put us in the delightful predicament of being alone in the tiger jungle with two empty guns. Not waiting to reload, he urged me to get upon his back, but I refused. So we started on the run, out of the woods, and into the center of the open plain.

After we had covered about a half mile, Ning Krawng carrying both guns, we reached the actual camp site of the soldiers. There we threw ourselves upon the ground and panted until I had recovered my wind. Crying out for water, I followed Ning Krawng back toward the bungalow. At the point where our morning path had crossed the ravine he made a cup from a big leaf and gave me a drink of water from the stream. It was the most refreshing drink that ever wet my lips.

Back at the bungalow, I fell exhausted on my cot, where Ning Krawng left me to go for our companions. Mr. Geis had heard the quick succession of our shots, had concluded that we were finding plenty of game, and therefore made no effort to come to our help.

The sun had set when Mr. Geis arrived. He washed my wounds, dressed me in pajamas, made a stretcher out of my cot and two bamboo poles, and ordered the four pumpers to carry me on their shoulders up the twelve miles of railway track to the nearest doctor. The swaying motion which the bearers gave to my stretcher soon lulled me to sleep, and for the most of the way I slept peacefully.

Within a few minutes of our arrival at the Mission House, the regimental surgeon from the military hospital appeared. His examination showed several scalp wounds, one deep incision near the crown, my left ear hanging in three strips, and a deep wound in the left shoulder just below the collar-bone. This last was made by my fall upon a stiletto-like stump. The pressure of the tiger's right forepaw had pushed me firmly down upon this "spit," and had also left five black-and-blue footprints upon my left breast. This wound in the shoulder, fortunately, injured neither my collar-bone nor my shoulder-blade, but the laceration of the muscles had caused my arm to be temporarily useless.

Having examined all my injuries, the doctor gave me ammoniated spirits to inhale (since he had no anesthetic), and proceeded to cleanse and dress my wounds. He took thirteen stitches in my head and ear. At this point for the first time I began to feel pain, and I felt it a-plenty.

I spent the next twelve hours in my own bed. For the next five or six days the doctor visited me daily. After that I was able to ride a bicycle to the hospital for the daily dressing. Thanks to my own clean blood and the doctor's skillful ministrations, no infection developed. This was a matter of relief to my friends and of surprise to the doctor, who declared that, in all his experience as an army surgeon in the tropics, he had never known a person to survive a tiger's mauling. In those rare cases where the victim had not been killed outright, blood-poisoning had set in, and death soon resulted.

At the end of the vacation period my wounds had all healed. I returned to my work at Rangoon according to the plan made six weeks before. At that time, few scars were discernible. Today a "dent" in my head, apparent only to the touch, a scar on my shoulder and two "seams" on my left ear are the only outward evidence of my first and only attempt to win fame as a big-game hunter.

This fearful experience is called to my mind every time I enter a barber shop, for barbers always want to know what made the "hole" in my head. I tell them but they never believe me.

15 The Scourge of a District

BY PARDESI

Aman-eating tiger is supremely bad; but a man-eating panther, hard-
ened in sin, is superlatively worse. The tiger waits by the wayside to
gather up what the gods of the jungle may send him. He will pull
down an unfortunate charcoal-burner as he passes on his lawful occasions along a jungle road in India. A villager's luck fails him as he returns home
one evening; and the next morning a shrill wailing in the village, and possibly a
cloud of vultures hovering over one particular spot in the jungle, announce that
the man-eater has found another meal. A scared herdsman will bolt in with the
news that the 'shere' has carried off his companion as they were driving out the
communal cattle in broad daylight; for the man-eating tiger loses the habits of
the more reputable of his kind, and seeks his prey at any hour of the twenty-four.

A man-eating panther does all these things, and more. He is more cunning than the tiger, and that is saying a very great deal. But what chiefly makes
him so terrible a scourge is his almost incredible boldness. He has no respect
for nor fear of human beings or human habitations. He will cheerfully enter a
house where half a dozen people are sleeping, and, quite unperturbed by the
alarm raised by the others, will seize and drag out a child, or even a woman, to
devour at his leisure. Indeed, on occasion, if he can find no other way in, he
will effect an entrance by tearing through the thatched roof. Nor at times can
he be held guiltless of killing for the sake of killing. A really bad man-eating
panther has been known to make his way into a hut and deliberately kill
everyone of the inmates on exactly the same principle as a fox in a chicken-
run. Finally, the beast will teach his progeny to follow in his own wicked ways;
and unless the whole line is extirpated, a district may continue indefinitely to
suffer wholesale depredations, involving the loss of hundreds of lives.

My own experience of the blatant contempt of a man-eating panther
for the human race occurred in a native state to the south of the Central

229

Provinces. I had received a permit to shoot in State territory, and an urgent request came along from the rajah to see what I could do towards ridding the land of one of these evil-doers, which was terrorising something like two hundred square miles of country. It had an evil record, this beast, dating back over a couple of years or so, in the course of which it had claimed some 150 victims. Latterly its depredations had become—there is no other word for it—appalling. Accordingly I went into camp on the outskirts of a largish village, where the local thana, or police-station, formed a convenient centre for the collection of information regarding the movements of the man-eater. Every two or three days news came in of a woman or child having been killed and eaten. The beast rarely, if ever, touched a man, or if it did, I never heard of it. All these kills, however, were reported from villages some fifteen or twenty miles from where I was, and successive reports would come from places perhaps twenty or thirty miles apart. The brute was ranging over a big beat, and it was little use going after him. The only thing to do was to possess my soul in patience until such time as the mountain came to Mahomet, or, at any rate, within reasonable distance of him.

The outlook was anything but the hopeful one which I in my innocence had at first imagined it would be. But there was nothing to be done but wait. In the meantime the whole countryside was scared thoroughly stiff. By day or night no one moved abroad alone. Now and again I used to meet parties of ten or fifteen, all armed with axes, making their way from one place to another, and keeping a wary eye on both sides of the road as they went. As these people were Gonds, this state of affairs meant a great deal. To begin with, the Gond is an eminently plucky individual in himself. Then he has the contempt born of the familiarity of a lifetime with the beasts of the jungle. And if a panther can throw the Gond inhabitants of some 200 square miles of territory into a state of abject fright, it must be a very evil beast indeed. After I had been in camp some ten days I had my first brush with the man-eater, and he took all the honours of the round. One morning an unkempt individual was brought into my camp who announced that the 'shaitan' had visited his house the previous night and attempted to carry off a small girl. Would the sahib give the matter his urgent and personal attention, and bring some medicine for the injured child? The sahib would, and as we went I heard the story of the attack.

It appeared that the girl was asleep in the middle of the hut, directly between the two doors. Near one door there was a group of three or four men sitting talking. Near the other, in the opposite wall of the hut, there was a single man whittling a stick for use as an axe-helve. Suddenly the panther bounded in through one door, past the group of conversationalists, picked up the child, and proceeded to walk out of the hut with her through the other door. The single man near the other door pluckily attacked the brute with the stick he was shaping. He managed to bring this unsatisfactory weapon hard down across the beast's hind-quarters, startling it into dropping its prey, and vanishing through the door into the night, to the accompaniment of a series of disappointed snarls. When we arrived at the village a mile away, I proceeded, so far as I could, to check the story. After a careful examination of the tracks, I came to the definite conclusion that it was correct in every detail. The panther had walked quietly up to the hut, and the scratches of its claws showed where it had made its bound through the front door. Other marks showed how it had picked up the child bodily, the drag of her heels along the ground alone being visible, and how it had dropped her when attacked by the man with the stick. The girl was torn about the throat, but not very badly. I dressed her wounds with carbolic, and up to the time I left that camp a fortnight or so later, she was doing well, and, I have no doubt, ultimately recovered.

The reputation of the panther left room for little hope that it would remain near the village. Accordingly I returned to my camp after a fruitless attempt to track the beast to its lying-up place, leaving word that any further developments were to be reported at once. As I expected, there were none, and two days later a kill was announced from a village miles away.

At the end of three weeks in that camp I was getting thoroughly tired of it. Day after day I scoured the neighbouring jungles for game, with a conspicuous lack of success. In the meantime reports of the man-eater's activities continued to come in, but they were all from different and widely-separated villages. Already the better part of a month of my hard-earned leave had been spent. The place where I was camping was undoubtedly convenient so far as getting the necessary khubbar of the panther was concerned. On the other hand, game was so scarce as to be to all intents and purposes nonexistent. Keen though I was to shoot the man-eater, I could not spend the whole of my leave doing nothing in this way on the offchance of getting it, and as the days went on my hopes sank lower and lower. One day I returned thoroughly disgusted from my customarily unsuccessful morning round. While I was waiting for breakfast, the wish to move on elsewhere deepened into a fixed determination, and I decided to start getting ready to shift camp as soon as the meal was over. But the powers that be had decreed otherwise. I was in the middle of breakfast when a thoroughly scared urchin bolted in with the news that a panther had killed one of his companions as they were driving out the village cattle a couple of hours earlier. His shivering limbs and dirty grey colour were sufficient *prima facie* evidence of the truth of his story. He and three other small boys, he said, were driving out the cattle, when a panther suddenly bounded out of the jungle, seized one of the boys and dragged him off. The body was lying in the jungle, and would not be removed until I had arrived and inspected it.

I promptly set out for the scene of the tragedy four miles away. When I arrived at the village I was met by the headman and the father of the dead boy. The corpse was exactly as it had been found, they told me, so I went down to reconnoitre. The kill had taken place on the edge of a strip of jungle bordering a widish nullah. On the other side of the nullah was a similar strip, and neither was more than twenty or thirty yards wide. The body of the dead boy, who must have been about nine or ten years old, was lying in the middle of one strip under a mass of creeper forming a sort of tent about six feet square. As in the previous case of the girl, the panther had seized its victim by the throat, and, as far as I could judge, death must have been practically instantaneous. It remained now to settle with the murderer—I hoped once and for all. Beating was out of the question. Apart altogether from the likelihood of its attacking the beaters, the devilish cunning of the panther and the fact that it might be lying up anywhere in either of the strips of jungle made any prospect of getting a shot at it by beating extremely remote. If I was to have any reckoning with the slayer, it meant sitting up over the body of the slain. It was very far from being a pleasant idea, but it had to be faced. The first thing to do was to persuade the father. He wanted to remove the body at once for decent cremation. After a lot of argument, however, he allowed it to remain, and I set about making what preparations I could for my vigil.

Now the body was lying under this mass of creeper, and close to it was the only decent-sized tree there was within reasonable distance. Accordingly I had a charpoy hoisted into its branches, whence I thought I could get a good view of the corpse just below me, and, taking my rifle and a kukri, established myself for the wait. It was about two o'clock in the afternoon when I got settled down. I did not expect an extended vigil. The panther, however, thought otherwise, and it was practically dark by the time he arrived. I just saw a shape glide in under the mass of creeper without giving me the chance of a shot, and the sound of rending flesh indicated that he had started his meal.

Then my troubles began. The corpse was lying under that mass of creeper with the panther tearing at it, and in the darkness I could see neither. There was no moon, and even if there had been, the opaque shadow of the creeper would still have been there. I waited for a long time, every minute expecting the beast to come out into the open, where I might get a chance at him. But he continued tearing at the body in a way that demonstrated very clearly that he was ravenous and had no intention of being interrupted until his hunger had been satisfied. Something had obviously to be done. Otherwise we might have remained as we were until morning. Eventually I decided to throw something down, in the hope that it might startle the man-eater into showing himself outside the shadow of the creeper. The only thing I could think of was my bunch of keys. Down they went, and I gripped my rifle steady for the expected shot; but not a bit of it. The panther growled, walked once or twice round the corpse, still keeping under the creeper, and calmly returned to his meal.

This came as a revelation to me of the fearlessness of a hungry man-eating panther. But there were many more revelations to come that night. The fact that a bunch of keys dropping out of the sky with a metallic jingle close to the beast's head was insufficient to disturb him was astonishing enough. Accordingly I cast about for something more drastic, and decided to try clapping my hands. The first time or two the panther growled his acknowledgments, and did his little circumambulation. Then he got bored, and did not deign to pay any attention at all to my efforts. So I tried shouting at him, with equally unsuccessful results. Occasionally he growled back; generally he did not bother to do that, even when I bawled at him with the full strength of my lungs. Now consider the ludicrousness of the position. Here on the machan was a man armed with a heavy rifle, and there below him, at a distance to be measured in feet, was the animal to shoot which he had expended so much time and trouble. But so far as getting a shot was concerned, those few feet might have been as many miles. If only the panther would show himself outside that six-feet-square patch of creeper—but it remained 'if only.' I was getting desperate by this time. Hacking off a branch with my kukri, I cut it up and hurled the pieces into the darkness below. The man-eater hardly troubled to growl back. Only one thing remained. I lifted my rifle and let drive into the middle of that infernal creeper, ripping another cartridge into the chamber as fast as I could work the bolt. The noise the shot made in the quiet jungle was extraordinary. My rifle was a .400 full-cordite, magazine one, and the seeming loudness of the report startled even me, used as I was to the weapon. But it did not disturb that panther—at least, not to the extent anyone would have expected. He gave a blood-curdling snarl or two, and I heard him walk around the body, keeping as always under the creeper. Then the noise of his feeding began again. Three more shots I fired, hurling down the empty cartridge-cases after each shot to the accompaniment of my shouted objurgations. Then I stopped abruptly. Never expecting anything of this nature, I had only brought ten rounds with me, and the realisation came very forcibly that I could not afford to waste any more of them on an entirely fruitless attempt to move a beast which had no intention of being moved.

I began to feel decidedly creepy. At the best the whole business had a very gruesome flavour about it; and when this amazing behaviour on the part of the panther came on top of everything else, all the local stories of the super-natural attributes credited to him began to come to mind. Cold clammy fin-gers began to tickle gently up and down my spine. In fact, not to put too nice a point on it, I was not very far from being in a state of what is commonly known as 'mortal funk.' It came as an immense relief, therefore, to hear human voices hailing me from the edge of the jungle. The villagers, hearing the shots, had come to the conclusion that the panther must be dead, and had come down in a body to hear all about it. I shouted back that the panther was very far from being dead, and that they had better clear out at once, advice which they lost no time in following.

The visit of the villagers had a soothing effect on nerves which, as I have said, were becoming more than a trifle strained. After they had departed, I dozed off, and the doze deepened into sleep. Just after one o'clock I snapped into sudden and complete wakefulness, and the realisation that the man-eater was clawing at the foot of my tree. I looked over the edge of the machan, but though the moon had risen, he was in the shadow and was invisible to me. I felt profoundly uncomfortable. The earlier behaviour of the brute had already instilled in my mind an intense respect for his uncanny contempt of my efforts to terminate his existence, not untinged, I admit, with a touch of superstitious awe. It may sound curious—to use no stronger term—that a man, armed with a rifle and perched on a machan some ten feet from the ground, should be scared by a large cat clawing at the foot of the tree in which he was situated. But this was no ordinary panther. It was so many cubic feet of concentrated activity, cunning, courage, deadly viciousness and utter contempt for the human race. Moreover, the whole circumstances of the vigil had been of a gruesomeness calculated to tax the strongest of nerves. I grabbed my kukri and made ready to smite as soon as the panther should make its appearance over the edge of the machan, which I expected every moment. However, after a few minutes, and very much to my relief, it moved off. Looking back on things, I have come to the conclusion that the panther was only cleaning its claws by scraping them up and down the bark of the tree. Still, at the time I was very far from realising that, and the sound of the animal's retreating footsteps was one of the things in my life for which I have felt most devoutly grateful. Another thing which I have often wondered, is whether the choice of my tree for those manicuring operations was not a deliberate act on the part of the panther to show his contempt for me. He knew well enough that I was in that tree. He must have realised that I had designs on his life. And he cared not one atom, except in so far as he consistently declined to come out into the open and to give me the chance of a shot at him.

I remained very much on the alert for the rest of the night, expecting him back at any moment. It was nearly four o'clock, however, before I heard him again. Keeping in the shadow the whole way, he slid in under the patch of creeper, and for ten minutes or so the sound of his feeding went on. Then he left again, this time, as it turned out, for good.

I was not feeling too happy. In the first place, the night had been an unholy one. But what was worse was the knowledge that I had to face the father of the dead boy in the morning. That, I think, was the least pleasing part of a wholly unpleasant business. At dawn I heard the villagers coming down, and stiffly descended from my machan. The sight was a horrible one. Only the hands and feet of the corpse remained. The rest was a litter of broken bones and fragments of flesh. The boy's father said never a word. He cast one look of unutterable reproach at me, gathered up the hands and feet, and walked quietly away, looking neither to the right nor to the left. It was a bad moment, and the memory of it has given me many bad moments since.

We made an attempt to track the panther in case he might be lying up in the neighbourhood. So far as we could gather, however, he seemed to have gone clean off across country, and after a mile or so of difficult tracking we had to give it up. There was obviously no prospect of seeing him again in that village, for the time being at any rate.

I came to the definite conclusion after this that the panther was not fated to die by my hand, and a day or two later I moved my camp to another village some ten miles away, where there was a chance of getting some of the shooting I had come for and hitherto had not got. Just before dawn on the second night after my arrival I was awakened by something bumping into my tent just behind my head as I lay in bed. I slept very lightly in those days: the presence in the district of the man-eater did not encourage heavy slumber, any more than it encouraged me to go to bed without my rifle and kukri ready to hand. There was a gentle scratching just outside the tent, and then two long sniffs. The hair started to bristle up at the back of my neck, and the palms of my hands became suddenly very cold and clammy. There was no mistaking the identity of the animal outside. It was a panther all right, and in the circumstances it could only be the man-eater. I grabbed my rifle and the

kukri, determined to sell my life as dearly as possible, and awaited developments. Just then there was a shout outside. With the approaching dawn my
camp was awakening into life, and one of my entourage was calling to the
bhisti in the village to bring water for the preparation of my chota hazri. The
scratching ceased, and I heard the intruder moving off. There was no undigni-
fied hurry about his retreat. Judging from the sound, his attitude was that he
was leaving because he wanted to, and not because he was frightened into
doing so. After a discreet interval I got up, and as soon as it was light enough
examined carefully the ground around my tent. The whole position was very
soon cleared up. The nocturnal visitor was the man-eater, sure enough. He
had prowled once or twice around the tent, evidently trying to make up his
mind what it was. A tentative scratch or two in the ground just outside
showed where he had tried a closer investigation of the queer object which
obviously contained a desirable meal, but which might at the same time have
been a trap. My follower's mercifully opportune shout had apparently decided
him that the chances of running into danger were too great to make an entrance worth while, and he had accordingly moved off with dignity. To this
day I am firmly convinced that the man-eater was suspicious that the tent was
a trap of some sort. If it had not been for that, he would certainly have come
in, and the chances of my being alive at the present time would not have been
worth considering. Even now the memory of those two long sniffs induces a
rather creepy feeling around my spine.

The sands of the man-eater's existence were, however, rapidly running
out. Three days later a Gond villager turned up at my camp with an old Tower
musket and the skin of a fine panther which he had shot in his compound the
previous night. As I prefer to shoot my own trophies, I was not at first interested in the prospective deal; but when he produced two things which he
found in the animal's stomach, my attitude changed. The things he showed me
were a black ball, which on closer inspection proved to consist of human hair,
and a silver anklet. There was no mistaking the identity of the panther after
that. This was the skin of the man-eater which had taken all the honours of our
three encounters, and incidentally given me some of the worst moments I have
had in a fairly extended experience of big game shooting in India. Glad as I
was that the land had been rid of the pest, the manner of its death was rather a
blow to my pride. After making an arrant fool of a sahib armed with modern
weapons of destruction, who had devoted more than a month to an effort to
compass its end, the man-eater had fallen to a charge of nondescript missiles
fired by a simple savage from a gas-pipe, which from its appearance threatened
greater danger to its user than to the intended victim. But that was just one of

the practical jokes which the gods of the jungle delight in playing as an anti-dote to sinful human pride.

The way in which the work of destruction had been accomplished was too beautifully simple. The Gond told me that a panther had come into his compound and killed one of his goats. He had frightened the animal away and ensconced himself in the door of his hut waiting for its return. It had duly returned, to be dropped dead by an assorted mixture of slugs, nails and heaven knows what besides, fired from the old muzzle-loader at a range of five yards. Had this stalwart realised the identity of the beast he had sat up for I have little doubt that he would never have waited for it as he did. All the characteristic pluck of the Gond notwithstanding, the man-eater had established its reign of terror far too firmly throughout the country for any of the local inhabitants to tackle it single-handed in this way. But the villager did not realise what he was doing, and the result was that one of the most cunning and most ruthless of all beasts in the Indian jungle had walked up to its death like any ordinary goat-killer. The whole thing was astonishing enough; but what has always puzzled me most of all is the way in which the panther consented to be driven off its kill. It had no fear of human beings, and its record showed that it preferred them for edible purposes to the normal food of its kind. Yet the man-eater, which had declined to be frightened off its kill by my missiles, shouted objurgations and rifle-shots, permitted itself to be driven off from a goat by the voice of an unarmed villager.

I bought the skin as a memento, and the Gond was delighted with the ten rupees he received for it. The panther was a large male, and, so far as it was possible to judge from the skin, in fine condition. One might have expected to find that the beast was an old and mangy one, but it was not. The skin was a beauty, and the claws did not suggest that their late possessor was in any way getting on in years. Nor were there any signs of a previous injury which might have accounted for the animal's original embarkation on its extended career of human destruction. To my lasting regret, I did not get the skull. It is possible that defective teeth may have accounted for its horrible proclivities. Failing that, the only explanation which suggests itself to me is that the panther acquired the taste for human flesh at an early age, having been educated to it by one of its parents which had been a man-eater before it.

As there was the possibility of a reward being forthcoming for the destruction of the panther, I wrote to the State Durbar giving the name of the man who had killed it, the circumstances of the shooting and details of the evidence that the dead animal was the dreaded man-eater. Whether the villager got his reward I never discovered. I certainly heard nothing more so far as that side of the matter was concerned. Long after, however, I learned that the panther's depredations had come to a sudden end at a time which coincided with the bringing of the skin to me. That removed any possible doubt there may have been that the skin I bought then, and still have, at one time belonged to one of the worst pests with which that particular part of India has ever been cursed.

16   Man-Eating Leopards

BY JIM CORBETT

Editor's Note: First published in the 1940s, Englishman Jim Corbett's Indian jungle stories rival Rudyard Kipling's popularity and exceed them in excitement. And they are all true! Corbett's classic *Man-Eaters of Kumaon*, concerning tigers, and *The Man-Eating Leopard of Rudraprayag,* from which this excerpt was taken, have been republished by Oxford University Press.

Terror

The word 'terror' is so generally and universally used in connexion with everyday trivial matters that it is apt to fail to convey, when intended to do so, its real meaning. I should like therefore to give you some idea of what terror—real terror—meant to the fifty thousand inhabitants living in the five hundred square miles of Garhwal in which the man-eater was operating, and to the sixty thousand pilgrims who annually passed through that area between the years 1918 and 1926. And I will give you a few instances to show you what grounds the inhabitants, and the pilgrims, had for that terror.

No curfew order has ever been more strictly enforced, and more implicitly obeyed, than the curfew imposed by the man-eating leopard of Rudraprayag.

During the hours of sunlight life in that area carried on in a normal way. Men went long distances to the bazaars to transact business, or to outlying villages to visit relatives or friends; women went up the mountain-sides to cut grass for thatching or for cattle-fodder; children went to school or into the jungle to graze goats or to collect dry sticks, and, if it was summer, pilgrims either singly or in large numbers toiled along the pilgrim routes on their way to and from the sacred shrines of Kedarnath and Badrinath.

As the sun approached the western horizon and the shadows lengthened, the behaviour of the entire population of the area underwent a very sudden and a very noticeable change. Men who had sauntered to the bazaars or to outlying villages were hurrying home; women carrying great bundles of grass were stumbling down the steep mountain-sides; children who had loitered on their way from school, or who were late in bringing in their flocks of goats or the dry sticks they had been sent out to collect, were being called to by anxious mothers, and the weary pilgrims were being urged by any local inhabitant who passed them to hurry to shelter.

When night came an ominous silence brooded over the whole area— no movement and no sound anywhere. The entire local population were behind fast-closed doors, and in many cases they had sought further protection by building additional doors. Those of the pilgrims who had not been fortunate enough to find accommodation inside houses were huddled close together in pilgrim shelters. And all, whether in house or shelter, were silent for fear of attracting the dread man-eater.

This is what terror meant to the people of Garhwal, and to the pilgrims, for eight long years.

I will now give a few instances to show you what grounds there were for that terror.

A boy, an orphan aged fourteen, was employed to look after a flock of forty goats. He was of the depressed—untouchable—class, and each evening when he returned with his charges he was given his food and then shut into a small room with the goats. The room was on the ground floor of a long row of double-storied buildings and was immediately below the room occupied by the boy's master, the owner of the goats. To prevent the goats crowding in on him as he slept, the boy had fenced off the far left-hand corner of the room.

This room had no windows and only the one door, and when the boy and the goats were safely inside, the boy's master pulled the door to, and fastened it by passing the hasp, which was attached by a short length of chain to the door, over the staple fixed in the lintel. A piece of wood was then inserted in the staple to keep the hasp in place, and on his side of the door the boy, for his better safety, rolled a stone against it.

On the night the orphan was gathered to his fathers his master asserts the door was fastened as usual, and I have no reason to question the truth of his assertion. In support of it, the door showed many deep claw-marks, and it is possible that in his attempts to claw open the door the leopard displaced the piece of wood that was keeping the hasp in place, after which it would have been easy for him to push the stone aside and enter the room.

Forty goats packed into a small room, one corner of which was fenced off, could not have left the intruder much space to manoeuvre in, and it is left to conjecture whether the leopard covered the distance from the door to the boy's corner of the room over the backs of the goats or under their bellies, for at this stage of the proceedings all the goats must have been on their feet.

It were best to assume that the boy slept through all the noise the leopard must have made when trying to force open the door, and that the goats must have made when the leopard had entered the room, and that he did not cry for help to deaf ears, only screened from him and the danger that menaced him by a thin plank.

After killing the boy in the fenced-off corner, the leopard carried him across the empty room—the goats had escaped into the night—down a steep hillside, and then over some terraced fields to a deep boulder-strewn ravine. It was here, after the sun had been up a few hours, that the master found all that the leopard had left of his servant.

Incredible as it may seem, not one of the forty goats had received so much as a scratch.

A neighbour had dropped in to spend the period of a long smoke with a friend. The room was L-shaped and the only door in it was not visible from where the two men sat on the floor with their backs to the wall, smoking. The door was shut but not fastened, for up to that night there had been no human kills in the village.

The room was in darkness and the owner of it had just passed the hookah to his friend when it fell to the ground, scattering a shower of burning charcoal and tobacco. Telling his friend to be more careful or he would set the blanket on which they were sitting on fire, the man bent forward to gather up the embers and, as he did so, the door came into view. A young moon was near setting and, silhouetted against it, the man saw a leopard carrying his friend through the door.

When recounting the incident to me a few days later the man said: 'I am speaking the truth, sahib, when I tell you I never heard even so much as the intake of a breath, or any other sound, from my friend who was sitting only an arm's-length from me, either when the leopard was killing him, or when it was carrying him away. There was nothing I could do for my friend, so I waited until the leopard had been gone some little while, and then I crept up to the door and hastily shut and secured it.'

The wife of the headman of a village was ill of a fever, and two friends had been called in to nurse her.

There were two rooms in the house. The outer room had two doors, one opening on to a small flagged courtyard, and the other leading into the inner room. This outer room also had a narrow slip of a window set some four feet above floor level, and in this window, which was open, stood a large brass vessel containing drinking-water for the sick woman.

Except for the one door giving access to the outer room, the inner room had no other opening in any of its four walls.

The door leading out on to the courtyard was shut and securely fastened, and the door between the two rooms was wide open.

The three women in the inner room were lying on the ground, the sick woman in the middle with a friend on either side of her. The husband in the outer room was on a bed on the side of the room nearest the window, and on the floor beside his bed, where its light would shine into the inner room, was a lantern, turned down low to conserve oil.

Round about midnight, when the occupants of both the rooms were asleep, the leopard entered by way of the narrow slip of a window, avoiding in some miraculous way knocking over the brass vessel which nearly filled it, skirted round the man's low bed and, entering the inner room, killed the sick woman. It was only when the heavy brass vessel crashed to the floor as the leopard attempted to lift its victim through the window that the sleepers awoke.

When the lantern had been turned up the woman who had been sick was discovered lying huddled up under the window, and in her throat were four great teeth-marks.

A neighbour, whose wife had been one of the nurses on that night, when relating the occurrence to me said, 'The woman was very ill of her fever and was like to have died in any case, so it was fortunate that the leopard selected her.'

Two Gujars were moving their herd of thirty buffaloes from one grazing-ground to another, and accompanying them was the twelve-year-old daughter of the older of the two men, who were brothers.

They were strangers to the locality and either had not heard of the man-eater or, which is more probable, thought the buffaloes would give them all the protection they needed.

Near the road and at an elevation of eight thousand feet was a narrow strip of flat ground below which was a sickle-shaped terraced field, some quarter of an acre in extent, which had long been out of cultivation. The men selected this site for their camp and having cut stakes from the jungle which surrounded them on all sides, they drove them deep into the field and tethered their buffaloes in a long row.

After the evening meal prepared by the girl had been eaten, the party of three laid their blankets on the narrow strip of ground between the road and the buffaloes and went to sleep.

It was a dark night, and some time towards the early hours of the morning the men were awakened by the booming of their buffalo-bells and by the snorting of the frightened animals. Knowing from long experience that these sounds indicated the presence of carnivora, the men lit a lantern and went among the buffaloes to quieten them, and to see that none had broken the ropes tethering them to the stakes.

The men were absent only a few minutes. When they returned to their sleeping-place they found that the girl whom they had left asleep was missing. On the blanket on which she had been lying were big splashes of blood.

When daylight came the father and the uncle followed the blood trail. After skirting round the row of tethered buffaloes, it went across the narrow field and down the steep hillside for a few yards, to where the leopard had eaten his kill.

'My brother was born under an unlucky star, sahib, for he has no son, and he had only this one daughter who was to have been married shortly, and to whom he looked in the fullness of time to provide him with an heir, and now the leopard has come and eaten her.'

I could go on and on, for there were many kills, and each one has its own tragic story, but I think I have said enough to convince you that the people of Garhwal had ample reason to be terrified of the man-eating leopard of Rudraprayag, especially when it is remembered that Garhwalis are intensely superstitious and that, added to their fear of physical contact with the leopard, was their even greater fear of the supernatural, of which I shall give you an example.

I set out from the small one-roomed Rudraprayag Inspection Bungalow one morning just as day was breaking, and as I stepped off the veranda I saw in the dust, where the ground had been worn away by human feet, the pug marks of the man-eater.

The pug marks were perfectly fresh and showed that the leopard had stepped out of the veranda only a few minutes in advance of me, and from the direction in which they were pointing it was evident that the leopard, after his fruitless visit to the bungalow, was making for the pilgrim road some fifty yards away.

Tracking between the bungalow and the road was not possible owing to the hard surface of the ground, but as I reached the gate I saw the pug marks were heading in the direction of Golabrai. A large flock of sheep and goats had gone down the road the previous evening, and in the dust they had kicked up the leopard's tracks showed up as clearly as they would have on fresh-fallen snow.

I had, by then, become quite familiar with the man-eater's pug marks and could with little difficulty have distinguished them from the pug marks of any hundred leopards.

A lot can be learnt from the pug marks of carnivora, as for instance the sex, age, and size of the animal. I had examined the pug marks of the man-eater very carefully the first time I had seen them, and I knew he was an outsized male leopard, long past his prime.

As I followed the tracks of the man-eater on this morning I could see that he was only a few minutes ahead of me, and that he was moving at a slow even pace.

The road, which had no traffic on it at this early hour of the morning, wound in and out of a number of small ravines, and as it was possible that the leopard might on this occasion break his rule of never being out after daylight, I crept round each corner with the utmost care until I found, a mile farther on, where the leopard had left the road and gone up a great track into dense scrub and tree jungle.

A hundred yards from where the leopard left the road there was a small field, in the centre of which was a thorn enclosure, erected by the owner of the field to encourage packmen to camp there and fertilize it. In this enclosure was the flock of sheep and goats that had come down the road the previous evening.

The owner of the flock, a rugged fellow who by the looks of him had been packing trade commodities up and down the pilgrim road for nigh on half a century, was just removing the thornbush closing the entrance to the enclosure when I came up. In reply to my inquiries he informed me that he had seen nothing of the leopard but that, just as dawn was breaking, his two sheepdogs had given tongue and, a few minutes later, a kakar had barked in the jungle above the road.

When I asked the old packman if he would sell me one of his goats, he asked for what purpose it was wanted; and when I told him it was to tie up for the man-eater, he walked through the opening in the fence, replaced the bush, accepted one of my cigarettes, and sat down on a rock by the side of the road.

We remained smoking for a while, with my question still unanswered, and then the man began to talk.

'You, sahib, are undoubtedly he whom I have heard tell of on my way down from my village near Badrinath, and it grieves me that you should have come all this long way from your home on a fruitless errand. The evil spirit that is responsible for all the human deaths in this area is not an animal, as you think it is, that can be killed by ball or shot, or by any of the other means that you have tried and that others have tried before you; and in proof of what I say I will tell you a story while I smoke this second cigarette. The story was told to me by my father, who, as everyone knows, had never been heard to tell a lie.

'My father was a young man then, and I unborn, when an evil spirit, like the one that is now troubling this land, made its appearance in our village, and all said it was a leopard. Men, women, and children were killed in their homes and every effort was made, as has been made here, to kill the animal. Traps were set, and far-famed marksmen sat in trees and fired ball and shot at the leopard; and when all these attempts to kill it had failed, a great terror seized the people and none dared leave the shelter of his home between the hours of sunset and sunrise.

'And then the headmen of my father's village, and of the villages round about, bade all the men attend a panchayat, and when all were assembled the panch addressed the meeting and said they were assembled to devise some fresh means to rid themselves of this man-eating leopard. Then an old man, fresh back from the burning-ghat, whose grandson had been killed the previous night, arose and said it was no leopard that had entered his house and killed his grandson as he lay asleep by his side, but one from among their own community who, when he craved for human flesh and blood, assumed the semblance of a leopard, and that such a one could not be killed by the methods already tried, as had been amply proved, and could only be killed by fire. His suspicions, he said, fell on the fat sadhu who lived in the hut near the ruined temple.

'At this saying there was a great uproar, some exclaiming that the old man's sorrow at the loss of his grandson had demented him, while others averred he was right. And these latter recalled that the sadhu had arrived at the village at about the time the killings had started, and it was further recalled that on the day succeeding a killing the sadhu had been wont to sleep all day, stretched on his bed in the sun.

'When order had been restored the matter was long debated and the panchayat eventually decided that no immediate action would be taken, but that the sadhu's movements should in future be watched. The assembled men were then divided into three parties, the first party to start its watch from the night the next kill could be expected; for the kills had taken place at more or less regular intervals.

'During the nights the first and the second parties were on watch, the sadhu did not leave his hut.

'My father was with the third party, and at nightfall he silently took up his position. Soon after, the door of the hut slowly opened, and the sadhu emerged and vanished into the night. Some hours later an agonized scream came floating down on the night air from the direction of a charcoal-burner's hut far up the mountain-side, and thereafter there was silence.

'No man of my father's party closed an eye that night, and as the grey dawn was being born in the east they saw the sadhu hurrying home, and his hands and his mouth were dripping blood.

'When the sadhu had gone inside his hut and had closed the door, the watchers went up to it, and fastened it from the outside by passing the chain that was dangling from it over the staple in the lintel. Then they went each to his haystack and returned with a big bundle of straw, and when the sun rose that morning there was nothing but smouldering ash where the hut had been. From that day the killing stopped.

'Suspicion has not yet fallen on any one of the many sadhus in these parts, but when it does the method employed in my father's time will be adopted in mine, and until that day comes, the people of Garhwal must suffer.

'You have asked if I will sell you a goat. I will not sell you a goat sahib, for I have none to spare. But if, after hearing my story, you still want an animal to tie up for what you think is a man-eating leopard, I will lend you one of my sheep. If it is killed you shall pay me its price, and if it is not killed no money shall pass between us. Today and tonight I rest here, and tomorrow at the rising of the Bhootia star I must be on my way.'

Near sundown that evening I returned to the thorn enclosure and my packman friend very cheerfully let me select from his flock a fat sheep which I considered was heavy enough to give the leopard two nights' feed. This sheep I tied in the scrub jungle close to the path up which the leopard had gone some twelve hours earlier.

Next morning I was up betimes. As I left the bungalow I again saw the pug marks of the man-eater where he had stepped off the veranda, and at the gate I found he had come up the road from the direction of Golabrai, and, after calling at the bungalow, had gone away towards the Rudraprayag bazaar.

The fact that the leopard was trying to secure a human kill was proof that he had no interest in the sheep I had provided for him, and I was therefore not surprised to find that he had not eaten any portion of the sheep which he had apparently killed shortly after I had tied it up.

'Go back to your home, sahib, and save your time and your money,' was the parting advice of the old packman as he whistled to his flock, and headed down the road for Hardwar.

A parallel case, happily without as tragic an ending, occurred a few years previously near Rudraprayag.

Incensed at the killing of their relatives and friends, and convinced that a human being was responsible for their deaths, an angry crowd of men seized an unfortunate sadhu of Kothgi village, Dasjulapatty, but before they were able to wreak their vengeance on him Philip Mason, then Deputy Commissioner of Garhwal, who was camping in the vicinity, arrived on the scene. Seeing the temper of the crowd, and being a man of great experience, Mason said he had no doubt that the real culprit had been apprehended but that before the sadhu was lynched justice demanded that his guilt should be established. To this end he suggested that the sadhu should be placed under arrest and closely guarded, night and day. To this suggestion the crowd agreed, and for seven days and seven nights the sadhu was carefully guarded by the police, and as carefully watched by the populace. On the eighth morning, when the guard and the watchers were being changed, word was brought that a house in a village some miles away had been broken into the previous night, and a man carried off.

The populace raised no objection to the sadhu being released that day, contenting themselves by saying that on this occasion the wrong man had been apprehended, but that next time no mistake would be made.

In Garhwal all kills by man-eaters are attributed to sadhus, and in the Naini Tal and Almora districts all such kills are attributed to the Bokhsars, who dwell in the unhealthy belt of grass at the foot of the hills called the Terai, living chiefly on game.

The sadhus are believed to kill for the lust of human flesh and blood, and the Bokhsars are believed to kill for the jewellery their victims are wearing, or for other valuables they have on their person. More women than men have been killed by man-eaters in the Naini Tal and Almora districts, but for this there is a better reason than the one given.

I have lived too long in silent places to be imaginative. Even so there were times a-many during the months I spent at Rudraprayag sitting night after night—on one occasion for twenty-eight nights in succession—watching bridges, or cross-roads, or approaches to villages, or over animal or human kills, when I could imagine the man-eater as being a big, light-coloured animal—for so he had appeared to me the first time that I saw him—with the body of a leopard and the head of a fiend.

A fiend who, while watching me through the long night hours, rocked and rolled with silent fiendish laughter at my vain attempts to outwit him, and licked his lips in anticipation of the time when, finding me off my guard for one brief moment, he would get the opportunity he was waiting for, of burying his teeth in my throat.

It may be asked what the Government was doing all the years the Rudraprayag man-eater menaced the people of Garhwal. I hold no brief for the Government, but after having spent ten weeks on the ground, during which time I walked many hundreds of miles and visited most of the villages in the affected area, I assert that the Government did everything in its power to remove the menace. Rewards were offered: the local population believed they amounted to ten thousand rupees in cash and the gift of two villages, sufficient inducement to make each one of the four thousand licensed gun-holders of Garhwal a prospective slayer of the man-eater. Picked shikaris were employed on liberal wages and were promised special rewards if their efforts were success-ful. More than three hundred special gun licenses over and above the four thou-sand in force were granted for the specific purpose of shooting the man-eater. Men of the Garhwal Regiments stationed in Lansdowne were permitted to take their rifles with them when going home on leave, or were provided with sporting arms by their officers. Appeals were made through the press to sports-men all over India to assist in the destruction of the leopard. Scores of traps of the drop-door type, with goats as bait, were erected on approaches to villages and on roads frequented by the man-eater. Patwaris and other Government of-ficials were supplied with poison for the purpose of poisoning human kills, and, last but not least, Government servants, often at great personal risk, spent all the time they could spare from their official duties in pursuit of the man-eater.

The total results from all these many and combined efforts were a slight gunshot wound which creased the pad of the leopard's left hind foot and shot away a small piece of skin from one of its toes, and an entry in Govern-ment records by the Deputy Commissioner of Garhwal that, so far from suffer-ing any ill effects, the leopard appeared to thrive on, and be stimulated by, the poison he absorbed via human kills.

Three interesting incidents are recorded in a Government report and I will summarize them here.

First: In response to the press appeal to sportsmen, two young British of-ficers arrived at Rudraprayag in 1921 with the avowed object of shooting the man-eater. What reason they had for thinking that the leopard crossed from bank to bank of the Alaknanda river by the Rudraprayag suspension bridge I do not know; anyway they decided to confine their efforts to this bridge and shoot the leopard as it was crossing at night. There are towers at each end of the bridge to carry the suspending cables, so one of the young sportsmen sat on the tower on the left bank of the river, and his companion sat on the tower on the right bank.

After they had been sitting for two months on these towers, the man on the left bank saw the leopard walk out on to the bridge from the archway below him. Waiting until the leopard had got well on to the bridge, he fired, and as it dashed across, the man on the tower on the right bank emptied the six chambers of his revolver at it. Next morning blood was found on the bridge and on the hill up which the leopard had gone, and as it was thought that the wound, or wounds, would be fatal, a search was kept up for many days. The re-port goes on to say that for six months after it was wounded the leopard did not kill any human beings.

I was told about this incident by men who had heard the seven shots, and who had assisted in trying to recover the wounded animal. It was thought by the two sportsmen, and also by my informants, that the leopard had been hit in the back by the first bullet and possibly in the head by some of the subsequent bullets, and it was for this reason that a diligent and prolonged search had been made for it. From the particulars given me of the blood trail I was of opinion that the sportsmen were wrong in thinking that they had inflicted a body and a head wound on the leopard, for the blood trail as described to me could only have been made by a foot wound, and I was very gratified to find later that my deductions were correct and that the bullet fired by the man on the tower on the left bank had only creased the pad of the leopard's left hind foot and shot away a portion of one of its toes, and that the man on the right bank had missed all his shots.

Second: After some twenty leopards had been caught and killed in traps of the drop-door type, a leopard which everyone thought was the man-eater was caught in one of these traps; and as the Hindu population were unwilling to kill it for fear the spirits of the people whom the man-eater had killed would torment them, an Indian Christian was sent for. This Christian was living in a village thirty miles away, and before he could arrive on the scene, the leopard had dug its way out of the trap, and escaped.

Third: After killing a man the leopard lay up with his kill in a small isolated patch of jungle. Next morning, when a search was being made for the victim, the leopard was detected leaving the jungle. After a short chase it was seen to enter a cave, the mouth of which was promptly closed with thorn-bushes heaped over with big rocks. Every day a growing crowd of men visited the spot. On the fifth day, when some five hundred were assembled, a man whose name is not given but whom the report describes as 'a man of influence' came, and, to quote the report, 'said scornfully "there is no leopard in this cave" and took the thorns off the cave. As he took the thorns up, the leopard suddenly rushed out of the cave and made his way safely through a crowd of some five hundred persons who had gathered there.'

These incidents took place shortly after the leopard had become a man-eater, and had the leopard been killed on the bridge, shot in the trap, or sealed up in the cave, several hundred people need not have died, and Garhwal would have been saved many years of suffering.

A Shot in the Dark

Mealtimes in India vary according to the season of the year and individual tastes. In most establishments the recognized times for the three principal meals are: breakfast 8 to 9, lunch 1 to 2, and dinner 8 to 9. During all the months I was at Rudraprayag my mealtimes were very erratic, and contrary to the accepted belief that health depends on the composition and regularity of meals, my unorthodox and irregular meals kept me fighting fit. Porridge supped at 8 p.m., soup taken at 8 a.m., one combined meal in the day or no meal at all, appeared to have no injurious effect beyond taking a little flesh off my bones.

I had eaten nothing since my breakfast the previous day, so as I intended spending the night out I had a nondescript meal on my return from Bhainswara, and after an hour's sleep and a bath set off for Golabrai to warn the pundit who owned the pilgrim shelter of the presence in his vicinity of the man-eater.

I had made friends with the pundit on my first arrival at Rudraprayag and I never passed his house without having a few words with him, for in addition to the many interesting tales he had to tell about the man-eater and the pilgrims who passed through Golabrai, he was one of the only two people—the woman who escaped with the lacerated arm being the other—whom I met during my stay in Garhwal who had survived an encounter with the man-eater.

One of his tales concerned a woman who had lived in a village further down the road, and with whom he had been acquainted. After a visit to the Rudraprayag bazaar one day this woman arrived at Golabrai late in the evening, and fearing she would not be able to reach her home before dark she asked the pundit to let her spend the night in his shelter. This he permitted her to do, advising her to sleep in front of the door of the store-room in which he kept the articles of food purchased by the pilgrims, for, he said, she would then be protected by the room on the one side, and by the fifty or more pilgrims who were spending the night in the shelter on the other.

The shelter was a grass shed open on the side nearest the road, and boarded up on the side nearest the hill; the store-room was midway along the shed, but was recessed into the hill and did not obstruct the floor of the shed, so when the woman lay down at the door of the store-room there were rows of pilgrims between her and the road. Some time during the night one of the women pilgrims screamed out and said she had been stung by a scorpion. No lights were available, but with the help of matches the woman's foot was examined and a small scratch from which a little blood was flowing was found on her foot. Grumbling that the woman had made a lot of fuss about nothing, and that in any case blood did not flow from a scorpion sting, the pilgrims soon composed themselves and resumed their sleep.

In the morning, when the pundit arrived from his house on the hill above the mango-tree, he saw a sari worn by hill-women lying on the road in front of the shelter, and on the sari there was blood. The pundit had given his friend what he considered to be the safest place in the shelter, and with fifty or more pilgrims lying all round her the leopard had walked over the sleeping people, killed the woman, and accidentally scratched the sleeping pilgrim's foot when returning to the road. The explanation given by the pundit as to why the leopard had rejected the pilgrims and carried off the hill-woman was that she was the only person in the shelter that night who was wearing a coloured garment. This explanation is not convincing, and but for the fact that leopards do not hunt by scent, my own explanation would have been that of all the people in the shelter the hill-woman was the only one who had a familiar smell. Was it just bad luck, or fate, or being the only one of all the sleepers who realized the danger of sleeping in an open shed? Had the victim's fear in some inexplicable way conveyed itself to the man-eater, and attracted him to her?

It was not long after this occurrence that the pundit had his own encounter with the man-eater. The exact date—which could if desired be ascertained from the hospital records at Rudraprayag—is immaterial, and for the purpose of my story it will be sufficient to say that it took place during the hottest part of the summer of 1921, that is, four years before I met the pundit. Late one evening of that summer ten pilgrims from Madras arrived weary and footsore at Golabrai, and expressed their intention of spending the night in the pilgrim shelter. Fearing that if any more people were killed at Golabrai his shelter would get a bad reputation, the pundit tried to persuade them to continue on for another two miles to Rudraprayag, where they would be ensured of safe accommodation. Finding that nothing he could say had any effect on the tired pilgrims, he finally consented to give them accommodation in his house, which was fifty yards above the mango-tree to which I have already drawn attention.

The pundit's house was built on the same plan as the homesteads at Bhainswara; a low ground-floor room used for storage of fuel, and a first-floor room used as a residence. A short flight of stone steps gave access to a narrow veranda, the door of the residential room being opposite to the landing at the top of the steps.

After the pundit and the ten guests that had been forced on him had eaten their evening meal, they locked themselves into the room, which was not provided with any means of ventilation. The heat in the room was stifling, and fearing that he would be suffocated the pundit some time during the night opened the door, stepped outside, and stretched his hands to the pillars on either side of the steps supporting the roof of the veranda. As he did so and filled his lungs with the night air, his throat was gripped as in a vice. Retaining his hold on the pillars, he got the soles of his feet against the body of his assailant and with a desperate kick tore the leopard's teeth from his throat, and hurled it down the steps. Then, fearing that he was going to faint, he took a step side-ways and supported himself by putting both hands on the railing of the ve-randa, and the moment he did so the leopard sprang up from below and buried its claws in his left forearm. The downward pull was counteracted by the rail-ing on which the pundit had the palm of his hand, and the weight of the leop-ard caused its sharp claws to rip through the flesh of his arm until they tore free at his wrist. Before the leopard was able to spring a second time, the pilgrims, hearing the terrifying sounds the pundit was making in his attempts to breathe through the gap torn in his throat, dragged him into the room and bolted the door. For the rest of that long hot night the pundit lay gasping for breath and bleeding profusely, while the leopard growled and clawed at the frail door, and the pilgrims screamed with terror.

At daylight the pilgrims carried the pundit, now mercifully uncon-scious, to a Kalakamli hospital at Rudraprayag, where for three months he was fed through a silver tube inserted in his throat. After an absence of over six months he returned to his home in Golabrai, broken in health and with his hair turned grey. Photographs were taken five years later, and scarcely show the leopard's teeth-marks on the left side of the pundit's face and in his throat, and its claw-marks on his left arm, though they were still clearly visible.

In his conversations with me the pundit always referred to the man-eater as an evil spirit, and after the first day, when he had asked me what proof I could give him in face of his own experience that evil spirits could not assume material form, I also, to humour him, referred to the man-eater as 'the evil spirit.'

On arrival at Golabrai that evening I told the pundit of my fruitless visit to Bhainswara, and warned him to take extra precautions for his safety and for the safety of any pilgrims who might be staying in his shelter; for the evil spirit, after its long excursion into the hills, had now returned to the vicinity.

That night, and for the following three nights, I sat on the haystack, keep-ing a watch on the road; and on the fourth day Ibbotson returned from Pauri.

Ibbotson always infused new life into me, for his creed, like that of the locals, was that no one was to blame if the man-eater had not died yesterday, for surely it would die today or maybe tomorrow. I had a lot to tell him, for though I had corresponded with him regularly—extracts from my letters being embod-ied in his reports to the Government, and by them made available to the press— I had not been able to give him all the details which he was now eager to hear. On his part Ibbotson also had a lot to tell me; this concerned the clamour being made in the press for the destruction of the man-eater, and the suggestion that sportsmen from all parts of India be encouraged to go to Garhwal to assist in killing the leopard. This press campaign had resulted in Ibbotson receiving only one inquiry, and only one suggestion. The inquiry was from a sportsman who said that, if arrangements for his travel, accommodation, food, and so on, were made to his satisfaction he would consider whether it was worth his while to come to Golabrai; and the suggestion was from a sportsman in whose opinion the speediest and easiest way of killing the leopard was to paint a goat over with arsenic, sew up its mouth to prevent it licking itself, and then tie it up in a place where the leopard would find and eat it, and so poison itself.

We talked long that day, reviewing my many failures in minutest detail, and by lunch-time, when I had told Ibbotson of the leopard's habit of going down the road between Rudraprayag and Golabrai on an average once in every five days, I convinced him that the only hope I now had of shooting the leopard was by sitting over the road for ten nights, for, as I pointed out to him, the leopard would be almost certain to use the road at least once during that period. Ibbotson consented to my plan very reluctantly, for I had already sat up many nights and he was afraid that another ten on end would be too much for me. However, I carried my point, and then told Ibbotson that if I did not succeed in killing the leopard within the stipulated time, I would return to Naini Tal and leave the field free for any new-comers who might consider it worth their while to take my place.

That evening Ibbotson accompanied me to Golabrai and helped me to put up a machan in the mango-tree a hundred yards from the pilgrim shelter and fifty yards below the pundit's house. Immediately below the tree, and in the middle of the road, we drove a stout wooden peg, and to this peg we tethered a goat with a small bell round its neck. The moon was nearly at its full; even so, the high hill to the east of Golabrai only admitted of the moon lighting up the deep Ganges valley for a few hours, and if the leopard came while it was dark the goat would warn me of his approach.

When all our preparations had been made Ibbotson returned to the bungalow, promising to send two of my men for me early next morning. While I sat on a rock near the foot of the tree and smoked and waited for evening to close down, the pundit came and sat down beside me; he was a bhakti and did not smoke. Earlier in the evening he had seen us building the machan, and he now tried to dissuade me from sitting all night in the tree when I could sleep comfortably in bed. Nevertheless, I assured him I would sit all that night in the tree, and for nine nights thereafter, for if I was not able to kill the evil spirit I could at least guard his house and the pilgrim shelter from attack from all enemies. Once during the night a kakar barked on the hill above me, but thereafter the night was silent. At sunrise next morning two of my men arrived, and I set off for the Inspection Bungalow, examining the road as I went for pug marks, and leaving the men to follow with my rug and rifle.

During the following nine days my programme did not vary. Leaving the bungalow accompanied by two men in the early evening, I took up my position in the machan and sent the men away in time for them to get back to the bungalow before dusk. The men had strict orders not to leave the bungalow before it was fully light, and they arrived each morning as the sun was rising on the hills on the far side of the river and accompanied me back to the bungalow.

During all those ten nights the barking of the kakar on the first night was all that I heard. That the man-eater was still in the vicinity we had ample proof, for twice within those ten nights it had broken into houses and carried off, on the first occasion, a goat and on the second occasion a sheep. I found both kills with some difficulty for they had been carried a long distance, but neither had been of any use to me as they had been eaten out. Once also during those ten nights the leopard had broken down the door of a house which, fortunately for the inmates, had two rooms, the door of the inner room being sufficiently strong to withstand the leopard's onslaught.

On return to the bungalow after my tenth night in the mango-tree, Ibbotson and I discussed our future plans. No further communications had been received from the sportsman, and no one else had expressed a desire to accept the Government's invitation, and no one had responded to the appeals made by the press. Neither Ibbotson nor I could afford to spend more time at Rudraprayag; Ibbotson because he had been away from his headquarters for ten days and it was necessary for him to return to Pauri to attend to urgent work; and I because I had work to do in Africa and had delayed my departure for three months and could not delay it any longer. Both of us were reluctant to leave Garhwal to the tender mercies of the man-eater and yet, situated as we were, it was hard to decide what to do. One solution was for Ibbotson to apply for leave, and for me to cancel my passage to Africa and cut my losses. We finally agreed to leave the decision over for that night, and to decide on our line of action next morning. Having come to this decision I told Ibbotson I would spend my last night in Garhwal in the mango-tree.

Ibbotson accompanied me on that eleventh, and last, evening, and as we approached Golabrai we saw a number of men standing on the side of the road, looking down into a field a little beyond the mango-tree; the men had not seen us and before we got up to them they turned and moved off towards the pilgrim shelter. One of them however looked back, and seeing me beckoning retraced his steps. In answer to our questions he said he and his companions had for an hour been watching a great fight between two big snakes down in the field. No crops appeared to have been grown there for a year or more, and the snakes had last been seen near the big rock in the middle of the field.

There were smears of blood on this rock, and the man said they had been made by the snakes, which had bitten each other and were bleeding in several places. Having broken a stick from a nearby bush, I jumped down into the field to see if there were any holes near the rock, and as I did so I caught sight of the snakes in a bush just below the road. Ibbotson had in the meantime armed himself with a stout stick, and as one of the snakes tried to climb up on to the road he killed it. The other one disappeared into a hole in the bank from where we were unable to dislodge it. The snake Ibbotson had killed was about seven feet long and of a uniform light straw colour, and on its neck it had several bites. It was not a rat snake, and as it had very pronounced poison fangs we concluded it was some variety of hoodless cobra. Cold-blooded creatures are not immune from snake poison, for I have seen a frog bitten by a cobra die in a few minutes, but I do not know if snakes of the same variety can poison each other, and the one that escaped into the hole may have died in a few minutes or it may have lived to die of old age.

After Ibbotson left, the pundit passed under my tree on his way to the pilgrim shelter, carrying a pail of milk. He informed me that a hundred and fifty pilgrims, who had arrived during the day, were determined to spend the night in his shelter and that he was powerless to do anything about it. It was then too late for me to take any action, so I told him to warn the pilgrims to keep close together and not on any account to move about after dark. When he hurried back to his house a few minutes later, he said he had warned the pilgrims accordingly.

In a field adjoining the road, and about a hundred yards from my tree, there was a thorn enclosure in which a packman—not my old friend—earlier in the evening had penned his flock of goats and sheep. With the packman were two dogs who had barked very fiercely at us as we came down the road, and at Ibbotson after he left me to go back to the bungalow.

The moon was a few days past the full, and the valley was in darkness when, a little after 9 p.m., I saw a man carrying a lantern leave the pilgrim shelter and cross the road. A minute or two later, he recrossed the road and on gaining the shelter extinguished the lantern and at the same moment the packman's dogs started barking furiously. The dogs were unmistakably barking at a leopard, which quite possibly had seen the man with the lantern and was now coming down the road on its way to the shelter.

At first the dogs barked in the direction of the road, but after a little while they turned and barked in my direction. The leopard had now quite evidently caught sight of the sleeping goat and lain down out of sight of the dogs—which had stopped barking—to consider his next move. I knew that the leopard had arrived, and I also knew that he was using my tree to stalk the goat, and the question that was tormenting me as the long minutes dragged by was whether he would skirt round the goat and kill one of the pilgrims, or whether he would kill the goat and give me a shot.

During all the nights I had sat in the tree I adopted a position that would enable me to discharge my rifle with the minimum of movement and in the minimum of time. The distance between the goat and my machan was about twenty feet, but the night was so dark under the dense foliage of the tree that my straining eyes could not penetrate even this short distance, so I closed them and concentrated on my hearing.

My rifle, to which I had a small electric torch attached, was pointing in the direction of the goat, and I was just beginning to think that the leopard—assuming it was the man-eater—had reached the shelter and was selecting a human victim, when there was a rush from the foot of the tree, and the goat's bell tinkled sharply. Pressing the button of the torch I saw that the sights of the rifle were aligned on the shoulder of a leopard, and without having to move the rifle a fraction of an inch I pressed the trigger, and as I did so the torch went out.

Torches in those days were not in as general use as they are now, and mine was the first I had ever possessed. I had carried it for several months and never had occasion to use it, and I did not know the life of the battery, or that it was necessary to test it. When I pressed the button on this occasion the torch gave only one dim flash and then went out, and I was again in darkness without knowing what the result of my shot had been.

The echo of my shot was dying away in the valley when the pundit opened his door and called out to ask if I needed any help. I was at the time listening with all my ears for any sounds that might come from the leopard, so I did not answer him, and he hurriedly shut his door.

The leopard had been lying across the road with his head away from me when I fired, and I was vaguely aware of his having sprung over the goat and gone down the hillside, and just before the pundit had called I thought I heard what may have been a gurgling sound, but of this I could not be sure. The pilgrims had been aroused by my shot but, after murmuring for a few minutes, they resumed their sleep. The goat appeared to be unhurt, for from the sound of his bell I could tell that he was moving about and apparently eating the grass of which each night he was given a liberal supply.

I had fired my shot at 10 p.m. As the moon was not due to rise for several hours, and as there was nothing I could do in the meantime, I made myself comfortable, and listened and smoked.

Hours later the moon lit up the crest of the hills on the far side of the Ganges and slowly crept down into the valley and a little later I saw it rise over the top of the hill behind me. As soon as it was overhead I climbed to the top of the tree, but found that the spreading branches impeded my view. Descending again to the machan, I climbed out on the branches spreading over the road, but from here also I found it was not possible to see down the hillside in the direction in which I thought the leopard had gone. It was then 3 a.m., and two hours later the moon began to pale. When nearby objects became visible in the light of the day that was being born in the east, I descended from the tree and was greeted by a friendly bleat from the goat.

Beyond the goat, and at the very edge of the road, there was a long low rock, and on this rock there was an inch-wide streak of blood; the leopard from which that blood had come could only have lived a minute or two, so dispensing with the precautions usually taken when following up the blood trail of carnivora, I scrambled down off the road and, taking up the trail on the far side of the rock, followed it for fifty yards, to where the leopard was lying dead. He had slid backwards into a hole in the ground, in which he was now lying crouched up, with his chin resting on the edge of the hole.

No marks by which I could identify the dead animal were visible, even so I never for one moment doubted that the leopard in the hole was the man-eater. But here was no fiend, who while watching me through the long night hours had rocked and rolled with silent fiendish laugher at my vain attempts to outwit him, and licked his lips in anticipation of the time when, finding me off my guard for one brief moment, he would get the opportunity he was waiting for of burying his teeth in my throat. Here was only an old leopard, who differed from others of his kind in that his muzzle was grey and his lips lacked whiskers; the best-hated and the most feared animal in all India, whose only crime—not against the laws of nature, but against the laws of man—was that he had shed human blood, with no object of terrorizing man, but only in order that he might live; and who now, with his chin resting on the rim of the hole and his eyes half-closed, was peacefully sleeping his long last sleep.

While I stood unloading my rifle, one bullet from which had more than cancelled my personal score against the sleeper, I heard a cough, and on looking up saw the pundit peering down at me from the edge of the road. I beckoned to him and he came gingerly down the hill. On catching sight of the leopard's head he stopped, and asked in a whisper whether it was dead, and what it was. When I told him it was dead, and that it was the evil spirit that had torn open his throat five years ago, and for fear of which he had hurriedly closed his door the previous night, he put his hands together and attempted to put his head on my feet. Next minute there was a call from the road above of, 'Sahib, where are you?' It was one of my men calling in great agitation, and when I sent an answering call echoing over the Ganges, four heads appeared, and catching sight of us four men came helter-skelter down the hill, one of them swinging a lighted lantern which he had forgotten to extinguish.

The leopard had got stiff in the hole and was extracted with some little difficulty. While it was being tied to the stout bamboo pole the men had brought with them, they told me they had been unable to sleep that night, and that as soon as Ibbotson's jemadar's watch showed them it was 4.30 a.m., they lit the lantern, and arming themselves with a pole and a length of rope had come to look for me, for they felt that I was in urgent need of them. Not finding me in the machan and seeing the goat unhurt, and the streak of blood on the rock, they concluded the man-eater had killed me, and not knowing what to do they had in desperation called to me.

Leaving the pundit to retrieve my rug from the machan, and give the pilgrims who were now crowding round his version of the night's happenings, the four men and I, with the goat trotting alongside, set off for the Inspection Bungalow. The goat, who had escaped with very little injury owing to my having fired the moment the leopard caught him, little knew that his night's adventure was to make him a hero for the rest of his life, and that he was to wear a fine brass collar and be a source of income to the man from whom I had purchased him, and to whom I gave him back.

Ibbotson was still asleep when I knocked on the glazed door, and the moment he caught sight of me he jumped out of bed and dashing to the door flung it open, embraced me, and next minute was dancing round the leopard which the men had deposited on the veranda. Shouting for tea, and a hot bath for me, he called for his stenographer and dictated telegrams to the Government, the press, and my sister, and a cable to Jean. Not one question had he asked, for he knew that the leopard which I had brought home at that early hour was the man-eater, so what need was there for questions? On that previous occasion—in spite of all the evidence that had been produced—I had maintained that the leopard killed in the gin-trap was not the man-eater, and on this occasion I had said nothing.

Ibbotson had carried a heavy responsibility since October of the previous year, for to him was left the answering of questions of Councillors anxious to please their constituents, of Government officials who were daily getting more alarmed at the mounting death-roll, and of a press that was clamouring for results. His position had for a long time been like that of the head of a police force who, knowing the identity of a noted criminal, was unable to prevent his committing further crimes, and for this was being badgered on all sides. Little wonder then that Ibbotson on that 2nd of May 1926 was the happiest man I had ever seen, for not only was he now able to inform all concerned that the criminal had been executed, but he was also able to tell the people from the bazaars, and from the surrounding villages, and the pilgrims, all of whom were swarming into the compound of the Inspection Bungalow, that the evil spirit that had tormented them for eight long years was now dead.

After emptying a pot of tea and having a hot bath I tried to get a little sleep, but fear of a repetition of the cramps that twisted my feet, and from which I was only relieved by the vigorous ministrations of Ibbotson, brought me out of bed. Then Ibbotson and I measured the leopard, and carefully examined it. The following are the results of our measurements and of our examination.

Measurements:

Length, between pegs   7 feet 6 inches
Length, over curves   7 feet 10 inches

[Note. These measurements were taken after the leopard had been dead twelve hours.]

Description:

Colour. Light straw.

Hair. Short and brittle.

Whiskers. None.

Teeth. Worn and discoloured, one canine tooth broken.

Tongue and mouth. Black.

Wounds. One fresh bullet-wound in right shoulder.

One old bullet-wound in pad of left hind foot, and part of one toe and one claw missing from same foot.

Several deep and partly healed cuts on head.

One deep and partly healed cut on right hind leg.

Several partly healed cuts on tail.

One partly healed wound on stifle of left hind leg.

I am unable to account for the leopard's tongue and mouth being black. It was suggested that this might have been caused by cyanide, but whether this was so or not I cannot say. Of the partly healed wounds, those on the head, right hind leg, and tail were acquired in his fight at Bhainswara, and the one on the stifle of his left hind leg was the result of his having been caught in the gin-trap, for the piece of skin and tuft of hair we found in the trap fitted into this wound. The injuries on the left hind foot were the result of the bullet fired on the bridge by the young army officer in 1921. When skinning the leopard later, I found a pellet of buckshot embedded in the skin of his chest which an Indian Christian—years later—claimed he had fired at the leopard the year it became a man-eater.

After Ibbotson and I had measured and examined the leopard it was laid in the shade of a tree, and throughout the day thousands of men, women, and children came to see it.

When the people of our hills visit an individual for any particular purpose, as for instance to show their gratitude or to express their thanks, it is customary for them not to go on their mission empty-handed. A rose, a marigold, or a few petals of either flower, suffices, and the gift is proffered in hands cupped together. When the recipient has touched the gift with the tips of the fingers of his right hand, the person proffering the gift goes through the motion of pouring the gift on to the recipient's feet, in the same manner as if his cupped hands contained water.

I have on other occasions witnessed gratitude, but never as I witnessed it that day at Rudraprayag, first at the Inspection Bungalow and later at a reception in the bazaar.

'He killed our only son, sahib, and we being old, our house is now desolate.'

'He ate the mother of my five children, and the youngest but a few months old, and there is none in the home now to care for the children or to cook the food.'

'My son was taken ill at night and no one dared go to the hospital for medicine, and so he died.'

Tragedy upon pitiful tragedy, and while I listened, the ground round my feet was strewn with flowers.

Part Six:
America's Lion
The Cougar
Mysteries and Mayhem!

17 Cougar Attacks on Humans

BY ROBERT H. BUSCH

Cougar predation on humans is even more rare, and is contrary to the cat's nature. In 1892, Francis Parkman wrote that "the mountain lion shrinks from the face of man"; even Theodore Roosevelt admitted in 1901 that instances of the cat having attacked humans "are exceedingly rare." Biologist Alan Rabinowitz, who has studied wild cats from Belize to Bhutan, describes the cougar as "a very unaggressive cat."

But there have been exceptions, and reports of cougar attacks on humans, in areas with large populations of both humans and cougars, have increased. In the past century, cougar attacks in North America have resulted in the deaths of eleven people. Three of these deaths occurred within a two-year period from 1994–1995.

In 1986, five-year-old Laura Small was searching for tadpoles in a creek in Caspers Wilderness Park in southern California when she was suddenly grabbed by a cougar and dragged off. A hiker beat off the animal with a stick and the terrified girl was rushed to the hospital. As a result of her encounter, Laura lost the sight in one eye and is partially paralyzed. Her family sued the county authorities and was awarded preliminary damages of $2 million, the jury ruling that the county had not adequately warned tourists of the potential danger of cougars in the park.

The award sent shock waves through the wildlife management community across North America, which scrambled to erect signs and issue booklets to wilderness hikers. Today, visitors to Caspers Wilderness Park must sign a liability waiver prior to hiking through the park, and minors are not allowed in certain park areas. Similarly, hikers in Montana's Glacier National Park are now often faced with foreboding signs stating: CAUTION: MOUNTAIN LION ON TRAIL. Park managers aren't taking any chances.

It has long been known that cougars will feed upon human flesh. Bernal Diaz del Castillo, who accompanied Cortéz to Mexico in 1519, reported that the cougars in Montezuma's zoo were fed "deer, chickens, little dogs, . . . and also on the bodies of the Indians they sacrifice." The first recorded lethal cougar attack on a white man in North America appears to have been upon one Philip Tanner in Pennsylvania in 1751.

Despite folklore to the contrary, rabies is almost unknown among cougars. Only one cougar attack in North America, a California case in 1923, may have been attributable to rabies. Of the over eight thousand cases of rabies in North America reported to the Centers for Disease Control and Prevention in Atlanta, Georgia, in 1995, there was not one instance of rabies in cougars.

Almost a third of all cougar attacks in North America have occurred on Vancouver Island. Dan Lay, the former predator control officer for Vancouver Island, described the island's cats as "by far the most vicious cougars in all of [British Columbia]. . . . Over 50 percent of the cougars I take from settled areas have been scarred up by fighting." Lay suggests that adult male cougars may be pushing juveniles out of occupied territories and into conflicts with humans.

However, Knut Atkinson, a carnivore biologist with the British Columbia Wildlife Branch, doesn't believe that the Vancouver Island cougars are more aggressive than any others. He explains the situation this way:

> Many of our attacks, and all of the fatalities, have taken place on the west coast of the Island. This is the area where our deer populations are the lowest, due to a combination of poorer habitat, logging, and wolf predation, and where people and their houses are right against the bush. There is no buffer zone. . . . Occasionally a child is in the wrong place at the wrong time and we have an attack.

Some of the early recorded "attacks" on Vancouver Island, however, are open to question. In 1934, a Vancouver Island hunter killed a cougar and was shocked to find scraps of blue cloth and brass buttons in the cat's stomach. He immediately assumed that a sailor had been eaten by a cougar and hunters began roaming the woods searching for more of the man-eaters. Three cougars were killed before a local resident came forth and sheepishly admitted that the scraps of cloth belonged to a whale-oil soaked jacket that he'd thrown away, and that had been scrounged from the garbage by an enterprising cougar. Despite his admission, old-timers still talk of the "man-eating cougars" that ravaged their community in the 1930s.

Of those attacks verified by biologists, many are made either by old, starving animals or by young cougars still learning to hunt. In one British Columbia study, most attacks were by juvenile cougars independent of their mothers but not yet proficient at catching prey.

Almost half of the cats known to have attacked humans were underweight juveniles, animals that were desperate for food. Half of the offending adult cats were also noticeably thin.

Other attacks have been made by female cougars attempting to protect their young. Ian Ross, a cougar researcher in southern Alberta, once came across a female cougar that uttered a low moan and began to walk slowly toward him. "Then she broke into two or three very fast steps toward me and I thought, 'This is it!' I just shrieked at her and waved my arms, and she stopped, . . . turned, and then very slowly walked out of my way," he says. He later found that she had two newborn kittens, and had just been trying to defend them. "I don't fault her at all," he adds.

By far the majority of attacks by cougars are on children, whose small size is not dissimilar to that of the cougar's natural prey. Cougar researcher Fred Lindzey has theorized that a child's "quicker, more erratic movements compared with adults" also make them vulnerable. Children between five and nine years of age seem to be at highest risk.

Kailash Sankhala, an Indian tiger biologist, found that "tigers start stalking as soon as they find a man in a bent position, but when he stands up they lose interest." R. L. Eton reached a similar conclusion in his studies of the cheetah.

The cougar, too, seems to find an adult human in a standing position just too tall to be considered fair game. Of the few adults who have been attacked, many have been crouching at the time. One hunter met a cougar a few years ago on a logging road near Vancouver, British Columbia. The two held a staring contest for a few minutes, but the cat made no move until the hunter bent over to pick up a rock. Only when he was in this crouched position did it attack. He was able to beat the cougar off with his hands; he wasn't even scratched.

In 1993, a female jogger near Sacramento was attacked and killed by a cougar, following a similar attack in Colorado three years earlier. The cat was tracked down and killed; she was found to be a lactating mother, with a 1-month-old cub hidden nearby. The reason the woman was killed, though, is likely because she was running.

Running triggers a chase instinct in almost all predators, even in cougars, which normally avoid standing, two-legged prey. The same instinct goes awry when the prey is confined and continues running in panic. There's a report from Arizona of a cougar entering a sheep pen and killing all twenty sheep in one night. One Alberta cougar similarly killed fourteen goats during a single evening. Although these are often cited as examples of the cougar's "bloodthirsty" nature, they're actually just examples of the cat obeying a predatory chase instinct under unusual conditions. Cougars simply don't understand that domestic animals are not fair game.

Dr. Paul Beier, Associate Professor, Wildlife Ecology Department, Northern Arizona University, made a study of cougar attacks on humans and presented his findings to the cougar conference sponsored by the Colorado Division of Wildlife in Denver in 1991. He found that most of the attacks came from behind, followed by a bite to the back of the neck. Most of the people who were attacked weren't aware of being stalked until the stab of pain. Dennis Pemble, a wildlife conservation officer in southern British Columbia, believes that "a cougar is most likely to attack when it believes its prey is not aware of its presence . . . or if the prey does not indicate it will fight back, such as someone running away."

Two things are notable about these attacks on humans: their rarity, and the reaction of many humans to the mere presence of cougars or other predators. After one cougar attack near Colorado Springs, a number of residents demanded that all cougars within 150 miles of town be shot. Following a recent grizzly attack in Alberta, an indignant citizen wrote to the local paper demanding that all the bears in the *entire province* be shot. "Why should the public have to put up with this when we only want to enjoy the countryside?" another complainant wrote. Luckily, most wilderness hikers take a more tolerant view of the wild predators they might meet on the trail.

It's interesting, though, that the mysterious nature of the cougar has in some cases led to an animosity that's not directed toward other, better-known predators. In 1991, a cougar attacked a dog in a kennel near Colorado Springs, but quickly left the scene when a neighbor fired shots at it. According to Robert B. Davies, of the Colorado Division of Wildlife, the first reaction of the dog's owners was "to request removal of all mountain lions." It was patiently explained to them that this was not possible. Davies noted that "these people had had black bears feeding out of the garbage cans the previous summer and were not concerned about bears."

In one Colorado study of cougar attacks, researchers found that of seventy-one interactions with pets, cougars attacked in 61 percent of the cases. In the interactions between cougars and humans without pets, the chance of a person being attacked was found to be about 1 in 2.2 million.

One of the most controversial problems today is that of the cougar population in California. In 1994, seven cougars in California were killed as nuisance animals; two of them had attacked humans. It's estimated that the state now contains about five thousand cougars, twice that of only twenty years ago.

Cougars in California were classed as varmints until 1963, under a very generous bounty program. Hunters received $50 to $60 per cat, plus expenses, which averaged an additional $500 to $600. The program was discontinued in 1963, when cougars were classed as nongame animals. In 1969, they were reclassed as game animals for a two-year period. After over a hundred cats were shot, the species was given protection until 1987. A sport-hunting season was then opened on cougars for a short period, until it was challenged under the California Environmental Quality Act. In 1990, California citizens passed Proposition 117, the California Wildlife Protection Act, which banned cougar hunting completely. The only cats that can now be legally shot under depredation permits are nuisance animals—those that have caused damage to humans, livestock, or property.

Theoretically the damage caused by a cougar in California must be reported and verified by Department of Fish and Game personnel before a depredation permit is issued. However, almost two hundred such permits have been issued annually since 1990, many of which are based on mere cougar sightings. For example:

- May 1994. A hiker in Cuyamaca Rancho State Park is followed by a curious cougar. Authorities deem it a threat and shoot it.
- August 1994. A cougar strolls into a parking lot in Montclair and hides under a car. It, too, is deemed "dangerous" and is shot by wildlife officers.
- August 1994. A young female cougar wanders into a backyard in Loomis. Local police surround the frightened animal and shoot it, stating that it's acting "aggressively."

Almost half of the depredation permits issued in California since 1990 have resulted in the destruction of a cougar.

Some of the killings of cougars, of course, were justified. There have been two recent deaths resulting from cougar attacks in California. A jogger was killed in a state park near Sacramento in 1993, and a hiker in Cuyamaca Rancho State Park was killed in late 1994. Since 1990, California has reported eight cougar attacks on humans, including these two deaths.

The problem is there is not room for five thousand cougars in California. With a human population of over thirty million, and rural development creeping up every available canyon, conflicts with wildlife are bound to occur. Some biologists also believe that the cougars are losing their fear of humans. "We're seeing a different kind of mountain lion," says Paul Wertz, information officer with the California Department of Fish and Game. "They used to stay in remote areas and had enough contact with hunters and dogs that they learned to avoid them. But today they are no longer threatened by those sources."

There is also a concern about the effect of cougar predation on the threatened California bighorn sheep, which was reintroduced to the state in 1971, at the exorbitant cost of over $2,200 per animal. Biologists are perhaps justifiably concerned about protecting their investment.

Inevitably, some people have called for the retraction of Proposition 117. Although amending this proposition requires a four-fifths vote in both houses of the legislature, it can be altered by the enactment of additional propositions. An attempt to retract the proposition in March 1996 failed by a narrow margin, despite a strong pro-hunting lobby.

Steve Torres, a biologist with the California Department of Fish and Game, has stated that "there is no biological reason not to hunt mountain lions. Lions in California are not endangered or threatened and are not in jeopardy." But supporters of the original Proposition 117 point out that California's high ratio of humans to cougars is the real problem; sparsely populated states like Oregon, which has over twenty-five hundred cougars, have never experienced a single mauling or fatality caused by cougars. The advocates would therefore prefer to see aggressive cats moved to remote parks to reduce human-cougar conflicts. They also point out that there's a small population of cougars living within the Santa Monica Mountains in Los Angeles County, within an hour's drive of one of the largest cities in the world, and that not one of these cats has ever harmed a human. Biologists theorize that these cats have learned that humans are dangerous and should be avoided.

Some wildlife officers in other states, however, believe that the opposite is happening—that their cougars are starting to lose some of their natural fear of humans due to the high numbers of hikers and people who live in rural areas. Keith Aune, of the Montana Department of Fish, Wildlife, and Parks, found that "habituated mountain lions . . . begin to feed on livestock, human refuse . . . and, in some cases, pets in residential areas. Several . . . completely lost fear of humans."

Many so-called cougar attacks are nothing more than examples of the cat's innate curiosity. Alberta cougar biologist Martin Jalkotzy documented one case in which a cougar chased a girl up a tree then ran up, touched her with its nose, and ran off, its curiosity satisfied. Recently, a young cougar strolled onto private land near the town of Priddis in southern Alberta only to be quickly repelled by a farmwife wielding a broom. In the ensuing scuffle, the woman was bitten. The headlines in the local paper the next day screamed: COUGAR ATTACKS WOMAN! Jalkotzy commented that this is the usual slant that the media takes. "It would be more accurate," he noted, "for the headline to have read WOMAN ATTACKS COUGAR!"

Another recent incident involved a man in southern British Columbia who fell asleep in the woods and awoke to find himself under scrutiny by a cougar only four yards away. The two watched each other surreptitiously for a few minutes, but when the man made direct eye contact, the cougar quietly walked away.

Eye contact seems to repel many members of the cat family. In India, residents of the Sundarban marshes were regularly preyed upon by tigers until researchers discovered a simple deterrent. It seemed that tigers wouldn't attack a person wearing a mask on the back of his or her head, and the foresters and honey collectors lived for a while without fear. But cats are intelligent, and as soon as they discovered that the staring faces were not real, the attacks resumed.

In *Wild Hunters: Predators in Peril,* American cougar researcher Jay Tischendorf has stated:

> Humans have a way of getting themselves into bad situations with any kind of wildlife from rattlesnakes to chipmunks and squirrels. I think probably every animal in the world at one point or another has "attacked humans," but probably it almost always relates to the person being in the wrong place at the wrong time.

And the hordes of hikers now inundating America's last wilderness areas ensure that such inadvertent encounters will continue.

So just what *do* you do if you come face to fang with a cougar? One British Columbia pioneer recommended, "Never run. . . . Bang two rocks together as loud as you can." Maurice Hornocker has similar advice: "Stand firm, fight back, and yell." Ken Russell, leader of the Colorado Cooperative Wildlife Research Unit, adds that "giving the lion sufficient time and room to escape is important."

However, the chance of such an encounter is very slim. Statistically, you're five hundred times more likely to be stung by a bee and almost a thousand times more likely to be zapped by lightning than you are to be attacked by a mountain lion.

Part Seven:
Tembo!
The African Elephant
When Bigger Is Scarier!

18   Rogue Elephant

BY J. A. HUNTER

Two natives were returning to their village one evening when they saw a great black mass standing motionless in the shadows of the huts. The men shouted to scare the thing away. At once the mass left the shadows and charged them at fearful speed. Then the men saw it was a huge bull elephant.

They ran for their lives, each going in a different direction. One man was wearing a red blanket and that blanket was his death warrant, for the elephant followed him. The villagers cowering in their huts listened to the chase, powerless to help their friend. They heard the man's screams as the elephant caught him. The great brute put one foot on his victim and pulled him to pieces with his trunk. Then he stamped the body into the ground and went away.

I was guiding two Canadian sportsmen through the Aberdare Forest in British East Africa when runners arrived from the chief of the murdered man's village to ask my help in killing the elephant. The natives in Kenya knew me well, for I had lived there many years as a white hunter—taking out sportsmen to shoot big game and killing dangerous animals at the request of the government. The chief sent me word that this bull was a rogue elephant that had been destroying farms and terrorizing the district for many months. If the animal were not destroyed, he was sure to kill someone else sooner or later.

I was under contract to my two sportsmen. They were brothers, Allen and Duncan McMartin, and we had been in the bush many weeks looking for bongo, a rare antelope not easily come by. If I took off time to track down the rogue, it would lessen the brothers' chances of getting a good trophy. Still, the McMartins told me to go ahead. I have seen other sportsmen who would not have been so generous. I started back at once with the runners, taking Saseeta, my Wakamba gunbearer who had been with me many years.

273

When we arrived at the village, I was met by the chief. His name was Ngiri and we were old friends. But we had little time to talk of past adventures for the village was in a panic. The natives were afraid to venture into the shambas, as their maize fields are called, and many of them would not even leave their huts although the wattle shacks would have been little enough protection against a rogue elephant. Ngiri told me the rogue moved from village to village, destroying the maize fields as he went, and unless he was killed the villagers would be in dire straits indeed.

With Saseeta, I went out to look for the body of the dead native. We picked up his tracks on the edge of the village where he had first seen the elephant and followed them through the bush. It was a sad sight to see how he had zigzagged and doubled, trying to throw off his pursuer. Well do I know how he felt, for I have often been chased by elephants. It is like running in a nightmare, for the wait-a-bit thorns hold you back and the creepers pull at your legs while the elephant goes crashing after you like a terrier after a rat. Not a second goes by but you expect to feel that snakey trunk close about your neck, yet you dare not look back for you must keep your eyes on the brush ahead.

We found what was left of the body, but there was no sign of the red blanket that the man had been wearing. The elephant had no doubt carried it off with him. This was not the first time I had heard of a native dressed in red being attacked by an elephant and I believe the color must attract them.

I was ready to start at once on the rogue's spoor but Ngiri told me to wait. The bull was sure to despoil another village that evening and runners would bring in word during the night. Then I could start out on the fresh spoor in the morning and save a day or more of hard tracking. Ngiri was right. I could only wait and hope that the rogue would ruin a shamba and not take another life.

A few hours before dawn, a runner arrived all breathless from a village in the uplands some five miles away. The rogue had entered the village in the evening but instead of going straight to the fields had wandered up and down among the huts. He stopped in front of one hut and stood there so long that he dropped a great mass of dung not six feet from the door. One can imagine the feelings of the wretched natives who were huddled together under the flimsy thatch roof while outside stood the rogue elephant, unafraid and forbidding in the darkness. After a time that must have seemed to the natives like an eternity, they heard the great beast move off in the direction of their shamba and listened despairingly while he destroyed the crop—their little all, the fruits of their sweat and labor. When he had gorged himself, he moved away into the bush to digest his feast and sleep during the day.

As soon as dawn broke, Saseeta and I started out for the village. We had a stiff, uphill climb of nine thousand feet and the going was hard on the lungs. In the village we picked up the bull's spoor at a trodden gap in the thorn-bush barricade around the shamba. The trail led us toward the deepest part of the great Aberdare Forest.

After the bright light of the open country, the forest seemed like a great building with a green roof and tree trunks for pillars. There was an eerie stillness about the place for the thick foliage deadened sounds. We walked noiselessly among the boles of the vast trees. I was glad there was little undergrowth. I could see twenty yards ahead; as much as one might ask or want.

I smelt the pungent odor of elephant droppings and saw ahead of us a pile of these unsightly dollops, surrounded by myriads of small forest flies. Saseeta kicked the heap and pointed to the kernels of undigested maize. The droppings were fresh. The bull was only a few hours ahead of us.

I had hoped to come up with the bull in this semi-open part of the forest. But he was cunning and had gone into the thicket to take his daytime rest. The tracks led us into a belt of dense bamboo, intergrowing with a tall plant like forest nettle that was anything but desirable to hunt in. We put up troops of Colibi and Sykes monkeys that bounded away through the trees and I prayed the rogue wouldn't hear their startled crashing. In any case, the rotting bamboo underfoot made it impossible to walk quietly. I tried to step in the deep impressions made by the bull but his great stride dwarfed the efforts of mere man. Every time a red-legged francolin or tiny duiker antelope burst out of the cover, my heart gave a jump and I clutched my rifle. This kind of work is very different from trophy hunting where you can locate a herd in open bush and pick your bull. If it hadn't been for my promise to Chief Ngiri, I would have turned back and tried again when the bull was in better country.

The bamboo opened out and we came on a spot where natives had been cutting wood. I swore to myself when I saw how the bull had shied away from the hated man smell and knocked the bamboos aside as he raced off through the grove. An elephant that has no fear of human scent at night in shambas will often grow panicky when he smells man in the jungle. So far the bull had been moving slowly, grazing as he went. Now he was trying to put as many miles as possible between him and the woodcutters' camp.

Saseeta and I looked at each other. He shrugged. It was hunting luck. Doggedly we set out on the great spoor which took us up an almost unbelievably steep slope to a high ridge. Here the tracks went through a tangle of wild briars and stinging nettles as if the rogue were determined to find the foulest cover in the whole Aberdare. The snarl was so bad we had to crawl under it on our hands and knees, a time-consuming business and hard on the back. Wriggling along, I suddenly came out into a place where the elephant had stopped to rest. I was most grateful to him for having moved on. Coming unexpectedly on a rogue when you are flat on your belly under a briar tangle is not pleasant.

Suddenly a distinct crackling sound came from ahead. Saseeta and I lay still. The noise came again. The bull was feeding in a grove of bamboo only a few feet ahead of us.

We crawled forward. Once in the bamboo, we could stand upright—a great relief. We moved toward the noises, stepping carefully on the ground already flattened by the bull's great imprints. The wind was uncertain. Cross drafts in the bamboo tossed it about in all directions. There was no way we could be sure of keeping downwind of the elephant and the growth was so thick we could move only by staying in his tracks. I knew we must be almost up with him but I could see little through the tall stalks of bamboo hemming us in on every side.

Saseeta stopped and pointed with his lips toward our left. I could still see nothing but I slowly raised my rifle. I was using a .475 Jeffery #2, double-barrel express—a reliable gun that has never failed me or I wouldn't be writing these notes. The crashing sounded again only a few feet away. I held my breath, waiting for a shot.

Suddenly the noises ceased. There was absolute silence. Saseeta and I stood motionless and I wished I could stop the noise of my heart. It sounded to me like a drum. Then we heard the bamboos crack and sway as the bull turned and ran through the grove at full speed. That accursed breeze had given him our scent.

Saseeta and I looked at each other. Poor fellow, there is no profanity in his language but I was more fortunate and swore for us both. But I did so silently, for even though the elephant was now far away, we never spoke in the bush unless absolutely necessary.

The sun was beginning to drop and I knew it must be about five o'clock. We had been going since dawn through very hard country, and the elephant was now definitely alarmed. He might go for miles before he stopped. A wise man would have given up and returned to camp, but I have never been very wise, as far as hunting is concerned and I motioned to Saseeta that we'd continue to track.

Light in the undergrowth was already failing but we had no trouble following the bull. He had trampled down the tough bamboos like so much grass in his fright. As we pressed on, the rotting surface of the ground became worse than ever. My shoes plunged through it, producing sounds that not even an unwary elephant would have stood for.

After an hour's tracking, Saseeta gave a low, birdlike whistle—the recognized bush signal for "attention." We stopped and listened. I could hear the bull moving through the bamboo to our left. He was going downwind, trying to pick up our scent. Then the sounds stopped and I knew he had paused to listen. Instead of our stalking the elephant, he was now stalking us, and in my experience an elephant is a better stalker than a man.

I again considered turning back but I hated to break my promise to old Ngiri. My chances of getting a shot at the rogue were now very slim but Saseeta and I kept on. He could not have caught our scent as yet for we didn't hear him crashing away. He was still standing there, probably testing the air with his raised trunk. If he waited a few more minutes, we would be up to him. My eyes ached from the constant strain of peering ahead through the greenish yellow bamboo poles.

Suddenly I saw an indistinct, shadowy shape through the bamboo. I stopped dead and slowly raised my rifle. In the thick cover I could not tell head from tail. There was no gleam of white or yellow ivory to guide me. I held my breath until I nearly strangled to avoid the slightest noise and I knew Saseeta behind me was doing the same. I wanted badly to fire but was afraid of only wounding him. If he moved a few feet one way or the other I could tell where to shoot.

Then a sudden breeze swept through the bamboo. In an instant the bull got our scent and was gone.

I felt a sickly feeling. If I had fired I might have brought him down. But if I had only injured him, he might have killed us both in the thick cover or raced off with the pain of the wound driving him for miles before he stopped. A wounded elephant is a terrible creature and I never like to shoot unless I can be sure of a kill.

There was no use in going on. Evening was falling and the camp many miles away. Saseeta and I slowly toiled back over the long route. In the village, everyone was bitterly disappointed at my failure. Hardly a word was spoken. Supper was served in complete silence.

After I had eaten and lit my pipe, I could regard this whole business more philosophically. The failures make hunting worth while. If you won every time, there would be no thrill to it. I hoped the natives whose shambas the rogue was destroying that night could view the affair equally impartially.

I went to bed and lay awake listening to the herd calls of the hyrax, a curious beast that looks like an overgrown guinea pig, and the steady beat of native drums in the village. I knew they were keeping up their courage by gulping quantities of home-made brew and I wished I could join them, but I needed a clear head for hunting in the morning. Then came the haunting grunt of a lion. The sound of the drums quickly petered out as the natives hurried to their huts. I heard the lion drinking at the stream a few feet from my camp and move off again. Then there was silence except for the occasional distant chatter of disturbed monkeys and the twitter of a drowsy bird. I fell asleep.

The next morning a heavy fog covered the forest. The grass was heavy with dew and the air was distinctly chilly. While I was drinking my hot tea, a half-naked runner rushed into camp. During the night the bull had raided a shamba three miles away and destroyed the crop. The rogue was so cunning that he never raided the same village twice in succession and this made hunting him far more difficult.

Saseeta and I started off at once. When we reached the raided village, some of the natives volunteered to go along as guides. We picked up the bull's trail. By now, I knew every toenail in his huge feet and was beginning to hate the sight of them. We followed him as fast as we could go. He was headed toward the hills and our guides assured me that the country was more open there. I hoped they were right.

The slopes were steep and I had to stop constantly for rests. I envied the local natives their remarkable staying power. Still, the brush was open and we made fair time. But this was too good to last. By noon we entered some of the most damnable cover it has ever fallen my lot to hunt in. Bamboo shoots and fallen stems were woven into a virtual mat. Boles of dead trees lay across the trail, some four feet high. They were hard to climb over and worse to crawl under. The elephant had taken all these obstructions in his stride but we were not so fortunate. Moving quietly was impossible. I scowled at Saseeta for making an unnecessary noise and a moment later made a much louder noise myself.

We came on a spot where the bull had lain down at full length to sleep. I could see the imprint of his hide on the soft earth. This was encouraging, for if he had kept going, we never would have caught up with him. At the same time, I hoped we would not meet him in this thick stuff. We were in a secondary growth of bamboo, the stalks barely half as high as the long poles we had struggled through the previous day, and their tufted tops made it impossible to see beyond muzzle range.

Gusts of wind began to spring up making the long bamboos clank together. We moved forward with the greatest caution as it is difficult to tell whether wind-borne noises are caused by stems or by beast. This was the last place I wanted to meet the rogue, for when an elephant charges in bamboo, he knocks down the long, springy stems in front of him and you may be pinned under them before getting a chance to shoot. Even Saseeta, generally afraid of nothing, made an ugly grimace when I looked back as if to say, "This is a sticky business."

Suddenly we heard a movement in the bamboo ahead of us. Saseeta and I both stopped dead and I raised my rifle, waiting for the charge. Instead of the elephant, a magnificent male bongo broke out of the cover and stood in front of us. This was the very trophy the McMartins and I had been after for many long weeks. Yet I could not shoot for fear of alarming the rogue. Often it happens you see the best trophies when you can't collect them.

We passed the fern-clad banks of a mountain stream and saw where the bull had been pulling up bracken with his tusks to get at the roots. The roots of the bracken seem to possess a medicinal quality that serves to keep the great beasts healthy. We knew the bull must be just ahead of us now for the turned-over earth was still moist.

While we were checking the signs, one of our native guides darted back to say he heard a noise in the bamboo ahead of us. This might mean much or little. Saseeta and I moved forward as quietly as possible. The wind was steady now and in our favor. We moved slowly through the high stalks. Then we heard the ripping noise of bamboo being torn apart. The bull was right ahead of us. He could not hear us above the noise of his own feeding, and if the wind held, we had him.

I saw his trunk appear above the stalks and pull a particularly succulent tip down to him. I crept along, trying to see through the stalks ahead and at the same time watch where I put my feet. Saseeta kept behind me, constantly testing the breeze with a small forest fungi puff. When shaken, these little puffballs give off a fine white powder almost like smoke and you can tell every shift of the wind by watching it. As we went deeper into the bamboo, the heavy growth cut off the breeze and the puffball dust hung motionless around Saseeta's hand. Then I saw the bull not fifteen yards from me.

I could hear him munching bamboo shoots as the line conveying elevator of his trunk hoisted them into his mouth. Between us was a network of bamboo poles through which I dared not shoot lest the bullet be deflected by one of the tough stems. Another of those terrible decisions. Should I take the chance and shoot? Or should I wait a few minutes and hope the bull would shift his position slightly and give me a shoulder shot? I would have to make up my mind quickly for we were so close that our smell would permeate to him in the absence of wind.

Suddenly the bull saw us. He did not run as he had the day before. Without the slightest hesitation or warning, he spun around and charged.

Almost before I could raise my rifle he was on top of us. His great ears were folded back close to his head and his trunk was held tight against the brisket. He was screaming with rage—a series of throaty *"urrs"* is the nearest I can describe the sound. I aimed the right barrel for the center of his skull, a point three inches higher than an imaginary line drawn from eye to eye, and fired. For an instant after the shot the bull seemed to hang in the air above me. Then he came down with a crash. He lay partly hidden by the bamboo, giving off high-pitched cries and low, gurgling sounds. I fired the second barrel through the center of his neck. Instantly the whole body relaxed, the hind legs stretched to their fullest. So ended the raider that had brought death and terror to Chief Ngiri's people.

Our local scouts had wisely vanished when the shooting started. Now they began to appear as if out of the earth. They gathered around the dead rogue and stood looking at him, so overjoyed that they could not speak. It must have seemed to them almost too good to be true that they could now work their fields in peace and security.

I sat down on one of the dead rogue's legs to fill my pipe. Everyone wanted to do something to express his gratitude, although all the poor fellows could do was to offer me a drink of cool water. Some of the sectional parts of the bamboo stems showed tiny openings bored by insects. The natives, selecting these sections, cut them down and pressed them on me. Each section contained a few mouthfuls of clean, cold water.

When I had finished my pipe, I examined the dead rogue's carcass. The ivory was very poor. The tusks were only about forty pounds each, whereas a really good bull will carry ivory weighing three times that much. Forest vegetation seems to lack calcium, for the forest elephants never have as good tusks as the bush dwellers. While examining the tusks, I found an old bullet hole at the base of the right hand tusk. With my knife I dug out a musket bullet, probably fired by an Arab ivory hunter years before. The bullet was embedded in the nerve center of the tusk and the pain must have been terrible. The constant suffering had driven the old bull mad and that was why he had become a rogue. No doubt the Arab who had fired the shot was now living comfortably with never a thought for the suffering he had caused to both man and beast.

We headed back toward camp. Everyone was in high spirits and elated with success. The leading scouts cut a path for us through the tangle with their knives, shouting and laughing as we progressed, a noisy contrast to the deathly stillness with which we had crept along that same trail a few hours before. As we came out into open country, I could see the hill slopes dotted with black figures who had heard the sound of the rifle shots and come hurrying to meet us. Our scouts yelled some guttural sounds across the valley. Native voices carry a surprising distance and I could see the black dots stop and then go scurrying back to the village with the good news.

Back in camp, a great welcome was given Saseeta and me. Even the old and sick tottered out of their huts to thank us. The white man had not failed them. I sent word to Chief Ngiri that the raider was dead and then sat down to a well-earned supper.

That evening, sitting in front of my campfire and smoking my pipe, I thought back over the many years I'd spent in Africa as a hunter. When I first came to Kenya, the game covered the plains as far as a man could see. I hunted lions where towns now stand, and shot elephants from the engine of the first railroad to cross the country. In the span of one man's lifetime, I have seen jungle turn into farmland and cannibal tribes become factory workers. I have had a little to do with this change myself, for the government employed me to clear dangerous beasts out of areas that were being opened to cultivation. I hold a world's record for rhino, possibly another record for lion (although we kept no exact record of the numbers shot in those early days) and I have shot more than fourteen hundred elephant. I certainly do not tell of these records with pride. The work had to be done and I happened to be the man who did it. But strange as it may seem to the armchair conservationist, I have a deep affection for the animals I had to kill. I spent long years studying their habits, not only in order to kill them, but because I was honestly interested in them.

Yet it is true I have always been a sportsman. Firearms have been my ruling passion in life and I would rather hear the crack of a rifle or the bang of a shotgun than listen to the finest orchestra. I cannot say that I did not enjoy hunting, but looking back I truly believe that in most cases the big game had as much chance to kill me as I had to kill them.

I am one of the last of the old-time hunters. The events I saw can never be relived. Both the game and the native tribes, as I knew them, are gone. No one will ever see again the great elephant herds led by old bulls carrying 150 pounds of ivory in each tusk. No one will ever again hear the yodeling war cries of the Masai as their spearmen swept the bush after cattle-killing lions. Few indeed will be able to say that they have broken into country never before seen by a white man. No, the old Africa has passed and I saw it go.

19 The Elephant Charge You Can Watch on TV

BY BRIAN HERNE

T he professional hunters had Papa Hemingway to thank in large part for the spotlight of world attention thrust upon them in the free-wheeling postwar years in Africa. The Great White Hunter became Hollywood's latest hero. Aspiring amateur hunters from all over the world clamored for a taste of Hemingway's feats with big game. To fulfill their dreams and follow in Ernest's footsteps, adventurers booked passage to East Africa.

Hollywood depended on the expertise of the safari fraternity to make African movies. While some hunters scoffed at the overblown melodramatic hoopla of it all, most good-naturedly participated whenever they could. For one thing it was good business. For another, it expanded their frontiers beyond mere hunting. The glamorizing and dramatizing of the white hunter's life was in full swing—and a good time was being had by all.

Just as *The Macomber Affair* had been a financial and publicity windfall for Ker and Downey Safaris, the movie *King Solomon's Mines* brought welcome capital to the newest of three major safari firms. Hunter David Lunan, who had the bearing of a tall, dark, and handsome movie actor, and his partner, Stan Lawrence-Brown, had recently registered Lawrence-Brown and Lunan Safaris Ltd. The firm's name had a nice ring to it, but the two partners were almost always broke. Wartime military pay had never made anybody rich, and Stan and Dave were in the same financial straits as other postwar hunters.

Stan Lawrence-Brown, born in India of British parents, had grown up in Kenya, and had worked for Ker and Downey before going into partnership with David Lunan. To the Africans Stan was known as Bwana Korongo (Mr. Roan Antelope) because of his broad, heavy shoulders, a build that to the humorous Africans likened him to the sturdy outline of the world's second-largest antelope.

David Lunan's boyhood neighbor had been Leslie Tarlton, the founder of Kenya's first safari company. Tarlton had taken Lunan and his brother on duck shoots, and kept the boys spellbound with tales of adventure as he taught them about hunting. As a result Lunan followed in Tarlton's footsteps.

The partners had great aspirations, but were held back by humble pocketbooks. In the end it was the financial windfall from two record-class elephants that enabled Lawrence-Brown and Lunan to join the professional ranks as outfitters. The two had purchased elephant licenses in Tanganyika in hopes of getting ivory heavy enough to pay for start-up expenses. With a modest fly-camp they hunted in south Masailand, where they soon found many hundreds of elephant, but no giant bulls carrying big ivory. After three weeks' hunting they were running low on supplies, and almost in despair, when they came upon the tracks of two big bulls near the Masai village of Kibaya. Stan and Dave spoored the bulls all day. Late that afternoon they caught up with the elephants in dense bush. Neither man could believe their good luck. Stan shot the first bull carrying tusks weighing 135 and 132 pounds. Dave immediately shot the second bull with tusks of 129 and 126 pounds. From the sale of the ivory Stan and Dave had enough money to purchase rudimentary safari equipment, and Lawrence-Brown and Lunan Safaris was launched.

The biggest obstacle for hunters was finding vehicles. For years after the war new cars were almost impossible to obtain in Africa. As luck would have it, Dave found four four-wheel-drive Dodge Power Wagons at a military disposal. The vehicles had seen rough service in the Abyssinian campaign, and all were fitted out as water tankers. The two hunters went to an Indian Sikh named Partap Singh, a coach builder in Nairobi. Singh replaced the water tanks with wooden shooting-brake bodies and the vehicles gleamed like brand-new, custom-built safari cars.

When the partners got word MGM was about to make *King Solomon's Mines* starring Deborah Kerr and Stewart Granger, the two hunters found the producer and landed a contract to take out a film unit consisting of twenty-four clients. The filming was to begin in three weeks' time, and after getting a substantial deposit they managed to buy enough equipment to outfit the safari.

The dramatic opening scene of *King Solomon's Mines* shows a bull elephant rushing toward the cameras in a genuine full-out charge, which is abruptly stopped by a bullet from Stan that hits the elephant between the eyes. The elephant goes down, poleaxed in a cloud of dust. At that moment the cameras cut to Stewart Granger portraying the hero Allan Quatermain. Granger is shown in profile as he fires a double rifle, and then the camera switches back to the downed elephant.

English Gypsy hunter Bunny Allen was also on the *Solomon's* set and witnessed the elephant charge. He thought Stan had pulled off a spectacular shot in dropping the elephant, for had it not been shot it would very likely have killed a cameraman. The relieved movie crews and actors sat upon the fallen elephant and posed for photographs. Then everybody went back to camp, and a crew was sent to get the ivory. But the elephant was nowhere to be found. It had simply vanished. Stan's "perfect shot" had not been so perfect after all, even though it looked great to all who had seen the animal knocked cold.

Stan's bullet had passed close to the brain—close enough to stun the animal. When it recovered the elephant hightailed it out of the country. Stan, Bunny Allen, and a team of trackers spoored the elephant for days. But they never caught up with it, for by then the elephant was fully recovered. An aircraft was hired for the search, but the elephant was never found. Following that incident Stan advised, "Always put an insurance shot into dangerous game." After the *Solomon's* debacle it was advice he fervently practiced himself.

With the advent of Hollywood in Africa hunters' salaries shot up. Stan recalled, "We paid good hunters 250 quid [pounds] per month on *Solomon's*. Before that hunters could be had for between £100 and £200." There had never been any cap on hunters' salaries, even before the war. Top-notch men did demand higher salaries, which they usually got, especially for risky or daring performances around dangerous game.

The considerable proceeds from *King Solomon's Mines* set up Lawrence-Brown and Lunan's new company, giving them an immediate jump-start. "It was money for jam," Stan gleefully commented. The resulting publicity attracted the attention of other major American moviemakers. Dave and Stan outfitted Twentieth-Century Fox's film unit for Hemingway's *The Snows of Kilimanjaro*, starring Gregory Peck, Susan Hayward, and Ava Gardner. This time Dave Lunan was hired not as a white hunter but as Gregory Peck's double. Even so, during filming Lunan had to shoot a charging rhino that nearly hammered crew members. Soon afterward Lunan was "scalped" by a leopard, whose dewclaw somehow trepanned Dave; his scalp was ripped off, hanging over his face by a thread of skin.

20   Close Calls

BY BRIAN HERNE

Stan Lawrence-Brown had his office in the Safari Hotel one hundred yards up the street from his rival, Russell Douglas. The Safari Hotel was newer, and probably fancier than the New Arusha, but it did not have the trout river frontage, lovely grounds, or the Old World charm of its rival. The Safari was a four-story rectangular box built of stone and concrete, and in its time the interior was comfortably appointed with lofty rooms. Even today, while the Safari has sunk into obscurity with the advent of newer hotels, one cannot help but notice that this large hotel has all its plumbing on the exterior of the structure, a result of an oversight by the contractors, who had forgotten to include plumbing. The hotel was owned by two aristocratic English sisters, Gladys and Margot Rydon. Both women owned prosperous coffee estates. Gladys lived in a magnificent mansion overlooking a mysterious crater lake called Duluti, seven miles east of Arusha. Margot's son, David, was killed by a buffalo near Arusha in 1964.

The Safari Hotel was masterfully managed for the Rydons by a pale-skinned Englishman named Ben Benbow. Benbow was a professional hotelier down to his manicured fingertips and slicked-down hair. He was the only man in Arusha who always wore a suit and tie. Among his dusty, khaki-clad safari clientele, he stood out like a catwalk mannequin in the Ituri forest. Rotund, jovial, and present when guests registered, day or night, Benbow was on a first-name basis with every white hunter as well as with celebrity actors such as Robert Taylor, John Wayne, and Hardy Kruger. The walls around the huge copper bar at the Safari were decorated with framed and signed photographs of white hunters with their clients and trophies.

Stan Lawrence-Brown wasted no time in recruiting lieutenants. He had brought with him from Kenya a young and talented hunter named David

Ommanney. Ommanney had worked for both Stan and Dave Lunan during their partnership, having begun his apprenticeship with them in 1952. At Arusha Jacky Hamman came on board, followed in 1957 by hunters George Six, Derrick Dunn, Brian Herne, Nick Swan, and, in 1960 a very good Kenya hunter, Mike Hissey, and Stan's brother, Geoff. On a casual basis Stan hired Douglas Collins, Lars Figgenshou, and, for a time, Greg Hemingway (youngest son of Ernest). Greg's older brother, Patrick Hemingway, was a hunter with Russell's Whores and Shauris, just down the road.

By any measure Stan Lawrence-Brown was one of the leading hunters of his day. He was an extremely good rifle shot, particularly with his Holland and Holland .470 double ejector. Back when Lawrence-Brown and Lunan began their hunting venture, their first major safari clients had been Marje and Donald Hopkins of Spokane, Washington. Don Hopkins was a very wealthy man and codeveloper of several different rifles known as O.K.H.s. The first Hopkins safari was a three-month trip in Kenya and Tanganyika. Both Marje and Don became grand safari aficionados, whose hunts often lasted six months, and sometimes much longer. At first both Marje and Don hunted with Stan, but as husband and wife became more competitive, subsequent hunts were arranged separately to keep the peace.

After his first trip Hopkins became fascinated with elephant hunting. He made a record eleven safaris averaging nine months apiece in search of an elephant (thought to be mythical by his hunters) with tusks weighing 150 pounds each. Stan was always nominally his white hunter, although a second, and sometimes a third hunter, was engaged at the same time. During the course of a Hopkins safari, Stan was often away, back in Arusha or Nairobi, and whoever was second hunter took over the show with Hopkins. I once hunted with Don for seven months, during which time Stan came and went, sometimes remaining away for a month at a time.

In pursuit of big elephant, Stan Lawrence-Brown had miraculously survived two maulings, though neither occurred on a Hopkins safari. Not surprisingly he regarded elephant with some caution, although he liked to be within at least thirty yards range before allowing a client to shoot. The first of Stan's elephant attacks occurred near the Tana River village of Saka, when Stan was hunting with a client named Francois Sommer, a demanding Frenchman.

Stan and Sommer forded the Tana at Saka, wading from sandbar to sandbar despite the crocodile population, and then entered the dense riverine jungle. Stan's trackers picked up the fresh spoor of three elephant bulls. In a short time they caught up with the bulls in acacia forest, and although they could not see the animals, they could hear the crack of branches as the elephant moved about feeding. Stan crept nearer followed by his client, and at a range of twenty yards the foliage parted to reveal a big elephant, its trunk held suspiciously high testing for alien scent. In a second the elephant dropped its trunk and charged the offensive human odor, smashing down bushes in its path.

Stan threw up his .470 and fired the first barrel, but the elephant came on as if nothing had happened. Sommer apparently fired a shot, too. As Stan's second barrel roared, the elephant grabbed for Stan with its trunk. He was knocked aside by the elephant's trunk, and instead of grabbing him it snatched Stan's wide-brimmed Borsalino hat off his head, flinging it violently to the ground. For some reason the elephant broke off the attack and crashed away, leaving a shaken and bruised Stan. Stan's gunbearer Mohammed and Tana River tracker Mwalimu Manza, who were unarmed, had somehow dodged the enraged elephant.

With Mwalimu's help Stan, despite a dozen broken ribs and severe bruising caused by the elephant's trunk, followed the spoor for weeks, but never caught up with the animal. Stan said there was no blood spoor and he was certain the elephant recovered from those head shots. Even after he had quit spooring the elephant Stan engaged extra Tana River trackers—led by legendary Borana tracker Gholo—to assist Mwalimu with the search, but even these experts were never able to catch up with the elephant, despite Stan's promise of a hefty bonus.

Stan said he never could figure out why the elephant had not finished him off when it had the chance. He concluded that his hat had saved his life when the elephant's attack was distracted by it. Stan Lawrence-Brown did not consider himself superstitious, but after that incident he wore a wide-brimmed Borsalino hat with a khaki *pugree* hatband. The Borsalino was his trademark, and he was rarely seen without it. Almost everybody in Stan's employ wore a similar hat and *pugree*.

Every now and then one reads fanciful accounts that mention "disappearing" African bearers who vanish when danger threatens. Nobody is denying that occasionally bearers disappear, and who can blame them for a quick retreat if their bwanas fail to knock down charging animals? Bearers are usually unarmed. In the experience of most professionals it is often the bearers who are the bravest of the brave. Many hunters, including Stan Lawrence-Brown, owed their lives to their bearers.

During his second mauling by an elephant, Stan's life was saved by the quick action of his gunbearer, a small Masai D'robo tracker named Longolla Lakiti. Subsequent to Sommer's safari, Stan was hunting with clients in Tanganyika's south Masailand. He and two clients, a husband and wife, found the spoor of four bulls that had crossed the sandy road during the night. Several miles of tracking brought them within earshot of the elephants, which were spread out and feeding in open brush. Beside a large baobab tree Stan left his lady client with her gunbearer, the nervous, strung-out Mohammed, who had been with Stan during the Saka elephant attack.

Stan, client, and tracker Longolla inched forward to inspect the bulls in turn. The first tusker broke out of a bush twenty yards from the hunters, and they saw his ivory, which Stan judged to be seventy pounds a side. They let him go, and worked their way toward another elephant feeding in a thicket fifty yards farther on. They got to within thirty yards of the elephant, which suddenly charged. The elephant's head broke out of the brush ten yards from Stan. He fired for a frontal brain shot with his .470, but the elephant grabbed Stan in its trunk, whirled him aloft, and tried to skewer him onto a tusk and impale him. Meantime, Longolla grabbed Stan's rifle out of the dust, pressed it against the side of the elephant's head, and fired the second barrel. The elephant collapsed with a brain shot but with the unfortunate Stan still gripped by its trunk. Longolla had saved Stan's life, but the fall injured Stan's back and he suffered from back pain for the rest of his life.

Part Eight:
Snake!
Cobra, Mamba, Rattlesnake, and Others
Don't Tread on These!

21   Aggressive Snakes

BY JAMES A. OLIVER

Anumber of years ago a story was circulated about a Boer farmer in South Africa who was ploughing with his team of oxen when his plough passed through the subterranean nest of a mamba. The aroused snake quickly glided up the furrow and set out after the farmer and his oxen. The gracefully curved body flowed rapidly over the ground, and the snake neatly nipped the farmer on the neck. It then proceeded to bite each ox on the flank, and as quickly returned to its lair. The hapless farmer and the oxen allegedly died almost immediately.

This tale strongly impressed on me the terribly aggressive nature and deadliness of the mamba. Later I read another story confirming these early impressions. In this story, a pair of the snakes were engaged in amorous pursuits when they were disturbed by a young couple on horseback. At the sight of the snakes, the couple galloped away from the spot. Although they urged the horses to their best efforts, the enraged male mamba swiftly overtook them and bit both horses and riders, all of whom died shortly after.

Another story has appeared about a young couple driving along a South African road in a small open sportscar. They ran over a large Black Mamba that was basking in the road. The impact merely annoyed the snake, which set out after the fleeing car, soon caught up with it, and bit both occupants fatally.

Each of these stories was presented at the time as a supposedly factual experience. In the light of present knowledge about this snake and its frequent role in fictitious or exaggerated stories of African adventure, however, it seems certain that none of the stories has much factual basis, and that the similarity among them is more than coincidental. A large number of stories—virtually all imaginary—feature the mamba as a real terror of the bush, THE great hazard of life and travel in Africa.

Few snakes have ever had such energetic press agents as the mamba. Its very name is symbolic of treacherous and sinister death. Such is the dreadful spell of this name that a best-selling novel by the African writer Stuart Cloete bears the single-word title, "Mamba." Is such an awe-inspiring and infamous reputation justified, or is it, like so many things about snakes, another exaggeration?

While the mamba is perhaps the best known symbol of serpentine aggression, all snakes are considered in the same light by some people, and a number of other species are widely believed to attack human beings on sight. We must, of course, consider what we mean by the terms "aggression" and "aggressive" before we examine some examples of snake behavior considered to be aggressive. For the individual killed by a falling airplane, it is of no consequence whether the plane was guided intentionally by a lunatic or whether it fell out of control of the hands of an inept student. However, the difference is of considerable interest to the rest of mankind. Similarly it makes a difference whether a snake makes an unprovoked attack, or whether it simply conducts an active defense when *it* is attacked.

Venomous snakes do not attack human beings for food. Only the rare giants among the largest species are physically capable of coping with prey as large as a man or woman. In the few cases where human beings have been killed by such giant snakes, the snake was either attacked or injured. Other than the necessity to defend itself, none but the larger snakes have any reason to attack human beings. Still the belief persists. Usually it is attributed to an inherent viciousness in snakes; occasionally it is linked to a strong territorial sense in which the snake is said to vigorously defend its home or nest. This notion involves a stronger sense of territorial rights or parental devotion than is known for snakes.

One of the most common reports of this supposed type of aggression is the tale of the enraged snake who comes to its murdered mate, usually seeking revenge. When Huckleberry Finn and his friend Jim were rafting down the Mississippi River, they camped on an island where Huck killed a rattlesnake and curled it up on the foot of Jim's blanket, hoping to have some fun at Jim's surprise when he found it. Huck forgot about the snake by nightfall, and poor Jim was bitten by the snake's mate. Remorsefully Huck says, "That all comes of my being such a fool as not to remember that wherever you have a dead snake its mate always comes there and curls around it." The widespread nature of this belief is indicated by the remarks of one of Stuart Cloete's characters, "Because you know, and I know, that if you kill a mamba its mate will look for it."

When two snakes are found near each other, their presence is usually coincidental; they are just as often of the same sex as of opposite sexes—and neither is likely to be interested in making an attack on the intruding human being. During the mating season snakes, particularly males, are alert to all movements and are more curious and bolder than at other times of the year. In some species the males locate females by following their scent. During this brief time a male could locate and remain near a freshly-killed female, but it would have no way of identifying the killer of the snake. And it would be no more likely to attack an intruder at such a time than it would before it encountered the dead snake.

Many other yarns about snakes elaborate beliefs of their supposedly aggressive nature. The Hoop Snake of the southern United States is alleged to launch its attacks by taking its tail in its mouth and rolling along like a hoop after its intended victim. When within striking distance, it supposedly releases its tail and hurls its body, tail first, inflicting a deadly sting with the tip of its tail. This story is entirely fictitious. No snake can roll along like a hoop, and no snake has a stinger in its tail. The Coachwhip Snake is another vicious attacker in American folklore. This speedy snake is said to be able to outrun the fastest horse. Supposedly when it overtakes its human victim it wraps the fore part of its body around the man's legs so that further running is impossible, and then it flogs him mercilessly with its long whiplike tail. The debunking of this belief, far more prevalent in the South than elsewhere, is said to have resulted in a widespread rise in juvenile delinquency. There *is* a snake known as the Coachwhip Snake because of its resemblance to a slender braided whip. It is a fast traveler, but any able-bodied boy or girl can outrun it with ease, and it does not use its tail as a whip.

A distinction should be made between an unprovoked attack and what can be termed "active defense." Technically there probably is no such thing as an *unprovoked* attack. However, if a snake attempts to rush toward a person and to bite *without having been disturbed,* this is, practically speaking, an unprovoked attack, and therefore a case of aggression. Striking at, hitting, stepping on, or suddenly threatening a snake constitutes provocation, and a snake reacting vigorously to any of these does so defensively and not aggressively. If you suddenly step beside a snake, or accidentally put your hand on one or close to it, such acts represent a threat to its welfare, and the snake's response, if any, is defensive. Since none but the largest snakes might eat human beings, the only reason for aggression would be malevolent viciousness or an easily-excited defensive behavior. The latter might be related to the defense of a territory against intruders, or the active guarding of a nest. All have been cited in relation to alleged attacks by snakes, but are definitely exceptional types of behavior.

Most snakes—both harmless and venomous—protect themselves from human beings by quickly crawling away or remaining completely still and being overlooked. Trouble often arises when snakes are cornered and cannot escape, when they are come upon suddenly and do not have time to escape, or when the intruder stands between them and the usual place of shelter. Being cornered is the primary reason for aggressive displays by snakes in captivity. Given the opportunity, most of the supposedly aggressive snakes escape. If they cannot rely on this normal means of protection, they are forced to defend themselves. Therefore, consideration here will be given primarily to snakes in the wild.

Often any movement toward a person is interpreted as an attack. This is especially true if the person is afraid of snakes. The greater the fear, the less the movement required to qualify as aggression in the mind of the person. In some instances this interpretation may be completely wrong. Twice when I have been snake-hunting I have had snakes try to escape by coming straight toward me and crawling between my legs *without* any attempt to bite. Another time, while I was watching some lizards in Florida, I had a Black Racer follow me for almost a hundred feet. As soon as I made a move in its direction, it departed in haste. Many herpetologists have had similar experience.

Arthur Loveridge, a longtime student of African wildlife both in the field and the laboratory, has written: "One day, I was standing on a large mass of smooth, but highly sloping rock, on a boulder-strewn hill. Below, and to the left of me, was a gunbearer searching for a hyrax which I had just shot. Above, and behind me, a second native was descending after going to retrieve a lizard which I had shot.

"Apparently, in descending he disturbed a mamba, possibly six feet in length, certainly not an inch less than five feet. It was so quick in its rush that he never saw it. I felt something bump and brush against my shoe, as I half-turned the snake was already in mid-air, having shot off the rock with the impetus of its descent. It landed twenty feet below on a mass of scrub and thorn, never paused, slid straight over another huge slab in full view, then dived into a tangle of vegetation beyond this rock and was seen no more. The boy on the rocks to the left below me, exclaimed: 'Did you see that big snake go right between your legs?'

"As a matter of fact it was not actually between; what happened was that it had side-slipped with the velocity with which it arrived on the rock, then carromed against my shoe. I was thankful that my back was not towards it, for had I been facing the other way I should doubtless have gone to swell the ranks of those who thought they had been attacked by a mamba."

The existence of one aggressive snake out of a thousand does not earn the designation "aggressive" for the entire species. However, if many individuals are truly aggressive, then the species can be considered generally aggressive.

Pride of place for aggression unquestionably goes to the mamba on the basis of its widespread infamy. There are four species of mambas, all living in Africa and found nowhere else. They are:

> Black or Brown Mamba—found throughout a wide area of Africa south of the Sahara. It attains a maximum length of 14 feet, and is the longest venomous snake in Africa.
>
> Green Mamba—occurs in central, eastern, and southern Africa. It reaches a maximum length of 9 feet.
>
> West African Mamba—inhabits western Africa and attains a length of 8 feet.
>
> Jameson's Mamba—found in the forest and scrub areas of central Africa. It reaches a maximum length of about 8 feet.
>
> A fifth form, called the Transvaal Mamba, is listed in some books, but it is a minor variant of the Black Mamba and should not be considered distinct from it.

All of these are long, slender, agile snakes found on the ground, as well as in the bushes and trees. The average person could not distinguish among the different species of mambas, and generally would confuse all of them with several other long and slender snakes. For years many herpetologists confused the Black (really a dark gray or brown and not a black-colored snake) and the Green Mambas because the young and half-grown individuals of the Black Mamba are green in color. However, there are important differences in structure and temperament. Because of its large size and excitable disposition, the Black Mamba is the scourge of the group, and especially aggressive individuals of this species have been reported frequently from South Africa. The others are generally shy and retiring except when injured or touched. Most field accounts do not distinguish accurately between these forms, and even if Black Mamba is specified, the identity is not certain in many instances.

F. W. Fitzsimons, for many years Director of the Port Elizabeth Museum and Snake Park in South Africa, had considerable experience with Black and Green Mambas, and related many stories about both in his book, *Snakes*. He says that the Green Mamba is shy and timid in disposition, always retreating when disturbed. He does not know of a single instance in which a Green Mamba has attacked without provocation. He does report cases where individuals were bitten when they brushed against a Green Mamba that was resting in a bush or stepped on one lying on the ground. In contrast to the Green Mamba, the Black Mamba is considered by Fitzsimons as a very excitable snake that will "invariably flee when disturbed" if given the opportunity.

Other herpetologists also have a great respect for this large snake, but all agree that it is not aggressive and will flee when given the chance. Walter Rose, in his book, *Snakes—Mainly South African,* wrote as follows: "Deadly it certainly is, having long fangs well to the front of the mouth, and venom of a highly toxic character; and in activity few if any snakes can surpass it; but it cannot be regarded as ferocious, being indeed an extremely nervous creature. Since we expressed this opinion in an earlier book, we have received letters from several correspondents, who have lived for years in mamba country and who have caught dozens of them, entirely agreeing with it. All lay stress on its inoffensiveness *unless molested,* deliberately or inadvertently" (italics the present author's).

He went on to say that deaths from mamba bite "are rare outside the pages of fiction, and then generally following some ill-advised, semi-hysterical attempt to kill one."

Arthur Loveridge has had many personal encounters with both Black and Green Mambas. His experiences confirm the statements already cited, but indicate that mambas are sometimes a hazard simply by their presence in the area and the fear they inspire in the human population. This is true wherever they may occur in abundance near human habitation. Sometimes trails or roads are closed merely because large mambas are regularly seen in a given location. In Nyasaland, Loveridge reports that mambas appear to be particularly troublesome in the vicinity of Mount Hora, a rocky hill beside the main road. A government agricultural officer driving in the neighborhood once had a large mamba rear up and hit the windshield of his car. Another district officer had a similar experience when a snake struck the door of the open touring car in which he and his family were driving. Loveridge quotes the acting provincial commissioner, whom he had queried about these snakes, as stating that what he assumed to be Black Mambas were fairly common in the district. "When surprised it rears up about chest high. Bus drivers stop if they see one on the road for fear it may strike a passenger."

This habit of rearing the head is common among racer-like snakes when disturbed or when investigating some movement. Loveridge cites an instance of a surprised mamba rearing up for a look and then going on its way. The group's headman was hurrying along after Loveridge "when he encountered a big snake that came sliding down the eroded, rock-strewn hillside and out on to the footpath within six feet of him. The startled snake reared up (allegedly higher than Thomas' face, a statement that may be discounted— Loveridge) and faced him for a few seconds, then dropping to the ground, it continued on downhill to a bush-choked ravine."

Loveridge reports other somewhat similar encounters with large Black Mambas. C. J. P. Ionides, Senior Game Ranger of Tanganyika territory and an experienced herpetologist, once suddenly came upon a large Black Mamba at close quarters. The snake raised its head about a foot off the ground and spread a hood so large that Ionides took a good look to be sure it was not a cobra. Meanwhile he retreated to get a stick, but the snake crawled off before he could catch it. On another occasion Ionides surprised a large female of the same species. The snake darted off, but when Ionides followed, the mamba turned, reared about two feet from the ground, and spread a hood. After remaining motionless for awhile, she slowly advanced towards a small patch of grass that lay between them. For a short time she continued to stare at him over the grass, then made for a termite hill. He took out after the snake and caught it. Ionides has given his opinion of the mamba: "I quite agree that the mamba is not an aggressive snake, being rather timid and anxious to avoid an encounter. If cornered, it will strike out in self defence, but prefers to get away if it can. I have caught scores during the last few years and consider them quite gentle but very nervous snakes."

How, then, do we explain the aforementioned reports of mambas striking cars? Probably the snakes raised their heads to see what was approaching, but the cars came on them so fast they didn't get out of the way in time, and either struck at, or were hit so hard their heads were jerked against, the cars. In either case, the action would be an unsettling and dangerous one to experience, but can scarcely be attributed to truly aggressive action by the snake.

Loveridge tells of another encounter with a mamba that might have ended quite differently, one hardly in keeping with the popular idea of standard behavior for a mamba. The episode occurred on Manda Island off the coast of Kenya Colony. Loveridge was leading his men along a trail through an acacia forest when he stooped and passed beneath a spreading bough, as he had done many times before on the trip. He was followed by a native carrying a small antelope in each hand. This man also stooped and moved on. Next came the gunbearer carrying a collecting gun in his right hand and with a rifle slung across his back, projecting above his left shoulder. He was a tall man, and did not stoop sufficiently, so the muzzle of the rifle became entangled in the branch. Without looking around he jerked his shoulder impatiently, but this failed to free the gun. Turning to see how he could best set it free, he found himself face to face with a large and surprised mamba, not more than six inches away! With a wild cry the man sprang forward, freeing the gun by his sudden, forceful movement. Loveridge rushed back to see what the commotion was about, and by the time he reached the spot the mamba was three trees away and traveling fast over the foliage at a height of 25 feet. He shot the snake and found it measured exactly 9 feet, but a few inches were missing from the tail.

A somewhat similar instance was reported in Uganda in 1952 when a native policeman was retrieving a guinea fowl he had shot. He accidentally stepped on a mamba, which coiled around his foot and ankle, but which fled precipitously as soon as the officer realized his predicament and jumped back. R. M. Isemönger, experienced collector of snakes in South Africa, has related a Zululand encounter with a large Black Mamba in which he had a most frightening escape. In his book *Snakes and Snake-catching in Southern Africa* he wrote, "Whilst groping my way through thick brush, I noticed the tail-end of a snake nearby, but at first did not realize what species it was, only about 12 inches were in view. As it happened, the tail belonged to an enormous Black Mamba lying in a semi-circular position, so that its head, instead of being about 12 feet away, was, in fact, barely a few feet from where I was standing.

"As I moved closer to get a better view in order to confirm the identification, my intentions were interpreted as definitely hostile, whereupon the snake struck at once, hooking its fangs into the khaki fabric of my slacks. It released its grip immediately but remained motionless, staring at me, rather as if it were about to say: 'Your move next!' I was wise enough (or frightened enough) to stand quite still, and it gently lowered its head and slithered off towards a crevice at the base of the cliff.

"Mambas usually slip away before you get too close, but as I had probably come upon it suddenly and too near to its home, its reaction was pardonable, if a little disturbing. Amongst the many I have caught, this was the only time one had actually struck at me before having been grabbed."

So much for the mambas. Judged by the unemotional opinions of men who have had wide experience with these snakes, they are not aggressive and rarely bite unless provoked, but they may defend themselves actively if wounded, suddenly threatened, or startled. How different from the terrible attacking demons of fiction!

But what of the cobras, particularly the King Cobra? Is it, too, the victim of fearful exaggerations, or is it perhaps deserving of its awesome reputation? From the point of size alone the King Cobra is worthy of respect, for it is the longest, and perhaps the heaviest, venomous snake in the world, reaching a maximum length of 18 feet 4 inches. It is equipped with a nerve-affecting venom powerful enough to knock out an elephant. In fact, there are records of elephants having been killed by King Cobras that bit them on the tip of the trunk—about the only place that such a snake could bite an elephant and penetrate its skin. Throughout southeastern Asia where this Cobra dwells, it is a common belief that King Cobras attack human beings on sight. A few more sophisticated souls claim these fits of aggressive behavior are indulged in only during the mating season or by females guarding their nests.

In 1903, in what was reported to be an unprovoked attack, a King Cobra 10 feet 1 inch in length bit and killed a coolie woman while she was picking tea on an estate in Assam. The snake retained its grip on the woman's leg for eight minutes while she remained "absolutely paralyzed with fear, and apparently did nothing to free herself." The snake finally released its grip when a group of men arrived on the scene. The snake crawled away, but when pursued by the men, it turned and attacked them but was killed. The woman died "about twenty minutes after being bitten."

This account has been cited on several occasions to prove that King Cobras occasionally attack without provocation and that they are extremely deadly snakes. However, it is quite unusual for death to occur in such a short time as the result of the effects of the venom. It seems more likely that the woman died as a result of a heart attack rather than from the venom, particularly since the story says she was so frightened. The snake was sent to authorities in Bombay for identification, and the sender was told it was "undoubtedly a Hamadryad or King Cobra." Hamadryad is another name for this snake, but the "undoubtedly" raises the possibility that the attacking snake was a harmless species, possibly the large Indian Rat Snake or Dhaman, which is a large, excitable snake. There also is the question of whether the attack *was* unprovoked. A woman picking tea would probably be concentrating on her work, and not watching where she was stepping. Thus she might approach close to or even step on a resting snake, which might be startled into biting. In any case, we cannot be certain this is a true account of an unprovoked attack by a King Cobra.

Colonel Frank Wall, a student of Asiatic snakes, collected a great deal of information on the King Cobra, and was convinced that it would "sometimes attack without provocation, other than being confronted in its natural haunts." The only specific instance of an allegedly unprovoked attack that Wall cites, however, is the one referred to above. He remarks that the "female when disturbed in the process of brooding her eggs, seems to be especially sensitive, and usually attacks the intruder at sight. Several instances are recorded where a jungle path has become closed to the wayfarer, owing to a brooding female and her mate attacking anyone attempting to pass. When actually molested the snake frequently accepts the challenge, and attacks with great determination and ferocity."

Colonel Wall has reported an adventure of a Major Fraser and his wife, who were driving in the Nilgiri Hills when they saw a large snake in the road in front of them. The Major at first thought the snake was a python, and tried to run over it, aiming to cross the snake's tail. Instantly it reared up on the side of Mrs. Fraser, who, seeing its head on a level with the door, threw herself across her husband on the opposite side of the car. Major Fraser stopped the car and got out to investigate further, armed only with a butterfly net. He found the snake in the middle of the road with its head raised and hood spread, turning right and left in a threatening manner. The Major hesitated, and the snake came down the road straight for him. He jumped back in the car, released the brake, rolled down the road for a hundred yards or so, and got out again. The snake was still in the middle of the road with head and hood raised. It remained in this position for a moment and then crawled away.

Colonel Wall's report also refers to the ferocity attributed to female King Cobras when guarding their nests. He does not cite any specific cases, although there are several reports of encounters with snakes on or in their nests. One of the earliest reports of a snake on its nest was made by George K. Wasey in 1892. He wrote, "Information was brought to me that a path into a village situated some 3 or 4 miles from here, was closed owing to a large and deadly snake having taken up his quarters close by the side of it. My informant also told me that the snake had made a chamber, upon the top of which it was sitting. This morning I went out to have a look at it, and sure enough within two yards of the path was a heap of dried leaves and on top of them the snake. The head seemed to be down in the leaves, but two coils were visible. After throwing a few stones at the heap, one of which hit the snake, it erected its head and on seeing us distended the hood, when I fired and killed it."

This snake was 9 feet 8 inches long and made no attempt to attack either before or after it was hit with the stone. The trail was closed, not because the snake was attacking the villages, but rather to keep them from going too close to the snake and possibly disturbing it.

All of the reports of personal encounters with King Cobras made by naturalists bear out the conclusion of Colonel G. H. Evans of Rangoon, who said, "I am more than ever convinced that Hamadryads as a rule are as glad to escape as most other snakes." Evans quotes an officer of the Indian Forest Department who had had considerable experience with these snakes in the wild, and who was skeptical of its aggressiveness. He said that, unless molested, this snake sought retirement in preference to hostilities in nine cases out of ten.

Two additional encounters can be cited here as further evidence of the lack of aggressiveness in the King Cobra. Both are taken from the *Journal of the Bombay Natural History Society.*

R. N. Champion Jones reported, "I was in the office one afternoon and heard my clerk's dog making a fiendish yapping down at his quarters. On enquiring the cause thereof I was informed that it was fighting a big cobra. Although cobras have been captured on the lower lying estates in this district I had not previously seen one here and was somewhat skeptical as there are plenty of very large rat snakes about. However, when I had finished my work in the office I went to investigate and found about four coolies standing round and the dog still keeping up its cacophony. Although at the first glance nothing was visible as the 'conflict' was in amongst some grown up tea, but upon a closer approach I was able to discern a section of the snake about 3 ft. off the ground between two bushes and it sent me hot foot back to the bungalow for my gun. I found I only had some old No. 8 shot cartridges and so took along my .380 revolver. On arriving back I thought I would see if I could see the head and to this end crawled on hands and knees under the tea and saw the dog barking only a few inches away from it. I drove it away and had four shots at the snake with the revolver but all missed—a lamentable occurrence. I then thought I would give it a shot with the gun and this did not have much effect other than to make it come down sluggishly to earth when I managed to hit it with a revolver bullet in the neck. One or two facts emerge from the hunt. Firstly the extreme sluggishness and apparent docility of the snake—I never saw its hood expanded once. Secondly the striking proof that a snake is deaf to ordinary sound; it never turned an inch at the four revolver shots fired a few feet away from its head, from which one presumes it neither heard the dog; and lastly the time it took to die, although the backbone was broken at the neck it took half an hour at least before it was dead. It taped 10 ft. 4 in. before skinning and 11 ft. 6 in. after and was a male. There were numerous ticks under its scales and a large leech was found adhering to it.

"I cannot account for the dog getting away with it as it did, as I was told the Hamadryad, which it proved to be, was in the open when the dog found it and the King Cobra is reputed to be the fiercest and most dangerous of Indian snakes. The bands on this snake were not well defined."

The account of H. C. Smith is of particular interest, since it involves a snake on its nest guarding eggs. "On 7th June 1936 I was walking through fairly open moist bamboo forest at about 2,000 ft. elevation near Ahisakan (some 8 miles from Maymyo) in the Mandalay District, Burma. Noticing a rather curious looking heap of dead leaves close to the rough track I was following I thrust a small cane into the heap. Immediately a snake's head shot out from the top of the heap and, as quickly disappeared. Having no gun and being with a picnic party I decided to leave well alone for the time being.

"On 11th June 1936 I returned to the place accompanied by Mr. T. S. Thompson, Divisional Forest Officer, Maymyo, and some followers. Mr. Thompson and I posted ourselves on one side of the heap whilst our men cautiously pushed a long bamboo into it from another quarter. The snake soon emerged from the top of the heap and we shot it. It was a hamadryad measuring 7 ft. 5 in.

"We then proceeded to examine the heap which was about 1 ft. 9 in. in height and 3 ft. 6 in. in diameter. Within this heap of dead leaves was the nest proper. It was placed on the ground and comprised a compact mass of dead bamboo and other leaves and a few small twigs and leaf stalks. Externally it measured about 1 ft. 7 in. in diameter and 9 in. deep. It was a comparatively solid structure and could be lifted off the ground without its falling to pieces. In the center was a cup about 8 in. in diameter and about 8 in. deep.

"Within the nest were twenty-seven eggs, white, soft-shelled and measuring about 55 by 27 mm. The eggs were comparatively fresh and in some cases stuck lightly together. Above the eggs there was a compact covering of dead bamboo leaves which filled in the cup of the nest flush with the edges. Upon this nest, though separated from the eggs the snake had evidently been lying coiled up. The leaves forming the mound covered the snake and nest and they were lying loosely as compared with the solid and almost woven nature of the nest proper.

"It is interesting to note that fourteen people accompanied by seven dogs twice passed at different times within two yards of the nest and yet the hamadryad failed to show itself and the nest remained undiscovered until I prodded the heap of leaves with a small cane."

From these and other similar reports the editors of the *Journal of the Bombay Natural History Society* concluded in 1936 that "while the King Cobra has a reputation for ferocity, for the making of immediate and unprovoked attacks, the sum of recorded evidence, supported now by these notes indicates that normally, the snake behaves in the manner of all snakes and usually endeavors to escape."

Thus the King Cobra, like the mamba, loses some of its malevolent character when carefully studied. Both snakes should be respected as dangerous adversaries when disturbed, but neither species can be considered aggressive. Undoubtedly part of the erroneous notions about these snakes have come from observations of the species in captivity. Under these abnormal conditions where escape is impossible and the snakes are usually in close confinement, they appear more aggressive than they are in the wild. Many snakes will defend themselves vigorously when cornered. The same snakes if given a chance to escape will do so rather than fight.

In 1953, three large King Cobras were received at the New York Zoological Park. The smallest, a male, measured 11 feet 6 inches, while the largest, also a male, taped 14 feet 4 inches. For some time after they arrived at the Zoo, all three would rush the keeper as soon as the cage door was opened. These were large snakes confined in a relatively small area from which they could not escape when disturbed. Their only alternative was to fight, and in doing so they lunged toward the obvious threat to their peace, the keeper. When they were proffered a plastic shield against which they could strike without danger, they soon tired of such action and quieted down. The snakes are now so accustomed to captivity and human beings that they rarely erect their hoods. For three years the smaller male and the female have mated, and the female has made a large nest in which she has laid her eggs each year. Most of the eggs have been removed to be incubated under artificial conditions. From these have hatched the first King Cobras bred in captivity. When the female is moved off the nest in order to remove the eggs, she makes no show of belligerence, and watches the procedure with no outward signs of excitement. Which of these attitudes indicates the true nature of the King Cobra—the excitable individuals of the early days of adjustment to captivity, or the calm, indifferent snakes of later months?

Tall tales of Bushmasters stalking and attacking unsuspecting hunters and explorers are commonplace in northern South America and lower Central America. There seems to be even less justification for considering this snake aggressive than for so viewing the mamba and King Cobra. I recently asked a South American herpetologist which of his native snakes he considered the most dangerous. Without hesitation he replied, "Bushmaster! Because it is so aggressive." When asked what he meant by "aggressive," he replied that "it won't run away like the other snakes do." This hardly qualifies as truly aggressive behavior, and indicates something of the varying connotations placed on the word.

Large size, a very high strike, and virtually no knowledge of its normal habits are responsible for the Bushmaster's sinister reputation. It is the longest venomous snake in the New World, attaining a length of more than 12 feet. When assuming a defensive position, the Bushmaster loops a large portion of the anterior part of its body into a series of S-shaped vertical coils. As a result, it has a long and high strike that makes it a dangerous adversary. In spite of its formidable size, its venom is not particularly potent in comparison to the venoms of some of its smaller relatives. Actually the Bushmaster appears to be a shy, retiring inhabitant of the upland tropical forests. Scientists and hunters who have frequently encountered this snake in the wild discount any aggressive tendencies on its part.

The Taipan of Australia is a large active snake attaining a length of 10 or 11 feet, and the possessor of relatively long fangs and copious quantities of venom. Four recorded bites on human beings all proved fatal, and a Taipan in North Queensland is said to have killed a horse in five minutes. Another report states that there appear to be only two cases of recovery from its bite. The Taipan occurs on the Cape York Peninsula of Australia and in eastern New Guinea—both regions of sparse human habitation. Within these areas it is considered to be a rare snake, and few specimens have been preserved in museum collections. Like all large venomous snakes about which little knowledge is available, there is considerable legend about the ferocity and aggressiveness of the Taipan, but there are few firsthand accounts of encounters with this snake. One recent story that was widely circulated in Australian newspapers related the death of Kevin Budden, a young snake collector from Sydney, who was bitten by a Taipan near Cairns. Budden was bitten after he had captured the snake and while he was putting it in a bag for safe carrying. Despite the fact that he had received what he knew was probably a fatal bite, he secured the snake and requested that it be sent to the Commonwealth Serum Laboratories in Melbourne where its venom could be studied.

Eric Worrell, Curator of the Ocean Beach Aquarium in Umina, is one of the few persons who have had personal experience with the Taipan in the wild. In his *Dangerous Snakes of Australia,* he said, "I saw several Taipans in the Cairns sugar-cane fields. We found Taipan to be extremely shy and surprisingly quick to vanish into heavy grass when we approached. We captured three, one of which was taken to Taronga Zoo (Sydney)."

The Australian naturalist David Fleay has also had personal experience with the Taipan both in the wild and in captivity. His opinion is that this snake, like all others, does not look for trouble and usually tries to get away. He says they characteristically "vanish in a flash, but, if suddenly encountered or provoked, the highly nervous creatures react with unequaled ferocity." It looks as if the Taipan also will have to be removed from its legendary role of a truly aggressive snake. What is true of these snakes is equally true of *all* species of venomous snakes; they seek to escape rather than to fight. No species of snake is aggressive in the sense that most or many individuals make unprovoked attacks on human beings.

While no species of snake can be considered generally aggressive, an occasional irascible individual does turn up. Just as there are occasionally dia-

bolical human beings, so there are misfit snakes—fortunately more often encountered in harmless than in venomous species. In the United States, Racers
and Whipsnakes are most frequently reported to show definite aggressive tendencies, especially in the spring. Many herpetologists have had experiences
with aggressive individuals of these species. Whether such attacks are stimulated by some types of territorial defense, or simply result from overexcite-
ment, is impossible to say. Certainly all cases of aberrant aggressiveness are not
limited to sexually mature individuals. A Long Island woman once brought
the Zoo a newly-born Eastern Garter Snake that was one of the most vicious
snakes I have ever seen. As soon as the lid was taken off the small box in which
it was carried, the tiny demon rushed at my finger, lunging vigorously with
open mouth and advancing farther with each lunge. I placed it on the floor
and backed away a distance of about four feet. Without hesitating, it started toward me, with a wonderful display of ferocity considering that my towering
figure was many times larger than its eight-inch length.

Others have reported similar exceptional performances, outstanding
because of their radical departure from the normal behavior of the species.
When E. Raymond Hall visited a large Rattlesnake den in eastern Nevada, he
found most of the snakes sluggish and lethargic in disposition, but one of the
many he saw was an exception. This grumpy individual was in the middle of
the road when the party drove up, and he immediately struck at the car. Hall
said, "On getting out of the car we found him coiled about 12 feet away. He almost instantly uncoiled and with surprising speed made directly for me with
his head and about seven inches of his neck slightly raised off the ground.
When two of us shifted our locations he changed his course and made directly
for another person until stopped with a charge of dust shot."

Similar unusually aggressive behavior has been reported in other Rattlesnakes in the vicinity of hibernating dens, usually when the human being
was between the snake and the den hole. Wilfred T. Neill has reported the case
of a surprisingly aggressive Cottonmouth Moccasin from Georgia. The moccasin is noted for its threatening behavior, which includes a fearsome gaping of
the white mouth and vibration of the tail. Despite this display, these snakes are
frequently quick to slink away, and I had never heard of nor seen one make an
effort to approach an intruder. Neill's mad moccasin was a real exception to
the rule. Neill wrote, "On the opposite bank we spied a Cottonmouth of perhaps a yard in length, basking on some cypress roots. The snake was separated
from us by a steep eight-foot bank overgrown with smilax and poison-ivy, and
by a sluggish stream about 12 feet wide and four feet deep. Having already collected a good series from the area, we were preparing to leave the Moccasin

undisturbed, when it shook its tail angrily for a moment and then lunged open-mouthed in our direction. Its strike carried it into the stream, where it floated with uplifted head. Piqued by such belligerency, I seized a stick and scrambled down the bank into the stream. To my surprise, the Cottonmouth swam to meet me. I waved the stick over its head; it did not strike at it until touched on the anterior part of the body. It embedded its fangs in the wood for a moment and then swam toward my legs. With the stick I pitched the snake onto the bank near the spot where it was first noted and, wading across, pinned it to the ground. This is the only Cottonmouth in my experience that made an entirely unprovoked attack when every opportunity for escape was presented."

These few examples indicate that an occasional individual snake may put on an aggressive display or actually come toward a person. The probability of anyone getting bitten by such an aberrant snake is a highly unlikely occurrence. One has a far better chance of being hit by lightning—actually neither is likely enough to cause you much concern.

Furthermore, *no* snake can crawl as fast as a man can run. The terrible tales of speedy mambas are sheer exaggerations. Mambas are about as fast and agile as any snakes, but probably no faster than a number of slender, racer-like species. The speeds of only a very few snakes have been accurately clocked with a stopwatch, and many highly erroneous ideas are based on *estimates* of their speed. The long, slim body of a snake moving smoothly and rapidly over stones and sticks, through weeds and grass, past bushes and trees, gives a completely false impression of fast movement relative to the small objects of the habitat. Because of this relative movement, it is extremely difficult to judge the speed of such a snake with any degree of accuracy. In Florida, my wife and I demonstrated this false impression by releasing a Black Racer on rough terrain and asking a group of people to guess the speed at which it moved. The estimates ran between 10 and 15 miles per hour, but the best speed measured with a stopwatch was 3.7 miles per hour—less than a good walking pace for a man.

Walter Mosauer measured the speed of several species of desert snakes in California. Using a stopwatch, the fastest speed he recorded was 3.6 miles per hour for the Colorado Desert Whipsnake. Most of the snakes traveled at a far slower speed. One of the fastest movements he measured was the sidewinding type of movement used by the Sidewinder Rattlesnake when on loose sand. When really warmed up, these Rattlesnakes can move at a clip of 2.04 miles per hour!

In discussing the speed of the mamba in his book, *A Guide to the Snakes of Uganda,* Captain Charles R. S. Pitman said, "One could only obtain a true estimate of the mamba's exceptional speed by practical test, though the writer can visualize no more suicidal form of amusement than that of deliberately provoking a large mamba in order to put it through its paces!" On at least one occasion this has been done, and a maximum speed of 7 miles per hour was measured by stopwatch. The figure was published recently by Colonel R. Meinertzhagen in connection with speeds of other animals. When I asked him how and where he had obtained this record Colonel Meinertzhagen kindly sent me the following account, the only one I have been able to locate which gives an actual measurement of a mamba's speed.

"The record was taken on April 23rd, 1906 near Mbuyuni on the Serengeti Plains between Voi and Taveta in Kenya. The terrain was recently burned grass. I first saw the snake crossing my path about 20 yards distant so I got my men to surround it as I wished to photograph it. The snake turned to bay with about a quarter of the head-end raised. We baited it with clods of earth until it was really angry. It kept making small rushes at my men so I tried to measure its pace, having been told that mambas could travel at the pace of a trotting horse. I waited, gun in hand to shoot if necessary and eventually got the snake to chase one of my men over a measured distance of 47 yards when I shot it as my man tripped up and fell. Timed with a stop-watch. The snake had not been handled, only baited. It measured five feet seven inches."

Mambas are similar in build and disposition to the harmless racers and whipsnakes of North America. They are agile and fast, as snakes go. Herpetologists estimate that no mamba can go more than twice as fast as these snakes, or a top speed of 8 miles per hour. Meinertzhagen's figure comes within this estimated range of speed.

Incidentally, the estimated and observed speeds of the mamba are well below the top figure for both man and the horse, both of which can run at a top speed of better than 20 miles per hour for short distances. If Colonel Meinertzhagen hadn't been sure of this, his method of measuring the mamba's speed would have been dangerous indeed.

Some people believe a venomous snake cannot bite unless it is coiled, while others believe the snake can hurl itself through the air a distance several times greater than its length. Neither of these beliefs is correct. A snake can bite at any time, from any position and even under water. Biting is simply opening the mouth and inserting the fangs or teeth into any accessible object. In fact, the severed head of a venomous snake has inflicted a fatal bite as a result of the marked reflex action of these animals.

The tongue is often thought to be the snake's "stinger." Actually it is perfectly harmless. It is used to pick up odors or chemical substances which are carried to the sense organs in the roof of the mouth. For this reason snakes flick their tongues out rapidly when they are excited. In doing so the snakes are just investigating the disturbance or the environment.

A strike is the lunging out of the head and anterior body from a coiled or defensive position. Snakes can inflict a venomous wound *only* by means of the mouth—either through enlarged, hollow teeth in front of the upper jaw, as in cobras, rattlesnakes, mambas, and vipers, or by means of en-larged, grooved teeth at the rear of the upper jaw, as in the rear-fanged snakes, such as the Boomslang. Pit vipers and true vipers normally strike from a coiled position, whereas cobras, mambas, and their relatives strike from an erect or drawn back position. These snakes usually strike more slowly than the vipers. For example, an Asiatic Cobra strikes about one-sixth as fast as a Timber Rattlesnake, or much slower than a man can punch with his fists. Skilled snake charmers can pat a cobra on the head in the middle of its strike without difficulty.

The speed of the strike of the Prairie Rattlesnake has been studied at length by Walker Van Riper by means of high-speed photography. He calcu-lated the speed of this "fast" motion at an average of 8 feet per second. Van Riper concluded, "It is one of the slowest of the animal movements we ordi-narily regard as being fast. The truth seems to be that we nearly always greatly over-estimate the speed of small animal movements near-by (they must be close to be seen at all clearly)."

Van Riper showed that a man of average ability could punch his fist out at a speed of 18 feet per second, or more than twice as fast as the rattler's strike. A golfer was shown to move his hands at 40.6 feet per second in a golf stroke. A trout swam at 7 feet per second; a bee flew at 8.3 feet per second; and a dragonfly went at 22.7 feet per second. This all makes the rattler look pretty slow—and other snakes even slower by comparison. Few venomous snakes have been calibrated for the speed of their strike, and it seems certain that some species will be found to strike much faster than the Prairie Rattler, but also many, particularly the relatives of the cobras and mambas, will be found to strike much slower than that. With Photographic Consultant Henry Lester, Staff Photographer Sam Dunton, and Curator of Publications William Bridges of the Bronx Zoo, I was once engaged in getting an ultra-highspeed colored movie of a rattlesnake striking, for an educational film we produced. After six months of ironing out technical difficulties, we obtained several records of the strike of the Western Diamondback Rattlesnake, a notoriously irascible snake. Where we were able to compute the speed of the strike, we got a figure about twice that for the Prairie Rattlesnake. Our data were inadequate to demonstrate whether this was an average or a maximum figure, but they do suggest the possibility, which is recognized by virtually all herpetologists, that the speed of the strike varies from species to species.

In a popular article on his observations in *Animal Kingdom,* Van Riper related the exploits of W. C. Bradbury who "liked to start an argument about the speed of the Rattlesnake—which he could always do by maintaining that it was slow, not fast. If a snake could be produced, he would make a demonstration. Holding a sack or something of the sort in his left hand to attract the snake's attention, and a sharp bowie-knife in his right, he would clip off the head of the snake when it reared to strike."

On level ground snakes generally strike one-third to one-half of their length. A viperine snake, such as a Timber Rattlesnake or a Fer-de-lance in a circular coil, with the anterior part of its body drawn back in a horizontal S-shape, will strike about one-third its length. If the fore part of the body is raised into a partially vertical coil, as an aroused Western Diamondback Rattlesnake or a Bushmaster is prone to do, the snake will strike farther and higher. Similarly, if the snake is resting on a rock ledge, a log, or the bank of a stream, the increased altitude may give it extra range.

This is a constant concern to hunters and woodsmen in hilly areas. For example, in the Northern Range in Trinidad the trails, or traces as they are called, are cut deep in the side of the hills in places so that the upper bank of the trail is as high as or higher than a man's head. One night in the Arima Valley, my East Indian companion, Otar Lal, entertained me by relating some of his encounters with Bushmasters on the high, uphill bank. He said, "When you meets them thar and they get stirred up, they flies right over you. And when they misses, as please God they do, they shoots right on down the hill." I can't vouch for the truth of his remarks, but it would be exciting to catch a large Bushmaster in such a position.

Cobras rear the anterior part of the body in a vertical position, and in a striking lunge forward a distance slightly greater than the vertical height to which the head is raised. An aggravated snake will strike farther than one that is just aroused from rest. A Western Diamondback Rattlesnake or a greatly excited Fer-de-lance can—but rarely does—actually strike a distance equal to its own length, and may momentarily leave the ground in so doing. If one estimates the length of a snake and stays that distance from it, there is little chance of being bitten—especially since the estimate is likely to be far more than the snake's length, and the creature cannot strike anywhere near such a distance.

Some of the cobras and their relatives have evolved the ability to "spit" or eject their venom. The venom is ejected in the general direction of a man's head, and can produce blindness if it gets into the eyes and is not treated promptly. The exact distance to which these snakes can "spit" their venom is somewhat uncertain. Certainly they can eject the venom a distance of six feet with good accuracy and eight feet with fair results; beyond that distance an effective hit is probably fortuitous.

Charles M. Bogert, Chairman and Curator of the Department of Amphibians and Reptiles of the American Museum of Natural History, in his scholarly study of the "spitting" snakes, shows that they are able to eject their venom in this fashion because of special modifications of their fangs. The Black-necked Cobra of Africa and the Asiatic Cobra in the eastern part of its range are the two cobras that practice this method of defense. The South African Ringhals, a close ally of the cobras, also possesses the ability to "spit." This is a purely defensive weapon and is not used in securing prey. Many individuals with this ability fail to use it until thoroughly aroused, and "spitting cobras" have been captured under the mistaken notion they were another species.

So much for the defensive behavior of snakes, which is sometimes so vigorous as to be mistaken for aggressive action. There is no scientific evidence to support the oft-cited, but erroneous, belief that any species of snake is habitually aggressive. Mambas, King Cobras, Bushmasters, and others do not indulge in unprovoked attacks on human beings. A rare, exceptional individual of any species *may* exhibit aggressive behavior and slowly approach a human being in a threatening manner, but this happens only in extraordinary instances, under highly unusual circumstances. In no instance can a snake crawl faster than an adult man or woman can run. Virtually all snakes will try to escape from an encounter with a human being if given the opportunity. When you walk through the countryside or forest, far more snakes see you than you see snakes. They are simply content to let you pass, or they silently crawl away.

22 Deadliest Creature on Earth

BY JACK DENTON SCOTT

Themaking me forget that I had a rifle. I was ready to turn
he natives were walking slowly abreast, hoping to drive a tiger before them. But today there was no cat. Suddenly one of the men
screamed and flew backward three feet as if pushed by a giant hand.
The others fled from him in terror.

The man was silent now; we could hear labored breathing as if he were
fighting suffocation. The shikari beside me went tense. He was an Indian
friend, a professional hunter, helping me research tigers for my novel, *Elephant
Grass,* in which a tiger is the hero. We had rifles and came down the tree fast.
As we neared the felled native, the ground before us began to wiggle. Mottled
green, twisting. Then it rose to face us. A huge snake, its head swollen into an
angry hood. It came for us in a lunging movement, head still high. It menaced,
striking viciously. Although it was still 50 feet from us, its size and obvious intent sent me backward, making me forget that I had a rifle. I was ready to turn
and establish a new track record when the shikari shot. He had an old .30–06
Winchester, almost as much a part of him as an arm. He shot four times into
the lifted hood of the creature. Head shredded, it went to the ground, tremors
shooting from head to tail. Life remained in the great snake for 20 minutes.

That was my first meeting with the king cobra or hamadryad (also
Naja hannah in India), the world's largest venomous snake. The record is 18 feet
4 inches; the one before us measured just over 11 feet. It hadn't the thick body
of the python, was an olive color crossbanded with black; the throat and chin
were light orange. Herpetologists consider it the most beautiful snake—and
the deadliest.

The action had taken just under a half hour. The native was dead. The
wound on his leg wasn't deep, and the shikari explained that the large amount
of neurotoxic poison injected by the giant didn't require a deep piercing. Cobras strike, bite, chew briefly and the victim has had it. The venom has an im-

313

mediate effect on the nerve centers, producing death by paralysis of the muscles that control the breathing mechanism.

The shikari was a university graduate who had become a hunter because he loved the jungle and hated the filth and noise of civilization. He had vast respect for the king cobra and, using his knife, showed me that the snake had fangs just over a half-inch long. He explained that what really made it deadly was its personality, plus the size and tremendous amount of venom it possessed.

"It is an insolent snake," he said. "The most aggressive of all. All snakes would rather slither off and hide when they see a man. The king cobra too. But if you happen on him, often he will attack immediately. And when they are nesting their eggs, both male and female will attack anyone approaching. Besides, they are moody creatures. Unpredictable. You never know what to expect."

He told of a 10-foot king cobra attacking a woman picking tea in Assam, holding the woman's leg for eight minutes. The snake released the woman and slithered off when five men came to her rescue. Chased by the men, it whirled and attacked. Now the pursuers were the pursued. They reported later that the snake, despite its size, was supple and very fast, and if one man hadn't had a shotgun and some courage, the king cobra might have performed a mass killing. The woman it had originally attacked, apparently without provocation, died in 20 minutes.

He gave me a classic example of the power of this venom. Last year he had been working with hunting elephants in the north of India, using them to drive a tiger before them in a beat, just as we today were using men. It was a photographic hunt, and not the right season to be moving about the jungle, but Indians declare no right and wrong seasons for themselves and they were trying to locate tigers before the clients arrived. Money is a powerful mover, the shikari said with a sad smile. They were beating through elephant grass and a scattering of trees near a hill pocked with rocky ledges. Suddenly a king cobra rose out of the grass before the lead elephant my shikari was riding.

"There was no provocation," the shikari said. "We didn't just happen on him and nearly step on him. He could have avoided us and escaped into the rock ledges where he probably lived. But no. He was obviously annoyed, as his hood was expanded. He struck quickly, biting my elephant on the tip of the trunk, one of the very few areas where the skin could be penetrated."

The shikari shook his head. "That was Kalu, one of our best hunting elephants, 25 years old, took five years to train."

The world's largest land mammal, weighing six tons, 70 times the size of a man, was dead from the incredible venom in less than three hours. The king cobra's venom is five times stronger than that of the Russell's viper, famed for its deadliness, and responsible for many of the 20,000 deaths by snake bite in India yearly.

Later, when traveling in Thailand and watching the training of the skilled tuskers in the teak forests, I saw an elephant in Chieng Mai that had been killed by a king cobra. This one had been bitten on the foot, at the juncture of the nail and the foot where the skin was soft. In this case, the big bull had killed the snake, crushing it with his feet. But usually they don't; king cobras frighten elephants. Everything else too. In Thailand several elephants are killed by them every year. This is an expensive loss. It takes several years to train an elephant to work skillfully in the teak forests, and they are valued at $5000 each.

Here he is, a giant with a temper, often attacking man on sight, quick, agile, fearless, with venom that can kill our largest animal in 180 minutes. What else does this creature have that sets him apart? Probably the most important attribute: Intelligence.

The king cobra is smart, a thinking animal. One example: Rodolphe Meyer de Schauense was returning from Asia to the Academy of Natural Sciences in Philadelphia with live zoo specimens. Among them was a 12-foot king cobra. Mr. de Schauense had observed the snakes in the Far East and had a marked respect for them. There was no receptacle for water in the cobra's box, and no one would open it to give it water. Not even de Schauense, who was an expert in transporting wild creatures. He tried giving the snake water from a pitcher. In minutes, the cobra learned to raise its head against the wire of the box and drink from the spout of the pitcher. More: The cobra even recognized the water pitcher and came to the wire when he saw anyone approaching with it.

Raymond L. Ditmars, former curator of Mammals and Reptiles at the New York Zoological Park, claims that he has observed many demonstrations of this singular intelligence of the king cobra. "I use the word 'singular,' " he says, "because other snakes do not act this way." He told of a newly arrived cobra discovering that the material covering the front of its zoo cage was glass. For a day it would strike at visitors pressing against the glass to view him. But that was all the nose-bumping it needed. From then on it stayed away from it, rearing and feinting, but not touching that hard glass. Other snakes would continue to punish themselves against it for weeks. King cobras also recognize the keepers who feed and care for them, and do not bother them, but always react antagonistically toward strangers. At feeding time the cobras come to the rear of their cages, and peer up and down the passageway for the keeper.

Brains, they've got. There is in the London Zoo a king cobra that daintily takes a freshly killed grass snake from her keeper's hands. That, though, is unusual. King cobras are cannibals, eating their own kind alive, both nonpoisonous and poisonous, sometimes even lizards, although lively snakes are their preference.

Again, intelligence is a force in the matter of food selection. They eat heartily once a week: one 14-foot male consuming in recorded test, from July to March, 145 feet of live snakes. If they are extremely hungry, they will eat the venomous snakes, agilely darting in and injecting their own brand of killer fluid before they can be bitten by their victim. But zoo king cobras seem to know they have a choice, and don't have to forage and take what they can get as they do in the wild.

In one test, a zoologist waited until the end of the week when his pair of king cobras would be very hungry, and then gave them a large water snake, and a poisonous water moccasin that looked very much like the harmless snake. The water moccasin was thrown into the cobra cage first. The hungry cobras rushed, then slammed to a stop a few feet from the hissing moccasin. This was the first time in years that the cobras had not pounced and demolished their wiggling meal immediately. They retreated to the other side of the cage and reared, regarding the moccasin cautiously. Were they really hungry? The moccasin was retrieved and they were each given a common grass snake. Gobbled. Again the moccasin was slipped into their cage. The cobras approached hungrily, recognized what it was, halted. Now the moccasin was angry, striking and hissing. The cobras raised straight up four feet and spread their hoods.

Now the real test: The moccasin was again removed and the harmless "double" placed in the cage without the cobras' seeing it accomplished. This large snake was also annoyed, and looked more dangerous than the water moccasin, hissing and striking. The cobras quieted and slithered in to examine the new snake. They attacked instantly, killed and ate it. Conclusion of the test: King cobras will not fight another venomous snake and risk getting bitten themselves unless hunger and circumstances drive them to it.

What about the hood we keep talking about, that swells when the king cobra is angry, and vanishes when he is not? Long movable ribs lie close to the backbone when the snake is not annoyed. When aroused, the king cobra (and his cousins, the smaller cobras) spreads this series of ribs laterally, and lo, the horrid hood. It is like a weird magician's trick designed to frighten.

Inhabiting India, Burma, Southeast Asia and the Philippines, there is nothing usual about the king cobra. They even protect their young, which is unheard of for the snake family. Like all snakes, though, they do hibernate. Mating can take place in spring or fall, before or after hibernation. Fertilization also can occur in the fall. However, due to the largely reduced metabolic activity during the low temperature of the hibernation, development is slowed to the point that the young are often born at the same time as those from the spring mating.

The king cobra lays eggs and hatches its young. Eggs are laid (anywhere from a couple dozen to a record clutch of 56) four to eight weeks after mating. The young, 18 inches long, black, with white and yellow-green crossband, complete with venom, are hatched in 12 to 18 weeks. Temperature influences the time; if it is warm it is speeded up; cool, retarded.

This astonishing snake is also the only one that carefully builds a large nest of vegetable matter or forest debris. In 1955, a female was observed and photographed building such a nest at the New York Zoological Park. It took the 13½-foot cobra two days to construct a nest 18 inches high and 36 inches in overall diameter. She pushed bamboo litter into a neat pile by looping the forward section of her body part way around it, then bringing her body gracefully back in an open loop.

She bulldozed sand into a foundation around the nest, moving her head at a 45-degree angle, then pushing. Leaves she grasped with a body loop, and carried to the nest. As the nest rose in height, she went inside, twisting around and around, probing and pushing and forming the nest, like a plasterer troweling a wall. A fantastic performance. She laid her eggs two days later, covered them with leaves, then coiled atop.

Most snakes lay their eggs, or give birth to their living young, then off they go; the kids are on their own. I can testify that both male and female cobras guard the nest and patrol the territory for a good distance around, attacking anyone on sight.

James A. Oliver, curator of reptiles, New York Zoological Society, in *Snakes in Fact and Fiction,* in a study of the world's most fearful snakes, narrows it to three: the black mamba of Africa, the taipan of Australia, and the king cobra of Asia. He bases this claim on several factors, among them large size, long fangs, powerful nerve-affecting venoms, and excitability and unpredictability. Also, the manner of striking. These snakes do not strike in short jabs as the vipers and pit vipers do, but in what Doctor Oliver calls a "gliding lunge" from which the snake can strike many times in close quarters. This ability, he believes, is what really makes them the top villains in the reptile world. Also, all three species defend themselves in a threateningly mobile manner (even chasing their foes), which makes them much more deadly than the feared varieties such as the rattler that rises from a stationary coiled position to strike.

Dr. Oliver says that a choice to name the deadliest of the three is difficult. "However," he says, "I have more respect for the king cobra, and whether it's just that I like the name, or whether it's based on something more subtle, I personally think he's 'king of snakes'—the most dangerous of all."

23   Mambas

BY C. J. P. IONIDES

I left the army in March 1943. I had not been able to go overseas to Europe so, feeling that I would be more useful in the Game Department than I could be in some depot doing office work inefficiently, I applied to be released. This was eventually sanctioned.

On my way through Nairobi I called at the Coryndon Museum and went to see Dr. L. S. B. Leakey, the Curator. During our discussion he mentioned that he needed various snakes for his snake park and asked if I could supply them.

'Yes, I'll try,' I said although I had had little experience of snakes apart from occasionally playing about with them. I had, however, always been interested in them. I can remember reading about them avidly at the age of six, and in one of those early books, in a fight between a long green snake, a Negro called Sambo and an elephant, I was always on the side of the snake. In Kipling's *Jungle Book* too I was always for Nag and Nagaina, never for Riki Tiki Tavi.

I asked Leakey what he wanted.

'Oh, boomslangs, cobras, mambas, that sort of thing,' he said casually. 'Anything you can get me.'

I then said, 'How do I send them?'

'Oh, the usual way—you'll find out all about that easily enough.' He jumped up. 'Now, if you'll excuse me, I've got things to do.' and walked out of the room, leaving me completely in the air.

That is how it was with snakes. I had to find out everything for myself right from scratch. With me it was a case of trial and—not error so much as near miss, as you will appreciate.

When I got back to Liwale, which was then my headquarters, there was quite a lot to be done in the initial stages to put things right again after my two years' absence. However, I did make a start with a few snakes. The first was a night adder which is not particularly poisonous.★ That was followed by a garter snake, a small rigid-fanged snake which, although ready to bite when first caught, settles down very quickly and soon becomes tame and pleasant tempered. Both snakes were put into a box and posted to Leakey. While at Kilifi, on the coast, during my war period in the army, I had caught two spitting cobras and sent them to a friend in Nairobi in a canvas bag in the boot of somebody's car. He wrote acknowledging the bag, which he said was a nice bag, only that there were no snakes in it. I never solved the mystery of their disappearance, so I was naturally a little anxious till I heard from Leakey that his snakes had arrived safely.

The snakes were caught with a forked stick. This simple device has its limitations however, as I discovered when I tackled my first black mamba. The black mamba is a magnificent animal. It is the longest venomous snake in Africa. I have taken one of 10 feet 6 inches at Voi, in the Tsavo National Park in Kenya, while individuals up to fourteen feet have been reported in South Africa. They have a sinister reputation. Though arboreal they are quite often seen on the ground, and this first one was lying across a path, its extremities in grass on either side.

Knowing very little about the game, I just walked up and applied my forked stick in the prescribed fashion to the back. It did not occur to me that there might be a good deal more snake on either side of the path than I had bargained for. The next thing I knew four feet of the anterior portion whipped out of the grass and I pulled one hand away just in time as the head with the mouth wide open struck violently at it. Fortunately the stick was just that little bit longer than the business end of the mamba so that I was able to hold it clear.

But where was I to go from there? The snake was very annoyed; if I let go it would certainly bite me. I knew that some of the stories of the black mamba's speed were gross exaggerations yet I was sure it certainly could move faster than I could run. I did not have any serum with me in those days; besides I was out of reach of any hospital, so there was quite a bit of sweating while servants hurried around looking for a suitable stick and kept coming back from time to time to report that there were no suitable sticks available.

★The only case of a death through a night adder bite that I know of was when a European was bitten and a friend sucked the wound. The friend, who had either a sore in his mouth or a gum infection, absorbed the poison. That caused his throat to swell up so that he actually died of suffocation, there being no doctor available to perform a tracheotomy. The man who was bitten was not seriously affected.

Some bad language was then used, which produced after further delay a piece of rotting log. I managed to get it over the neck of the mamba and it was held down long enough for me to take off the old felt hat I was wearing and with it grab the head and neck. This large, powerful snake had then to be boxed, a job which at first I did not think we could manage as the coils, as taut as a tempered steel spring, were extremely difficult to control. However the animal suddenly seemed to give up the struggle, and I realise now that it must have been partially strangled by the grip I had on its neck. The lid of the box, hinged sideways on a nail, was slid over to where I was still grimly hanging on to the head, and with a muttered prayer from one of my good Moslems it was pushed down and the lid slipped over.

Something was obviously wrong with my technique. After thinking about it quite a good deal I devised what I considered a really ingenious instrument that I thought could fittingly be named after myself. The Ionides snake-catcher was a sophisticated forked stick, one with a hole bored in the base of the fork and threaded with a string having a noose which could be tightened by pulling the end of it that was brought up the handle of the stick. This remained my basic snake catcher for several years. What astonishes me now is that I not only caught snakes with it but also survived.

I remember three black mambas we located in a hole under a dead tree on a disused ant heap, quite a favourite kind of hide-out for the black mamba as it is for the black and white cobra and the Egyptian cobra, particularly during the seasonal burning of the dried grass which had just been completed. My forked stick worked perfectly for the first of the three mambas, the largest. It was boxed and got out of the way, and my men and I then turned our attention to the other two.

There were two holes into the hide-out, a bigger one with two entrances and, round the other side, a single small hole. First we thought we would wait for them to come out in the hope of being able to noose them, and we nearly succeeded right away. I was standing above the small hole ready with my snake-catcher with the noose open in front of it. The head of one of the mambas appeared and tentatively looked out. It was about to slide further, and all I had to do was wait till there was enough of it before pulling the noose tight, when some rubberneck of a villager of the sort you always get on these occasions came wandering along in front of the hole; the snake saw him and dodged straight back inside.

After that there was a good deal of bad language and poking about with the snake-catcher through the entrances of the bigger hole. The mambas could not get away, but as they were writhing and winding about a good deal it was extremely difficult to put a noose round either of them. They were furious of course, expending a lot of their venom on the forked sticks which probably had a lot to do with what happened subsequently.

One of my assistants that day was a mature man named Mahomedi Ngelelo who claimed to possess immunity from snake bite. I knew that in showing off to local people he cheerfully let himself get bitten by small puff adders and night adders, and twice I had myself seen him take bites from small spitting cobras. He would have a swollen hand all right, for a few days, but otherwise it seemed to do him no harm.

After a while he succeeded in getting a noose round one of the black mambas, so I dropped the stick with which I had been poking about and went to his assistance. I told him to pull out the snake so that I could get hold of the neck with my hand, the idea being to box it before proceeding to deal with the remaining mamba. Mahomedi managed to extract about two feet of the snake and I grabbed the neck, removing the noose which then had to be worked under the hand finger by finger. We then found that the snake had wound its prehensile tail round a root and could not be budged.

In the middle of the tug-o-war the head of another mamba appeared at the second entrance of the hole before which I was squatting with my feet against the tree on either side of it. Opening its mouth wide, it started shaking its head at me, which I took to be an expression of displeasure. So turning to Mahomedi I said, 'Let us get this snake back in the noose where it can be held. It would be better if I caught the other one before we go any further.'

The mamba at the entrance remained demonstrating while I released my captive to Mahomedi's noose, but the moment I was ready the head disappeared. Rushing round to the other side I put a noose over the small hole. I saw the head emerge, hesitating, then the snake came out fast and I was able to nab it round the neck. By keeping the string tight, and reaching down the stick hand-over-hand, I got hold of the neck and successfully removed the noose.

Meanwhile Mahomedi had been busy on his side. He had given his stick with the noosed mamba to a porter to hold and, putting his hand into the hole, had unhooked the tail from the root to which it still clung. The snake was then eased out, but it seems that in returning the head to Mahomedi, the porter let the string get a little slack, and the black mamba, twisting its head round, cut at Mahomedi's hand with one fang and drew blood.

'Bwana,' he called to me, 'I've been bitten.'

'Well,' I replied, 'what do you expect me to do about it? My hands are full of mamba.'

I was, in fact, engaged in a Laocoönic struggle in which the body had coiled round both forearms and I was having to exert all my strength to prevent my left hand being drawn towards the head which was straining forward to give it a nip.

'There is only one thing to do,' I said. 'If you feel any faintness, or that you are losing control of the snake, you must kill it because I cannot help you.'

That was not necessary however as our camp was very near. We boxed the snakes without further incident. I then asked the man how he was feeling. It was one thing to flirt with death with juveniles of less poisonous species, but this time it was an adult black mamba, the most deadly snake in Africa.

'Oh, perfectly all right. Nothing wrong,' was his reply.

He certainly was not afraid, which was fortunate as it never helps in cases of snake bite for the patient to be alarmed.

'All right, just let me know if there is anything,' I said in a casual way.

I then got my orderly and gave him strict instructions. 'You have got to keep a careful watch on this man, but you must not fuss him as that will only make him scared. If he gets worse, particularly if he starts getting breathless, or having trouble with his breathing, or his speech starts slurring, you must call me at once.'

Not that there was anything I could possibly have done. We were on a foot safari in the bush, miles from any sort of medical help.

In the afternoon I went out pretending to look for birds, passing close to where my men were camped about fifty yards from my tent. Seeing me the orderly came up and said, 'He seems all right—he has eaten a good meal. He had a little diarrhoea, otherwise nothing to worry about.'

'Keep watching him,' I said. 'Report to me again at sundown.'

At sundown the orderly reported all was still well, so I then sent for two other men and instructed the three of them that they must take turns to watch all night and to call me at once in case of emergency. I went to bed very uneasy in mind, though there was, of course, comfort in the thought that the man had demonstrated obvious immunity to bites of other snakes.

Next morning with my coffee I asked after Mahomedi and was told he was out taking a walk round looking for more snakes.

Apparently at 9 p.m. the night before he had suddenly begun to get rigors and my watch party were debating whether or not to call me when the shivering wore off. As the patient had shown no further untoward symptoms they had not disturbed me. And that, I am happy to relate, is the end of the story. Beyond a handsomely swollen hand which subdued after two days, Mahomedi suffered no other ill effects.

In looking at his case the factors to be considered are: first, that all he got was a glancing cut with one fang, not a full bite which is in fact a proper double injection of two fairly long fangs⋆; and secondly, that the snake had expended a good deal of its poison in attacking the forked sticks. On the other hand to kill a man a black mamba only needs to inject two minims of its deadly venom, against which serums, good for cobras, puff adders and the other snakes that had bitten Mohamedi, are of minimal value. To me his continued good health was nothing short of remarkable.

I have noted that people seem to find it extremely difficult to think clearly and dispassionately the moment they touch on the subject of snakes. To most of those whom I have met in Africa every black snake they have seen is a black mamba and every green snake is a green mamba. There was a Game Warden, who ought to have known better, who even talked of a spitting mamba. No other species appears to exist. The reason for this, I think, is that the mambas haunt African literature, particularly the accounts of some of the more imaginative travellers who perhaps listened to natives rather than observed for themselves. Take the question of the black mamba's speed. There is, for instance, the story of a black mamba overtaking and biting a man on a horse at full gallop. Another writer reported that the snake moved so fast as to be invisible.

There is something about this snake that spontaneously generates fable. I remember one day on safari when we stopped to camp and the porters, in clearing a patch of grass for my tent, put up a black mamba which hid in a bush. On being informed I went to the place, and, seeing the bush surrounded by people, warned them to leave an obvious gap for the snake to escape otherwise somebody was going to get bitten. I then sent two men round to the other side to start throwing things into the bush. They did this and the snake came out in a hurry. It came in my direction, but on seeing me it flinched aside and went through the gap. We followed it carefully in extended order, caught it up, pinned it down and got it into a box.

That was all that happened, yet to this day Makabui, my major domo, always says, 'Don't you remember when that black mamba bit your trousers?'

He is my servant. I can tell him not to be a fool, because the mamba did no such thing. It is an entirely different matter when a writer comes and you tell him a story. The story is of how one day I was meditating in a bush latrine, an affair with a hole in the ground surrounded by a screen of leaves and

---

⋆Not as long as is generally imagined. Actually in proportion to its length the mamba has more slender and somewhat shorter fangs than most of the cobras.

branches, when in the tail of my eye I noticed a movement just behind me and on looking round saw the head and anterior part of a large black mamba coming through the screen. The snake and I each took one look at the other and parted company in opposite directions.

In an anxiety to help a writer one thinks of anything, though it did occur to me that Father's flight in such circumstances might be amusing. Yet in print this commonplace incident became a harrowing yet erotic experience in a dark, enclosed lavatory with the snake sliding over my bare thighs, titillating my gooseflesh with his forked tongue. I believe, if I remember rightly, that I did adjust my dress before leaving. That was not all. Next morning, lo the snake is still waiting in the lavatory—nothing less than a black mamba which, of course, is duly subdued.

If poetic licence must be taken why not pick a suitable snake for the occasion? I could imagine perhaps an amiable, sluggish gaboon viper behaving like that. Oh no, mamba is the only really fabulous stuff from which yarns are spun.

Many years before I was born a frightful mamba accident is reported to have occurred in a village in South Africa. A black mamba dropped out of the grass roof of a hut on to a sleeping family, a man, his wife and four children. The family woke up, and in the panic the snake bit five of them before escaping through the door. All five died. That incident has now been translated to Newala where I live, the number of people killed has increased to eight, the black mamba has become a green mamba and I am the five-star hero who captured it.

For the record, although the green mamba is certainly a deadly snake, it is far from being aggressive. It will invariably try to retreat. Presented with a situation in which it suddenly found itself among a number of people in a confined space, provided no attempt were made to catch or handle it, I believe a green mamba would do its utmost to get out of the way. This has been my experience of the animal.

In Newala, and within a radius of five or six miles of the town, I have within the last few years taken over 3,000 green mambas, which will give some indication of the number of these snakes in the area. These beautiful creatures live in trees. In the mango season the boys of the district spend half their days climbing up after the fruit in the lofty branches of mango trees where most of my green mambas are caught. Yet I have never heard of anyone being bitten by a green mamba in the Newala area. I beg your pardon, there was one person— myself, when I mistook a juvenile green mamba for a grass snake, pounded on it and got a nip on the finger for not being more careful. This happened last year when I was out with Sally Anne Thompson, the animal photographer, who promptly injected me in the arm and posterior with a total of 30 c.c. of the appropriate serum. There were no serious aftereffects.

It is sometimes difficult to pick out the thread of fact about the mamba from the tangle of fiction that has made them like some fabulous creatures you might see in a horror comic. The three mambas I know, namely the black, the green and Jameson's, are all arboreal. They are tree cobras, or rather that is the theory to account for their similarity to the cobra family yet with specialised characteristics which adapt them better for arboreal life, such as their slenderness and lightness and their long, prehensile tail.

Jameson's mamba, like the green, lives mainly on small birds and small mammals. I know of one instance of a green mamba eating a chameleon, but I think such an item of diet would be rare. Probably like the black mamba the other two may on occasion eat bats. The green is a beautiful mamba with an iridescent green back and a distinctly yellowish-green belly, for colouring and grace second only to the Jameson's which is a wonderful velvety blue with dark green interspersed with black on the anterior portions, and a black tail in the case of those found in East Africa.

The black mamba is not black as the name suggests, but brown or an olive-slate colour on top and white underneath. All three mambas are aristocrats, fast moving and immeasurably graceful. The eyes are a reddish brown of moderate size, the head being straight-sided, coffin-shaped and abnormally small in proportion to the body. The fangs are very far forward, more so than any other African snake, and situated just under the nose in the upper jaw, no other teeth being near the fangs. They do not carry as much venom as the large-headed vipers, but the venom is extremely potent. The black mamba, the most poisonous of the mambas, on being milked yields only about sixteen drops, but as I have mentioned before this is roughly eight times the normal deadly dose for a man. It is not the custom of the mambas to hang on when they bite, like the cobras which strike and chew. The mambas strike and release in a very quick movement, striking possibly twice or a multiple number of times.

Every movement of this snake is quick when it needs to be. You might see one in a tree moving with a fluid grace through the branches to stretch out hanging on by its tail and uncoiling stealthily towards some bird perched on a high twig. But disturb the mamba and it becomes a shimmering streak. Opinions differ about the top speed of the black mamba which is the fastest of the three mambas. I have seen it assessed by several sound observers as low as 7 m.p.h. and by one sound observer as high as 20 m.p.h.

I am personally not fond of guessing the speed of creatures in miles per hour, and will not attempt to do so here. All I will say is that from my own observations the black mamba is extremely fast and probably the fastest snake in Africa. Again, it would be difficult to suggest speeds for either of its two very fast cousins, the Jameson's, which is a rain forest snake, or the green, which is more generally distributed in savannah country and riverine forest. Although it is primarily arboreal, I have on one occasion taken a Jameson's mamba on the ground where it was hiding in a bush like a puff adder. A few I took in Kakamega disgorged rats, suggesting a rather more terrestrial habit than the green which is seldom found on the ground, though it will come down into the grass roofs of houses looking for geckos and lizards.

I have noticed that when disturbed the Jameson's mamba is more sensitive, nervous and alert, and is more inclined to drop down from a tree and make off on the ground than the green mamba which seldom does that; at the same time I should explain that my experience of the Jameson's mamba is confined to those I took in Kakamega district, in a spot where there were not many big trees. I noticed in catching them that if the first attempt to grab them proved abortive, instead of running away they would jerk themselves up in rather an indignant manner, looking round as much as to say, 'Who threw that brick?' which often gave one another opportunity to nab them.

This happened on one occasion when we found two Jameson's mambas courting, chasing each other all over the place, while we watched these goings on in the trees in a valley from the hillside above. On going down we crossed a small stream to the other side, to a spot where we anticipated they would pass. We were lucky because the female came flashing by through the bushes, diving straight into thick stuff, and Rashidi, one of my snake team, was able to get a grab-stick on the male as he tried to follow. The grab-stick I should explain was designed for me by the late Norman Mitton, who was Keeper of Exhibitions in the Coryndon Museum. It was, as it were, my breakthrough in the mechanics of snake-catching: it is simply a pincers at the end of a long pole operated by a handle at the base and used especially for catching snakes in trees.

Rashidi had the snake firmly in the grab when the remote control wire broke and the mamba instead of immediately making straight off, turned, got up and looked round, which gave me my chance with a second grab-stick.

This rearing up may indicate a certain tendency towards an aggressive retaliation, but I have noted no such behaviour in the green mamba which I have seldom known to bite unless restrained or cornered. On the other hand the black mamba is definitely a bolder snake, readier to resist interference than the other two species though in view of its unfortunate image in Africa it is necessary to qualify this statement very carefully.

It will sometimes treat you with a sort of insolence, have a good look at you, then slowly get out of the way, preferring to go up a tree if one is available rather than along the ground. However, if the tree is not large enough for it to manoeuvre it will come down again. Early in my snake-catching career, before I had my grab-sticks, we used to pelt black mambas with things as they circled round and round a tree, till in the end they would slant out of the branches and try to get away. When chased like that their one intention always appeared to be to make good their escape; they seldom if ever looked like attacking. Of course had one of them ever thought itself to be cornered I have no doubt it would have struck without hesitation.

I took 120 black mambas on one safari in Kenya in 1965, between July 17th and October 20th. Some were caught in trees, some on low, isolated bushes; some on low thickets; some on the ground; two under rocks. Some were dug out of disused termite nests, some out of rat holes, some out of ant-bear holes, some out of hollow trees. In the case of those in hollow trees, if the hole was within reach of the ground with my short grab-sticks, the tree was opened up with an axe until the snake was visible, when it was pulled out with a grab-stick; if out of reach, the hole was blocked up, the tree or branch cut down, and the snake then extracted on the ground with a grab-stick.

The mambas were always very reluctant to emerge from a hollow tree or branch, and it was often necessary to prod them with sticks to induce them to do so. Even when cornered in a low bush, they only tried to escape normally, and, in fact, one sometimes had to play 'round and round the mulberry bush' with them. They were inclined to come fast out of ant-bear holes when cornered in them. Twice one just stood its ground and demonstrated with its tongue, in one case under a low bush and in the other case at the edge of an ant bear hole which had previously been dug out. In both instances I simply walked up and caught the snake. Neither attacked me and both were adults. The locality was the Baringo area of Kenya, and I am indebted to Jonathan Leakey for putting me on to the areas concerned. I disposed of all the snakes caught to him. He milks snakes for their venom and is a great expert at this work.

It was noticeable that when a black mamba was disturbed in a tree, it often descended and made a bee-line for a hole, either in a tree or on the ground. In this it differs from the green and Jameson's mambas which normally go higher up the tree, if it is a reasonably high one. This habit of the black mamba's may be mistaken for aggression if the snake descends in the direction of a man, though it is usually merely trying to get away.

I rather think that most of the people who are bitten by black mambas have unwittingly provoked them in some way. A typical case is that of Nanjati, a young man I knew well as he used to act as my guide whenever I went to his village, which was in Liwale district. The incident occurred when the grass was being burnt off, a good time incidentally for tracking down black mambas as they leave an easy spoor in the ash.

Nanjati was looking for cane rats, a large rodent, a near relative of the porcupine with rudimentary quills and very good for eating. During the grass burning they are to be found in holes in the ground where they seek refuge from the fire, and he, as is usual, went about with a stick poking in all the likely holes he could find. One of these was an ant-bear hole, out of which a black mamba suddenly shot, travelled up the stick and struck him on the hand. Poor Nanjati died.

Another case in Liwale district was that of two natives who came upon two black mambas on the ground apparently fighting; I suspect the snakes were copulating. The mambas, becoming aware of the intrusion, separated and one of them attacked one man, striking him twice on the leg. He too died.

It is said, though I have no personal experience of it, that black mambas and other fierce members of the cobra family are particularly edgy at mating time.

Of alleged entirely unprovoked attacks by the black mamba I have little reliable evidence. There is the account by my friend Charles Pitman in his book *The Snakes of Uganda,* in which he gives the case in Northern Rhodesia many years ago of a rogue black mamba that started by chasing sheep and goats and ended by killing eleven people, most of whom died within half an hour. The nearest I ever got to that sort of multiple killer was at a place in Mtwara district where four people were killed in one year and three in the following year, all attacked in one particular spot which seemed to be the haunt of a snake or snakes. I was passing through the village and asked the headman about snakes.

At first he seemed reluctant to speak; I suspect there was a witchcraft scare or something very near it. However in the end he said, 'Bwana, it is late now, but tomorrow I will take you to a little patch of forest where two people have recently been bitten by a large snake. Both died.' He said nothing at the time of the previous deaths; I only heard about those later.

I thanked the man, adding that I looked forward to the opportunity of ridding his village of a dangerous neighbour.

'But we should thank you,' he replied.

Next morning we set out with similar expressions of mutual admiration and cordiality. We arrived at the spot and after a short search found a big black mamba curled up on a low branch. It was just after I had received the first of my grab-sticks—one long one with the pincers operated by a hand grip of the sort used for a brake on a bicycle, and two short ones which could be locked. Using the long one, I put the grab on the snake which nearly yanked the thing out of my hand as it tried to get away. I had made a mistake in not selecting a clear approach, because I next found I could not get the mamba out on account of branches in the way, and the stick then started to bend like a fishing rod. During all this my hand on the grip had begun to tire, but there was nothing I could do about that except hang on until the intervening growth was cut away.

Eventually the mamba was brought down to the ground and into the open, its head rearing up four feet from the grab and looking very hard-boiled. I then had to get one of my servants to relieve me of the grip on the snake by gradually moving my hand forward as he took over the pressure. I then gripped the snake with two grab-sticks and locked them. By then my hand was so tired I had to rest it for a while, flexing the fingers, before I could go on to sex and bag the snake. It was a female, a nice snake over 10 feet in length, in colour a beautiful dark purple above and white below with a lovely bloom on her. She had been freshly sloughed and looked intensely beautiful and, I thought, very proud of herself for having killed those two people and perhaps the others, which I think we can assume she did as no further deaths from snake bite have been reported from the village, and the date of that capture was March 7, 1954.

She went to the London Zoo and is still there, doing very well. If I may be permitted one lapse into modern hyperbole, quite a *fabulous* mamba, don't you think?

24   How It Feels to Die

BY BEN EAST

T he elk hunt had been a good one, in spite of the fact that no trophies had been taken. The time was September of 1953, and the
party was camped in northwestern Wyoming, in the high country
between Jackson Lake and Two Ocean Pass, about 10 miles south of
Yellowstone.

Ted Adams was outfitter. The three hunters were Dr. Judd Grindell, a
40-year-old physician and surgeon with a general practice at Siren in north-
western Wisconsin; Dr. Lyle French, a well known neurosurgeon from Min-
neapolis; and Judd's brother, Jack Grindell, a legal assistant in the Adjutant General's Department of the Army, with the rank of captain, then stationed at
Camp Carson, Colorado. None of them had the slightest inkling that Lyle and
Jack were about to see Judd through the most horrible ordeal of his life.

Elk were plentiful and they saw several fine racks that would have
been easy to take with a rifle, but they were using bows and that's another matter. Dr. Grindell had hunted with a bow for 18 years and greatly preferred it to
any other method, for its wonderful challenges and the high quality of sports-
manship it calls for. In his book, the hunter who takes a good trophy that way
has met his game on even terms, and that's how Judd Grindell liked it best.

"Most bowhunters don't feel too unhappy even when they miss a shot,"
he explained afterward. "At least they've had the keen delight of stealing to
within a few yards or even a few feet of whatever animal they are after. The hunt
itself, the love of the outdoors at its best, becomes their goal, rather than the kill."

The three men had had the usual minor frustrations on this hunt.
Judd had missed one fairly decent shot at an elk. Jack had used all his arrows
one forenoon in a vain attempt to take a big mule deer, then had a fine bull
elk walk nonchalantly out in front of him and start grazing while he watched

helplessly. "But I had a wonderful morning anyway," he told the others when he got back to camp.

They killed a deer for camp venison and then were joined by Fred Bear, the well known Michigan bowhunter, and Fred brought along an antelope he had killed east of the mountains on the way out. They were living high on wild meat, which Judd rated the best of all, and enjoying every minute. But time was running out, and on the 20th Jack and Lyle and Judd packed out and headed east for the antelope country around Gillette.

They got to the little town of Recluse, 40 miles north of Gillette, the next afternoon. One of the guides at the elk camp had given them a letter of introduction to a rancher there, Mayne Lester. He invited them to stay overnight at the ranch and start the antelope hunt the next morning, and when he told them what the prospects were he didn't have to twist their arms.

They turned in early and were roused at daylight with a cheery banging on the bedroom door. Half an hour later they sat down to an old-fashioned ranch breakfast, plates heaped with eggs, fried potatoes, toast, coffee, jam and honey.

Their host was too busy to go with them but he gave them detailed information on the lay of the ranch and how to hunt it (it covered 13 square miles, more than 8,000 acres), and they started out. Because it's extremely difficult to get within bow range of antelope in the open country where they are found, the hunters were falling back on rifles for this hunt.

They spent a couple of hours in a 4-section area without seeing game, then crossed the highway and entered a chunk of arid ranch land that covered nine more sections. Lyle saw an antelope and started after it. Jack and Judd walked up a rolling, sage-covered hill about a mile from the road, where they could look across a wide valley, and sat down on a rock outcrop to rest and use their binoculars. They didn't know it, but they were very close to bad trouble.

Within four or five minutes they spotted a pair of ears that they took to be an antelope's, sticking up out of the sage a quarter mile away. They studied the situation and agreed that Jack would try the stalk. By making a big circle he could keep out of sight of the animal and come up behind it, with the wind in his face. He walked away and Judd lay down behind the outcrop to watch through the binoculars.

The animal was so well hidden in the sage that, even though he knew exactly where it was, it disappeared completely whenever it lowered its ears. For a long time nothing happened. Then suddenly it raised its head and looked in the direction from which Jack Grindell was approaching. Judd saw then that it was a doe mule deer rather than an antelope. She got to her feet, listened and looked for a moment, and went rocking off.

The game was up, and Judd stood up to signal his brother. Without the slightest warning something struck him a sharp blow on the back of his right leg just below the knee, and he looked down to see a four-foot prairie rattlesnake, its fangs tangled in the coveralls he was wearing and still imbedded in his flesh, twisting and thrashing to get loose. He reached down, grabbed it behind the head, drew the fangs out, and threw it as far as he could, all in one swift motion.

Up to that minute he had not given rattlers too much thought, although he knew they were present in the area.

"That's the wrong attitude to take anywhere in snake country," he told me long afterward.

He felt no real pain, such as many snakebite victims describe. The strike was like a blow from a branch that has been bent and whips back against your leg, accompanied by two sharp but not very painful pricks, as if he had been jabbed mildly with a pair of hypodermic needles. Actually, that was what had happened. But although the bite did not hurt much, Dr. Grindell knew, even as he pulled the rattler's teeth out of his leg and flung it away, that he had been seriously bitten by a snake that accounts for many cases of terrible suffering and a few human deaths each year.

Dr. French was off somewhere after his antelope, probably two or three miles away by now. Jack was out of sight across the valley and because of the hard wind that was blowing there was no chance he could hear his brother's shouts. For the moment Judd was entirely on his own.

His first thought was of first aid. As a physician, he knew exactly what needed to be done. (A bad accident with a horse on another elk hunt ten years later forced him into early retirement, and his wife Arline and he live now on the Totogatic Flowage, a beautiful north-country impoundment between Spooner and Superior, Wisconsin.)

He knew what to do but couldn't do it. He realized with a sudden shock that he had no snakebite kit, no hunting knife or other sharp instrument with which to make cuts over the bite, nothing that would serve as an effective tourniquet. His boots were the pull-on kind, without laces, his coveralls were beltless, and because the day was very hot his underwear consisted only of shorts. And he had no way to resort to mouth suction, since the bite was behind his knee where he couldn't reach it.

For an experienced and, he had always believed, a reasonably sensible doctor, he had gotten himself into a sorry predicament. The only first aid he could manage was to lock his hands around the leg and use both thumbs for compression just above the bite.

Jack finally came into sight, half a mile way, and Judd signalled him frantically. But he thought his brother was trying to let him know the location of the animal he had gone after, and he was a long time getting close enough to realize that Judd was pointing to his own bared leg and yelling "Snakebite! Snakebite!" at the top of his voice. Jack ran the rest of the way, so hard that when he got to the scene he was barely able to talk.

Just as he started to run, Judd glanced at the spot where he had thrown the snake, to see what had become of it. It was no longer there. Next he saw it only a few feet away, crawling slowly but steadily straight at him. He could hardly believe his eyes. He knew the rattler was not coming back to attack him. In all likelihood it had a hole under the small outcrop from which it had struck, and was bent on getting back into that retreat. Later he learned that that is typical snake behavior.

The outcrop formed a flat shelf a foot or two above the ground. Apparently the snake had been lying there and had stayed motionless and silent, without rattling, while Jack and Judd walked up, sat down only a few feet away, and even when Judd lay behind the rock to watch what he thought was an antelope. He must have been within a foot or two of it at that time, but it did nothing to reveal its presence and because of its natural camouflage among the rocks and dry grass, he failed to see it. It was only when he got to his feet that it finally lashed out. Had it been lying on the ground instead of on the rock shelf, it would have hit his boot and probably done him no harm.

Whatever its intentions were now, however, he wanted nothing more to do with it. He brought his rifle up and blew it almost in half, and then resumed the tight hand-lock above the bite. Right after that Jack panted up.

But when Judd asked him for his hunting knife he looked blank. He wasn't carrying one, either. The doctor knew that cutting was essential, to drain the wound and get rid of part of the venom, but they still had no way to do it. The two brothers had hunted together since Judd was 13, and had cleaned plenty of game in the field. That was the first time they could remember that either of them had been without a knife.

Jack was wearing laced boots, however. They could at least make a tourniquet. They tied one of the boot thongs in place, tightening it just enough to impede the circulation of lymph, and Jack fired three slow-spaced shots to let Lyle know that they were in trouble. He repeated that signal two or three times and then, as soon as he recovered his breath, he hurried off to find their partner and bring him back. Judd was by himself once more.

He lay there on the ground and faced the fact that he might die. He remembers thinking, "Well, what better place, with the sun and wind in your face?" He even saw a certain element of justice in it. They were hunting wild things, and a wild thing had struck him down. "That's only fair," he reminded himself.

He had felt no pain from the bite itself, but now he became aware that his scalp, lips, tongue and hands were getting numb, and speech was becoming difficult. That meant the venom was spreading through his body. Next he looked off into the distance and everything he saw was doubled, as when you look through the range finder of an unfocused camera. Only by the greatest effort could he make the two images coincide. In a few more minutes even that became impossible, and his vision faded gradually into a series of crazily unrelated and momentary images.

His ordeal was beginning, and although he had never treated a case of snakebite he knew enough about it to realize that what was coming would be one of the most terrible experiences a human being can endure.

"It's matched in my opinion only by the agony of severe and extensive burns," he says today.

Once the general symptoms appeared they progressed with frightening swiftness. The numbness and tingling and weakness grew worse. He remembered that he must loosen the tourniquet for 20 or 30 seconds at regular intervals, but the third time he did that he realized that after each loosening he was experiencing an increasing wave of weakness and a strange sensation of floating. It was as if invisible hands were pushing him sideways. He knew it all resulted from the release of more venom into the general circulation.

There is some question in medical circles as to the benefits of first-aid procedures in snakebite, especially the use of a tourniquet, and a few doctors have suggested that it might be better to omit both cutting and constriction. But Judd Grindell is sure that that boot lace of Jack's saved his life in the first 90 minutes after he was bitten, and he strongly advises the victim of any such mishap to take first-aid measures at once if possible.

Next he became aware of nausea and a deep pain in the abdomen, which was relieved by a session of terrific vomiting. For two or three minutes he felt a little better, but then the floating-away sensation returned and this time it was accompanied by a roaring, rushing sound in his ears. He knew what that meant, too. His blood pressure was falling below shock levels and into the critical survival range. He was going into shock.

Then he must have a fast, thready pulse, he reminded himself, and he mustered strength to try to check it. His hands waved weakly and without much co-ordination, but finally settled in the right position. He could feel nothing. His fingers were too numb to detect a pulse beat.

That bit of activity had called for tremendous effort and somehow the tourniquet had slipped loose. He could expect a real jolt now. He tightened and tied the lace again, and just in time. The roaring and illusion of floating came once more, much louder and faster, and he realized his chances of survival were growing very slim.

In his years as a doctor he had seen a lot of life begin and a lot of life end. He delivered some 4,000 babies before he retired from practice, and he had spent almost four years overseas as an Army doctor in World War II.

But now for the first time he knew firsthand how it feels to die. Fragments and scraps of thought went through his mind, as they apparently do in the closing minutes of life:

> This must be what it's like—just peaceful floating away and the most delicious tiredness—what of Arline and the three girls—fine wife, wonderful kids—they need you—too tired, can't—you're a quitter, you can try.

He fought back then, in brief flashes of crystal-clear and lightning-fast thinking, resisting the feel of drifting off, refusing to be pushed into the oblivion that seemed to be waiting for him.

Then belly pain racked him once more and he vomited again. He noticed that his mind cleared briefly each time that happened. The effort of the retching was raising his blood pressure for a minute or so, and his brain was getting more oxygen. He decided to try breathing deeply, but he kept vomiting and the drawing in of deep breaths deliberately became too much of an effort. Then he heard footsteps, and Dr. French was bending over him.

French had a knife. "Turn a little," he said gently. But nothing happened, and Judd realized that he was hesitant about making the needed cuts through the fang punctures. Sick as Judd was, it struck him as odd that such a small thing should give pause to a surgeon who was used to the most intricate brain surgery. Later, when the whole thing was over with, he asked Lyle about that moment of reluctance.

"That was the first time in my life I had ever cut into flesh while the patient was conscious," Dr. French told him with a smile, "and I confess I didn't like the idea."

But at last Judd felt severe pain in his leg, grinding and burning. He could measure the length of each cut, and feel the knife rip out. He asked Lyle if the incisions were bleeding.

"Yes, good flow," was the reply.

Then the furious roaring again, even faster now—pain in abdomen worse—
whole leg numb and heavy—trying to see Lyle's face—no use—balanced on
a tightrope—going to fall off—vomit and vomit and vomit.

And then, on the top of everything else, he suffered the misery and
embarrassment of diarrhea.

He was hardly aware that Jack had left, to make a fast hike down to the
car and race back to the ranch to summon a doctor from Gillette. Judd lost
track of time, but finally heard voices all around. Jack's and Lyle's and a
stranger's, and then a girl's, and he understood dimly that the doctor from
Gillette had arrived and had brought a nurse along.

He heard someone mention Antivenin, and the doctor said, "I'll put
part above the bite where the leg is swelling, and the rest higher up." Then to
his nurse, "Mix up that other vial right away."

Judd felt pain as the needle went in near the wound, but none from
the rest of the shots, and did not even know when the second vial was injected.

The Antivenin took effect far more quickly than the venom itself had,
and with equally dramatic results.

More vicious vomiting—the taste of bile—bitter—can't see—the roaring and
floating back again—somebody's opening my eyes with fingers—remember
to breathe—pain in belly more and more severe—more diarrhea—wish I
could see Jack—touching him in a blinding, dazzling cloud—can't hold arm
up—floating away faster and faster—this is curtains.

If the phrase more dead than alive is ever justified, it would have applied to Judd Grindell at that point.

Then in the midst of it all there was a sudden lurch, the dizzying sense
of motion was gone, the roaring in his ears subsided, and he came back to
where he was, lying on the ground in the sagebrush. He could hear better, and
the interval before he vomited again was longer. He heard the young doctor (it
was many hours before Judd learned his name, Dr. R.V. Plehn) ask about blood
in the vomit, and when somebody answered no, Dr. Plehn said quietly, "He
may have a chance then."

Next they made ready to start for the hospital, and suddenly Judd was
sure he could endure the trip, just as he had been sure only a short time before
that to move him at all meant certain death. But he had to try twice to get out
a very weak, "Okay, Jack."

Somehow a car had been driven up to the hillside, and he was laid on the
back seat. The 40-mile ride to Campbell County Memorial Hospital in Gillette

was fast, but something that to this day he would just as soon forget. Thirst began, not ordinary thirst but a burning, cottony clogging of mouth and throat. Lyle French gave him water from a canteen, but Judd was unable to swallow. His chest cramped so he could hardly breathe and he asked to have all the car windows opened. The rush of wind on his face gave him some relief, but he remembers vomiting two or three times, and feeling dirty and ashamed. His mind seemed clearer, but he still saw everything outside the car window only as a gray fog.

He heard Lyle's voice again, "Nearly there, Judd. Hang tough!" Then the car stopped, there were more voices, and someone said, "Bring the bed right out to the car." Judd felt himself between cool, soft sheets, being rolled down a hospital corridor. He was aware of an increasing and intense craving for sweetened fluids, reflecting dehydration and lowered blood sugar level from the vomiting and diarrhea.

"If I were ever to treat a snakebite of this type in the future, where those symptoms had been present, I'd take special care to supply additional sugar and fluids," he says. "I tried to tell one of the nurses walking beside me how terribly I wanted a cold sweet drink, but I could no longer speak."

Next he was aware of new pain developing in his lower abdomen, sharp and intense, as if he were being pulled apart. He sensed that another doctor had come into the room—he proved to be an older associate of Dr. Plehn—and Judd heard him exclaim, "My god, look at that swelling!"

Grindell's eyes were pried open again and he tried to let them know that he could hear what they said, but it was no use. The torture in his belly grew and the whole abdominal wall turned rigid as a board. Every breath became a fight against pain and knotted muscles, and for the second time he knew what it is like to die. But he was too tired and had suffered too much to care. Dying would bring relief. At last, five hours after the snake struck him, he passed out.

It was six hours before he regained consciousness. In the meantime Jack had rustled up the additional Antivenin that saved his life. A third vial was available at the hospital and was injected at once. There was no more in Gillette, but Jack located two vials in Billings, Montana, and the Montana State Highway Patrol rushed them south. Jack met the patrol car and brought them the rest of the way, and Judd got them at once. Without them, he is sure he would have died in that venom-induced coma.

He returned to the world of awareness to hear his doctors discussing "the optimum level for amputation." Should they take his leg off below the knee or above, and how far? He tried to let them know that he was against the whole idea, but it was half an hour before he could open his eyes, roll his head and move an arm enough to alert a nurse to the fact that he was conscious. An hour after that he had his first look at the bitten leg.

"There is no adequate way to describe the consequences of such a snakebite as I had received," Dr. Grindell says now. The whole leg looked more like an elephant's than a man's, both in size and color. It was slate gray, with patches of pink, and he no longer had either a foot or ankle. Swelling had engulfed everything, clear to the base of his toes.

He has been asked since whether the severity of his experience might have been due to the fact that one of the snake's fangs penetrated a vein, introducing venom directly into the blood. Bites of that kind have unusually grave and dangerous consequences, for obvious reasons. But he does not think that happened in his case. It was about 20 minutes after he was bitten before he felt the first effects of the spreading poison. If a vein had been punctured the general symptoms would have appeared almost at once.

Instead, Judd believes he got an abnormally large dose of venom in comparison with the size of the snake, probably almost the entire contents of its poison sacs, as a result of it hanging on and struggling to free itself.

"I'm sure that before I got his half-inch-long fangs out of my leg he must have pumped in far more than he would have delivered with one lightning stroke, and I think that accounted for what happened to me," Grindell told me years afterward.

He was not going to part with that leg if it could be avoided. As he pointed out to Jack and Lyle, he thought he might have quite a few years left after he got over this thing, and he contemplated spending some of his time at the same kind of activity that had gotten him into this fix. For that an artificial leg would hardly do.

They did some judicious pin-sticking in the swollen member and learned that fairly normal sensation was still scattered over most of it, and the amputation was postponed. In the end it proved unnecessary. In fact, in view of the severity of swelling and general symptoms, and the very close call Judd had had, the final outcome was a most fortunate one. The rattler did him no permanent damage at all.

He left the hospital at the end of 10 days, and headed home to Wisconsin. The arrangements for the drive were a bit strange. Judd was settled comfortably on pillows laid across the back seat, with a bulky and highly unusual looking leg protruding out of a rear window. He rode all the way from Gillette to Siren that way, too.

But right then he was the most thankful antelope hunter in the whole United States. He still is.